# The Psychobiology of Trauma and Resilience Across the Lifespan

# The Psychobiology of Trauma and Resilience Across the Lifespan

Edited by Douglas L. Delahanty

JASON ARONSON

*Lanham • Boulder • New York • Toronto • Plymouth, UK*

Published in the United States of America
by Jason Aronson
An imprint of Rowman & Littlefield Publishers, Inc.

A wholly owned subsidiary of
The Rowman & Littlefield Publishing Group, Inc.
4501 Forbes Boulevard, Suite 200, Lanham, Maryland 20706
www.rowmanlittlefield.com

Estover Road
Plymouth PL6 7PY
United Kingdom

British Library Cataloguing in Publication Information Available

**Library of Congress Cataloging-in-Publication Data**

The hardback edition of this book was previously cataloged by the Library of Congress
as follows:

The psychobiology of trauma and resilience across the lifespan / edited by
    Douglas L. Delahanty.
        p. ; cm.
    Includes bibliographical references.
    1. Post-traumatic stress disorder—Age factors. I. Delahanty, Douglas L., 1970–
[DNLM: 1. Stress Disorders, Post-Traumatic. 2. Adaptation, Psychological.
3. Adolescent. 4. Adult. 5. Child. 6. Risk Factors. WM 170 P97326 2008]

RC552.P67P7595 2008
616.85'21—dc22                                              2008020160

ISBN: 978-0-7657-0536-5 (cloth : alk. paper)
ISBN: 978-0-7657-0535-8 (pbk. : alk. paper)
ISBN: 978-0-7657-0608-9 (electronic)

Printed in the United States of America

♾ ™ The paper used in this publication meets the minimum requirements of American
National Standard for Information Sciences—Permanence of Paper for Printed Library
Materials, ANSI/NISO Z39.48-1992.

# Contents

# Preface

On April 22, 2007, a group of twelve experts were brought together in the picturesque Amish country of north central Ohio to begin a three-day forum on the state-of-the-science in our understanding of posttraumatic stress disorder (PTSD). A number of graduate students, postdoctoral fellows, and collaborators were also in attendance. The following chapters were generated from presentations by the experts and discussion of all attendees. The researchers were selected for their expertise in PTSD at different stages of development. Up to now, child and adult PTSD researchers operated relatively autonomously, with little communication between the two groups. Our hope was to bridge this gap in research, establish collaborative relationships, and increase our understanding of how developmental influences impact risk and resilience for PTSD and comorbid disorders at all stages, from childhood to older age.

I wish to thank many people without whom this conference and book would not have been possible. First, the presenters who openly gave of their time and expertise—I would like to extend my personal thanks for your enthusiasm and support of this project as well as your thoughtful contributions to this work. Next, to the forum attendees for their lively discussion and thought-provoking contributions, which are reflected in the content of the following chapters. Special thanks go to my graduate students (Aaron Armelie, Jessica Boarts, Crystal Gabert, Leah Irish, Ihori Kobayashi, Sarah Ostrowski, Keri Pinna, and Suhrida Yadavalli) for their help with organizational logistics and transporting of participants. I would also like to thank Stevan Hobfoll and the Applied Psychology Center for organizing the Kent Forum series and funding the conference. Finally, an extra-special thanks goes to Kathy Floody, who took on the task of organizing all aspects of the forum and book preparation. Without her tireless help and support neither would have been a possibility.

Preparation of this book was facilitated by National Institute of Mental Health grants R34 MH 73014 and R34 MH 71201.

Douglas L. Delahanty

# Introduction

Since the introduction of posttraumatic stress disorder (PTSD) as a diagnosis in the third edition of the *Diagnostic and Statistical Manual of Mental Disorders* (*DSM-III*, American Psychiatric Association, 1980), research into risk and resilience factors for the disorder has focused primarily on adult male veterans. More recently, research has expanded to include victims of a variety of traumas, at times findings similarities and at times differences in predictors and correlates of PTSD dependent upon the index trauma experienced. However, the vast majority of PTSD research, to this date, has continued to focus on adult samples. That said, the importance of examining risk/resilience factors in PTSD across the lifespan has become increasingly obvious. Recent research has consistently demonstrated that childhood experiences confer risk/resilience for reactions to trauma in adulthood, and predictors and correlates of PTSD appear to differ developmentally.

Large-scale studies prospectively following children through young adulthood and beyond are costly and time-consuming, and require a large amount of resources to conduct. Therefore, our understanding of developmental influences on responses to trauma and risk for posttraumatic distress are often hindered by retrospective designs and limited follow-up assessments. Perhaps due to differing training requirements of child and adult psychologists and psychiatrists, and decreased comfort in expansion of one's research program into areas of different variables and complexities, few researchers have examined predictors and correlates of posttraumatic responses in both child and adult samples. Further, PTSD research has typically been conducted by either child or adult researchers with relatively little overlap or communication between the two camps. However, we are at the point where developmental models of PTSD are necessary to fully understand the complex constellation of responses to trauma across the lifespan. Such models can inform study designs and lead to novel, developmentally appropriate interventions. To this end, this book is organized in such a way to present and integrate research into child, adult, and older adult trauma samples in an attempt to culminate in a testable model of PTSD risk and resilience across the lifespan. Each author incorporated a developmental slant to their individual chapter, and the chapters are organized to highlight potential differences in our understanding of risk and resiliency between children and adults.

The book begins with an overview discussion by Michael R. McCart and colleagues of differences in PTSD prevalence rates and symptom presentation between children and adults with PTSD, with a specific focus on factors that increase risk for developing PTSD in childhood (chapter 1). The next section focuses on pre- and peritraumatic risk factors for the development of PTSD. Karestan C. Koenen et al. examine pretrauma genetic and biological risk factors for the development of PTSD (chapter 2), while Nnamdi Pole presents research from a number of longitudinal studies of police officers, highlighting differences in risk factors through the officers' service, from cadet training to mid-career to retirement (chapter 3).

The next section focuses on work conducted in child trauma victims with Daniel W. Smith and colleagues examining risk factors and treatment issues related to childhood PTSD (chapter 4). Glenn N. Saxe and colleagues highlight biological risk and resilience factors in studies of child trauma victims (chapter 5).

Parallel chapters are presented in the next section, although with a focus on research findings in adults. However, as mentioned, even in the adult chapters, authors have attempted to take a developmental approach to their presentations by examining the impact of childhood trauma and experiences on findings in adults. Stevan Hobfoll et al. examine the importance of resource loss in increasing risk for trauma and posttraumatic distress in abuse victims, with a specific focus on trauma experiences across the lifespan (chapter 6). In contrast, Ann Rasmusson reviews and synthesizes the literature on biological risk and resilience factors in adulthood PTSD (chapter 7). Prior research has largely examined just factors that increase risk for posttraumatic psychopathology; therefore, Rasmusson has focused more on timely findings concerning biological resilience variables. The final chapter in this section focuses on the psychobiology of PTSD in older adults, with special attention to partialling out the influence of age-related trauma reactions from normal psychobiological changes in aging (chapter 8). In this chapter, Rachel Yehuda draws on her extensive work in the psychobiology of trauma and PTSD to examine differences in biological correlates of PTSD as a function of aging in adults.

The impact of comorbid disorders is examined in the next two chapters. A recurring theme in the PTSD literature is that "pure" PTSD is rarely seen, and a specific focus on PTSD without examination of the impact of comorbid conditions is overly simplistic. In order to address this shortcoming, Daphne Simeon and Ashley Braun examine the incidence of dissociative disorders in children and adults highlighting the role of trauma in the development of both dissociation disorders and PTSD (chapter 9). Dean G. Kilpatrick and colleagues examine the incidence and impact of PTSD and comorbid depression, with a specific focus on the extent to which prior interpersonal trauma may increase risk for developing these comorbid symptoms (chapter 10).

The final section examines ways in which PTSD treatments may need to be adjusted when dealing with children versus adults. Norah C. Feeny and colleagues draw on their experience in treating both adults and children with PTSD to highlight implications for the psychosocial treatment of PTSD across the lifespan (chapter 11). In chapter 12, Douglas L. Delahanty and Sarah A. Ostrowski review pharmacological treatment for PTSD and differences between child and adult pharmacotherapy for PTSD. Finally, in chapter 13, we attempt to synthesize the prior chapters into a workable model for guiding psychobiological research in PTSD. We particularly note areas in need of research as well as points at which intervention seems most appropriate.

# Developmental Issues in Diagnosing PTSD

*Michael R. McCart, Genelle K. Sawyer, and Daniel W. Smith*

Posttraumatic stress disorder (PTSD) involves a collection of psychiatric symptoms that can occur following exposure to traumatic events. Examples of traumatic events that place individuals at risk for developing PTSD include physical or sexual assault, combat exposure, motor vehicle accidents, and natural disasters. The prevalence of PTSD in the general population is high, with as many as one in ten adults and one in fifteen children meeting criteria for this disorder at some point during their lifetime (Kessler, Sonnega, Bromet, Hughes, and Nelson, 1995; Kilpatrick, Saunders, and Smith, 2003). In this chapter, we provide a brief overview of the historical development of the PTSD diagnosis. Research is also reviewed exploring potential differences in the development and manifestation of this disorder across the lifespan.

## HISTORY OF PTSD

The diagnosis of PTSD was first introduced in the third edition of the Diagnostic and Statistical Manual of Mental Disorders (DSM-III; American Psychiatric Association, 1980). As noted by Lasiuk and Hegadoren (2006a; 2006b), the creation of this diagnostic construct was informed by more than a century of clinical observation on the psychological responses of individuals following exposure to various traumatic stressors. Some of the earliest

Address correspondence concerning this chapter to Michael R. McCart, Ph.D.; National Crime Victims Research and Treatment Center; Department of Psychiatry and Behavioral Sciences; Medical University of South Carolina; 165 Cannon Street; Charleston, SC 29425. E-mail: mccartm@musc.edu.

writings on traumatic stress reactions date back to the nineteenth century, during the heart of the Industrial Revolution. During that time, medical professionals began documenting symptoms that were commonly experienced by individuals who had been involved in railway crashes, including sleep difficulties, avoidance of trauma cues, and persistent anxiety. Interest in this area grew during World War I and World War II, as clinicians started to observe comparable symptoms among men returning from combat. Military physicians initially believed that these symptoms were the result of neurological damage stemming from exposure to exploding shells on the battlefield. This hypothesized etiology was later called into question, however, when similar symptom patterns were observed among war veterans with no direct combat exposure (Lamprecht and Sack, 2002).

Although clinical attention to the effects of trauma faded somewhat following World War II, interest mounted again in the late 1960s and early 1970s. Around that time, Vietnam veterans were petitioning the federal government for reparation owing to the physical and psychological injuries that they sustained in the war. The mental health community responded by devoting increased attention to research on the psychological experiences of war veterans, as well as survivors of other types of trauma, including rape, severe burns, and the Holocaust (Lasiuk and Hegadoren, 2006a). The synthesis of these diverse bodies of work ultimately led to the development and inclusion of the PTSD diagnosis in the DSM-III.

The inclusion of PTSD in the DSM-III is significant because contrary to prevailing assumptions in psychiatry at the time, the diagnosis specifies that an external stressful event, rather than some individual weakness, is responsible for the disorder (Lasiuk and Hegadoren, 2006b). For example, DSM-III specified that in order to meet criteria for PTSD, an individual had to encounter an event that was outside the range of normal human experience and that would be markedly distressing to almost anyone (criterion A). In addition, the individual had to report at least one re-experiencing symptom (e.g., intrusive recollections of the traumatic event, nightmares; criterion B), at least three avoidance symptoms (e.g., efforts to avoid trauma cues, affective numbing; criterion C), and at least two hyperarousal symptoms (e.g., sleep difficulties, irritability; criterion D). Symptoms had to persist for at least one month and cause distress in social, occupational, or some other important area of functioning (American Psychiatric Association, 1980).

In 1987, a revised version of DSM-III was published that retained the original structure of PTSD, but expanded the list of potential re-experiencing, avoidance, and hyperarousal symptoms from twelve to seventeen (DSM-III-R; American Psychiatric Association, 1987). In addition, the DSM-III-R began including reference to child-specific symptom manifestation. More specifically, the DSM-III-R noted that children's re-experiencing symptoms may present as repetitive play, and symptoms of avoidance may manifest as a loss of recently acquired developmental skills (e.g., toilet training). Further, this revision commented on the importance of obtaining reports from parents and teachers when assessing symptoms of avoidance in children.

The symptoms in DSM-III-R were retained in DSM-IV (American Psychiatric Association, 1994), although some changes were made to the diagnosis (see table 1.1). Criterion A was revised and expanded to cover both objective and subjective aspects of the traumatic event. Criterion A1 states that an individual must have experienced, witnessed, or been confronted with an event or events that involved actual or threatened death or serious injury, or threat to the physical integrity of self or others, and criterion A2 requires that the individual must have responded to the event with intense fear, helplessness, or horror. This revision was guided by research showing that an individual's acute fear response and perceived threat of harm or death during a traumatic event represented some of the strongest predictors of poor outcome (Lasiuk and Hegadoren, 2006b; March, 1993).

In the years preceding publication of the DSM-IV, research examining child trauma victims indicated that while the reactions of traumatized children and adults were remarkably similar, children also tended to respond in unique ways (e.g., Blom, 1986; Pynoos et al., 1987; Terr, 1983, 1991). Thus, the second substantive revision in DSM-IV involved a more thorough description of how PTSD symptoms may manifest differently among youth. As shown in table 1.1, DSM-IV currently notes that a child's criterion A symptoms of fear, helplessness, and horror may be expressed as disorganized or agitated behavior. Regarding criterion B, the DSM-IV states that a child may relive their trauma by reenacting certain aspects of the event through repetitive play. In addition, dreams about the traumatic event may be present in children as frightening dreams without recognizable content. DSM-IV further specifies that because there may be challenges in assessing criterion C symptoms of cognitive and behavioral avoidance among youth, clinicians are advised to evaluate these symptoms through direct observation or reports from parents and teachers. In reference to criterion D symptoms, it is recognized that for some children, persistent hyperarousal may be manifest as somatic complaints such as headaches or stomachaches.

Despite the inclusion of symptoms in the DSM-IV that reflect attention to developmental concerns, the conceptualization of PTSD and the suitability of its diagnostic criteria for children have recently been called into question (Scheeringa, Zeanah, Drell, and Larrieu, 1995; Scheeringa, Zeanah, Myers,

**Table 1.1. DSM-IV Posttraumatic Stress Disorder Diagnostic Criteria**

A. The person has been exposed to a traumatic event in which both of the following were present:
  1. The person experienced, witnessed, or was confronted with an event or events that involved actual or threatened death or serious injury, or a threat to the physical integrity of self or others.
  2. The person's response involved intense fear, helplessness, or horror. (In children, this may be expressed by disorganized or agitated behavior.)
B. The traumatic event is persistently reexperienced in one or more of the following ways:
  1. Recurrent and intrusive distressing recollections of the event, including images, thoughts, or perceptions. (In young children, repetitive play may occur in which themes or aspects of the trauma are expressed.)
  2. Recurrent distressing dreams of the event. (In children, there may be frightening dreams without recognizable content.)
  3. Acting or feeling as if the traumatic event were recurring. (In young children, trauma-specific reenactment may occur.)
  4. Intense psychological distress at exposure to internal or external cues that symbolize or resemble an aspect of the traumatic event.
  5. Physiological reactivity on exposure to internal or external cues that symbolize or resemble an aspect of the traumatic event.
C. Persistent avoidance of stimuli associated with the trauma and numbing of general responsiveness (not present before the trauma), as indicated by three or more of the following:
  1. Efforts to avoid thoughts, feelings, or conversations associated with the trauma.
  2. Efforts to avoid activities, places, or people that arouse recollections of the trauma.
  3. Inability to recall an important aspect of the trauma.
  4. Markedly diminished interest or participation in significant activities.
  5. Feeling of detachment or estrangement from others.
  6. Restricted range of affect (e.g., unable to have loving feelings).
  7. Sense of foreshortened future (e.g., does not expect to have a career, marriage, children, or a normal life span).
D. Persistent symptoms of increased arousal (not present before the trauma), as indicated by two or more of the following:
  1. Difficultly falling or staying asleep.
  2. Irritability or outbursts of anger.
  3. Difficulty concentrating.
  4. Hypervigilance.
  5. Exaggerated startle response.
E. Duration of the disturbance (symptoms in Criterion B, C, and D) is more than 1 month.
F. The disturbance causes clinically significant distress or impairment in social, occupational, or other important areas of functioning.

and Putnam, 2003). Furthermore, data regarding the prevalence rates for the disorder during childhood have been mixed. In the following section, we review some of the more recent epidemiological studies on the prevalence of PTSD in youth. This section also summarizes the current debate on the validity of the PTSD symptom criteria for children and discusses various developmental factors that may influence children's responses to traumatic events.

## PTSD IN CHILDHOOD

### Prevalence

Epidemiological studies of the prevalence of PTSD in childhood have yielded variable results. In a probability sample of over four thousand youth (aged twelve to seventeen years) participating in the National Survey of Adolescents, 6.3 percent of the female and 3.7 percent of the male adolescents met criteria for PTSD within the past six months (Kilpatrick et al., 2003). Among a sample of ten thousand children and adolescents (aged five to fifteen years) participating in the British National Survey of Mental Health, it was reported that 0.4 percent of the eleven- to fifteen-year-olds met criteria for PTSD while negligible rates of PTSD were observed among the youth aged five to ten years (Meltzer, Gatward, Goodman, and Ford, 2000). Finally, in a multistage sample design from the Great Smoky Mountains Study, three cohorts of children (aged nine, eleven, and thirteen years) were followed over eight years and assessed for various mental health outcomes. Lifetime prevalence of PTSD in the sample was rare (0.4 percent), while subclinical levels of PTSD were more common (2.2 percent) (Copeland, Keeler, Angold, and Costello, 2007). Adolescents were more likely to report subclinical levels of PTSD than were children.

While only a few studies have examined the population prevalence of PTSD among children and adolescents, multiple studies have estimated the rates of PTSD among youth following exposure to specific traumatic stressors. Studies suggest that prevalence rates vary significantly depending upon a number of factors, including the type of trauma experienced, the severity of the traumatic event, the child's proximity to the trauma, the time elapsed since the event, and the method of assessment (e.g., Cohen, 1998; Fletcher, 1996).

Exposure to natural disasters typically produces lower rates of PTSD than other traumas. In a recent review of the disaster literature, La Greca and Prinstein (2002) found that 5–10 percent of youth met full criteria for PTSD following exposure to traumatic events such as earthquakes, hurricanes, or tornadoes. Rates of PTSD tend to be much higher in children exposed to warfare, with estimates ranging between 27 percent (Saigh, 1991) and 33 percent (Arroyo and Eth, 1985). The prevalence of PSTD in children exposed to intimate partner violence has been found to range from 3 percent to 60 percent, with most studies yielding rates somewhere in between (e.g., Graham-Bermann and Levendosky, 1998; Graham-Bermann, DeVoe, Mattis, Lynch, and Thomas, 2006; Kilpatrick and Williams, 1998; Levendosky, Huth-Bocks, Semel, and Shapiro, 2002). Similarly, rates of PTSD following sexual abuse are variable and range from 0 percent (Sirles, Smith, and Kusama, 1989) to 90 percent (Kiser et al., 1988). In a meta-analysis of thirty-four samples that included 2,697 children exposed to varying types of trauma, Fletcher (1996) examined whether the differing incidence rates observed for PTSD might vary by age. Approximately one-third of the total sample met criteria for PTSD and rates of PTSD did not differ markedly across developmental levels. That is, PTSD was diagnosed in 39 percent of youth under age seven, 33 percent of youth aged six to twelve, and 27 percent of adolescents aged twelve and older. These findings indicate that children of all ages can and do experience significant PTSD symptoms following exposure to multiple types of trauma.

Prevalence rates have also been found to vary depending on the severity of the traumatic event. For instance, Pynoos and colleagues (1993) found that youth who were exposed to particularly gruesome experiences during an earthquake evidenced relatively high rates of PTSD symptoms when compared to youth with less gruesome experiences. Additionally, following a sniper attack, children who were closer to the shooting scene experienced significantly more PTSD symptoms immediately following the traumatic event (Pynoos et al., 1987) and fourteen months later (Nader, Pynoos, Fairbanks, and Frederick, 1990).

## Age Differences

Despite the consistent finding that children of all ages experience PTSD symptoms, there has been considerable debate in the literature about the manifestation of symptoms in children vs. older adolescents and adults and the diagnostic validity of the current PTSD criteria and algorithm thresholds for children. In general, research has demonstrated that children exposed to traumatic events respond in a manner similar to adults, supporting the relevance of the DSM-IV symptom clusters for pediatric populations. Fletcher's meta-analysis (1996) suggests that many of the specific DSM-IV criteria occur with comparable frequency in child and adult populations, including intrusive memories (34 percent vs. 45 percent, respectively), bad dreams (31 percent vs. 36 percent), reliving the event (39 percent vs. 29 percent), avoidance of reminders (32 percent vs. 33 percent), loss of interest in activities (36 percent vs. 28 percent), detachment or withdrawal (25 percent vs. 34 percent), irritability (23 percent vs. 29 percent), difficulty concentrating (41 percent vs. 41 percent), hypervigilance (25 percent vs. 27 percent), and exaggerated startle response (28 percent vs. 38 percent). Further, Yule (1992) compared symptom profiles from children following the Jupiter cruise ship disaster with those of adults following similar types of disasters and found comparable rates of intrusion and avoidance symptoms in both populations.

There has been some speculation that despite the similarities between adult and child symptom presentation, the current PTSD algorithm thresholds may be too stringent for children, resulting in an underdiagnosis of PTSD in young children (Scheeringa et al., 1995). In a sample of sixty-two traumatized children aged twenty months to six years, none met full diagnostic criteria for PTSD, primarily due to the stringent threshold of criterion C requiring three symptoms of numbing/avoidance (Scheeringa et al., 2003). More recently, Scheeringa, Wright, Hunt, and Zeanah (2006) examined the validity of the current PTSD algorithm thresholds for children across three developmental stages: six and younger, seven to eleven, and twelve to eighteen. Results indicated that current thresholds for criterion B (re-experiencing) and criterion D (hyperarousal) were appropriate across age groups and that rates of criterion D were similar regardless of whether one or two symptoms were required. However, there was significant disparity in criterion C symptoms with 4.8 percent of children under age six, 9.1 percent of youth ages seven to eleven, and 17.2 percent of adolescents ages twelve to eighteen meeting the threshold of three symptoms. The authors concluded that the threshold of three criterion C symptoms is likely inappropriate for children under age six and may be inappropriate for children under age eleven.

Based on findings that PTSD symptoms may appear different in very young children, Scheeringa and colleagues (1995, 2003) recently proposed an alternative set of diagnostic criteria for preschool-aged youth. Specifically, they suggested that several traditional symptoms be excluded (e.g. sense of foreshortened future, inability to recall important aspects of the trauma) because they may be developmentally inappropriate for this age group. Furthermore, they proposed the addition of a new symptom cluster (criterion E) that is specific to the developmental uniqueness of young children, including new separation anxiety, new onset of aggression, and new fears that do not have an obvious link to the trauma (e.g., fear of the bathroom, dark, etc.). Finally, given the obvious difficultly in assessing symptoms of emotional and cognitive avoidance among young children with little or no verbal abilities, they argued for a reduction in the number of criterion C symptoms that are required to make the diagnosis.

In sum, research suggests that there may be some differences in the manifestation of PTSD symptoms, particularly avoidance symptoms, among children aged six and younger. Somewhere between the ages of seven and eleven, however, children's reactions to traumatic events start to approximate those manifested by adults. This is likely due to important changes in cognition, emotional regulation, and language abilities that occur throughout childhood. These and other relevant developmental factors are described in more detail below.

## Developmental Factors

Cognitive abilities are continuously changing and developing throughout childhood, and these cognitive skills likely play a role in children's understanding and appraisal of traumatic events (for a review see Salmon and Bryant, 2002). For instance, children have a limited knowledge base from which to draw upon when they are attempting to understand and make sense of a traumatic event. This is important because prior knowledge has a significant impact on how information enters memory and is encoded (Ornstein, Shapiro, Clubb, Follmer, and Baker-Ward, 1997; Schneider and Bjorklund, 1998). Specifically, events are encoded with less detail for young children, making them more likely to forget details than are older children or adults. Further, events that are outside the child's usual experience may not be appraised as traumatic, which is likely to impact their understanding and emotional reaction to the event (Pollak, Cicchetti, and Klorman, 1998; Saarni, Mumme, and Campos, 1998). For instance, children under the age of eight who lived on Three Mile Island and were exposed to the nuclear incident generally displayed minimal distress (Handford et al., 1986). Given the complex nature of the event, it is possible that these children did not understand the danger posed to them, resulting in minimal emotional reactions. This is important because theorists have posed that if an event is not perceived as threatening, feelings of fear and symptoms of PTSD are less likely to develop (e.g., Fletcher, 1996).

As cognitive abilities develop, so does the ability to regulate thought and emotion. With age and cognitive development, children are better able to engage in cognitive restructuring, thought suppression, and intentional forgetting (e.g., Eisenberg, 1998; Fletcher, 1996; McNally, Metzger, Lasko, and Clancy, 1998). More effective use of these strategies is likely to affect emotional and behavioral responses (Eisenberg, 1998). Salmon and Bryant (2002) suggest that due to children's immature understanding of their cognitions, the relationship of cognition to emotion, and their inability to manage cognitions, emotions, and memories, they are likely to have poor coping strategies and, therefore, are more vulnerable to intrusive thoughts and other cognitive aspects of trauma. This is consistent with literature that suggests that younger children report more symptoms of re-experiencing (Fletcher, 1996).

The level of a child's language development significantly affects their ability to describe the traumatic event, complicating the assessment of PTSD symptoms in pre-verbal and young children. Children's narratives about events are generally brief, and because of their language limitations, they generally do not fully reflect the extent of information that has been encoded in memory (e.g., Hudson and Fivush, 1990). Children's verbal abilities are particularly limited when describing unfamiliar, traumatic events. For instance, Poole and Lamb (1998) found that young children do not have the vocabulary or language abilities to describe the sexual experiences endured during sexual abuse. Additionally, children's emotion vocabulary and understanding of their emotions is limited. Even at age eight or nine, children incorporate little information about their affect in their reports of emotionally laden experiences (Wesson and Salmon, 2001).

Language related factors also have important consequences for children's memory and understanding of traumatic events. Given their limited language and cognitive abilities, young children tend not to initiate conversations about past events (Fivush and Hamond, 1990; McDonald and Hayne, 1996). Therefore, due to the lack of communication regarding a specific event, the event may not be encoded into memory, and details of the event may be gradually forgotten (e.g., Nelson, 1993). As such, language abilities impact not only the child's immediate ability to describe the traumatic event, but also may have a longer-term impact on the child's memory of the event.

Because of their cognitive, emotional, and language limitations, children are particularly dependent upon their parents to help them regulate their emotions and understand traumatic events. However, given the infrequency of young children's conversations about such events, they may be at greater risk for misappraising the experience and having incorrect perceptions and attributions (Fivush, Pipe, Murachver, and Reese, 1997). Therefore, accurate understanding of the traumatic event in young children may depend on the parents' or caretakers' willingness to initiate conversations with their children about the event. For instance, McGuigan and Salmon (2005) found that children aged three to six made fewer recall errors when their parents engaged in elaborative discussions two to three days following participation in a staged, neutral event.

Evidence suggests, however, that at least some parents avoid such discussions due to the difficult nature of the conversation and/or as a means of protecting their children. In medical contexts, parents may not inform children of their diagnosis or may inadequately prepare them for painful medical procedures (Steward, 1993). Further, parents may avoid discussions because of their own distress related to the traumatic event itself or discomfort in discussing the event. Numerous studies have demonstrated that parents themselves can develop symptoms of PTSD following their child's disclosure of sexual abuse (e.g., Kelley, 1990; Manion et al., 1996; Timmons-Mitchell, Chandler-Holtz, and Semple, 1996) or diagnosis of a chronic medical illness (e.g., Kazak et al., 1997). In these instances, parents may avoid talking about the event due to their own desire to avoid reminders, which may also interfere with parents' ability to support their child. Following an Australian bush fire, McFarlane, Policansky, and Irwin (1987) found that children's reactions to the event were fully accounted for by the mothers' own reactions and mental health, rather than by the exposure to the fires themselves. More recent studies have not replicated this finding, but continue to find that maternal reactions have important influences on child symptoms following exposure to traumatic events (Mannarino and Cohen, 1996; Smith, Perrin, Yule, Rabe-Hesketh, 2001). Research has also demonstrated that parents tend to underestimate the severity of stress reactions evidenced by their children (e.g., Gordon and Wraigh, 1993; McCloskey, Figueredo, and Koss, 1995), which may be a function of the lack of direct conversations about the event or the parents lack of awareness of their children's symptoms due to their own stress reactions.

The importance of family factors on the development of posttraumatic stress symptoms has been continually demonstrated in the literature. For instance, Scheeringa and colleagues (1995, 2006) found that children and adolescents were more likely to develop PTSD when they witnessed a threat to their primary caregiver. Further, parental support following the event has been linked to reduced symptoms of psychopathology (e.g., Everson, Hunter, Runyon, Edelsohn, and Coulter, 1989; Kliewer, Lepore, Oskin, and Johnson, 1998). Additionally, children whose parents provide a positive, nurturing environment and set constructive limits tend to be more stress resilient than those whose parents are more rigid and less warm in their caregiving (Wyman et al., 1992). Numerous other family factors have been linked to child outcomes and recovery following exposure to traumatic events, including family cohesion (Conte and Schuerman, 1987; Loar et al., 1996), parental distress (Deblinger, Steer, and Lippmann, 1999; Sack, Clarke, and Seeley, 1995), parental rejection (Ruchkin, Eisemann, and Hagglof, 1998), and parental conflict (Wasserstein and LaGreca, 1998).

## PTSD IN ADULTHOOD

There is less debate regarding the validity of PTSD among adults. Indeed, most factor analytic studies of PTSD symptoms in adult samples generally support a three- or four-factor solution that at least partly corresponds to the re-experiencing, avoidance/numbing, and hyperarousal symptom clusters in DSM-IV. In this section, we provide a brief overview of the epidemiological literature documenting the prevalence of PTSD in adulthood. This section also includes a review of research exploring whether the rates of PTSD among adults might vary as a function of age.

### Prevalence

Population prevalence estimates of lifetime PTSD among adults range from 7.8 percent to 12.3 percent (Breslau, Davis, Andreski, and Peterson, 1991; Kessler et al., 1995; Resnick, Kilpatrick, Dansky, Saunders, and Best, 1993). Interpersonal victimization tends to be associated with higher rates of PTSD than other traumatic events—particularly those that do not involve intentionality—such as motor vehicle accidents and natural disasters (Resnick et al., 1993). In the National Women's Study, a longitudinal survey of a national probability sample of 4,008 adult women, 32 percent of adult rape victims had lifetime PTSD, and 12.4 percent had current (past six months) PTSD (Resnick et al., 1993). Rates of lifetime and current PTSD in physical assault victims were also high: 38.5 percent and 17.8 percent respectively. Furthermore, crime victims had higher rates of lifetime (25.8 percent) and current (9.7 percent) PTSD than non-crime victims (9.4 percent lifetime PTSD and 3.4 percent current PTSD).

Women tend to experience higher rates of PTSD than men, and the primary index events differ by gender. For example, while combat exposure and witnessed violence are the most common causes of PTSD for men, physical and sexual assault represent the most common precipitating events for women (Kessler et al., 1995; Kilpatrick and Resnick, 1993). Adults exposed to multiple traumatic events are also at greater risk for PTSD than those exposed to a single stressor (Hedtke, Ruggiero, Saunders, Resnick, and Kilpatrick, 2007; Ozer, Best, Lipsey, and Weiss, 2003). Other variables that have been shown to predict higher risk of PTSD among adults include family history of psychopathology, incurred injury and perceived life threat during the trauma, lower levels of perceived social support, peritraumatic emotional responses, and Hispanic ethnicity (e.g., Brewin, Andrews, and Valentine, 2000; Galea et al., 2002; Ozer et al., 2003).

**Age Differences**

Recently, researchers have started to explore whether age might moderate the relationship between exposure to trauma and PTSD among adults. The results of these studies have been largely inconclusive. Some studies report no age differences in adults' reactions to traumatic events (e.g., Galea et al., 2002; Goenjian, Najarian, Pynoos, and Steinberg, 1994; Hagstrom, 1995). Other studies, however, reveal greater vulnerability among older adults following exposure to traumatic stressors (e.g., Carr et al., 1995; Ohta et al., 2003; Tanida, 1996; Ticehurst, Webster, Carr, and Lewin, 1996). For instance, when Ohta and colleagues (2003) measured symptoms of psychological distress among a sample of adults exposed to a volcanic eruption in Japan, participants over age fifty reported significantly higher levels of trauma symptoms when compared to their younger counterparts. Older age was also associated with elevated posttraumatic stress symptoms among a sample of adults exposed to the 1989 Australian Newcastle earthquake (Carr et al., 1995). A number of hypotheses have been proposed to explain these findings. Some suggest that older adults are at heightened risk for psychopathology owing to the concurrent stressors that are commonly faced during this developmental period, such as retirement, widowhood, and physical health problems (Higgins and Follette, 2002). Others hypothesize that older individuals are more vulnerable because they have experienced more negative life events, and therefore possess compromised coping abilities (Dohrenwend and Dohrenwend, 1981).

A separate body of literature, however, appears to support an opposite view, suggesting that elderly individuals are more resilient in the face of traumatic stressors (Norris, Friedman, et al., 2002). Acierno and colleagues (2002) examined the prevalence of interpersonal assault and symptoms of PTSD among a national probability sample of adult women. Participants aged fifty-five and older reported lower levels of PTSD symptoms compared to participants aged eighteen to thirty-four. This apparent resilience has also been observed among older combat veterans (Hyer, Summers, Braswell, and Boyd, 1995) and elderly adults exposed to natural or technological disasters (Bolin, and Klenow, 1983; Epstein, Fullerton, and Ursano, 1998; Kato, Asukai, Miyake, Minakawa, and Nishiyama, 1996; Palinkas, Petterson, Russell, and Downs, 1993). One explanation for these findings is that older individuals may be less likely to report symptoms of psychological distress. This may be due to generational differences in attitudes toward mental health care (Acierno et al., 2002), or to higher levels of shame and embarrassment among older adults exposed to trauma (Falk, Van Hasselt, and Hersen, 1997). Consistent with this view, data from several studies suggest that older adults are relatively less likely than younger adults to seek mental health services (Koenen, Goodwin, Struening, Hellman, and Guardino, 2003) or to acknowledge past criminal victimizations (Kalra, Wood, Desmarais, Verberg, and Senn, 1998; Falk et al., 1997).

Another hypothesis is that older individuals may be more resilient in the face of trauma because of past experiences with certain stressful life events (Gibbs, 1989). Norris and Murrell (1988) tested this hypothesis with a sample of adults (aged fifty-five and older) who were either direct or indirect victims of major flooding in Kentucky. Analyses examined whether the relationship between flood exposure and self-reported trait anxiety was moderated by an individual's prior experience with severe flooding. Results revealed an interaction between prior flood experience and degree of exposure to the Kentucky flood in predicting symptoms of anxiety. More specifically, individuals who had never experienced a flood before were more strongly affected by the Kentucky flood, compared to those who had previously lived through this type of natural disaster.

In contrast to natural disasters, prior experience with interpersonal violence does not appear to buffer the effects of future victimization. In fact, data consistently reveal higher rates of PTSD among individuals exposed to multiple instances of violence compared to those exposed to a single event (Hedtke et al., 2007; McCart et al., 2007). Considering data from the National Women's Study, Kilpatrick, Acierno, Resnick, Saunders, and Best (1997) noted that women who endured multiple physical or sexual assaults were more likely to develop PTSD than women who experienced fewer than two traumas. Specifically, these investigators found that 3 percent of non-assaulted women had current PTSD, compared to 19 percent of women with one prior assault, and 53 percent of women with two prior assaults.

There are some qualitative differences between natural disasters and interpersonal violence that may help explain these divergent findings. First, individuals who reside in disaster-prone areas likely possess a greater awareness of their risk of harm, and they can take active steps to reduce this risk via improved disaster preparedness (Norris, Friedman, et al., 2002). It is far more difficult, however, to anticipate and prepare oneself for interpersonal assault. Second, while victims of a natural disaster may be more likely to assign blame for the event to some external agent (e.g., the weather), victims of violence are more likely to make internal attributions for their victimization (i.e., believing that the event was caused by one's own characteristics or behavior), and these attributions are likely reinforced during each subsequent assault. This distinction is important because research has consistently documented a strong relationship between feelings of self-blame and PTSD symptom severity among individuals exposed to trauma (Chaffin, Wherry, and Dykman, 1997; Crouch, Smith, Ezzell, and Saunders, 1999; Koss, Figueredo, and Prince, 2002).

Finally, all of the studies that have separated middle-aged adults from younger and older adults suggest that this former age group is at highest risk for negative outcomes following a traumatic event (Phifer, 1990; Shore, Tatum, and Vollmer, 1986; Thompson, Norris, and Hanacek, 1993). Thompson and colleagues measured symptoms of psychological distress among a sample of younger (eighteen to thirty-nine years), middle-aged (forty to fifty-nine years), and older (sixty+ years) adults exposed to Hurricane Hugo. Participants were interviewed twelve, eighteen, and twenty-four months following the hurricane to assess the impact of this traumatic event on self-reported symptoms of anxiety, depression, and somatization. Results supported a positive curvilinear relationship between disaster exposure and age at each time point, reflecting higher levels of distress among middle-aged adults compared to younger and older participants. According to these investigators, traumatic events may have a disproportionate impact on middle-aged adults owing to the higher levels of parenting, financial, and occupational stress commonly faced by this age cohort (Thompson et al., 1993).

In sum, research examining the relationship between age and PTSD among adults has yielded an array of contradictory findings. These inconsistencies may be explained by methodological differences in the abovementioned studies (Norris, Kaniasty, Conrad, Inman, and Murphy, 2002). One potentially important methodological factor discussed by Norris, Kaniasty, and colleagues (2002) pertains to the timing of assessment. For example, research suggests that while younger and older adults do not differ with regard to distress levels immediately following a traumatic event, symptoms among older adults tend to decrease faster resulting in age differences at later assessments (Kato et al., 1996). Thus, studies may produce a widely different pattern of results depending on the amount of time that has passed since the traumatic event. In addition, Norris and colleagues note that researchers have not consistently controlled for gender when examining the effects of age, which is potentially problematic given research revealing consistently higher rates of PTSD among women compared to men following exposure to traumatic events (Kessler et al., 1995). Greater attention to these methodological issues is likely needed before definitive conclusions can be drawn about the relationship between age and PTSD among adults. It is also worth noting that a majority of the abovementioned studies have focused on individuals exposed to natural disasters. Additional research with adults exposed to other types of traumatic events (e.g., motor vehicle accidents, interpersonal violence) is needed to explore whether the relationship between age and PTSD may vary as a function of trauma type.

## CONCLUSION

Most extant data suggest that individuals at all levels of development are exposed to potentially traumatic events, and that responses to these events are generally consistent with the symptom clusters described within the DSM-IV: re-experiencing, avoidance, and hyperarousal. Less clear, however, is the degree to which cognitive and emotional development factors in young children influence the development, assessment, and expression of these symptoms, given that many symptoms require the ability to report on internal states and recognize departures from "normal" states of functioning. These issues have led some researchers to call for either modifying diagnostic algorithms for determining PTSD in very young children, or for developing distinct diagnostic entities apart from PTSD. With older populations, PTSD research has focused less on the applicability of the diagnosis for young, middle-aged, and older adults and more on the relative risks for PTSD across such age ranges. These areas of investigation are exciting and potentially informative from both theoretical and clinical perspectives. Greater understanding of how the process of development influences risk for, and expression of, PTSD may inform developmentally sensitive approaches to intervention, as well as improved understanding of how trauma affects cognitive, neurobiological, and emotional development at various ages.

## REFERENCES

Acierno, R., Brady, K., Gray, M., Kilpatrick, D. G., Resnick, H., and Best, C. L. (2002). Psychopathology following interpersonal violence: A comparison of risk factors in older and younger adults. *Journal of Clinical Geropsychology, 8*, 13–23.

American Psychiatric Association. (1980). *Diagnostic and statistical manual of mental disorders* (third ed.). Washington, DC: American Psychiatric Association.

———. (1987). *Diagnostic and statistical manual of mental disorders* (third ed., rev.). Washington, DC: American Psychiatric Association.

———. (1994). *Diagnostic and statistical manual of mental disorders* (fourth ed.). Washington DC: American Psychiatric Association.

Arroyo, W., and Eth, S. (1985). Children traumatized by Central American warfare. In S. Eth and R. S. Pynoos (Eds.), *Posttraumatic stress disorder in children* (101–20). Washington, DC: American Psychological Association.

Blom, G. E. (1986). A school disaster—intervention and research aspects. *Journal of the American Academy of Child and Adolescent Psychiatry, 25*, 336–45.

Bolin, R., and Klenow, D. (1983). Response of the elderly to disaster: An age-stratified analysis. *International Journal of Aging and Human Development, 16*, 283–96.

Breslau, N., Davis, G. C., Andreski, P., and Peterson, E. (1991). Traumatic events and posttraumatic stress disorder in an urban population of young adults. *Archives of General Psychiatry, 48*, 216–22.

Brewin, C. R., Andrews, B., and Valentine, J. D. (2000). Meta-analysis of risk factors for posttraumatic stress disorder in trauma-exposed adults. *Journal of Consulting and Clinical Psychology, 68*, 748–66.

Carr, V. J., Lewin, T. J., Webster, R. A., Hazell, P. L., Kenardy, J. A., and Carter, G. L. (1995). Psychosocial sequelae of the 1989 Newcastle earthquake: Community disaster experiences and psychological morbidity 6 months post-disaster. *Psychological Medicine, 25*, 539–55.

Chaffin, M., Wherry, J. N., and Dykman, R. (1997). School age children's coping with sexual abuse: Abuse stresses and symptoms associated with four coping strategies. *Child Abuse and Neglect, 21*, 227–40.

Cohen, J. A. (1998). Practice parameters for the assessment and treatment of children and adolescents with posttraumatic stress disorder. *Journal of the American Academy of Child and Adolescent Psychiatry, 37*, 997–1001.

Conte, J. R., and Schuerman, J. R. (1987). Factors associated with an increased impact of child sexual abuse. *Child Abuse and Neglect, 11*, 201–11.

Copeland, W. E., Keeler, G. Angold, A., and Costello, J. (2007). Traumatic events and posttraumatic stress in childhood. *Archives of General Psychiatry, 64*, 577–84.

Crouch, J. L., Smith, D. W., Ezzell, C. E., and Saunders, B. E. (1999). Measuring reactions to sexual trauma among children: Comparing the Children's Impact of Traumatic Events Scale and the Trauma Symptom Checklist for Children. *Child Maltreatment, 4*, 255–63.

Deblinger, E., Steer, R., and Lippmann, J. (1999). Maternal factors associated with sexually-abused children's psychosocial adjustment. *Child Maltreatment, 4*, 13–20.

Dohrenwend, B. S., and Dohrenwend, B. P. (1981). *Stressful life events and their context*. New York: Neale Watso.

Eisenberg, N. (1998). Introduction. In W. Damon and N. Eisenberg (Eds.), *Handbook of child psychology: vol. 3. Social, emotional and personality development* (fifth ed., 1–24). New York: Wiley.

Epstein, R. S., Fullerton, C. S., and Ursano, R. J. (1998). Posttraumatic stress disorder following an air disaster: A prospective study. *American Journal of Psychiatry, 155*, 934–38.

Everson, M. D., Hunter, W. M., Runyon, D. K., Edelsohn, G. A., and Coulter, M. I. (1989). Maternal support following disclosure of incest. *American Journal of Orthopsychiatry, 59*, 197–207.

Falk, B., Van Hasselt, V., and Hersen, M. (1997). Assessment of posttraumatic stress disorder in older victims of rape. *Journal of Clinical Geropsychology, 3*, 157–71.

Fivush, R., and Hamond, N. R. (1990). Autobiographical memory across the preschool years. In R. Fivush and J. A. Hudson (Eds.), *Knowing and remembering in young children* (223–48). New York: Cambridge University Press.

Fivush, R., Pipe, M. E., Murachver, T., and Reese, E. (1997). Events spoken and unspoken: Implications of language and memory development for the recovered memory debate. In M. Conway (Ed.), *False and recovered memories* (34–62). London: Oxford University Press.

Fletcher, K. E. (1996). Childhood posttraumatic stress disorder. In E. J. Mash and R. Barkley (Eds.), *Child psychopathology* (242–76). New York: Guilford Press.

Galea, S., Ahern, J., Resnick, H., Kilpatrick, D., Bucuvalas, M., Gold, J., et al. (2002). Psychological sequelae of the September 11 terrorist attacks in New York City. *New England Journal of Medicine, 346*, 982–87.

Gibbs, M. (1989). Factors in the victim that mediate between disaster and psychopathology: A review. *Journal of Traumatic Stress, 2*, 489–514.

Goenjian, A., Najarian, L., Pynoos, R., and Steinberg, A. (1994). Posttraumatic stress disorder in elderly and younger adults after the 1988 earthquake in Armenia. *American Journal of Psychiatry, 151*, 895–901.

Gordon, R., and Wraith, R. (1993). Responses of children and adolescents to disasters. In J. P. Wilson and B. Raphael (Eds.), *International handbook of traumatic stress syndromes* (561–75). New York: Plenum.

Graham-Bermann, S. A., DeVoe, E. R., Mattis, J. S., Lynch, S., and Thomas, S. A. (2006). Ecological predictors of traumatic stress symptoms in Caucasian and ethnic minority children exposed to intimate partner violence. *Violence Against Women, 12*, 663–92.

Graham-Bermann, S. A., and Levendosky, A. A. (1998). Traumatic stress symptoms in children of battered women. *Journal of Interpersonal Violence, 14*, 111–28.

Hagstrom, R. (1995). The acute psychological impact on survivors following a train accident. *Journal of Traumatic Stress, 8*, 391–402.

Handford, H. A., Mayes, S. D., Matterson, R. E., Humphrey, F. J., Bagnato, S., Bixler, E. O., et al. (1986). Child and parent reaction to the Three Mile Island nuclear accident. *Journal of the American Academy of Child and Adolescent Psychiatry, 25*, 346–56.

Hedtke, K. A., Ruggiero, K. J., Saunders, B. E., Resnick, H. S., and Kilpatrick, D. G. (2007). A longitudinal analysis of the relation between interpersonal violence types and mental health outcomes: Results from the National Women's Study. Forthcoming.

Higgins, A. B., and Follette, V. M. (2002). Frequency and impact of interpersonal trauma in older women. *Journal of Clinical Geropsychology, 8*, 215–26.

Hudson, J. A., and Fivush, R. (1990). What children remember and why. In R. Fivush and J. A. Hudson (Eds.), *Knowing and remembering in young children* (1–8). New York: Cambridge University Press.

Hyer, L., Summers, M., Braswell, L., and Boyd, S. (1995). Posttraumatic stress disorder: Silent problem among older combat veterans. *Psychotherapy, 32*, 348–64.

Kalra, M., Wood, E., Desmarais, S., Verberg, N., and Senn, C. (1998). Exploring negative dating experiences and beliefs about rape among younger and older women. *Archives of Sexual Behavior, 27*, 145–53.

Kato, H., Asukai, N., Miyake, Y., Minakawa, K., and Nishiyama, A. (1996). Posttraumatic symptoms among younger and elderly evacuees in Japan. *Acta Psychiatrica Scandinavica, 93*, 477–81.

Kazak, A. E., Barakat, L. P., Meeske, K., Christiakis, D., Meadowns, A. T., Casey, R., et al. (1997). Posttraumatic stress, family functioning, and social support in survivors of childhood cancer and their mothers and fathers. *Journal of Consulting and Clinical Psychology, 65*, 120–29.

Kelley, S. J. (1990). Parental stress response to sexual abuse and ritualistic abuse of children in day-care centers. *Nursing Research, 39*, 25–29.

Kessler, R. C., Sonnega, A., Bromet, E., Hughes, M., and Nelson, C. B. (1995). Posttraumatic stress disorder in the National Comorbidity Survey. *Archives of General Psychiatry, 52*, 1048–60.

Kilpatrick, D. G., Acierno, R., Resnick, H. S., Saunders, B. E., and Best, C. L. (1997). A two year longitudinal analysis of the relationship between violent assault and alcohol and drug use in women. *Journal of Consulting and Clinical Psychology, 65*, 834–47.

Kilpatrick, D. G., and Resnick, H. S. (1993). PTSD associated with exposure to criminal victimization in clinical and community populations. In J. R. Davidson and E. B. Foa (Eds.), *Post-traumatic stress disorder in review: Recent research and future directions* (113–43). Washington, DC: American Psychiatric Press.

Kilpatrick, D. G., Ruggiero, K. J., Acierno, R., Saunders, B. E., Resnick, H. S., and Best, C. L. (2003). Violence and risk of PTSD, major depression, substance abuse/dependence, and comorbidity: Results from the National Survey of Adolescents. *Journal of Consulting and Clinical Psychology, 71*, 692–700.

Kilpatrick, D. G., Saunders, B. W., and Smith, D. W. (2003). *Child and adolescent victimization in America: Prevalence and implications.* Washington, DC: National Institute of Justice—Research in Brief.

Kilpatrick, D. G., and Williams, L. M. (1998). Potential mediators of post-traumatic stress disorder in child witnesses to domestic violence. *Child Abuse & Neglect, 22*, 319–30.

Kiser, L. J., Ackerman, B. J., Brown, E., Edwards, N. B., McColgan, E., Pugh, R., et al. (1988). Posttraumatic stress disorder in young children: A reaction to purported sexual abuse. *Journal of the American Academy of Child and Adolescent Psychiatry, 27*, 645–49.

Kliewer, W., Lepore, S. J., Oskin, K., and Johnson, P. D. (1998). The role of social and cognitive processes in children's adjustment to community violence. *Journal of Consulting and Clinical Psychology, 66*, 199–209.

Koenen, K. C., Goodwin, R., Struening, E., Hellman, F., and Guardino, F. (2003). Posttraumatic stress disorder and treatment seeking in a national screening sample. *Journal of Traumatic Stress, 16*, 5–16.

Koss, M. P., Figueredo, A. J., and Prince, R. J. (2002). Cognitive mediation of rape's mental, physical and social health impact: Tests of four models in cross-sectional data. *Journal of Consulting and Clinical Psychology, 70*, 926–41.

La Greca, M. A., and Prinstein, M. J. (2002). Hurricanes and earthquakes. In A. M. La Greca, W. K. Silverman, E. M. Vernbery, and M. C. Roberts (Eds.), *Helping children cope with disasters and terrorism.* Washington, DC: American Psychological Association.

Lamprecht, F., and Sack, M. (2002). Posttraumatic stress disorder revisited. *Psychosomatic Medicine, 64*, 222–37.

Lasiuk, G. C., and Hegadoren, K. M. (2006a). Posttraumatic stress disorder part I: Historical development of this concept. *Perspectives in Psychiatric Care, 42*, 13–20.

———. (2006b). Posttrauamtic stress disorder part II: Development of the construct within the North American psychiatric taxonomy. *Perspectives in Psychiatric Care, 42*, 72–81.

Levendosky, A. A., Huth-Bocks, A. C., Semel, M. A., and Shapiro, D. L. (2002). Trauma symptoms in preschool-age children exposed to domestic violence. *Journal of Interpersonal Violence, 17*, 150–64.

Loar, N., Wolmer, L., Mayes, L. D., Golomb, A., Siverberg, D. S., Weizman, R., et al. (1996). Israeli preschoolers under Scud missile attacks. *Archives of General Psychiatry, 53*, 416–23.

Manion, G., McIntyre, J., Firestone, P., Ligezinska, M., Ensom, R., and Wells, G. (1996). Secondary traumatization in parents following the disclosure of extrafamilial child sexual abuse: Initial effects. *Child Abuse & Neglect, 20*, 1095–1109.

Mannarino, A. P., and Cohen, J. A. (1996). A follow-up study of factors that mediate the development of psychological symptomatology in sexually abused girls. *Child Maltreatment, 1*, 246–60.

March, J. S. (1993). What constitutes a stressor? The "criterion A" issues. In J. R. T. Davidson and E. B. Foa (Eds.), *Posttraumatic stress disorder: DSM-IV and beyond* (37–54). Washington, DC: American Psychiatric Press.

McCart, M. R., Smith, D. W., Saunders, B. E., Kilpatrick, D. G., Resnick, H. S., and Ruggiero, K. J. (2007). Do urban adolescents habituate to interpersonal and community violence? Data from a national survey. *American Journal of Orthopsychiatry, 77*, 434–42

McCloskey, L. A., Figueredo, A. J., and Koss, M. P. (1995). The effects of systemic violence on children's mental health. *Child Development, 66*, 1239–61.

McDonald, S., and Hayne, H. (1996). Child-initiated conversations about the past and memory performance by preschoolers. *Cognitive Development, 11*, 421–42.

McFarlane, A. C., Policansky, S., and Irwin, C. P. (1987). A longitudinal study of the psychological morbidity in children due to a natural disaster. *Psychological Medicine, 17*, 727–38.

McGuigan, F., and Salmon, K. (2005). Pre-event discussion and recall of a novel event: How are children best prepared? *Journal of Experimental Child Psychology, 91*, 342–66.

McNally, R., Metzger, L. J., Lasko, N. G., and Clancy, S. A. (1998). Directed forgetting of trauma cues in adult survivors of childhood sexual abuse with and without posttraumatic stress disorder. *Journal of Abnormal Psychology, 107*, 596–601.

Meltzer, H., Gatward, R., Goodman, R., and Ford, T. (2000). *Mental health of children and adolescents in Great Britain.* London: The Stationery Office.

Nader, K., Pynoos, R., Fairbanks, L., and Frederick, C. (1990). Children's PTSD reactions one year after a sniper attack at their school. *American Journal of Psychiatry, 147*, 1526–30.

Nelson, K. (1993). The psychological and social origins of autobiographical memory. *Psychological Science, 4*, 7–14.

Norris, F. H., Friedman, M. J., Watson, P. J., Byrne, C. M., Diaz, E., and Kaniasty, K. (2002). 60,000 disaster victims speak: Part I. An empirical review of the empirical literature, 1981–2001. *Psychiatry, 65*, 207–39.

Norris, F. H., Kaniasty, K., Conrad, M. L., Inman, G. L., and Murphy, A. D. (2002). Placing age differences in cultural context: A comparison of the effects of age on PTSD after disasters in the United States, Mexico, and Poland. *Journal of Clinical Geropsychology, 8*, 153–73.

Norris, F. H., and Murrell, S. A. (1988). Prior experience as a moderator of disaster impact on anxiety symptoms in older adults. *American Journal of Community Psychology, 16*, 665–83.

Ohta, Y., Araki, K., Kawasaki, N., Nakane, Y., Honda, S., and Mine, M. (2003). Psychological distress among evacuees of a volcanic eruption in Japan: A follow-up study. *Psychiatric and Clinical Neurosciences, 57*, 105–11.

Ornstein, P. A., Shapiro, L. B., Clubb, P. A., Follmer, A., and Baker-Ward, L. (1997). The influence of prior knowledge on children's memory for salient medical procedures. In N. Stein, P. A. Ornstein, B. Tversky, and C. Brainerd (Eds.), *Memory for everyday and emotional events* (83–112). Hillsdale, NJ: Lawrence Erlbaum and Associates.

Ozer, E. J., Best, S. R., Lipsey, T. L., and Weiss, D. S. (2003). Predictors of posttraumatic stress disorder and symptoms in adults: A meta-analysis. *Psychological Bulletin, 129*, 52–73.

Palinkas, L. A., Petterson, J. S., Russell, J., and Downs, M. A. (1993). Community patterns of psychiatric disorders after the Exxon Valdez oil spill. *American Journal of Psychiatry, 150*, 1517–23.

Phifer, J. (1990). Psychological distress and somatic symptoms after natural disaster: Differential vulnerability and older adults. *Psychology and Aging, 5*, 412–20.

Pollak, S., Cicchetti, D., and Klorman, R. (1998). Stress, memory, and emotion: Developmental consideration from the study of child maltreatment. *Development and Psychopathology, 10*, 811–28.

Poole, D. A., and Lamb, M. (1998). *Investigative interviewing of children: A guide for professionals.* Washington, DC: American Psychological Association.

Pynoos, R. S., Frederick, C., Nader, K., Arroyo, W., Steinberg, A., Eth, S., et al. (1987). Life threat and posttraumatic stress in school-age children. *Archives of General Psychiatry, 44*, 1057–63.

Pynoos, R. S., Goenjian, S., Tashijian, M., Karakashian, M., Manjikian, R., Manoukian, G., et al. (1993). Post-traumatic stress reactions in children after the 1988 Armenian earthquake. *British Journal of Psychiatry, 163*, 239–47.

Resnick, H. S., Kilpatrick, D. G., Dansky, B. S., Saunders, B. E., and Best, C. L. (1993). Prevalence of civilian trauma and PTSD in a representative national sample of women. *Journal of Consulting and Clinical Psychology, 61*, 984–91.

Ruchkin, V. V., Eisemann, M., and Hagglof, B. (1998). Juvenile male rape victims: Is the level of post-traumatic stress related to personality and parenting? *Child Abuse & Neglect, 22*, 889–99.

Saarni, C., Mumme, D. L., and Campos, J. J. (1998). Emotional development: Action, communication and understanding. In W. Damon and N. Eisenberg (Eds.), *Handbook of child psychology: vol. 3. Social, emotional and personality development* (fifth ed., 237–310). New York: Wiley.

Sack, W. H., Clarke, G. N., and Seeley, J. (1995). Posttraumatic stress disorder across two generations of Cambodian refugees. *Journal of the American Academy of Child and Adolescent Psychiatry, 34,* 1160–66.

Saigh, P. A. (1991). On the development of posttraumatic stress disorder pursuant to different modes of traumatization. *Behavior Research and Therapy, 29,* 213–16.

Salmon, K., and Bryant, R. A. (2002). Posttraumatic stress disorder in children: The influence of developmental factors. *Clinical Psychology Review, 22,* 163–88.

Scheeringa, M. S., Wright, M. J., Hunt, J. P., and Zeanah, C. H. (2006). Factors affecting the diagnosis and prediction of PTSD symptomatology in children and adolescents. *American Journal of Psychiatry, 163,* 644–51.

Scheeringa, M. S., Zeanah, C. H., Drell, M. J., and Larrieu, J. A. (1995). Two approaches to the diagnosis of posttraumatic stress disorder in infancy and early childhood. *Journal of the American Academy of Child and Adolescent Psychiatry, 34,* 191–200.

Scheeringa, M. S., Zeanah, C. H., Myers, L., and Putnam, F. W. (2003). New findings on alternative criteria for PTSD in preschool children. *Journal of the American Academy of Child and Adolescent Psychiatry, 42,* 561–70.

Schneider, W., and Bjorklund, D. F. (1998). Memory. In W. Damon, D. Kuhn, and R. S. Siegler (Eds.), *Handbook of child psychology: vol. 2. Cognition, perception and language* (fifth ed., 467–522). New York: Wiley.

Shore, J., Tatum, E., and Vollmer, W. (1986). Evaluation and mental effects of disaster. Mount St. Helens eruption. *American Journal of Public Health, 76,* 76–83.

Sirles, E. A., Smith, J. A., and Kusama, H. (1989). Psychiatric status of intrafamilial child sexual abuse victims. *Journal of the American Academy of Child and Adolescent Psychiatry, 28,* 225–29.

Smith, P., Perrin, S., Yule, W., and Rabe-Hesketh, S. (2001). War exposure and maternal reactions in the psychological adjustment of children from Bosnia-Herzegovina. *Journal of Child Psychology and Psychiatry, 42,* 395–404.

Steward, M. S. (1993). Understanding children's memories of medical procedures: "He didn't touch me and it didn't hurt." In C. A. Nelson (Ed.), *Memory and affect in development* (171–225). Hillsdale, NJ: Lawrence Erlbaum and Associates.

Tanida, N. (1996). What happened to elderly people in the great Hanshin earthquake? *British Medical Journal, 313,* 1133–35.

Terr, L. C. (1983). Chowchilla revisited: The effects of psychic trauma four years after a school-bus kidnapping. *American Journal of Psychiatry, 140,* 1543–50.

———. (1991). Childhood trauma: An outline and overview. *American Journal of Psychiatry, 148,* 10–20.

Thompson, M. P., Norris, F. H., and Hanacek, B. (1993). Age differences in the psychological consequences of Hurricane Hugo. *Psychology and Aging, 8,* 606–16.

Ticehurst, S., Webster, R. A., Carr, V. J., and Lewin, T. J. (1996). The psychosocial impact of an earthquake on the elderly. *International Journal of Geriatric Psychiatry, 11*, 943–51.

Timmons-Mitchell, J., Chandler-Holtz, D., and Semple, W. E. (1996). Posttraumatic stress disorder symptoms in mothers following children's reports of sexual abuse. *American Journal of Orthopsychiatry, 66*, 463–67.

Wasserstein, S. B., and LaGreca, A. (1998). Hurricane Andrew: Parent conflict as a moderator of children's adjustment. *Hispanic Journal of Behavioral Sciences, 20*, 212–24.

Wesson, M., and Salmon, K. (2001). Drawing and showing: Helping children to report emotionally laden events. *Applied Cognitive Psychology, 15*, 301–20.

Wyman, P. A., Cowen, E. L., Work, W. C., Raoof A., Gribble, P. A., Parker, G. R., et al. (1992). Interviews with children who experienced major life stress: Family and child attributes that predict resilient outcomes. *Journal of the American Academy of Child and Adolescent Psychiatry, 31*, 904–10.

Yule, W. (1992). Posttraumatic stress disorder in child survivors of shipping disasters: The sinking of the "Jupiter." *Psychotherapy and Psychosomatics, 57*, 200–205.

# 2

# Genetic Risk Factors for PTSD

*Karestan C. Koenen, Ananda B. Amstadter,
and Nicole R. Nugent*

> There was evidence that the terrifying stresses of war tended to provoke
> anxiety states to a significantly preferential extent, but they did so far from
> regularly. A more important determinant of the type of response was the
> constitution of the individual, as shown by his family history, previous
> life, and personality.
>
> —Eliot Slater (Slater and Slater, 1944)

## INTRODUCTION

Twenty years of epidemiologic studies of trauma exposure and posttraumatic
stress disorder (PTSD) have established two important findings. We now
know that exposure to potentially traumatic events is common. In fact, the
overwhelming majority of individuals will experience a potentially traumatic
event at some point in their lives. However, only a minority of those exposed
will develop PTSD (Breslau, Davis, Andreski, and Peterson, 1991; Bromet,
Sonnega, and Kessler, 1998; Davidson, Hughes, Blazer, and George, 1991;
Helzer, Robins, and McEnvoy, 1987; Kessler, Sonnega, Bromet, Hughes, and
Nelson, 1995; Koenen et al., 2002; Norris, 1992; Perkonigg, Kessler, Storz,
and Wittchen, 2000). This apparent discrepancy between the prevalence
of exposure to traumatic events and the prevalence of PTSD among those
exposed has motivated a key question of traumatic stress research: Why do

Address correspondence to Karestan C. Koenen, Ph.D.; Department of Society, Human Development, and Health; Harvard School of Public Health, 677 Huntington Avenue, Kresge 613; Boston, MA 02115. E-mail: kkoenen@hsph.harvard.edu some individuals develop PTSD following exposure to potentially traumatic events when others appear to experience few negative effects?

This chapter reviews the current evidence for the role of genetic risk factors in the etiology of PTSD. Modern studies of genetic risk factors for PTSD are relatively new; the first genetic study of PTSD was published in 1991 (Comings et al., 1991). However, empirical research on the role of "constitutional" factors in the etiology of mental disorders in combat troops dates much earlier. Dr. Eliot Slater (1904–1983), a psychiatrist and researcher at the Maudsley Hospital, Institute of Psychiatry, in London, conducted much of this work in his studies of British World War I veterans. In fact, the results of Dr. Slater's studies suggested combat-related mental disorders resulted from an interaction between pre-existing "constitutional" vulnerability and severity of trauma (combat) exposure (Slater and Slater, 1944). This diathesis-stress model remains the foundation for current research on genetic risk factors for PTSD.

Extant research suggests genetic factors shape individuals' responses to trauma and play a role in determining who develops PTSD. However, many trauma researchers have largely neglected the role of genetic risk factors in the etiology of PTSD. The aim of this chapter is to review current evidence for the role of genetic risk factors in PTSD etiology in a way that is broadly accessible to the trauma field. We conclude our chapter by reflecting on future research needed to better understand the role of genetic risk factors in PTSD etiology.

## EVIDENCE FOR GENETIC INFLUENCES ON RISK FOR PTSD

An individual's genotype, or DNA sequence, is determined at conception. Thus, genetic variants associated with PTSD qualify as risk factors, or as a "measurable characterization of each subject in a specified population that precedes the outcome of interest and which can be used to divide the population into two groups (the high-risk and the low-risk groups that comprise the total population)" (Kraemer et al., 1997).[1] Evidence for genetic influences on PTSD comes from family, twin, and molecular genetic studies. Below, we summarize the evidence for genetic influences on risk of PTSD. Readers interested in more detail on this topic might wish to consult one of the recent review articles available (Koenen, 2007; Segman and Shalev, 2003).

If risk for PTSD is partially explained by genetic factors, biological relatives (family members) of individuals with PTSD should have a higher prevalence of PTSD than non-relatives. Moreover, among biological relatives of individuals with PTSD, the prevalence of the disorder should be higher in first-degree (parents, siblings) than second-degree (grandparents) relatives. The major limitation of family studies is that they cannot tell us whether a disorder, such as PTSD, runs in families for genetic or environmental reasons. Twin studies are needed to disentangle the roles of genetic and environmental influences in disorder etiology. However, twin studies are limited in that they cannot specify which genes actually increase risk for the disorder. Molecular genetic studies are needed to accomplish this aim. However, to date there have been strikingly few molecular genetic studies of PTSD.

## PTSD Runs in Families

Standard family studies generally seek to examine whether the prevalence of PTSD is higher in relatives of individuals with PTSD (called probands in genetic studies) than in relatives of similarly trauma-exposed individuals who did not develop PTSD. Family studies in PTSD are complicated by the practical reality that PTSD cannot be assessed in relatives who have not experienced a traumatic event. It is unknown whether these relatives would have developed PTSD if they were exposed. Thus, family studies of PTSD have focused on genetically related dyads who have known (often shared) trauma exposure. Most often these studies have examined the association between parent and child PTSD in trauma-exposed samples.

Extant research suggests that relatives of probands with PTSD are at elevated risk of the disorder as compared to relatives of similarly trauma-exposed controls who did not develop PTSD. For example, adult children of Holocaust survivors with PTSD had a higher risk of PTSD following trauma compared to adult children of Holocaust survivors without PTSD (Yehuda, Halligan, and Bierer, 2001). Similarly, Cambodian refugee children whose mother and father both had PTSD were five times more likely to receive the diagnosis than refugee children whose parents did not have PTSD (Sack, Clarke, and Seeley, 1995).

Increasingly common are family studies that examine the association between child and parent posttraumatic stress symptoms (PTSS) following child traumatic exposure. Parent-child PTSS correlations following child traumatic exposure have been mixed, with some studies reporting a significant correlation between child PTSS and parent PTSS (Barakat et al., 1997; de Vries et al., 1999; Hall et al., 2006; Pelcovitz et al., 1998) whereas other studies have found no relationship (Landolt, Vollrath, Ribi, Gnehm, and Sennhauser, 2003; McDermott and Cvitanovich, 2000; Stuber, Christakis, Houskamp, and Kazak, 1996). Attempts to resolve this apparent discrepancy have highlighted the importance of time lapsed between traumatic exposure and assessment (Pfefferbaum and Pfefferbaum, 1998). Studies examining acute distress levels soon after the trauma typically find no association between parent and child PTSS (Bryant, Moulds, and Guthrie, 2004; Winston et al., 2002), while longitudinal studies show increases in parent-child PTSS associations over time (Koplewicz et al., 2002; Ostrowski, Christopher, and Delahanty, 2007; Smith, Perrin, Yule, and Rabe-Hesketh, 2001). Initial symptoms in the child have been found to impact subsequent symptoms in the parent (Koplewicz et al., 2002) and initial parent symptoms have been found to predict subsequent child symptoms (Daviss et al., 2000; McFarlane, Policansky, and Irwin, 1987; Nugent, Ostrowski, Christopher, and Delahanty, 2007).

Research has further indicated that the impact of parental PTSS on subsequent child PTSS is not simply accounted for by overall levels of general parental distress (Nugent, Ostrowski, Christopher, and Delahanty, 2007). Thus, parent PTSS appear to influence child PTSS through a more specific mechanism than merely parental availability or child concern for global parental distress. Parents may model poor adjustment to trauma, may directly alter their child's avoidance behaviors, or may share underlying genetic vulnerabilities to the development of PTSD. These investigations illustrate the challenge inherent in using family study paradigms to examine genetic factors in PTSD, as children share not only genes with their parents, but also many environmental factors.

## PTSD is Heritable

Twin studies help to disentangle the role of genetic and environmental factors in risk of developing PTSD. The twin design has been used to calculate the proportion of the variance in a trait or disorder explained by genetic factors; the resultant variance attributed to genetic factors is termed heritability. The basic twin method compares the degree of similarity within identical or monzygotic (MZ) pairs with the degree of similarity within fraternal or dizygotic (DZ) pairs. It is assumed that, whereas MZ twins share 100 percent of their genes and 100 percent of the shared environment, DZ twins share approximately 50 percent of their genes and 100 percent of the shared environment. If MZ twins are significantly more similar on a characteristic than DZ twins, then this phenotype (observed characteristic) is interpreted as being genetically influenced. The heritability estimate is derived from the equation $2(rMZ - rDZ)$, where r = the intraclass twin correlation (Plomin, DeFries, McClearn, and McGuffin, 2001). For categorical phenotypes, such as PTSD diagnosis, the tetrachoric correlation, which assumes an underlying normal distribution of liability, is used to calculate heritability (Falconer, 1960).

*Gene-Environment Correlation*

Twin studies have made three major contributions to our understanding of the genetic etiology of PTSD. First, they indicate that genetic factors influence exposure to potentially traumatic events. This is referred to as gene-environment correlation, whereby selection of environment, and subsequently potential for exposure to trauma, is partly determined by genetic factors (Kendler and Eaves, 1986). A recent review of genetic influences on environmental measures including stressful life events, parenting, and social support, found that heritability estimates fell between 7 and 39 percent with a weighted heritability estimate for all environmental measures of 27 percent (Kendler and Baker, 2006).

Twin studies have demonstrated that genetic factors influence exposure to potentially traumatic events such as combat exposure (Lyons et al., 1993) and assaultive violence (Stein, Jang, Taylor, Vernon, and Livesley, 2002). Figure 2.1 presents the heritability of several different types of traumatic events. The Lyons et al. (1993) study included members of the Vietnam Era Twin (VET) Registry and thus focused on indicators of war-related trauma including volunteering for service in Southeast Asia, service in Southeast Asia, combat exposure, and being awarded a combat medal. Heritability estimates ranged from 35 percent for Southeast Asia service to 54 percent for being awarded

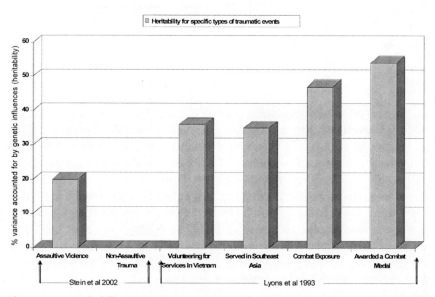

**Figure 2.1.  Heritability (% Variance Accounted for by Genetic Influences) for Specific Types of Traumatic Events**

a combat medal. The Stein et al. (2002) study was conducted on a community sample of twins; heritability estimates in this sample were lower than those in the VET Registry sample and ranged from zero, for non-assaultive violence events such as car accidents and natural disaster to 20 percent for assaultive violence. However, it is difficult to make strong inferences about the differences in heritability estimates for the traumatic events in the Lyons et al. (1993) vs. Stein et al. (2002) studies. Heritability estimates are affected by the reliability of the phenotype assessed; measurement error is included in estimates of non-shared environmental variance. Thus, being awarded a combat medal or Southeast Asia service may be more heritable in part because they can be assessed more reliably from military records than other types of trauma exposure that depend on retrospective recall.

These gene-environmental correlations are likely mediated individual differences in personality. Personality characteristics are moderately heritable and influence the tendency for individuals to select themselves into potentially harmful environments. For example, longitudinal investigations have found that childhood adjustment and neuroticism predicted subsequent stressful life events in adulthood (Van Os and Jones, 1999). Similarly, research has found that childhood externalizing is prospectively associated with both risk of trauma exposure and with PTSD in adulthood (Koenen, Moffitt, Poulton, Martin, and Caspi, 2007). One investigation found that genetic factors partially mediated the association between personality variables (such as antisocial personality traits, psychoticism, and openness to novelty) and exposure to violent traumatic events (Jang, Stein, Taylor, Asmundson, and Livesley, 2003).

*Genetic Influences on PTSD*

The second major contribution of twin studies is the suggestion that genetic influences explain a substantial proportion of vulnerability to PTSD even after accounting for genetic influences on trauma exposure. The first twin study to estimate heritability of PTSD was conducted by True and colleagues on members of the VET Registry (True et al., 1993). The authors found that approximately 30 percent of the variance in reported PTSD symptoms was accounted for by genetic factors, even after controlling for combat exposure. This genetic influence on PTSD symptoms was also found in a group of twins who did not serve in Southeast Asia, suggesting heritability of PTSD has generalization to traumatic events other than combat exposure. Interestingly, shared environmental experiences did not contribute to the variance in PTSD symptoms.

The second twin study of PTSD was conducted on a sample of male and female civilian volunteers (Stein et al., 2002). Consistent with True et al. (1993), the authors found moderate heritability in PTSD symptoms, with additional variance accounted for by non-shared environmental factors. The findings from these two twin studies suggest that genetic factors play a substantial role in vulnerability to developing PTSD.

## Common Genetic Vulnerability to PTSD and Other Mental Disorders

The third major contribution of twin studies is the demonstration that genetic influences on PTSD overlap with those for other mental disorders. The extent of the overlap varies with the disorder studied. For example, genetic influences on major depression account for the majority of the genetic variance in PTSD (Koenen et al., 2008). Genetic influences common to generalized anxiety disorder and panic disorder symptoms account for approximately 60 percent (Chantarujikapong et al., 2001) and those common to alcohol and drug dependence (Xian et al., 2000) and nicotine dependence (Koenen, Hitsman, et al., 2005) account for over 40 percent of the genetic variance in PTSD. Thus, the limited data available suggest that the majority of genes that affect risk for PTSD also influence risk for other psychiatric disorders and vice versa.

### Specific Genetic Variants May be Risk Factors for PTSD

Human beings are over 99 percent genetically identical. Research aimed at identifying genes that explain individual differences in risk for PTSD focuses on the tiny fraction (1 percent) of the DNA sequences that differs among individuals. Almost 90 percent of human genetic variation is made up of single nucleotide polymorphisms (SNPs, pronounced "snips"), which occur when a single nucleotide (A, T, C, or G) in the DNA sequence is altered. An example of a SNP is a change in the DNA sequence from CGTTGG to CGATGG. By definition, the frequency of SNPs must be at least 1 percent of the population. There are approximately three million SNPs in the human genome. Although other types of polymorphisms in the human genome exist, SNPs are most commonly used in molecular genetic studies. Readers interested in learning more about SNPs are encouraged to obtain a SNP factsheet from the Human Genome Project website: http://www.ornl.gov/sci/techresources/Human_Genome/faq/snps.html.

Molecular genetic studies of PTSD have used a case-control candidate gene association design. The association method detects genes with small effects on risk and has been, until very recently, the method of choice for molecular genetic studies of complex disorders (Risch and Merikangas, 1996). Disorders are referred to as "complex" when their etiology is thought to involve a combination of many genes and environmental factors such as is the case in PTSD. Association studies correlate a DNA marker's alleles, which are different sequences of DNA at a specific position (or locus) on the chromosome, with an outcome. Table 2.1 summarizes the findings from the eleven candidate gene studies of PTSD to date.

*Dopamine System*

Nearly half of these PTSD genetic studies have focused on dopamine (DA) system genes. Both animal and human studies have implicated the dopaminergic system in the etiology of PTSD. Higher levels of plasma (Hamner and Diamond, 1993) and urinary (De Bellis, Baum, Birmaher, Keshavan, Eccard, and Boring, 1999; Lemieux and Coe, 1995; Spivak et al., 1999; Yehuda, Southwick, Giller, Ma, and Mason, 1992) DA have been associated with PTSD in humans. In animal studies limbic system innervation of DA has been found to be reactive to stress (Goldstein, Rasmusson, Bunney, and Roth, 1996; Inglis and Moghaddam, 1999).

Four out of the five investigations examining dopamine system genes studied the association between marker alleles at the D2 dopamine receptor gene (*DRD2*) and PTSD. Whereas initial investigations found a positive association with the DRD2A1 allele (Comings et al., 1991; Comings, Muhleman, and Gysin, 1996), a subsequent investigation found no association with the DRD2A1 allele or with any combination of alleles for the *DRD2* locus (Gelernter, Southwick, Goodson, Nagy, and Charney, 1999). However, it is important to note that the investigation conducted by Gelernter and colleagues (1999) did not assess for trauma exposure in the control group. The Comings and colleagues (1996) investigation consisted of a relatively small sample of substance abusers with PTSD ($n = 37$) compared with substance abusers without PTSD ($n = 19$); limiting generalizability to a substance abusing population. Comorbid PTSD and substance abuse was also addressed in a subsequent investigation of combat veterans with and without PTSD, with analyses revealing a positive association between DRD2A1 and PTSD only in the subset of PTSD cases who engaged in harmful drinking (Young et al., 2002). The final study examined a slightly different facet of dopaminergic transmission in patients with chronic PTSD and trauma-exposed healthy controls, reporting a positive association between of the DA transporter *SLC6A3* (*DAT1*) 3' polymorphism and chronic PTSD (Segman et al., 2002).

**Table 2.1.  Review of Published Case-Control Candidate Gene Associations Studies of PTSD**

| First Author | Year | Cases N (% male) | Controls N (% male) | Trauma Type | Gene Name (Symbol) | Finding |
|---|---|---|---|---|---|---|
| Comings | 1991 | 35 (100) | 314 (100) | Combat | Dopamine Receptor D2 (DRD2) | Excess D2A1 Allele in PTSD cases p = .007 |
| Comings | 1996 | 24 (100) | 9 (100) | Combat | Dopamine Receptor D2 (DRD2) | Excess D2A1 Allele in PTSD cases p = .041 |
| Comings | 1996 | 13 (100) | 11 (100) | Combat | Dopamine Receptor D2 (DRD2) | Excess D2A1 Allele in PTSD cases p = .002 |
| Gelernter | 1999 | 52 (100) | 87 (100) | Combat | Dopamine Receptor D2 (DRD2) | No significant association between D2A1 allele/DRD2 haplotypes and PTSD |
| Lappalainen | 2002 | 77 (100) | 202 (100) | Combat | Neuropeptide Y (NPY) | No significant association between Leu7Pro polymorphism and PTSD |
| Segman | 2002 | 102 (56) | 104 (47) | Various | Dopamine Transporter (DAT1) | Excess 9-repeat allele in PTSD cases p = .012 |
| Young | 2002 | 91 (100) | 53 (100) | Combat | Dopamine Receptor D2 (DRD2) | Excess D2A1 allele only in PTSD cases with harmful drinking p < .001 |
| Bachman | 2005 | 118 (100) | 42 (100) | Combat | Glococorticoid Receptor (GCCR) | No significant association between GCCR polymorphisms and PTSD |
| Lee | 2005 | 100 (43) | 197 (39) | Various | Serotonin Transporter (SLC6A4) | Excess s allele in PTSD cases p = .04 |
| Zhang | 2006 | 96 (76) | 250 (41) | Not specified | Brain derived neurotrophic factor (BDNF) | No significant association between three BDNF variants and PTSD |
| Kilpatrick | 2007 | 19 (32) | 570 (37) | Hurricane | Serotonin Transporter (SLC6A4) | Significant association between s/s genotype and PTSD in adults with high hurricane exposure and low social support |

PTSD = posttraumatic stress disorder; D2DA1 = Al one allele of DRD2 gene; s allele = short version (versus long) of the serotonin transporter promoter polymorphism.

*Alternative Neurobiological Pathways*

One study examined the association between a common variable number of tandem repeats (VNTR) polymorphism in the promoter region of the serotonin transporter gene (*SLC6A4*), designated as 5-HTTLPR, and PTSD. The 5-HTTLPR is a functional polymorphism, the short ("s") 5-HTTLPR allele is less transcriptionally efficient than the long ("l") allele (Lesch et al., 1996). An excess of s/s genotypes has been reported in Korean PTSD patients as compared with normal controls (Lee et al., 2005). The six remaining studies explored genetic polymorphisms across alternative neurobiological pathways, with the majority of studies reporting no association between specific genes and chronic PTSD. More specifically, one investigation found no association between polymorphisms in the brain derived neurotrophic factor (*BDNF*) gene and chronic PTSD (Zhang et al., 2006). Similarly, no significant association was found between chronic PTSD and either the Leu7Pro polymorphism in the neuropeptide Y (*NPY*) gene (Lappalainen et al., 2002) or two glucocorticoid receptor polymorphisms (N363S and BclI) (Bachmann et al., 2005).

*Evidence for Gene-Environment Interaction in PTSD*

Emerging evidence supports the role of gene-environment interactions in the etiology of common mental disorders such as major depression (Moffitt, Caspi, and Rutter, 2005). However, only one study of which we are aware has specifically examined the role of gene-environment interaction in the etiology of PTSD.

This study is of note both because of the methodology used and its findings. Kilpatrick et al. (Kilpatrick et al., 2007) examined whether 5-HTTLPR variation moderated risk of developing PTSD in an epidemiologic sample of 589 adults exposed to the 2004 Florida hurricanes (see Acierno et al., at press; Acierno, Ruggiero, Kilpatrick, Resnick, and Galea, 2006). This is the first study to collect genetic samples by mail in the context of a large epidemiological telephone survey. Other studies have collected saliva samples for DNA analyses by mail (Freeman et al., 1997), but this has been in the context of studies in which investigators had ongoing research relationships with participants. Likelihood of returning a saliva sample did not differ in relation to sex, level of hurricane exposure, level of social support, or PTSD status. Additional details on response rate and correlates of participation are summarized elsewhere (Galea et al., 2006). The success of the Kilpatrick et al. study suggest that it is both feasible and useful to add genetic components to studies using telephone interviews to collect data about exposure to traumatic events and PTSD.

Kilpatrick et al. (2007) found the low expression(s) variant of the 5-HTTLPR increased risk of post-hurricane PTSD only under the conditions of high hurricane exposure and low social support. Figure 2.2 presents the prevalence of post-hurricane PTSD by *SLC6A4* genotype, level of social support, and level of hurricane exposure. High risk ($n = 27$) were those with the s/s genotype, low social support, and high hurricane exposure. Medium risk ($n = 54$) were those with the l/s (long/short) genotype, low social support, and high hurricane exposure. Low risk ($n = 498$) were all others. There was a strong association between risk group and prevalence of PTSD ($\chi^2(2, n = 579) = 19.94, p < .001$). High-risk individuals (high hurricane exposure, the low expression 5-HTTLPR variant, low social support) had 4.5 times (95 percent CI = 1.2, 17.9) the risk of developing PTSD as compared to low-risk individuals. Additional research is needed to replicate the Kilpatrick et al. findings. Such studies can add to our knowledge of how genetic and environmental risk and protective factors interact to foster resilience or increase psychopathology following trauma.

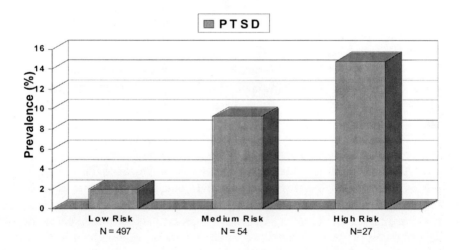

Adapted from Kilpatrick et al., under review.

Figure 2.2. Prevalence of post-hurricane PTSD by SLC6A4 genotype, level of social support, and level of hurricane exposure in adults exposed to 2004 Florida hurricanes. High risk (n = 27) were those with the s'/s' genotype, low social support, and high hurricane exposure. Medium risk (n = 54) were those with the l'/s' genotype, low social support, and high hurricane exposure. Low risk (n − 497) were all others ($x^2(2, n − 598) = 19.94, p < .001$).

*Genetic Studies of Comorbid Phenotypes Among Individuals with PTSD*

Several other studies have examined the association between variation in specific genes and phenotypes among individuals diagnosed with PTSD. In a recent study of male Vietnam veterans with PTSD the *DRD2* A1 allele was associated with comorbid conditions (Lawford, Young, Noble, Kann, and Ritchie, 2006). Specifically, those with the *DRD2* A1 allele had higher levels of anxiety/insomnia, social dysfunction, and depression compared to those without the A1 allele. Similarly, in an open label treatment study for PTSD, male veterans with the *DRD2* A1 allele had higher baseline levels of anxiety/insomnia, social dysfunction, and depression, compared to those without the A1 allele (Lawford et al., 2003). Following an eight-week paroxetine trial, all patients improved in terms of anxiety/insomnia, depression, and social dysfunction regardless of A1 allele status; however, those with the A1 allele improved to a greater degree on social dysfunction than did those without the allele.

In addition to investigations of candidate genes within dopaminergic systems, gamma-aminobutyric acid (*GABA*) neurotransmitter systems, and Apoliprotein E (*APOE*) systems have also been targets of genetic studies of comorbid conditions of PTSD. Feusner and colleagues (2001) examined the *GABAA* receptor β3 subunit gene (*GABRB3*) in relation to comorbid conditions in male Caucasians with PTSD. The risk genotype for *GABRB3* is the heterozygote (G1+G1−). Those with a heterozygote genotype had greater somatic symptoms, anxiety/insomnia, depression, and social dysfunction symptoms compared to those with a homozygote genotype (G1−G1− or G1+G1+) (Feusner et al., 2001).

*APOE* has been associated with psychiatric conditions marked by cognitive disturbances (Gallagher-Thompson, O'Hara, Simmons, Kraemer, and Murphy, 2001). Given the association between PTSD and neurocognitive deficits (e.g., Gilbertson et al., 2006), Freeman and colleagues (2005) investigated the association between *APOE* genotype and PTSD. Patients with the *APOE2* allele had higher PTSD re-experiencing symptoms and performed poorer on several facets of memory function compared to those without the *APOE2* allele (Freeman, Roca, Guggenheim, Kimbrell, and Griffin, 2005).

*Specific Genes Associated with PTSD and Other Mental Disorders*

As noted above, twin studies suggest comorbidity between PTSD and other mental disorders can largely be explained by a shared genetic diathesis. The presence of a common genetic diathesis between major depression and PTSD is further supported by molecular genetic studies, which have implicated the 5-HTTLPR S allele in both PTSD and depression (Caspi et al., 2003; Lee et al.,

2005; Kilpatrick et al., 2007). Polymorphisms in *FKBP5* have been associated with recurrence of major depressive episodes and *response* to antidepressant treatment (Binder et al., 2004) as well as with peritraumatic dissociation, an acute predictor of PTSD (Koenen, Saxe et al., 2005). DA system genes, such as *DAT1*, which have been associated with PTSD, have also been associated with ADHD (e.g., Brookes et al., 2006) and alcohol use (e.g., Kohnke et al., 2005).

## SUMMARY

Research to date has yielded a number of findings that provide a foundation for our current knowledge regarding the genetics of PTSD. We know that PTSD runs in families and that genetic factors influence both exposure to trauma and the development of PTSD. We also know that the association between PTSD and other mental disorders is largely explained by a shared genetic diathesis. Few molecular genetic studies of PTSD have been conducted at this writing and, therefore, we know little about which specific genes influence risk for developing PTSD.

An additional unexplored area is that of gene-environment interaction in PTSD. The only molecular genetic study of PTSD to move beyond the main effect model is that by Kilpatrick and colleagues (2007). Using a gene-environment interaction model, Kilpatrick and colleagues (2007) found that the s/s genotype for 5-HTTLPR conferred increased risk for the development of PTSD under conditions of low social support and high hurricane exposure (see figure 2.2). Findings from Kilpatrick et al. (2007) suggest collecting genetic data as part of a traditional epidemiologic study of PTSD is not only feasible but offers the opportunity to better understand the interplay of genetic and environmental factors in the etiology of the disorder.

## CONCLUSIONS AND FUTURE DIRECTIONS

Rigorous studies of genetic risk factors for PTSD will improve our ability to answer one of the key questions motivating the trauma field: Why do some individuals develop PTSD following exposure to potentially traumatic events when others appear to experience few negative effects? Although extant evidence suggests that genetic factors are important in the etiology of PTSD, our understanding of genetic risk factors for PTSD is still in the early stages. For example, we know little about the specific genes that might be important with respect to increasing or buffering risk or the mechanisms by which they operate. In this section, we present our views on promising directions for future research in this area.

## Integrating Genetics into Biologically-Informed PTSD Studies

Thus far, molecular genetic studies of PTSD have focused on whether specific genetic variants are more prevalent in PTSD cases than controls. Such studies represent important first steps in understanding the genetics of PTSD, but tell us little about the mechanisms by which specific genes may increase risk of PTSD. One way of learning more about such mechanisms is to incorporate genetics into studies that assess participants shortly after trauma exposure (e.g., in the emergency room) and follow them over some period of time, usually one to two years, to determine who develops PTSD. These prospective exposed cohort designs often include rich multidimensional assessments of acute biological and psychological responses to trauma and aim to test how variation in acute response predicts the development of PTSD. Obtaining DNA from participants in such studies is efficient and feasible since biological specimens, such as saliva, are often already being collected.

Obtaining genetic data on participants in prospective exposed cohort studies offers the opportunity to test whether the association between variation in specific genes and PTSD is mediated by acute biological and/or psychological response to trauma. For example, investigators can test whether genes involved in regulation of the hypothalamic-pituitary-adrenal (HPA) axis are associated with PTSD and, if they are, whether the association is mediated by peritraumatic cortisol rhythms, which are thought to be a marker of HPA axis dysregulation in response to stress.

Alternatively, acute biological and psychological response to trauma could be viewed as an "endophenotype" of PTSD and an outcome in itself for genetic studies. Endophenotypes are defined as "measurable components unseen by the unaided eye along the pathway between disease and distal genotype" (Gottesman and Gould, 2003, 636). We speculate, in the absence of evidence either way, that acute response to trauma may be more strongly determined by genetic influences than the ultimate diagnosis of PTSD. Unlike acute trauma response, numerous intervening environmental factors, such as social support following the trauma, medical care received, medications administered, and so on, will influence the development of PTSD. These environmental factors may complicate the ability to detect the effect of genetic influences on risk of PTSD.

At the time of this writing, we are aware of only one study that has examined the association between variation in specific genes and acute trauma response. Koenen, Saxe and colleagues (2005) examined whether variation in *FKBP5*, a glucocorticoid receptor-regulating co-chaperone of stress proteins, was associated with peritraumatic dissociation in a pediatric sample of forty-six children hospitalized for physical injury (Koenen, Saxe, et al., 2005;

Saxe et al., 2005). The authors examined the association between *FKBP5* and peritraumatic dissociation because this gene is involved in HPA axis regulation through influencing glucocorticoid receptor activity. Animal models support genetically influenced individual differences in HPA axis regulation that produce variation in acute behavioral responses to stress (Bakshi and Kalin, 2000). Moreover, the specific polymorphisms in *FKBP5* (rs3800373, rs1360780) examined were posited to result in "more rapid onset of stress hormone hyperactivity after stressful life events" (Binder et al., 2004, 1323). Peritraumatic dissociation has been shown to increase risk of developing PTSD in children and adults (Ozer, Best, Lipsey, and Weiss, 2003).

Koenen et al. (2005) found a significant association between these SNPs and peritraumatic dissociation. For rs3800373, each C allele was associated with .5 standard deviation increase in dissociation during the accident and a .7 standard deviation increase in dissociation since the accident ($p < .001$). Marker rs3800373 uniquely explained 14 percent of the variance in dissociation over and above race, gender, age, and injury severity. These results are very preliminary as the study was conducted on a small sample and have not yet been replicated. However, this study supported the feasibility of gathering genetic data as part of a prospective exposed cohort study and the potential for identifying specific genes that influence acute response to trauma.

## Disentangling Genetic Risk Factors for Onset vs. Course of PTSD

Studies of genetic risk factors for PTSD have largely included only PTSD cases with current PTSD, although current PTSD often involves a chronic disorder extending over many years or even decades. When considering disorder etiology, it is useful to distinguish between risk factors for onset or development of the disorder and risk factors for course or chronicity of the disorder. Factors that influence who develops the disorder in the first place may differ from those that influence who recovers from the disorder once it develops. For example, members of disadvantaged ethnic groups are not at higher risk for the development of psychiatric disorders; however, if the disorder is developed, these disadvantaged individuals may display greater chronicity compared to non-disadvantaged individuals. For example, Breslau and colleagues found that for Hispanic individuals who develop a psychiatric disorder, their disorders are more chronic than those of non-Hispanic whites (Breslau, Kendler, Su, Gaxiola-Aguilar, and Kessler, 2005).

Twin studies have relied almost exclusively on diagnoses of lifetime PTSD and therefore heritability estimates from such studies explain the proportion of variation in risk for developing PTSD explained by genetic factors. It is not known whether genetic factors explain as much of the variance in chronicity of PTSD or whether the same genes that influence risk for developing PTSD affect PTSD chronicity. Studies are needed that distinguish between genetic influences on risk for developing PTSD vs. persistence of the disorder.

## Considering Genetic Risk Factors from a Developmental Perspective

The effect of genetic risk factors in the etiology of PTSD may depend on developmental timing of trauma exposure. Childhood trauma has been associated with a variety of long-term deleterious consequences across social, emotional, and cognitive/academic functioning (Lansford et al., 2002). Research has suggested that children may be more vulnerable to developing PTSD than adults, with one meta-analysis concluding that traumatized children were 1.5 times more likely to develop PTSD following a traumatic event than were similarly traumatized adults (Fletcher, 1996). Developmental stage at time of trauma exposure may be an important factor in determining level, or possibly even type, of risk conferred.

Sensitivity to developmental stage may be particularly important in neurobiological aspects of PTSD, as animal research has suggested that early life events may be particularly relevant for subsequent cortisol reactivity (Anisman, Zahoria, Meaney, and Merali, 1998; Vasquez, 1998). This is consistent with evidence that women with PTSD who experienced childhood sexual abuse excreted higher levels of cortisol than both non-PTSD adults with childhood sexual abuse and non-abused controls (Lemieux and Coe, 1995). Moreover, different patterns of acute and chronic cortisol response have been reported in children with PTSD relative to adults with PTSD (De Bellis, et al., 1999; De Bellis, Hall, Boring, Frustaci, and Moritz, 2001; Delahanty, Nugent, Christopher, and Walsh, 2005; Ostrowski et al., 2007). It is possible that the lower cortisol levels seen in many adults with PTSD may be a long-term developmental consequence of trauma exposure during childhood (De Bellis, Chrousos, and Dorn, 1994).

In addition to developmental stage at the time of trauma exposure, studies of genetic risk factors for PTSD might benefit from studying the effects of repeated trauma exposure. A recent meta-analysis found prior trauma history to be one of the most consistent predictors of PTSD (Ozer et al., 2003). In a sample of rape victims, Resnick and colleagues (1995) found that those with a prior history of trauma were 6.7 times more likely to develop PTSD than victims without a prior history of trauma. Furthermore, prior trauma has been shown to be associated with altered HPA axis responses to subsequent stressors (Delahanty et al., 2005; Delahanty, Raimonde, Spoonster, and Cullado, 2003; Heim et al., 2000; Resnick et al., 1995).

## Genetics of PTSD—Clinical Implications

Future examinations of the genetics of PTSD are further encouraged to prioritize investigations with the potential to inform PTSD treatment. For example, depression research has found that both SSRI efficacy (e.g., Arias, Catalán, Gastó, Blanca Gutiérrez, and Fañanás, 2005; Cusin et al., 2002; Eichhammer et al., 2003; Murphy, Kremer, Rodrigues, and Schatzberg, 2003; Rausch et al., 2002) and side effects (Bishop, Moline, Ellingrod, Schultz, and Clayton, 2006; Murphy et al., 2003) may be associated with polymorphisms of the serotonin receptor and/or transporter genes. To the degree that genetic factors may play a role in biological concomitants and/or underlying mechanisms in pharmacologic treatments for PTSD, genetic investigations may inform treatment-matching as well as the development of novel treatments.

## ACKNOWLEDGEMENTS

From the Departments of Society, Human Development, and Health and Epidemiology, Harvard School of Public Health (Dr. Koenen). From the Departments of Psychiatry and Behavioral Science, Medical University of South Carolina, and Department of Psychology, Auburn University (Ananda Amstadter). From the Departments of Psychiatry and Behavioral Science, Medical University of South Carolina, and Department of Psychology, Kent State University (Nicole Nugent). Dr. Koenen is supported in part by US-NIMH K08 MH070627 and MH078828. Ananda Amstadter is supported by US-NIAAA T32 AA007474. Nicole Nugent is supported by US-NIMH T32 MH18869.

## ENDNOTE

1. Please note, for the purpose of this chapter, we are speaking of genetic influences only in terms of DNA sequence variation. We do not consider epigenetic modifications of the genome that may occur as the result of environmental input.

## REFERENCES

Acierno, R., Ruggiero, K. J., Galea, S., Resnick, H. S., Koenen, K. C., Rotizsch, J., et al. (at press). Psychological sequelae of the 2004 Florida hurricanes: Implications for post-disaster intervention. *American Journal of Public Health*.

Acierno, R., Ruggiero, K. J., Kilpatrick, D. G., Resnick, H. S., and Galea, S. (2006). Risk and protective factors for psychopathology among older versus younger adults after the 2004 Florida hurricanes. *American Journal of Geriatric Psychiatry, 14*, 1051–59.

Anisman, H., Zahoria, M., Meaney, M. J., and Merali, Z. (1998). Do early life events permanently alter behavioural and emotional response to stressors? *International Journal of Developmental Neuroscience, 16*, 149–64.

Arias, B., Catalán, R., Gastó, C., Blanca Gutiérrez, B., and Fañanás, L. (2005). Evidence for a combined genetic effect of the 5-HT1A receptor and serotonin transporter genes in the clinical outcome of major depressive patients treated with citalopram. *Journal of Psychopharmacology, 19*, 166–72.

Bachmann, A. W., Sedgley, T. L., Jackson, R. V., Gibson, J. N., Young, R. M., and Torpy, D. J. (2005). Glucocorticoid receptor polymorphisms and post-traumatic stress disorder. *Psychoneuroendocrinology, 30*, 297–306.

Bakshi, V. P., and Kalin, N. H. (2000). Corticotropin-releasing hormone and animal models of anxiety: gene-environment interactions. *Biological Psychiatry, 48*, 1175–98.

Barakat, L. P., Kazak, A. E., Meadows, A. T., Casey, R., Meeske, K., and Stuber, M. L. (1997). Families surviving childhood cancer: a comparison of posttraumatic stress symptoms with families of healthy children. *Journal of Pediatric Psychology, 22*, 843–59.

Binder, E. B., Salyakina, D., Lichtner, P., Wochnik, G. M., Ising, M., Putz, B., et al. (2004). Polymorphisms in FKBP5 are associated with increased recurrence of depressive episodes and rapid response to antidepressant treatment. *Nature Genetics, 36*, 1319–25.

Bishop, J. R., Moline, J., Ellingrod, V. L., Schultz, S. K., and Clayton, A. H. (2006). Serotonin 2A-1438 G/A and G-protein Beta3 subunit C825T polymorphisms in patients with depression and SSRI-associated sexual side-effects. *Neuropsychopharmacology, 31*, 2281–88.

Breslau, J., Kendler, K. S., Su, M., Gaxiola-Aguilar, S., and Kessler, R. C. (2005). Lifetime risk and persistence of psychiatric disorders across ethnic groups in the United States. *Psychological Medicine, 35*, 317–27.

Breslau, N., Davis, G. C., Andreski, P., and Peterson, E. (1991). Traumatic events and posttraumatic stress disorder in an urban population of young adults. *Archives of General Psychiatry, 48*, 216–22.

Bromet, E., Sonnega, A., and Kessler, R. C. (1998). Risk factors for DSM-III-R posttraumatic stress disorder: Findings from the National Comorbidity Survey. *American Journal of Epidemiology, 147*, 353–61.

Brookes, K. J., Mill, J., Guindalini, C., Curran, S., Xu, X., Knight, J., et al. (2006). A common haplotype of the dopamine transporter gene associated with attention-deficit/hyperactivity disorder and interacting with maternal use of alcohol during pregnancy. *Archives of General Psychiatry, 63*, 74–81.

Bryant, R. A., Moulds, M., and Guthrie, R. M. (2004). Cognitive strategies and the resolution of acute stress disorder. *Journal of Traumatic Stress, 14*, 213–19.

Caspi, A., Sugden, K., Moffitt, T. E., Taylor, A., Craig, I., Harrington, H., et al. (2003). Influence of life stress on depression: Moderation by a polymorphism in the 5-HTT gene. *Science, 301*, 386–89.

Chantarujikapong, S. I., Scherrer, J. F., Xian, H., Eisen, S. A., Lyons, M. J., Goldberg, J., et al. (2001). A twin study of generalized anxiety disorder symptoms, panic disorder symptoms and post-traumatic stress disorder in men. *Psychiatry Research, 103*, 133–45.

Comings, D. E., Comings, B. G., Muhleman, D., Dietz, G., Shahbahrami, B., Tast, D., et al. (1991). The dopamine D2 receptor locus as a modifying gene in neuropsychiatric disorders. *Journal of the American Medical Association, 266*(13), 1793–1800.

Comings, D. E., Muhleman, D., and Gysin, R. (1996). Dopamine D2 receptor (DRD2) gene and susceptibility to posttraumatic stress disorder: A study and replication. *Biological Psychiatry, 40*, 368–72.

Cusin, C., Serretti, A., Zanardi, R., Lattuada, E., Rossini, D., Lilli, R., et al. (2002). Influence of monoamine oxidase A and serotonin receptor 2A polymorphisms in SSRI antidepressant activity. *The International Journal of Neuropsychopharmacology, 5*, 27–35.

Davidson, J. R., Hughes, D., Blazer, D. G., and George, L. K. (1991). Post-traumatic stress disorder in the community: An epidemiological study. *Psychological Medicine, 21*, 713–21.

Daviss, W. B., Mooney, D., Racusin, R., Ford, J. D., Fleischer, A., and McHugo, G. J. (2000). Predicting posttraumatic stress after hospitalization for pediatric injury. *Journal of the American Academy of Child and Adolescent Psychiatry, 39*, 573–83.

De Bellis, M. D., Baum, A. S., Birmaher, B., Keshavan, M. S., Eccard, C. H., and Boring, A. M. (1999). A. E. Bennett Research Award. Developmental traumatology. Part I: Biological stress symptoms. *Biological Psychiatry, 45*, 1259–70.

De Bellis, M. D., Baum, A. S., Birmaher, B., Keshavan, M. S., Eccard, C. H., Boring, A. M., et al. (1999). Developmental traumatology. Part I: Biological stress systems. *Biological Psychiatry, 45*, 1237–58.

De Bellis, M. D., Chrousos, G. P., and Dorn, L. D. (1994). Hypothalamic-pituitary-adrenal axis dysregulation in sexually abused girls. *Journal of Clinical Neuroendocrinology and Metabolism, 78*, 249–55.

De Bellis, M. D., Hall, J., Boring, A. M., Frustaci, K., and Moritz, G. (2001). A pilot longitudinal study of hippocampal volumes in pediatric maltreatment-related posttraumatic stress disorder. *Biological Psychiatry, 50*, 305–9.

de Vries, A. P. J., Kassam-Adams, N., Cnaan, A., Sherman-Slate, E., Gllagher, P. R., and Winston, F. K. (1999). Looking beyond the physical injury: posttraumatic stress disorder in children and parents after pediatric traffic injury. *Pediatrics, 104*, 1293–99.

Delahanty, D. L., Nugent, N. R., Christopher, N. C., and Walsh, M. (2005). Initial urinary epinephrine and cortisol levels predict acute PTSD symptoms in child trauma victims. *Psychoneuroendocrinology, 30*, 121–28.

Delahanty, D. L., Raimonde, A. J., Spoonster, E., and Cullado, M. (2003). Injury severity, prior trauma history, urinary cortisol levels and acute PTSD in motor vehicle accident victims. *Journal of Anxiety Disorders, 17*, 149–64.

Eichhammer, P., Langguth, B., Wiegand, R., Kharraz, A., Frick, U., and Hajak, G. (2003). Allelic variation in the serotonin transporter promoter affects neuromodulatory effects of a selective serotonin transporter reuptake inhibitor (SSRI). *Psychopharmacology, 166*, 294–97.

Falconer, D. S. (1960). *Introduction to quantitative genetics.* Glasgow: R. MacLehose and Com.

Feusner, J., Ritchie, T., Lawford, B., Young, R. M., Kann, B., and Noble, E. P. (2001). GABA(A) receptor beta 3 subunit gene and psychiatric morbidity in a posttraumatic stress disorder population. *Psychiatry Research, 104*, 109–17.

Fletcher, K. E. (1996). Childhood posttraumatic stress disorder. In E. J. Mash and R. A. Barkley (Eds.), *Child psychopathology* (242–76). New York: Guilford Publications, Inc.

Freeman, B., Powell, J., Ball, D., Hill, L., Craig, I., and Plomin, R. (1997). DNA by mail: An inexpensive and noninvasive method for collecting samples from widely dispersed populations. *Behavior Genetics, 27*, 251–57.

Freeman, T., Roca, V., Guggenheim, F., Kimbrell, T., and Griffin, W. S. (2005). Neuropsychiatric associations of apolipoprotein E alleles in subjects with combat-related posttraumatic stress disorder. *Journal of Neuropsychiatry Clinical Neuroscience, 17*, 541–43.

Galea, S., Acierno, R., Ruggiero, K., Resnick, H., Tracy, M., and Kilpatrick, D. (2006). Social context and the psychobiology of posttraumatic stress. *Annals of the New York Academy of Sciences, 1071*, 231–41.

Gallagher-Thompson, D., O'Hara, R., Simmons, A., Kraemer, H. C., and Murphy, G. M., Jr. (2001). Apolipoprotein E epsilon4 allele affects the relationship between stress and depression in caregivers of patients with Alzheimer's disease. *Journal of Geriatric Psychiatry Neurology, 14*, 115–19.

Gelernter, J., Southwick, S., Goodson, S., Morgan, A., Nagy, L., and Charney, D. S. (1999). No association between D2 dopamine receptor (DRD2) "A" system alleles, or DRD2 haplotypes, and posttraumatic stress disorder. *Biological Psychiatry, 45*, 620–25.

Gilbertson, M. W., Paulus, L. A., Williston, S. K., Gurvits, T. V., Lasko, N. B., Pitman, R. K., et al. (2006). Neurocognitive function in monozygotic twins discordant for combat exposure: relationship to posttraumatic stress disorder. *Journal of Abnormal Psychology, 115*, 484–95.

Goldstein, L. E., Rasmusson, A. M., Bunney, B. S., and Roth, R. H. (1996). Role of the amygdala in the coordination of behavioral, neuroendocrine, and prefrontal cortical monoamine responses to psychological stress in the rat. *The Journal of Neuroscience, 16*, 4787–98.

Gottesman, I. I., and Gould, T. D. (2003). The endophenotype concept in psychiatry: Etymology and strategic intentions. *American Journal of Psychiatry, 160*, 636–45.

Hall, E., Saxe, G., Stoddard, F., Kaplow, J., Koenen, K., Chawla, N., et al. (2006). Posttraumatic stress symptoms in parents of children with acute burns. *Journal of Pediatric Psychology, 31*, 403–12.

Hamner, M. B., and Diamond, B. I. (1993). Elevated plasma dopamine in posttraumatic stress disorder: a preliminary report. *Biological Psychiatry, 33*, 304–6.

Heim, C., Newport, J. J., Heit, S., Graham, Y. P., Wilcox, M., and Bonsall, R. (2000). Pituitary-adrenal and autonomic responses to stress in women after sexual and physical abuse in childhood. *Journal of the American Medical Association, 284*, 592–97.

Helzer, J. E., Robins, L. N., and McEnvoy, L. (1987). Post-traumatic stress disorder in the general population: Findings of the epidemiologic catchment area survey. *New England Journal of Medicine, 317*, 1630–34.

Inglis, F. M., and Moghaddam, B. (1999). Dopaminergic innervation of the amygdala is highly responsive to stress. *Journal of Neurochemistry, 72*, 1088–94.

Jang, K. L., Stein, M. B., Taylor, S., Asmundson, G. J., and Livesley, W. J. (2003). Exposure to traumatic events and experiences: Aetiological relationships with personality function. *Psychiatry Research, 120*, 61–69.

Kendler, K. S., and Baker, J. H. (2006). Genetic influences on measures of the environment: a systematic review. *Psychological Medicine*, 1–12.

Kendler, K. S., and Eaves, L. J. (1986). Models for the joint effects of genotype and environment on liability to psychiatric illness. *American Journal of Psychiatry, 143*, 279–89.

Kessler, R. C., Sonnega, A., Bromet, E., Hughes, M., and Nelson, C. B. (1995). Posttraumatic stress disorder in the National Comorbidity Survey. *Archives of General Psychiatry, 52*, 1048–60.

Kilpatrick, D. G., Koenen, K. C., Ruggiero, K. J., Acierno, R., Galea, S., Resnick, H. S., et al. (2007). Serotonin transporter gene and social support moderate PTSD and depression in hurricane-exposed adults. *American Journal of Psychiatry, 164*, 1693–99.

Koenen, K. C. (2007). Genetics of posttraumatic stress disorder: Review and recommendations for future studies. *Journal of Traumatic Stress, 20*, 737–50.

Koenen, K. C., Fu, Q., Ertel, K., Lyons, M. J., Goldberg, J., True, W., et al. (2008). Genetic overlap between major depression and posttraumatic stress disorder in men. *Journal of Affective Disorders, 105*, 109–15.

Koenen, K. C., Harney, R., Lyons, M. J., Wolfe, J., Simpson, J. C., Goldberg, J., et al. (2002). A twin registry study of familial and individual risk factors for trauma exposure and posttraumatic stress disorder. *Journal of Nervous and Mental Disease, 190*, 209–18.

Koenen, K. C., Hitsman, B., Lyons, M. J., Niaura, R., McCaffery, J., Goldberg, J., et al. (2005). A twin registry study of the relationship between posttraumatic stress disorder and nicotine dependence in men. *Archives of General Psychiatry, 62*, 1258–65.

Koenen, K. C., Moffitt, T. E., Poulton, R., Martin, J., and Caspi, A. (2007). Early childhood factors associated with the development of post-traumatic stress disorder: results from a longitudinal birth cohort. *Psychological Medicine, 37*, 181–92.

Koenen, K. C., Saxe, G., Purcell, S., Smoller, J. W., Bartholomew, D., Miller, A., et al. (2005). Polymorphisms in FKBP5 are associated with peritraumatic dissociation in medically injured children. *Molecular Psychiatry, 10*, 1058–59.

Kohnke, M. D., Batra, A., Kolb, W., Kohnke, A. M., Lutz, U., Schick, S., et al. (2005). Association of the dopamine transporter gene with alcoholism. *Alcohol & Alcoholism, 40*, 339–42.

Koplewicz, H. S., Vogel, J. M., Solanto, M. V., Morrissey, R. F., Alonso, C. M., Abikoff, H., et al. (2002). Child and parental response to the 1994 World Trade Center bombing. *Journal of Traumatic Stress, 15*, 77–85.

Kraemer, H. C., Kazdin, A. E., Offord, D. R., Kessler, R. C., Jensen, P. S., and Kupfer, D. J. (1997). Coming to terms with the terms of risk. *Archives of General Psychiatry, 54*, 337–43.

Landolt, M. A., Vollrath, M., Ribi, K., Gnehm, H. E., and Sennhauser, F. H. (2003). Incidence and associations of parental and child posttraumatic stress symptoms in pediatric patients. *Journal of Child Psychology & Psychiatry, 44*, 1199–1207.

Lansford, J. E., Dodge, K. A., Pettit, G. S., Bates, J. E., Crozier, J., and Kaplow, J. (2002). A 12-year prospective study of the long-term effects of early child physical maltreatment on psychological, behavioral, and academic problems in adolescence. *Archives of Pediatric and Adolescent Medicine, 156*, 824–30.

Lappalainen, J., Kranzler, H. R., Malison, R., Price, L. H., Van Dyck, D., Krystal, J. H., et al. (2002). A functional neuropeptide Y *Leu7Pro* polymorphism associated with alcohol dependence in a large population sample from the United States. *Archives of General Psychiatry, 59*, 825–31.

Lawford, B. R., Young, R., Noble, E. P., Kann, B., Arnold, L., Rowell, J., et al. (2003). D2 dopamine receptor gene polymorphism: paroxetine and social functioning in posttraumatic stress disorder. *European Neuropsychopharmacol, 13*, 313–20.

Lawford, B. R., Young, R., Noble, E. P., Kann, B., and Ritchie, T. (2006). The D2 dopamine receptor (DRD2) gene is associated with co-morbid depression, anxiety and social dysfunction in untreated veterans with post-traumatic stress disorder. *European Psychiatry, 21*, 180–85.

Lee, H. J., Lee, M. S., Kang, R. H., Kim, H., Kim, S. D., Kee, B. S., et al. (2005). Influence of the serotonin transporter promoter gene polymorphism on susceptibility to posttraumatic stress disorder. *Depression and Anxiety, 21*, 135–39.

Lemieux, A. M., and Coe, C. L. (1995). Abuse-related posttraumatic stress disorder: Evidence for chronic neuroendoctrine activation in women. *Psychosomatic Medicine, 57*, 105–15.

Lesch, K. P., Bengel, D., Heils, A., Sabol, S. Z., Greenberg, B. D., Petri, S., et al. (1996). Association of anxiety-related traits with a polymorphism in the serotonin transporter gene regulatory region. *Science, 274*, 1527–31.

Lyons, M. J., Goldberg, J., Eisen, S. A., True, W., Tsuang, M. T., and Meyer, J. M. (1993). Do genes influence exposure to trauma? A twin study of combat. *American Journal of Medical Genetics B: Neuropsychiatric Genetics, 48*, 22–27.

McDermott, B. M., and Cvitanovich, A. (2000). Posttraumatic stress disorder and emotional problems in children following motor vehicle accidents: An extended case series. *Australian and New Zealand Journal of Psychiatry, 34*, 446–52.

McFarlane, A. C., Policansky, S. K., and Irwin, C. (1987). A longitudinal study of the psychological morbidity in children due to natural disaster. *Psychological Medicine, 17*, 727–38.

Moffitt, T. E., Caspi, A., and Rutter, M. (2005). Strategy for investigating interactions between measured genes and measured environments. *Archives of General Psychiatry, 62*, 473–81.

Murphy, G. M., Kremer, C., Rodrigues, H. E., and Schatzberg, A. F. (2003). Pharmacogenetics of antidepressant medication intolerance. *American Journal of Psychiatry, 160,* 1830–35.

Norris, F. R. (1992). Epidemiology of trauma: Frequency and impact of different potentially traumatic events on different demographic groups. *Journal of Consulting and Clinical Psychology, 60,* 409–18.

Nugent, N. R., Ostrowski, S., Christopher, N. C., and Delahanty, D. L. (2007). Parental posttraumatic stress symptoms as a moderator of child's acute biological response and subsequent posttraumatic stress symptoms in pediatric injury patients. *Journal of Pediatric Psychology, 32,* 309–18.

Ostrowski, S. A., Christopher, N. C., and Delahanty, D. L. (2007). Brief report: The impact of maternal posttraumatic stress disorder symptoms and child gender on risk for persistent posttraumatic stress disorder symptoms in child trauma victims. *Journal of Pediatric Psychology, 32,* 338–42.

Ozer, E. J., Best, S. R., Lipsey, T. L., and Weiss, D. S. (2003). Predictors of posttraumatic stress disorder and symptoms in adults: A meta-analysis. *Psychological Bulletin, 129,* 52–73.

Pelcovitz, D., Libov, B. G., Mandel, F., Kaplan, S., Weinblatt, M., and Septimus, A. (1998). Posttraumatic stress disorder and family functioning in adolescent cancer. *Journal of Traumatic Stress, 11,* 205–21.

Perkonigg, A., Kessler, R. C., Storz, S., and Wittchen, H.-U. (2000). Traumatic events and post-traumatic stress disorder in the community: Prevalence, risk factors, and comorbidity. *Acta Psychiatrica Scandinavica, 101,* 46–59.

Pfefferbaum, B., and Pfefferbaum, R. L. (1998). Contagion in stress: An infectious disease model for posttraumatic stress in children. *Child and Adolescent Psychiatric Clinics of North America, 7,* 183–94.

Plomin, R., DeFries, J. C., McClearn, G. E., and McGuffin, P. (2001). *Behavioral genetics.* New York: Worth Publishers.

Rausch, J. L., Johnson, M. E., Fei, Y., Li, J. Q., Shendarkar, N., Hobby, H. M., et al. (2002). Initial conditions of serotonin transporter kinetics and genotype: Influence on SSRI treatment trial outcome. *Biological Psychiatry, 51,* 723–32.

Resnick, H. S., Yehuda, R., Pitman, R. K., and Foy, D. W. (1995). Effects of previous trauma on acute plasma cortisol level following rape. *American Journal of Psychiatry, 152,* 1675–77.

Risch, N. J., and Merikangas, K. (1996). The future of genetic studies of complex human diseases. *Science, 273,* 1516–17.

Sack, W. H., Clarke, G. N., and Seeley, J. (1995). Posttraumatic stress disorder across two generations of Cambodian refugees. *Journal of the American Academy of Child and Adolescent Psychiatry, 34,* 1160–66.

Saxe, G. N., Miller, A., Bartholomew, D., Hall, E., Lopez, C., Kaplow, J., et al. (2005). Incidence of and risk factors for acute stress disorder in children with injuries. *Journal of Trauma: Injury Infection and Critical Care, 59,* 946–53.

Segman, R. H., Cooper-Kazaz, R., Macciardi, F., Goltser, T., Halfon, Y., Dobroborski, T., et al. (2002). Association between the dopamine transporter gene and posttraumatic stress disorder. *Molecular Psychiatry, 7,* 903–7.

Segman, R. H., and Shalev, A. Y. (2003). Genetics of posttraumatic stress disorder. *CNS Spectrums, 8,* 693–98.

Slater, E., and Slater, P. (1944). A heuristic theory of neurosis. In J. Sheilds and I. I. Gottesman (Eds.), *Man, mind & heredity: Selected papers of Eliot Slater on psychiatry and genetics* (216–27). Baltimore: Johns Hopkins Press.

Smith, P., Perrin, S., Yule, W., and Rabe-Hesketh, S. (2001). War exposure and maternal reactions in the psychological adjustment of children from Bosnia-Hercegovina. *Journal of Child Psychology and Psychiatry, 42,* 395–404.

Spivak, B., Vered, Y., Graff, E., Blum, I., Mester, R., and Weizman, A. (1999). Low platelet-poor plasma concentrations of serotonin in patients with combat-related posttraumatic stress disorder. *Biological Psychiatry, 45,* 840–45.

Stein, M. B., Jang, K. J., Taylor, S., Vernon, P. A., and Livesley, W. J. (2002). Genetic and environmental influences on trauma exposure and posttraumatic stress disorder: A twin study. *American Journal of Psychiatry, 159,* 1675–81.

Stuber, M. L., Christakis, D. A., Houskamp, B., and Kazak, A. E. (1996). Posttrauma symptoms in childhood leukemia survivors and their parents. *Psychosomatics, 37,* 254–61.

True, W. J., Rice, J., Eisen, S. A., Heath, A. C., Goldberg, J., Lyons, M. J., et al. (1993). A twin study of genetic and environmental contributions to liability for posttraumatic stress symptoms. *Archives of General Psychiatry, 50,* 257–64.

Van Os, J., and Jones, P. B. (1999). Early risk factors and adult person-environment relationships in affective disorder. *Psychological Medicine, 29,* 1055–67.

Vasquez, D. M. (1998). Stress and the developing limbic-hypothalamic-pituitary-adrenal axis. *Psychoneuroendocrinology, 23,* 663–700.

Winston, F. K., Kassam-Adams, N., Vivarelli-O'Neill, C., Ford, J., Newman, E., Baxt, C., et al. (2002). Acute stress disorder symptoms in children and their parents after pediatric traffic injury. *Pediatrics, 109,* 90–99.

Xian, H., Chantarujikapong, S. I., Shrerrer, J. F., Eisen, S. A., Lyons, M. J., Goldberg, J., et al. (2000). Genetic and environmental influences on posttraumatic stress disorder, alcohol, and drug dependence in twin pairs. *Drug and Alcohol Dependence, 61,* 95–102.

Yehuda, R., Halligan, S. L., and Bierer, L. M. (2001). Relationship of parental trauma exposure and PTSD to PTSD, depressive and anxiety disorders in offspring. *Journal of Psychiatric Research, 35,* 261–70.

Yehuda, R., Southwick, S., Giller, E. L., Ma, X., and Mason, J. W. (1992). Urinary catecholamine excretion and severity of PTSD symptoms in Vietnam combat veterans. *Journal of Nervous and Mental Disorders, 180,* 321–25.

Young, B. R., Lawford, B. R., Noble, E. P., Kanin, B., Wilkie, A., Ritchie, T., et al. (2002). Harmful drinking in military veterans with posttraumatic stress disorder: Association with the D2 dopamine receptor A1 allele. *Alcohol and Alcoholism, 37,* 451–56.

Zhang, H., Ozbay, F., Lappalainen, J., Kranzler, H. R., van Dyck, C. H., Charney, D. S., et al. (2006). Brain derived neurotrophic factor (BDNF) gene variants and Alzheimer's disease, affective disorders, posttraumatic stress disorder, schizophrenia, and substance dependence. *American Journal of Medical Genetics B: Neuropsychiatric Genetics, 141,* 387–93.

# 3

## Predictors[1] of PTSD Symptoms in Police Officers: From Childhood to Retirement

*Nnamdi Pole*

**R**esearch into predictors and correlates of PTSD is often limited due to pseudoprospective designs. That is, the majority of studies have examined participants following exposure to a traumatic event and attempted to determine differences between trauma victims who subsequently did and did not develop PTSD. Few studies have been able to examine variables prior to trauma exposure that could confer risk or resilience to individuals who subsequently experienced trauma. However, studies of individuals at high risk for trauma exposure have more recently shed light on pre-, peri-, and posttraumatic predictors and correlates of PTSD and have allowed for an examination of these factors across the lifespan. Urban police officers represent such a high-risk sample. Urban police officers have stressful lives (Alexander and Wells, 1991; Pole, 2004) and more than their share of stress-related problems, such as alcoholism (Russell and Beigel, 1982), poor physical health (Beutler, Nussbaum, and Meredith, 1988), and divorce (Roberts and Levenson, 2001). Part of the stress of urban policing comes in the form of exposure to "critical incidents" involving threats to their lives or the lives of others; responding to disasters, hostage situations, sexual and physical assaults; and encountering mutilation, carnage, and death (Henry, 2004; McCafferty, Domingo, and MacCafferty, 1990; Paton and Violanti, 1996; Pole et al., 2001). Exposure to such interpersonal violence has been linked to posttraumatic stress disorder (PTSD) in the general population (Breslau et al., 1998; Pole, at press) and in police officers (Brown, Fielding, and

Address correspondence concerning this chapter to Nnamdi Pole, Ph.D.; Department of Psychology; Clark Science Center; Smith College; Northampton, MA 01060. E-mail: npole@email.smith.edu

Grover, 1999; Kopel and Friedman, 1999; Robinson, Sigman, and Wilson, 1997). Rates of PTSD in police have been estimated between 7 percent and 19 percent (Carlier, Lamberts, and Gersons, 1997; Gersons, 1989; Marmar et al., 2006; Robinson et al., 1997). Thus, police officers appear to have more current PTSD than the general population (3.9 percent; Kessler et al., 1999) and perhaps even more than Vietnam veterans (i.e., 15 percent; Kulka et al., 1990). In addition, police officers often suffer from clinically significant PTSD symptoms that fail to meet the full diagnostic criteria for the disorder (Carlier et al., 1997; Stein, Walker, Hazen, and Forde, 1997). Because urban police officers are exposed to trauma over a significant proportion of their adulthood, they present a unique opportunity for examining PTSD over the adult lifespan.

This chapter summarizes findings from an ongoing program of research on predictors of PTSD in police officers. Taking a developmental perspective, the chapter will review findings from police officers at the beginning, middle, and end of their careers. The research on early and mid-career officers is being led by Charles Marmar at the University of California, San Francisco (e.g., Marmar et al., 2006). The research on police officers at the end of their careers is being conducted under my direction at the University of Michigan (e.g., Pole, Kulkarni, Bernstein, and Kaufman, 2006).

A conceptual model articulated by Marmar and our group (2006) guides all of this research. In this model, cumulative exposure to duty-related trauma is viewed as less important for the development of PTSD than the magnitude and quality of the officers' responses during and immediately after the trauma (i.e., so called "peritraumatic" responses). Intense peritraumatic distress (e.g., helplessness, fear, horror) is assumed to facilitate fear-conditioning and to overconsolidate traumatic memories (Pitman, Shalev, and Orr, 2000). Intense peritraumatic dissociation (e.g., depersonalization, derealization, and disorientation) is thought to interfere with the appropriate integration of trauma memories (e.g., Zoellner, Alvarez-Conrad, and Foa, 2002) and to dysregulate physiological arousal (e.g., Griffin, Resick, and Mechanic, 1997; Pole, Cumberbatch et al., 2005). Once these peritraumatic risk factors are in place, the path to duty-related PTSD is thought to be further paved by dysfunctional posttraumatic coping (e.g., avoidant coping), poor social support (e.g., lack of people with whom to discuss traumatic experiences), and additional stressors (e.g., non-traumatic work stress: Liberman et al., 2002). The present chapter will build on this conceptual model by examining factors that may predispose intense peritraumatic responses; factors such as ethnicity, gender, and childhood trauma. It will also integrate findings regarding psychobiological factors that may contribute to or result from abnormal peritraumatic responses.

## EARLY CAREER PREDICTORS OF POLICE PTSD

### Sample Characteristics

We are in the process of prospectively studying early-career urban police officers before and after they are exposed to duty-related trauma. Our goal is to assess officers prior to police work and then repeatedly over the first few years of their police service. All cadets of participating police departments have been invited into the study except those with prior combat, emergency services, or law enforcement experience. Though only approximately one-third of eligible cadets have accepted the invitation, the achieved sample is thus far similar to the full academy classes in terms of age, gender, and ethnic distribution. The sample is currently on average approximately thirty years old, predominantly male, and about half ethnic minority.

In order to increase the likelihood of honest and accurate reporting, we have offered each participant a federal certificate of confidentiality. This certificate assures that our research will never be used to personally identify officers or to interfere with their career trajectories. In addition, we assess social desirability reporting bias and control for its influence on their self-report data. At the time of their enrollment in the study, the sample had very low rates of current Axis I psychopathology and no current PTSD according to results of Structured Clinical Interviews for DSM-IV (First, Spitzer, Gibbon, and Williams, 1997). This is not surprising because these cadets were screened for psychopathology before being admitted to their police academies. After one year of police service, their rates of PTSD continue to be low (close to 0 percent), but some officers report clinically significant PTSD symptoms.

### Ethnicity

Emerging genetic findings indicate that elevated risk for PTSD may begin even before birth (see Koenen, at press). Some provocative evidence suggests that an accelerated trajectory toward PTSD may begin at the moment that an individual's ethnoracial status is determined (Pole, 2006b; Pole, Gone, and Kulkarni, 2008). Though it is true that ethnic minority status has been only weakly associated with PTSD in the broader PTSD literature (Brewin, Andrews, and Valentine, 2000), Hispanic ethnicity appears to be robustly associated with higher rates of PTSD and more severe PTSD symptoms (Pole, Best, Metzler, and Marmar, 2005; Ruef, Litz, and Schlenger, 2000). In our prospective data, ethnic minority status is associated with more severe PTSD symptoms after one year of police service. Both African American and Hispanic American beginning officers report more severe PTSD symptoms than their European American counterparts.

## Gender

Female gender is another demographic variable that is established at birth and that has been associated with elevated risk for PTSD in the broader PTSD literature (Brewin et al., 2000; Pole and Gross, at press). In our early career sample, we found some evidence of more severe PTSD symptoms in female officers.

## Childhood Trauma

After birth, a number of experiences may elevate risk for PTSD. Experiencing trauma during childhood may be particularly deleterious (Brewin et al., 2000). In our work, we have been pursuing the possibility that childhood trauma may confer risk for adult psychopathology by permanently altering biological systems involved in responding to subsequent stressors (Otte et al., 2005; Pole, Neylan, et al., 2007). Most studies examining this theory have assessed adults with childhood trauma histories and concurrent Axis I disorders (e.g., Heim et al., 2000). Thus, it has been unclear whether the observed abnormal biological reactivity to adult stressors is a consequence of early trauma, current psychopathology, or both.

Christian Otte and our group (2005) studied seventy-six police academy cadets who were free of Axis I disorders. In the course of a trauma history interview, sixteen of these cadets disclosed experiencing an event in childhood during which she or he believed that death or serious injury was likely and during which she or he experienced intense helplessness, horror, or fear. The age of exposure ranged from four to thirteen years with the average being ten years (SD = 2.5) old. Disaster was the most commonly endorsed childhood trauma followed by physical assault, illness, accident, abuse, neglect, and sexual assault. Most cadets reported exposure to only one event and that their exposure only occurred once. Furthermore, cadets with and without childhood trauma did not differ in their subsequent exposure to traumatic events.

All cadets watched videotaped scenes of police officers experiencing actual duty-related critical incidents (e.g., an officer being hit by a car or being killed by a detonated bomb). Saliva and subjective ratings of distress were collected prior to the video, immediately after the video, and twenty minutes after the video. The saliva was subsequently assayed for cortisol and 3-methoxy-4-hydroxy-phenylglycol (MHPG, the major metabolite of norepinephrine). Because all participants were in training to begin careers in law enforcement, we anticipated that they would find the video personally salient and distressing. The resulting data showed that the childhood trauma (CT) group found the video more distressing than their counterparts without childhood trauma (NCT). The CT group also showed significantly greater MHPG increases during the video than the NCT group. However, the two groups did not differ in salivary cortisol responding. These findings were not substantially altered by excluding females and participants taking psychoactive medications from the analyses. In sum, the study's results are consistent with the interpretation that childhood trauma increased catecholamine responding to a personally relevant stressor.

In a similar study, we examined the effects of childhood trauma on adult psychophysiological responding in twenty-five police cadets with childhood trauma and sixty-five of their colleagues without childhood trauma (Pole, Neylan, et al., 2007). Psychophysiological measures have the advantage over neuroendocrine measures of being able to capture nearly instantaneous reactions to acute stressors, which may better approximate responses to sudden traumatic stressors. In this particular study, cadets were exposed to startling sounds under low, medium, and high proximity of a mild electric shock. Under low threat, cadets were notified that they would be shocked later in the experiment. Under medium threat, they were fitted with the device that would administer the shock but they were signaled that the shock would not yet occur. Under the high threat condition, they were first signaled that the shock would occur and then shocked. Eyeblink electromyogram (EMG) and skin conductance (SC) were recorded during a resting baseline period prior to the experiment and in response to each startling sound. Subjective positive and negative emotions were assessed prior to the experiment and following each threat condition. This complex procedure has been shown to elicit a reliable relationship between psychophysiological startle measures and PTSD (e.g., Grillon, Morgan, Davis, and Southwick, 1998; Pole, Neylan, Best, Orr, and Marmar, 2003).

Prior to the experiment, cadets with childhood trauma (CT) did not differ from their counterparts without childhood trauma (NCT) in social desirability reporting, trait anxiety, or current general psychiatric distress. The CT group showed trends for more negative affect in the week prior to the experiment and less positive emotions in the minutes prior to participating in the experiment. The CT group also showed higher skin conductance (SC) levels during the resting baseline period than the NCT group. We interpreted these differences as resulting from threats encountered during their ongoing police training and anticipatory anxiety about facing threat in the experiment. When exposed to the startling sounds under threat, the CT group reported experiencing less positive emotion (safety, pleasure, calm, and contentment) and showed larger skin conductance responses than the NCT group regardless of threat level. The relationship between childhood trauma and greater skin conductance (SC) responding was fully explained in a covariance analysis by baseline differences in skin conductance level thereby suggesting that group differences in SC responding resulted from chronic hyperactivity of the sympathetic nervous system (SNS). This conclusion is consistent with similar findings in studies of non-human animals (e.g., Coplan et al., 1998), human children (e.g., DeBellis et al., 1994), and our own MHPG findings in these same cadets as they watched the stressful video (Otte et al., 2005).

In addition to main effects of childhood trauma on skin conductance and positive emotions, we found interaction effects between childhood trauma and threat level on eyeblink EMG and reported negative emotions. Basically, whereas the CT group showed a progressive increase in eyeblink EMG response and negative emotions (fear, danger, and helplessness) at every level of threat increase, the NCT group only showed differences between the low and high threat conditions. The apparent sensitivity of the CT group to the medium threat condition is interesting because this condition presented both danger cues (e.g., being fitted with a shock-eliciting device) and safety cues (e.g., being told that they would not be shocked). Individuals in the CT group appeared to preferentially respond to the danger cues rather than the safety cues. In this respect, they behaved similarly to individuals with posttraumatic stress disorder (PTSD) (Grillon et al., 1998; Pole et al., 2003).

Taken together, these subjective, catecholamine, and psychophysiological results are consistent with our hypothesis that, even in the absence of current Axis I psychopathology, childhood trauma can lead to long-lasting aberrations in psychobiological processes that mediate the response to environmental threat. These alterations may contribute to greater peritraumatic distress in these individuals and therefore serve as a basis for the development of PTSD.

### Duty-Related Trauma Exposure

As noted earlier, interest in PTSD in police officers has been primarily inspired by their high exposure to duty-related trauma. Within their first year of police service, we found that the average officer reported exposure to more than a dozen potentially traumatic duty-related critical incidents including: seeing someone dying or encountering dead bodies, encountering a physically assaulted child or adult, encountering a sexually assaulted child or adult, being threatened with a deadly weapon, witnessing a fellow officer injured or killed, being seriously injured in the line of duty, having to shoot or kill someone in the line of duty, being involved in a potentially life-threatening disaster, and making a mistake that led to the injury or death of a fellow officer or a bystander. Interestingly, cumulative exposure to critical incidents was not significantly related to current PTSD symptoms at one year. However, Henn-Haase, McCaslin, Metzler, Pole, and Marmar (2006) found that officers who faced more personal life threat on duty during their first year also reported more severe PTSD symptoms.

## Peritraumatic Responses

Consistent with Marmar et al.'s (2006) conceptual model, the broader literature has found that peritraumatic distress and dissociation are among the strongest correlates of PTSD (Ozer, Best, Lipsey, Weiss, 2003). We found that officers with more severe PTSD symptoms after one year of police service reported more peritraumatic dissociation and more peritraumatic distress during their worst duty-related critical incident. The effect sizes associated with these findings were similar to the effect sizes in the broader literature. Furthermore, Henn-Haase et al. (2006) found that peritraumatic dissociation partially mediated the above-mentioned relationship between life threatening critical incident exposure and increased PTSD symptom severity.

## Psychobiological Predictors

The diagnostic criteria for PTSD include a number of psychophysiological symptoms such as elevated reactivity to trauma cues and exaggerated responses to startling stimuli (DSM-IV-TR; American Psychiatric Association, 2000). These subjective and clinically observed symptoms have been largely corroborated by laboratory evidence (Orr, Metzger, Miller, and Kaloupek, 2004; Pole, 2006a; Pole, 2007). My own work has focused on laboratory startle measures as correlates of PTSD symptom severity in police (e.g., Pole et al., 2003). It is unclear whether exaggerated startle is a pre-existing vulnerability factor or an acquired result of posttraumatic neuronal sensitization. Both possibilities have been supported by empirical evidence (Guthrie and Bryant, 2005; Shalev et al., 2000).

In a study of police cadets, I found that after accounting for age and general psychiatric distress, more severe PTSD symptoms at twelve months were prospectively and independently predicted by larger eyeblink responses under medium threat, larger skin conductance responses under high threat, and slower skin conductance habituation. This model accounted for more than one-third of the variance in twelve-month PTSD symptom severity. The findings suggest that pretrauma differences in (a) sensitivity to threatening contexts (i.e., larger eyeblink under medium threat), (b) sympathetic nervous system reactivity (i.e., skin conductance responses under high threat), and (c) capacity to adapt to adversity (i.e.,

skin conductance habituation) all prospectively contribute to elevated
PTSD symptom severity. In the context of the broader conceptual model
of PTSD in police (Marmar et al., 2006), these factors can be viewed as facilitating unusually intense peritraumatic responses, which in turn increase
the likelihood of PTSD (Ozer et al., 2003).

## MID-CAREER PREDICTORS OF POLICE PTSD

### Sample Characteristics

Prior to undertaking the prospective study of police, Marmar and colleagues
completed a survey of over seven hundred mid-career police officers from
New York and the San Francisco Bay Area. Potential participants were identified from departmental personnel rosters and were sent letters of invitation
from their police commissioner, their police union, and our project team along
with the federal certificate of confidentiality. The officers were sampled to
assure ethnoracial and gender diversity. The average officer in the study was
about forty years old and had more than a dozen years of police service. The
estimated rate of PTSD in this sample was 5 percent with an additional 2 percent reporting clinically salient but subthreshold PTSD symptom levels.

### Ethnicity

Comparing Hispanic American police officers with African American and
European American officers, we found that Hispanic American officers reported more severe PTSD symptoms than either their African American or
European American counterparts (Pole et al., 2001). These differences were
not explained by differences in social desirability reporting. In fact, Hispanic
officers were found to be more concerned with social desirability than the
other groups, which may have led them to underreport their true symptom
severity. We were able to explain the difference between Hispanic and other
officers in PTSD symptom severity using a regression model involving elevated peritraumatic dissociation, greater wishful thinking and self-blame
coping, lower social support, and greater workplace discrimination in the Hispanic group (Pole, Best, et al., 2005). These findings imply that the Hispanic
risk for PTSD may not be present from birth but may rather be a function of
discrimination experiences and learned cultural styles of responding to and
coping with stress. Importantly for our conceptual model, these cultural styles
appear to include increased propensity for peritraumatic dissociation, which
in turn contributes significantly to elevated PTSD symptom severity. It should
be emphasized, however, that the relationship between ethnic minority status

and PTSD symptom severity is very small in magnitude. Thus, it is unlikely that ethnic designation alone will serve as a useful predictor of PTSD.

## Gender

We also found that female police officers did not differ from their male counterparts in PTSD symptom severity (Pole et al., 2001). This was true even though male and female officers had similar levels of exposure to duty-related trauma. This result differs from our observation that female officers in the first year of police service reported more severe PTSD symptoms than their male counterparts. It is possible that experience or socialization factors neutralized gender differences in PTSD in police over time. This may be why mid-career female police officers in our research bear a resemblance to female military samples, which also tend not to differ in PTSD symptom severity from their counterpart male military samples (Brewin et al., 2000). The idea that socialization factors may play a role in this process is supported by Ballenger et al.'s (at press) finding that mid-career female police officers come to engage in alcohol use that is similar to their male police counterparts but substantially higher than their female civilian counterparts. Much of the informal socialization and stress reduction among officers occurs in settings involving alcohol (Miller, 2006). The absence of gender differences in PTSD symptom severity and alcohol use suggests that these differences may not be biologically "hardwired" but may rather be open to external influence. We speculate that during the course of their police careers female officers encounter pressure to alter their expression and management of emotions to mimic their male counterparts. Such a change in emotional expressivity could reduce peritraumatic responding and subsequent PTSD symptoms. Michelle Gross and I found that mid-career female officers report less peritraumatic distress than their female civilian counterparts and that this, in part, accounts for why they report less severe PTSD symptoms (Gross and Pole, 2006).

## Childhood Trauma

We have not directly examined the relationship between childhood trauma and PTSD in our mid-career officers. However, McCaslin, Metzler et al. (2006) surveyed a subsample of these officers and found that police officers who reported histories of childhood emotional abuse and neglect had elevated alexithymia (i.e., difficulty identifying and describing their emotions). Alexithymia was not related to the amount of critical incident exposure. However, greater alexithymia was associated with more severe PTSD symptoms. Moreover, in a prospective analysis of a smaller subsample of these officers, greater alexithymia predicted post–September 11 PTSD symptoms in New York City police officers above and beyond their pre–September 11 PTSD symptoms. These findings point to another way that childhood trauma may alter emotional responding and perhaps alter peritraumatic responses to duty-related critical incidents.

## Exposure to Duty-Related Trauma

Mid-career officers reported exposure to an average of approximately 150 duty-related critical incidents. However, their cumulative trauma exposure was only weakly associated with PTSD symptom severity (Pole et al., 2001; Liberman et al., 2002). On the other hand, McCaslin, Rogers, et al. (2006) found that officers whose worst duty-related traumatic event involved personal threat had more severe current PTSD hyperarousal symptoms. The finding that personal threat trauma is a more useful predictor of PTSD than cumulative exposure is consistent with Henn-Haase et al.'s (2006) similar finding in early-career officers and other findings in the literature (e.g., Green, 1993). Moreover, the specific association with hyperarousal symptoms may be important because other investigators have suggested that hyperarousal symptoms maintain other PTSD symptoms (Carlier et al., 1997; Schell, Marshall, and Jaycox, 2004).

## Peritraumatic Responses

Consistent with our findings in early-career officers and with our conceptual model, more severe PTSD symptoms among mid-career officers were associated with both elevated peritraumatic dissociation and elevated peritraumatic distress (Brunet et al., 2001; Pole et al., 2001). McCaslin, Rogers, et al. (2006) found that officers whose worst duty-related trauma involved high personal threat or violence reported more peritraumatic dissociation but not more peritraumatic distress than those whose worst trauma primarily involved encountering physical or sexual assault. Brunet et al. (2001) found that peritraumatic distress continued to predict PTSD symptom severity even after statistically controlling for peritraumatic dissociation, suggesting that peritraumatic distress contributes uniquely to the prediction of police-related PTSD over and above peritraumatic dissociation.

## Coping

Mid-career officers with elevated PTSD symptoms were significantly more likely to endorse a range of coping strategies (e.g., self control, distancing, etc.). Of these, escape-avoidant and planful problem-solving coping emerged as most strongly related to PTSD. The latter finding runs counter to the general expectation than active coping would be a buffer against negative post-traumatic sequelae. It is possible that this finding reflects a general increase in several types of coping behavior when more adaptive types of coping behavior have proven unsuccessful (Marmar et al., 2006). Though police officers are commonly assumed to use alcohol as a coping strategy, Ballenger et al. (at press) found that only a small fraction of the sample reported past alcohol abuse or dependence. Furthermore, their alcohol use was neither related to cumulative duty-related trauma exposure nor PTSD symptom severity.

## Social Support

Marmar et al. (2006) and the broader PTSD literature (Brewin et al., 2000; Ozer et al., 2003) view posttrauma social support as being an important buffer against PTSD symptoms. On a measure of both emotional and instrumental support, mid-career officers reported moderate levels of social support. Officers with poorer social support reported more severe PTSD symptoms.

## Non-traumatic Work Stress

Additional non-traumatic life stressors are thought to exacerbate risk for PTSD (Brewin et al., 2000). For police officers one important source of such stress comes from their work environment. These stressors include those that are part of virtually any occupation, such as poor management and paperwork, and some that are relatively specific to police work (e.g., hostility from the communities that they serve). Liberman et al. (2002) found that, for mid-career officers, greater PTSD symptom severity was much more strongly related to routine work stress than cumulative exposure to duty-related trauma. After accounting for minority status, social support, social desirability, routine work stress, and time elapsed since the worst traumatic event, routine work stress was the strongest predictor of PTSD symptoms. However, because routine work stress was assessed at the same time as PTSD symptoms, it is unclear whether routine work stress serves as a prospective indicator or merely another indicator of current psychological distress.

## Sleep

One component of routine work stress for police officers is shift work. Late shifts tend to disrupt natural biological cycles including sleeping patterns. Neylan et al. (2002) found that 64 percent of mid-career officers had clinically significant sleep problems, which were related to their exposure to duty-related trauma and routine work stress. Interestingly, both officers with stable work shifts and those with variable shifts were found to have poorer sleep quality than a peer-nominated comparison group of non–police officers. Officers who had more sleep problems reported significantly more severe PTSD symptoms even after taking into account the sleep symptoms that are known to accompany PTSD (Neylan et al., 2002). In addition, Mohr et al. (2003) found that sleep dysfunction mediated the relationship between PTSD symptoms and somatic symptoms, such as dizziness, headaches, and muscle soreness.

## Psychobiological Predictors of PTSD

We have also examined biological correlates of PTSD in mid-career officers. I led a study of startle reactivity in a subsample of these officers who were selected to represent extremes of exposure to critical incidents and PTSD symptom severity (Pole et al., 2003). We found that officers with more severe PTSD symptoms showed elevated physiological reactivity to startling sounds under low and medium threat but not high threat. Neither subjective reports of emotions nor subjective reports of exaggerated startle accounted for these physiological findings. In fact, the psychophysiological measures improved upon the prediction of overall PTSD symptom severity beyond self-report measures alone (Pole et al., 2003). These findings point to the potential utility of laboratory measures in the assessment of duty-related PTSD and indicate that mid-career officers with elevated PTSD symptoms show persisting inappropriate sensitivity to contextual threat.

Because previous research found that PTSD is associated with lower basal cortisol (e.g., Yehuda et al., 2000), Neylan et al. (2005) assessed salivary cortisol in mid-career officers before and after they took a low dose of dexamethasone. Results revealed that lower pre-dexamathasone cortisol levels were associated with higher peritraumatic distress, higher reported peritraumatic dissociation, and more severe PTSD symptoms. After controlling for age, gender, shift work, routine work stress, salivary dexamethasone levels, and peritraumatic dissociation, the authors found that the relationship between lower basal cortisol and higher PTSD symptoms still held. These results replicate earlier findings of lower cortisol in PTSD but also link these findings to elevated peritraumatic distress and dissociation. It is possible that lower cortisol reflects a broader failure of hypothalamic-pituitary-adrenal (HPA) axis regulation in officers with PTSD (Yehuda et al., 2000). It remains to be seen whether such dysregulation predates exposure to duty-related trauma or is merely a consequence of having PTSD symptoms.

## Multivariate Model

Marmar et al. (2006) constructed a multivariate model designed to explain current PTSD symptoms in mid-career officers. Each of the following variables accounted for significant variance in PTSD symptoms in the model: Hispanic ethnicity, duty- and non-duty-related trauma exposure, peritraumatic distress and dissociation, escape-avoidant and problem-solving coping, routine work stress, and social support. Due to missing data, neither the biological variables nor alexithymia were entered into the model. The five variables that were significant in the final model were greater peritraumatic distress, greater peritraumatic dissociation, greater problem solving coping, greater routine work environment stress, and lower levels of social support. This model accounted for approximately 40 percent of the variance in PTSD symptoms.

## POST-RETIREMENT PREDICTORS OF POLICE PTSD

### Sample Characteristics

Retired officers from all over the United States have completed my study of risk and resilience factors for post-retirement duty-related PTSD. The participants were recruited via newsletters and other media targeting the retired law enforcement community. Most are male, Caucasian, married, and had previously served in the military. The average participant was sixty years old, had worked in law enforcement for almost a quarter-century, and had been retired for more than a dozen years. Retired police officers bring important advantages to the study of duty-related PTSD. For example, because they are no longer exposed to duty-related trauma, they are ideal candidates to study factors that distinguish among individuals with chronic PTSD, those who recovered from PTSD, and those who never developed PTSD. Approximately 15 percent of our sample met criteria for posttraumatic stress disorder (PTSD) in relation to their accumulated police related experiences.

### Ethnicity and Gender

The lack of ethnic and gender diversity in the retired police sample prevented any meaningful examination of ethnicity and gender as correlates of PTSD symptom severity.

### Childhood (and Other) Trauma

Retired officers with a history of childhood trauma also reported more current duty-related PTSD symptoms associated with their worst duty-related traumatic experience. There was a trend for childhood trauma to be associated with greater peritraumatic distress during the incident but not greater peritraumatic dissociation. Thus, these results are broadly consistent with findings in the early career and mid-career officer samples linking childhood trauma to current PTSD symptoms. In terms of trauma occurring after childhood, neither military service nor participation in military combat was a significant predictor of post-retirement duty-related PTSD symptoms.

### Exposure to Duty-Related Trauma

As would be expected, the retired officers reported substantially more exposure to duty-related trauma than the early career and mid-career officers. The retirees reported exposure to an average of 250 duty-related critical incidents during their careers. Duty-related trauma included being threatened with a gun or knife, seeing someone dying or dead, encountering a child who had been assaulted or neglected, being seriously injured, witnessing a fellow officer injured or killed, having to kill or seriously injure someone, being involved in a large scale disaster (e.g., plane crash, tornado), and making a mistake that led to the injury or death of an officer or bystander. According to the respondents, the most stressful of these incidents were making a mistake that led to serious injury or death of an officer or a bystander, being present when a fellow officer was killed, and encountering a child who had been assaulted. Consistent with the other police samples, current PTSD symptoms were not associated with more cumulative duty-related trauma exposure. However, officers who were seriously injured in the line of duty reported more severe PTSD symptoms.

### Peritraumatic Responses

Consistent with the other police samples, retired officers who reported experiencing more severe current PTSD symptoms also reported more peritraumatic distress and peritraumatic dissociation during their worst duty-related incident.

### Coping

After their critical incident, most respondents managed their distress by exerting self-control (e.g., "I tried not to act too hastily"), distancing (e.g., "I didn't let it get to me; I refused to think too much about it"), and planful problem-solving (e.g., "I made a plan of action and I followed it"). A minority of officers endorsed escape avoidance coping (e.g., "I tried to make myself feel better by eating, drinking, or using drugs"). Those who had ongoing PTSD symptoms in retirement reported significantly more distancing, self-control, and escape avoidance coping. However, as with our mid-career sample, we found no relationship between alcohol use and current PTSD symptoms.

## Social Support

Surprisingly and in contradiction with both the broader literature and our other police samples, social support was not significantly related to post-retirement PTSD symptom severity. For the purposes of this particular study, retirees were asked to rate their social support at the time of their worst incident. Some earlier studies including our earlier police work assessed posttrauma social support, which may be a result rather than a cause of PTSD symptoms.

## Non-traumatic Work Stress

Retirees also rated their routine work stress at the time of their worst critical incident including stress arising from shift work (e.g., having to work overnight), administration (e.g., "The management caused pressure and job stress"), pay (e.g., "I was not paid enough for what I did"), court decisions (e.g., judges overturning decisions that were helpful to law enforcement), keeping professional matters secret (e.g., "I did not let my neighbors know what I did for a living"), equipment (e.g., "My personal equipment was not satisfactory for my safety and effectiveness"), and public attitudes (e.g., "Compared to other jobs with similar pay and educational requirements, the public viewed my job as lower in status"). We found that greater routine work stress at the time of the incident was associated with more current PTSD symptoms. Among these stressors, keeping police work secret was most strongly associated with more severe PTSD symptoms.

## Sleep

In the retired police sample, 62 percent reported ongoing clinically significant sleep problems (a figure that closely matched the data from the mid-career sample). Also paralleling our findings in the active duty sample, poor sleep hygiene was weakly related to cumulative critical incident exposure but was significantly related to more severe current PTSD symptoms.

## Multivariate Model

After adjusting for an acquiescent reporting bias that appeared to influence PTSD symptom reporting, significant variance in current PTSD symptom severity was explained by exposure to childhood trauma, serious injury in the line of duty, peritraumatic responses, escape avoidant coping, and keeping work secret from family and friends. In the full model, which explained approximately 40 percent of current PTSD severity variance, childhood trauma exposure was a marginally significant predictor. Only escape avoidance coping and keeping work secret were statistically significant predictors in the final model. Assuming that these results are not unduly influenced by greater retrospective reporting difficulties in an aging sample, they imply that poor coping and ongoing routine work stress may be more important than peritraumatic responses in maintaining long-term post-retirement PTSD symptoms.

## CONCLUSIONS

Consistent with Marmar et al.'s (2006) conceptual model, we found that cumulative duty-related trauma exposure poorly predicts PTSD symptoms in beginning, mid-career, and retired police officers. This is good news because it implies that mere exposure to the duty-related trauma of urban police work alone is not particularly pathogenic. On the other hand, police officers exposed to life threatening or personally injuring duty-related experiences appear to be significantly more likely to report PTSD symptoms. Also consistent with the conceptual model, we repeatedly found that more intense peritraumatic responses were associated with more severe PTSD symptoms. In this chapter, I have provided empirical support for the idea that childhood trauma and other factors like ethnicity and gender may set the stage for increased peritraumatic responding, which, in turn, accelerates the path to PTSD. However, posttraumatic coping, social support, and additional stressors appear to play an important moderating role. In fact, whereas peritraumatic responses continued to predict mid-career PTSD in a multivariate model that included posttrauma coping and support, peritraumatic responses no longer predicted post-retirement PTSD once coping and routine work stress were included in the model. This result reminds us that who gets and who keeps PTSD are two different questions. It also implies that intervention at the level of posttrauma coping and work environment could prevent post-retirement PTSD symptoms.

It is not clear whether and to what extent these results would generalize to civilian populations. It is likely that police officers differ in important ways from the general population especially with regard to their training and expectation of encountering traumatic stress. Even if these findings are not broadly generalizable they are still of value for their potential benefit to police officers and other people like them (e.g., soldiers, firefighters, and other emergency services personnel). Given the tremendous service that these people perform for society, it is important to understand the factors that predict PTSD in these groups. Thus, these findings provide an important step toward serving and protecting those who serve and protect the rest of us.

## ACKNOWLEDGEMENTS

The work described in the chapter was supported by grants from the National Institute of Mental Health (R01-MH056350-01A1) and the University of Michigan. The author thanks his collaborators (Charles R. Marmar, Thomas Neylan, Thomas Metzler, Christian Otte, Suzanne Best, Daniel Weiss, Jeffrey Fagan, Alain Brunet) and his students (Wendy D'Andrea, Madhur Kulkarni, and Michelle Gross Lilly) for their contributions to this chapter. Delores Carter Pole is also thanked for her special contributions.

## ENDNOTE

1. In this chapter, the term "predictors" should be taken to mean either prospective indicators or contemporaneous correlates.

## REFERENCES

Alexander, D. A., and Wells, A. (1991). Reactions of police officers to body handling after a major disaster: A before and after comparison. *British Journal of Psychiatry, 159*, 517–55.

American Psychiatric Association. (2000). Diagnostic and statistical manual of mental disorders (fourth ed., rev.). Washington, DC: American Psychiatric Association.

Ballenger, J. F., Best, S. R., Metzler, T. J., Wasserman, D. A., Mohr, D. C., Liberman, A., et al. (at press). Patterns and predictors of alcohol use in male and female urban police officers. *Journal of Addictive Behaviors.*

Beutler, L. E., Nussbaum, P. D., and Meredith, K. E. (1988). Changing personality patterns of police officers. *Professional Psychology: Research and Practice, 19*, 503–7.

Breslau, N., Kessler, R. C., Chilcoat, H. D., Schultz, L. R., Davis, G. C., and Andreski, P. (1998). Trauma and posttraumatic stress disorder in the community: The Detroit area survey of trauma. *Archives of Generals Psychiatry, 55*, 626–32.

Brewin, C. R., Andrews, B., and Valentine, J. D. (2000). Meta-analysis of risk factors for posttraumatic stress disorder in trauma-exposed adults. *Journal of Consulting and Clinical Psychology, 68*, 748–66.

Brown, J., Fielding, J., and Grover, J. (1999). Distinguishing traumatic, vicarious and routine operational stressor exposure and attendant adverse consequences in a sample of police officers. *Work & Stress, 13*, 312–25.

Brunet, A., Weiss, D. S., Metzler, T. J., Best, S. R., Neylan, T. C., Rogers, C., et al. (2001). The peritraumatic distress inventory: A proposed measure of PTSD criterion A2. *American Journal of Psychiatry, 158*(9), 1480–85.

Carlier, I., Lamberts, R., and Gersons, B. (1997). Risk factors for posttraumatic stress symptomatology in police officers: A prospective analysis. *Journal of Nervous and Mental Disease, 185*, 498–506.

Coplan, J. D., Trost, R. C., Owens, M. J., Cooper, T. B., Gorman, J. M., Nemeroff, C. B., et al. (1998). Cerebrospinal fluid concentrations of somatostatin and biogenic amines in grown primates reared by mothers exposed to manipulated foraging conditions. *Archives of General Psychiatry, 55*, 473–77.

DeBellis, M. D., Lefter, L., Trickett, P. K., and Putnam, F. W. (1994). Urinary catecholamine excretion in sexually abused girls. *Journal of the American Academy of Child and Adolescent Psychiatry, 33*, 320–27.

First, M. B., Spitzer, R. L., Gibbon, M., and Williams, J. B. W. (1997). Structured clinical interview for DSM-IV axis I disorders (SCID-I; clinician version). Washington, DC: American Psychiatric Press.

Gersons, B. P. (1989). Patterns of PTSD among police officers following shooting incidents: A two-dimensional model and treatment implications. *Journal of Traumatic Stress, 2*, 247–57.

Green, B. L. (1993). Identifying survivors at risk: Trauma and stressors across events. In J. P. Wilson and B. Raphael (Eds.), *International handbook of traumatic stress syndromes. The plenum series on stress and coping* (135–44). New York: Plenum Press.

Griffin, M. G., Resick, P. A., and Mechanic, M. B. (1997). Objective assessment of peritraumatic dissociation: Psychophysiological indicators. *American Journal of Psychiatry, 154*, 1081–88.

Grillon, C., Morgan, C. A., Davis, M., and Southwick, S. M. (1998). Effects of experimental context and explicit threat cues on acoustic startle in Vietnam veterans with posttraumatic stress disorder. *Biological Psychiatry, 44*, 1027–36.

Gross, M. M., and Pole, N. (2006). Gender and emotional distress: What cops tell us about disparities in PTSD symptoms. Poster presented at the annual meeting of the Anxiety Disorders Association of America, Miami, Florida.

Guthrie, R. M., and Bryant, R. A. (2005). A study of auditory startle response in firefighters before and after trauma exposure. *American Journal of Psychiatry, 162*, 283–90.

Heim, C., Newport, D. J., Heit, S., Graham, Y. P., Wilcox, M., Bonsall, R., et al. (2000). Pituitary-adrenal and autonomic responses to stress in women after sexual and physical abuse in childhood. *Journal of the American Medical Association, 284*, 592–97.

Henry, V. E. (2004). *Death work: Police, trauma, and the psychology of survival.* New York: Oxford University Press.

Henn-Haase, C., McCaslin, S. E., Metzler, T. J., Pole, N., and Marmar, C. R. (2006, November). Exposure to critical incidents and PTSD symptom in officers during the first year of police service. Paper presented at the International Society for Traumatic Stress Studies Conference, Hollywood, CA.

Kessler, R., Sonnega, A., Bromet, G., Hughes, M., Nelson, C., and Breslau, N. (1999). Epidemiologic risk factors for trauma and PTSD. In R. Yehuda (Ed.), *Psychological trauma*. Washington, DC. American Psychiatric Press.

Koenen, K. C. (at press). Genetics of posttraumatic stress disorder: Review and recommendations for future studies. *Journal of Traumatic Stress*.

Kopel, H., and Friedman, M. (1999). Effects of exposure to violence in South African police. In J. M. Violanti and E. D. Paton (Eds.), *Police trauma: Psychological aftermath of civilian combat* (xxiv, 327). Springfield, IL: Charles C. Thomas Publisher, LTD.

Kulka, R. A., Schlesenger, W. E., Fairbank, J. A., Hough, R. L., Jordan, B. K., Marmar, C. R., et al. (1990). *Trauma and the Vietnam War generation: Report of findings from the National Vietnam Veterans Readjustment Study*. New York: Brunner/Mazel.

Liberman, A. M., Best, S. R., Metzler, T. J., Fagan, J. A., Weiss, D. S., and Marmar, C. R. (2002). Routine occupational stress as and psychological distress in police. *Policing: An International Journal of Police Strategies and Management, 25*, 421–39.

Marmar, C. R., McCaslin, S., Metzler, T., Best, S., Weiss, D. S., Fagan, J., et al. (2006). Psychobiology of post-traumatic stress disorder: A decade of progress. Predictors of posttraumatic stress in police and other first responders. *Annals of the New York Academy of Sciences, 1071*, 1–18.

McCafferty, F. L., Domingo, G. D., and McCafferty, E. A. (1990). Posttraumatic stress disorder in the police officer: Paradigm of occupational stress. *Southern Medical Journal, 83*, 543–47.

McCaslin, S. E., Metzler, T. J., Best, S. R., Liberman, A., Weiss, D. S., Fagan, J., Marmar, C. R. (2006). Alexithymia and PTSD symptoms in urban police officers: Cross-sectional and prospective findings. *Journal of Traumatic Stress, 19*, 361–73.

McCaslin, S. E., Rogers, C., Metzler, T. J., Best, S. R., Weiss, D. S., Fagan, J. A., et al. (2006). The impact of personal threat on police officers' responses to critical incident stressors. *Journal of Nervous and Mental Disease, 194*, 591–97.

Miller, L. (2006). *Practical police psychology: Stress management and crisis intervention for law enforcement*. Springfield, IL: Charles C. Thomas.

Mohr, D., Vedantham, K., Neylan, T., Metzler, T. J., Best, S., and Marmar, C. R. (2003). The mediating effects of sleep in the relationship between traumatic stress and health symptoms in urban police officers. *Psychosomatic Medicine, 65*, 485–89.

Neylan, T., Brunet, A., Pole, N., Best, S. R., Metzler, T. J., Yehuda, R., et al. (2005). PTSD symptoms predict waking salivary cortisol levels in police officers. *Psychoneuroendocrinology, 30*, 373–81.

Neylan, T. C., Metzler, T. J., Best, S. R., Weiss, D. S., Fagan, J. A., Liberman, A., et al. (2002). Critical incident exposure and sleep quality in police officers. *Psychosomatic Medicine, 64*, 345–52.

Orr, S. P., Metzger, L. J., Miller, M. W., and Kaloupek, D. G. (2004). Psychophysiological assessment of PTSD. In J. P. Wilson and T. M. Keane (Eds.), *Assessing psychological trauma and PTSD* (second ed.) (289–343). New York: Guilford.

Otte, C., Neylan, T. C., Pole, N., Metzler, T., Best, S., Henn-Haase, C., et al. (2005). Association between childhood trauma and catecholamine responses to psychological stress in police academy recruits. *Biological Psychiatry, 57*, 27–32.

Ozer, E. J., Best, S. R., Lipsey, T. L., and Weiss, D. S. (2003). Predictors of posttraumatic stress disorder symptoms in adults: A meta-analysis. *Psychological Bulletin, 129*, 52–73.

Paton, D., and Violanti, J. M. (1996). *Traumatic stress in critical occupations: Recognition, consequences, and treatment.* Springfield, IL: Charles C. Thomas.

Pitman, R. K., Shalev, A. Y., and Orr, S. P. (2000). Posttraumatic stress disorder: Emotion, conditioning, and memory. In M. D. Corbetta and M. S. Gazzaniga (Eds.), *The new cognitive neurosciences* (687–700). New York: Plenum Press.

Pole, N. (at press). Post-traumatic Stress Disorder (PTSD). In C. M. Renzetti and J. L. Edleson (Eds.), *Encyclopedia of interpersonal violence.* Thousand Oaks, CA: Sage.

———. (2004). In the line of fire: Posttraumatic stress disorder in police officers. *ADAA Reporter, 15*, 3–4.

———. (2006a). Moderators of PTSD-related psychophysiological effect sizes: Results from a meta-analysis. Psychobiology of post-traumatic stress disorder: A decade of progress. *Annals of the New York Academy of Sciences, 1071*, 422–24.

———. (2006b). Posttraumatic stress disorder. In Y. Jackson (Ed.), *Encyclopedia of multicultural psychology* (359–67). Thousand Oaks, CA: Sage.

———. (2007). The psychophysiology of posttraumatic stress disorder: A meta-analysis. *Psychological Bulletin, 133*, 725–46.

Pole, N., Best, S. R., Metzler, T., and Marmar, C. R. (2005). Why are Hispanics at greater risk for PTSD? *Cultural Diversity and Ethnic Minority Psychology, 11*, 144–61.

Pole, N., Best, S. R., Weiss, D. S., Metzler, T., Liberman, A. M., Fagan, J., et al. (2001). Effects of gender and ethnicity on duty-related posttraumatic stress symptoms among urban police. *Journal of Nervous and Mental Disease, 189*, 442–48.

Pole, N., Cumberbatch, E., Taylor, W. M., Metzler, T., Marmar, C. R., and Neylan, T. (2005). Comparisons between high and low peritraumatic dissociators in cardiovascular and emotional activity while remembering trauma. *Journal of Trauma and Dissociation, 6*, 51–67.

Pole, N., Gone, J., and Kulkarni, M. (2008). Posttraumatic stress disorder among ethnoracial minorities in the United States. *Clinical Psychology: Science and Practice, 15*, 35–61.

Pole, N., and Gross, M. M. (at press). Posttraumatic Stress Disorder (PTSD). In J. O'Brien (Ed.), *Encyclopedia of gender and society.* Thousand Oaks, CA: Sage.

Pole, N., Kulkarni, M., Bernstein, A., and Kaufman, G. (2006). Resilience in retired police officers. *Truumatology, 23*, 1–10.

Pole, N., Neylan, T., Best, S. R., Orr, S. P., and Marmar, C. R. (2003). Fear-potentiated startle and posttraumatic stress symptoms in urban police officers. *Journal of Traumatic Stress, 16*, 471–79.

Pole, N., Neylan, T. C., Otte, C., Metzler, T. J., Best, S. R., Henn-Haase, C., et al. (2007). Associations between childhood trauma and emotion-modulated psychophysiological responses to startling sounds: A study of police cadets. *Journal of Abnormal Psychology, 116*, 352–61.

Roberts, N. A., and Levenson, R. W. (2001). The remains of the workday: Impact of job stress and exhaustion on marital interaction in police couples. *Journal of Marriage and Family, 63*, 1052–67.

Robinson, H. M., Sigman, M. R., and Wilson, J. P. (1997). Duty-related stressors and PTSD symptoms in suburban police officers. *Psychological Reports, 81*, 835–45.

Ruef, A. M., Litz, B. T., and Schlenger, W. E. (2000). Hispanic ethnicity and risk for combat-related posttraumatic stress disorder. *Cultural Diversity and Ethnic Minority Psychology, 6*, 235–51.

Russell, H. E., and Beigel, A. (1982). *Understanding human behavior for effective police work*. New York: Basic Books.

Schell, T., Marshall, G., and Jaycox, L. (2004). All symptoms are not created equal: The prominent role of hyperarousal in the natural course of posttraumatic psychological distress. *Journal of Abnormal Psychology, 113*, 1115–19.

Shalev, A. Y., Peri, T., Brandes, D., Freedman, S., Orr, S. P., and Pitman, R. K. (2000). Auditory startle response in trauma survivors with posttraumatic stress disorder: A prospective study. *American Journal of Psychiatry, 157*, 255–61.

Stein, M., Walker, J., Hazen, A., and Forde, D. (1997). Full and partial posttraumatic stress disorder: Findings from a community survey. *American Journal of Psychiatry, 154*, 1114–19.

Yehuda, R., Bierer, L. M., Schmeidler, J., Aferiat, D. H., Breslau, I., and Dolan, S. (2000). Low cortisol and risk for PTSD in adult offspring of holocaust survivors. *American Journal of Psychiatry, 157*, 1252–59.

Zoellner, L. A., Alvarez-Conrad, J., and Foa, E. B. (2002). Peritraumatic dissociative experiences, trauma narratives, and trauma pathology. *Journal of Traumatic Stress, 15*, 49–57.

# 4

## PTSD in Children and Adolescents: Risk Factors and Treatment Innovations

*Daniel W. Smith, Michael R. McCart,*
*and Benjamin E. Saunders*

### PTSD IN CHILDREN AND ADOLESCENTS: RISK FACTORS AND TREATMENT INNOVATIONS

Although retrospective assessments of prior trauma have shed light on the role of trauma history in increasing risk for PTSD in adult trauma victims, the retrospective nature of these studies is a limitation. Research examining risk factors and correlates of PTSD in children has greatly informed developmental models of PTSD risk and resilience. The study of traumatic stress and PTSD originated in attempts to understand the impact of combat and rape on adults; however, it remains a sad truth that children and youth are among the most highly victimized segments of society (Finkelhor and Hashima, 2001). Epidemiological research on trauma exposure in youth indicates that, in the United States, 50–70 percent of respondents below age eighteen report experiencing at least one type of direct or indirect victimization (cf., Fitzgerald, Danielson, Saunders, and Kilpatrick, 2007). Our own National Survey of Adolescents (e.g., Kilpatrick, Saunders, and Smith, 2003), a telephone survey of over four thousand twelve- to seventeen-year-olds, suggested very high rates of trauma exposure. Extrapolating to the U.S. population, our results suggest that 1.8 million adolescents have experienced a sexual assault, 3.9 million experienced a physical assault, 2.1 million experienced physically abusive punishment by parents or caregivers, and 8.8 million witnessed an incident of serious violence in their homes, neighborhoods, or communities. Another

Address correspondence concerning this chapter to Daniel W. Smith, Ph.D.; National Crime Victims Research and Treatment Center; Department of Psychiatry and Behavioral Sciences; Medical University of South Carolina; 165 Cannon St.; Charleston, SC 29425. E-mail: smithdw@musc.edu epidemiological telephone study, the Developmental Victimization Survey (Finkelhor, Ormrod, Turner, and Hamby, 2005), examined victimization rates in children and adolescents ages two to seventeen, and also found high rates of exposure to sexual abuse, physical assault, and witnessed violence. Moreover, youth who reported victimization experiences often reported experiencing or witnessing more than one type of violence, or multiple instances of exposure to the same type. For example, the Developmental Victimization Survey (which assessed over thirty possible types of victimization) found that of the youths who reported any victimization experiences, nearly 70 percent reported experiencing more than one type of direct or indirect victimization. Using a smaller subset of four possible violence exposure types, the National Survey of Adolescents still found that over 50 percent of trauma-exposed youth reported exposure to more than one type of trauma.

Numerous studies have documented that violence and trauma exposure are associated with higher levels of mental health and behavior problems. However, no studies suggest that rates of severe mental health problems in the national population of adolescents approach the rates of reported violence exposure. Despite the rather discouraging findings about the prevalence of trauma exposure in American youth, evidence suggests that most youth who are exposed to trauma are either resistant (i.e., they never develop violence-related mental health problems) or resilient (i.e., they may develop short-term symptoms but recover naturally) to the trauma exposure. Rates of PTSD in the National Survey of Adolescents, for example, were 10.1 percent for female and 6.2 percent for male adolescents (Kilpatrick et al., 2003). Identifying factors associated with both healthy and maladaptive functioning in young people is a critical task for researchers concerned with understanding the development of trauma-related psychopathology, and for policymakers and providers of treatment who seek to allocate limited service resources where they can do the most good.

## Risk Factors for PTSD

A wide range of stressful life events has been shown to place children and adolescents at risk for developing PTSD. Different types of events appear to produce different prevalence rates for the disorder. For example, clinical and epidemiological data estimate that PTSD occurs in 29–50 percent of youth exposed to sexual assault (Giaconia et al., 1995; Kilpatrick et al., 2003), 12–50 percent of physically abused children (Giaconia et al., 1995; Kilpatrick et al., 2003; Pelocovitz et al., 1998), 8–50 percent of youth who witness domestic or community violence (Giaconia et al., 1995; Kilpatrick et al., 2003; Pynoos and Nader, 1989), 6–34 percent of youth involved in motor vehicle accidents (Aaron, Zaglul, and Emery, 1999; Kassam-Adams and Winston, 2004; Stallard, Velleman, and Baldwin, 1998), 7–30 percent of burn patients (Stoddard, 1995; Stoddard, Norman, Murphy, and Beardslee, 1989), and 2–20 percent of pediatric cancer survivors (Kazak et al., 1997; Pelcovitz et al., 1998). These prevalence rates reveal a general trend toward higher PTSD risk among youth exposed to interpersonal violence when compared to other traumatic stressors. Similar findings are commonly observed among adults. That is, researchers have consistently documented higher rates of PTSD among adult victims of sexual or physical assault compared to those who experience other types of trauma (Resnick, Kilpatrick, Dansky, Saunders, and Best, 1993; Vrana and Lauterbach, 1994). The prevalence rates for PTSD also highlight considerable variability in outcome among youth exposed to traumatic events. While a sizable percentage of these youth develop symptoms of PTSD, a majority remain resilient and display little or no distress in the aftermath of a trauma.

Considerable effort has been expended to identify factors that distinguish children and adolescents who experience minimal or transient distress from those who develop longer-term psychopathology (particularly PTSD) following exposure to a traumatic stressor. As noted by Bryant (2003), acutely traumatized individuals who are at risk for developing poor outcomes may be good candidates for early intervention. This section provides a review of the literature on risk factors for PTSD among children and adolescents. Consistent with previous reviews in this area (Pine and Cohen, 2002), we categorize risk factors into three broad domains: characteristics of the trauma, characteristics of the individual, and characteristics of the social environment.

*Trauma Characteristics*

Certain characteristics of the trauma appear to increase the probability of negative outcomes among youth. For example, data from the traumatic stress literature suggest that youth are more likely to develop PTSD if the traumatic event elicits extreme fear of injury or death (McDermott and Cvitanovich, 2000; Stoppelbein, Greening, and Elkin, 2006). Individuals exposed to multiple traumatic events are also at greater risk for PTSD than those exposed to a single stressor (Hedtke, Ruggiero, Saunders, Resnick, and Kilpatrick, 2007). Notably, many victims of assault have experienced multiple types of violence. In a recent population-based study of youth aged two to seventeen years, 97 percent of those who had experienced sexual assault also reported exposure to one or more incidents of physical assault, abuse, or neglect by a caregiver, property victimization, or witnessing violence in the previous year (Finkelhor et al., 2005). A meaningful percentage of victims of violence have also experienced events that occur repeatedly over time (e.g., ongoing physical or sexual abuse: Saunders, 2003). Such chronicity of exposure leads to greater severity of PTSD symptoms (McCart et al., 2007). These features distinguish crime victims from those exposed to other traumatic events where repeated exposure to the same or different stressors is less common.

Among victims of childhood sexual assault, risk of PTSD is especially elevated when the assault involves a higher level of physical contact. Lynskey and Fergusson (1997) examined the relation between sexual assault in childhood and symptoms of PTSD among a birth cohort of 1,265 youth participating in the Christchurch Health and Development study. Among these youth, exposure to increasingly severe forms of sexual assault was associated with a linear increase in the number of self-reported PTSD symptoms. That is, youth experiencing childhood sexual assault involving attempted or completed oral, anal, or vaginal intercourse reported the highest number of PTSD symptoms, followed by individuals experiencing contact sexual assault without intercourse (i.e., fondling), non-contact sexual assault (i.e., exhibitionism), and those without any history of sexual assault in childhood.

Among victims of interpersonal violence, severity of physical injury is often correlated with higher levels of PTSD symptoms (Boney-McCoy and Finkelhor, 1995). However, the relationship between physical injury and PTSD among victims of nonviolent traumas is less clear. In one study, injury severity was shown to predict PTSD symptoms among youth exposed to a natural disaster (LaGreca, Silverman, Vernberg, and Prinstein, 1996). In another study, injury status among victims of motor vehicle accidents emerged as one of the strongest predictors of PTSD symptoms, after controlling for youth demographic characteristics (Keppel-Benson, Ollendick, and Benson, 2002). Others, however, have reported little to no association between measures of PTSD and physical injury among youth hospitalized following motor vehicle accidents or other accidental injuries (e.g., falls, burns: Aaron et al., 1999; Daviss et al., 2000; Kassam-Adams and Winston, 2004).

*Individual Characteristics*

**Demographic Characteristics.** The data are somewhat mixed regarding the role of demographic characteristics in predicting PTSD outcomes among youth. According to data from the National Survey of Adolescents, a population-based survey of 4,023 adolescents (aged twelve to seventeen years) residing in the United States, girls were significantly more likely than boys to meet criteria for a lifetime diagnosis of PTSD (10.1 percent vs. 6.2 percent: Kilpatrick et al., 2003). The prevalence of PTSD in this sample also rose significantly with increasing age. Another study explored predictors of PTSD among a sample of 171 youth admitted to a pediatric emergency department for treatment of traffic-related injuries (Winston, Kassam-Adams, Garcia-Espana, Ittenbach, and Cnaan, 2003). Older children and girls in the sample reported significantly higher levels of PTSD symptoms at a follow-up assessment conducted three to thirteen months post-injury. Similar age and/or gender differences have been reported in studies of youth with closed head injuries (Gerring et al., 2002) and among youth exposed to interpersonal and community violence (Singer, Anglin, Song, and Lunghofer, 1995; Springer and Padgett, 2000). In contrast, others have found no evidence of a relationship between age (Aaron et al., 1999; Daviss et al., 2000), gender (Scheeringa, Wright, Hunt, and Zeanah, 2006; Stoppelbein et al., 2006) and PTSD among youth exposed to various traumatic stressors. It is noteworthy, however, that some of these latter studies included very small samples, and others included an overrepresentation of girls and a restricted age range, limiting statistical power to detect potential group differences. Less attention has been paid to the role of ethnicity in predicting risk for PTSD, although a few studies have reported significantly higher rates of this disorder among African American and Hispanic youth compared to white, Native American, and Asian youth (Kilpatrick et al., 2003; LaGreca et al., 1996).

***Biological Mechanisms.*** There is some evidence indicating that early biological mechanisms may represent powerful predictors of longer-term psychological functioning among youth exposed to traumatic events. Delahanty, Nugent, Christopher, and Walsh (2005) explored the relationship between urinary hormone levels and PTSD among a sample of youth presenting to a pediatric emergency department with injuries secondary to motor vehicle accidents, sports accidents, or physical assault. Urine samples were collected during the first twelve hours of admission to the hospital and PTSD was assessed six weeks post-injury. Initial urinary cortisol and epinephrine levels were positively associated with PTSD symptoms, even after controlling for youth demographic variables and depression. These findings reveal potentially altered functioning of the hypothalamic-pituitary-adrenal axis and sympathetic nervous system among youth with PTSD (DeBellis et al., 1999). Chronic alteration of these neural systems can be harmful to childhood brain development and functioning, highlighting the importance of early identification and treatment of youth with PTSD (see Cohen, Perel, DeBellis, Friedman, and Putnam, 2002).

Data also support a link between physiological arousal shortly following a trauma and elevated risk for the development of PTSD. Kassam-Adams, Garcia-Espana, Fein, and Winston (2005) explored the relationship between heart rate and PTSD outcomes among a sample of youth who sustained traffic-related injuries. Youth with an elevated heart rate upon hospital admission were approximately two times more likely to develop partial or full PTSD six months post-injury, after controlling for youth demographic characteristics and the presence of a severe injury. In a similar study, Nugent, Christopher, and Delahanty (2006) examined whether heart rate levels predicted PTSD symptoms among a sample of youth hospitalized with an accidental or violence-related injury. Heart rate recorded during emergency medical service transport and heart rate averaged over the first twenty minutes following hospital admission predicted PTSD symptoms at six weeks post-injury, after controlling for demographic variables and depression. In sum, these findings suggest that routine assessment of physiological arousal among victims of acute trauma may help identify individuals at risk for developing PTSD.

*Cognitive Factors.*    Researchers have begun to consider cognitive factors that place traumatized individuals at risk for maladaptive outcomes. Ehlers and Clark (2000) recently proposed a cognitive model of PTSD. According to this model, individuals with PTSD appraise re-experiencing symptoms as dangerous, and these appraisals of danger lead to elevated levels of anxiety, anger, and distress. Victims of trauma may attempt to reduce this distress by engaging in maladaptive cognitive coping strategies, such as avoidance of intrusive memories. A recent study explored whether the cognitive variables specified in the Ehlers and Clark model would predict PTSD symptoms in a sample of youth involved in motor vehicle accidents (Ehlers, Mayou, and Bryant, 2003). Several cognitive responses assessed two weeks after the accident were associated with higher PTSD symptom severity at three and six months post-injury. Significant predictors of PTSD included negative appraisals of the trauma and its sequelae (negative interpretation of intrusive memories, perceived alienation from others, and anger) and dysfunctional cognitive strategies (rumination, cognitive avoidance, and persistent dissociation). Others have found elevated rates of PTSD among youth who engage in higher levels of thought suppression (Aaron et al., 1999) and cognitive minimization (downplaying of stressful life events: Springer and Padgett, 2000) following exposure to traumatic events. In several studies, youths' internal attributions for sexual abuse (i.e., believing that the event was caused by one's own characteristics or behavior) have also been shown to correlate positively with PTSD symptom severity (Chaffin, Wherry, and Dykman, 1997; Crouch, Smith, Ezzell, and Saunders, 1999; Feiring, Taska, and Chen, 2002). These findings are important because when compared to other risk factors for PTSD, cognitions are much more amenable to intervention. Indeed, existing empirically supported interventions for PTSD regularly employ cognitive components that help victims become more aware of their dysfunctional thoughts and beliefs, and attempt to modify them via cognitive restructuring techniques (described later).

***Acute Emotional Response.*** Studies indicate that youths' emotional response during or shortly following a traumatic event may be indicative of risk for later psychological problems. In 1994, the diagnosis of Acute Stress Disorder (ASD) was introduced in the DSM-IV as a way to identify individuals who display symptoms of acute distress at a level that might suggest risk for eventually developing PTSD. The diagnostic criteria for ASD include three or more dissociative symptoms, one re-experiencing symptom, marked avoidance of stimuli that arouse recollections of the trauma, and symptoms of anxiety or increased arousal that occur within one month of a traumatic event (American Psychiatric Association, 2002). The ASD diagnosis has been shown in a number of studies to have limited predictive validity for adult victims of trauma (see Bryant, 2003; Keane, Kaufman, and Kimble, 2001). Thus far, only a few studies have examined the utility of this diagnosis with pediatric populations. Kassam-Adams and Winston (2004) explored whether ASD was predictive of PTSD among a sample of youth hospitalized for injuries sustained in a traffic crash. ASD was assessed one month after the accident and PTSD was assessed three to twelve months post-injury. Of those who went on to develop PTSD, only 40 percent met criteria for ASD or subsyndromal ASD within the first month of injury. Thus, ASD does not appear to be an optimal categorical predictor of PTSD in either children or adults. Higher severity of ASD symptoms, however, was correlated with later PTSD symptom severity, suggesting an association between acute and longer-term distress. Indeed, other studies examining specific symptoms of acute distress have noted strong associations between measures of anxiety/arousal and dissociation administered immediately following a trauma and the development of PTSD over time (Kaplow, Dodge, Amaya-Jackson, and Saxe, 2005; Saxe et al., 2005).

***Prior Psychological Problems.*** The presence of prior psychological problems also appears to increase one's risk for developing PTSD (Breslau, Lucia, and Alvarado, 2006; Daviss et al., 2000; Gerring et al., 2002). Gerring and colleagues (2002) explored whether premorbid psychological problems would predict risk for PTSD among a sample of youth who suffered closed head injuries. Injuries were sustained due to a variety of events, including motor vehicle accidents, bicycle accidents, falls, or physical assault. Parents' retrospective reports of their youth's premorbid anxiety and depressive symptoms predicted PTSD severity at one year post-injury. Breslau and colleagues (2006) examined whether intelligence, anxiety disorders, and externalizing behavior problems assessed in childhood would influence risk for developing PTSD later in life. Participants included a randomly selected sample of low-birth-weight and normal-birth-weight youth assessed at six, eleven, and seventeen years of age. Youth with anxiety disorders and those with elevated externalizing behavior problems at age six were roughly twice as likely to meet criteria for PTSD at age seventeen. Notably, participants with an IQ greater than 115 at age six had decreased risk for PTSD later in life.

## Characteristics of the Social Environment

Trauma exposure results in elevated risk of longer-term psychopathology when the event causes disruption in the youth's family or social environment. For example, when Labor, Wolmer, and Cohen (2001) assessed the long-term impact of a SCUD missile attack on a sample of Israeli children, lower levels of family cohesion and being displaced as a result of the attack resulted in significantly higher levels of PTSD symptoms. A similar study examined social and family predictors of PTSD among a sample of youth exposed to a hurricane (Lonigan, Shannon, Taylor, Finch, and Sallee, 1994). Elevated PTSD symptoms were observed among youth whose families experienced more extensive home damage, displacement, and parental unemployment as a result of this natural disaster. Youth also tend to be at higher risk for PTSD if they are separated from their parents for a period of time following a trauma (Winston et al., 2003). In contrast, studies have reported reduced distress among youth when their parents are available to provide both physical and emotional support in the acute aftermath of a traumatic event (Kliewer, Lepore, Oskin, and Johnson, 1998; Overstreet, Dempsey, Graham, and Moely, 1999). Finally, aspects of parental mental health also appear to predict PTSD symptoms levels among youth. Daviss and colleagues (2000) found that youth victims of motor vehicle accidents were at much higher risk for PTSD if one of their parents showed signs of emotional distress after the accident. In another study, youth were at higher risk for experiencing symptoms of PTSD following a motor vehicle accident if their parents also experienced elevated PTSD symptoms (Landolt, Vollrath, Timm, Gnehm, and Sennhauser, 2005).

Overall, the extant body of research does little to help us understand the variability of PTSD development among youth exposed to traumatic stress. No individual risk factors identified to date consistently explain, across studies, who develops PTSD and who does not. As noted, most of these studies have been relatively small clinic or convenience samples, and as such are underpowered to detect the interactions of multiple risk factors. However, even very large studies will lack power when examining the multiplicity of factors that might be relevant for understanding a particular individual (e.g., female, racial minority, IQ status, history of depression, multiple victimizations, sexual penetration, separation from parents, etc.). One research avenue that offers some promise with respect to understanding risk and resilience is behavior genetics (cf., Koenen et al., this volume). Perhaps by incorporating more genetic and/or biological variables into our predictive models of who develops PTSD we can gain increased levels of certainty. However, these models are in their infancy, and despite the great strides made in understanding the genetics of complex disorders in the past decade, we are still a long way from understanding precisely how genes and environmental variables interact to produce mental disorders, especially complex phenotypes like PTSD. Therefore, until behavior genetics or some other research methodology is sufficiently developed to help clarify the picture, it is our view that the prediction of PTSD development among children and adolescents will remain frustratingly out of our grasp.

### Treatment of PTSD in Children and Youth: What Works? What Gets Delivered?

Despite our pessimism concerning the ability to predict which children or adolescents who are exposed to trauma will develop PTSD, we have much greater optimism about our increasing knowledge about how to treat the disorder effectively. Elsewhere in this volume, Feeny and her colleagues provide a thorough review of the treatment literature for PTSD in adults and children. We will offer a brief précis of their review before moving on to discuss the delivery of treatments. Reasonably good review articles published in the past several years regarding the treatment of PTSD in young people (e.g., Feeny, Foa, Treadwell, and March, 2004; Ruggiero, Morris, and Scotti, 2001) conclude that there is a growing research base documenting successful treatment of PTSD in children exposed to a range of traumatic events, from natural disasters to child sexual abuse. Most of the treatment interventions for pediatric PTSD that have been subjected to systematic evaluation stem from the cognitive-behavioral framework, which might be broadly construed to include eye movement desensitization/reprocessing (EMDR; Shapiro, 2001), though there is considerable controversy regarding EMDR's mechanism of action (Davidson and Parker, 2001). Multiple treatment interventions have been developed based on cognitive and/or behavioral conceptualizations of PTSD symptoms, and these interventions span individual (e.g., March, Amaya-Jackson, Murray, and Shulte, 1998; Saigh, 1986), group (e.g., Stein et al., 2003), and parent-child (e.g., Cohen, Mannarino, and Deblinger, 2006) treatment modalities. Both single-case and controlled, randomized clinical trial research designs support (to varying degrees) the use of cognitive-behavioral interventions for youth who have PTSD. It is important to note that other treatment models (e.g., psychodynamic intervention, non-directive intervention, psychopharmacology) may also be useful in treating PTSD; however, at this point there is either very limited or no controlled data supporting the effectiveness of these intervention modalities.

Although research data regarding clinical efficacy for some treatment models appears to be promising, data about the actual delivery of treatment services to trauma-exposed youth are less so. For example, Cohen, Mannarino, and Rogal (2001) surveyed both physicians and non-physicians who provided treatment to children with PTSD about the providers' preferred modes of intervention. Physicians indicated that they utilized psychopharmacological interventions most often (primarily selective serotonin reuptake inhibitors and alpha-adrenergic agonists), followed by psychodynamic therapy and cognitive-behavior therapy. There is little or no efficacy data regarding the psychopharmacological and psychodynamic interventions that were frequently endorsed by physicians, though it is encouraging that cognitive-behavioral therapy, for which efficacy data are available, was among the top three choices.

For non-physicians (e.g., social workers, psychologists, other psychotherapists), the most commonly endorsed interventions were cognitive-behavioral therapy, family therapy, and non-directive play therapy. Again, it is encouraging that an intervention with an evidence base was the most frequently endorsed practice; however, the frequent mentions of two interventions that lack clear support, when another, better validated intervention is available, is a matter of some concern. Several authors have described the "research-to-practice" gap in mental health service delivery (e.g., Chadwick Center, 2004), and these data suggest that service delivery for PTSD in children is no exception.

### Dissemination of Treatment:
### Trauma-Focused Cognitive-Behavioral Therapy (TF-CBT *Web*)

There are certainly several reasons that effective treatments might not be widely available (Chadwick Center, 2004), not the least of which is lack of clinician access to training in treatment delivery. It has been our experience that most graduate programs in clinical psychology and social work teach the basic principles of many different systems of psychotherapy, including cognitive-behavioral theory. However, we believe that many fewer training programs train their students to competence in specific treatment protocols for PTSD. For example, our clinical psychology internship training program includes a specific track for applicants interested in traumatic stress; yet, even among the applicants to this track, presumably interested and trained in trauma treatment, we estimate that fewer than 50 percent report pre-internship use of an empirically supported, structured treatment protocol for PTSD, let alone a protocol for PTSD in youth.

If mental health professionals do not receive instruction in PTSD treatment during their graduate training, they must rely on continuing professional education to fill in gaps in their training. However, in most forms of continuing education in mental health, at least one important element of learning is absent. Training clinicians to adopt and conduct empirically supported treatments is a complex enterprise (Chadwick Center, 2004). Several factors significantly limit the availability of adequate training. First, clinicians are busy doing clinical work, often with high caseloads and substantial quotas for productivity. Finding time for training in new treatment methodologies can be very difficult. Second, training methods tend to be time-intensive. Reading a book or treatment manual thoroughly requires hours; similarly, attending a training workshop—even one presented nearby—often requires more than a day away from the office, not to mention travel and registration costs. Clinical programs often must select one or two staff members to attend such trainings because it is impractical and financially prohibitive to shut down clinical operations entirely, even for brief periods, and pay for the training costs. Third, typical training methods (workshops, books) have their own limitations. Books and manuals, for example, do not typically allow the consumer to interact with the author or to observe or engage in simulated practice exercises. Also, books often include extensive scientific information about the theoretical and research basis for a treatment that, while clearly important from the perspective of the treatment developer, lacks relevance and practicality for the frontline clinician.

Workshop training, in contrast, typically allows for interaction with an expert and often includes role-playing and other experiential exercises that can facilitate learning. However, workshop training is typically presented by an expert who visits for one or two days and then leaves. Workshop attendees often leave trainings very excited about the information presented and in possession of excellent handouts. But when the clinicians return to their practices, they do not have access to the expert, cannot always remember the key points or tips presented at the training, and cannot ask about unexpected situations that commonly arise in treatment but were not necessarily covered specifically during training. Finally, neither books nor workshops typically provide opportunities for supervised practice in the interventions being presented.

The challenge facing the field of mental health is a way of disseminating meaningful training experiences to practitioners that contain practical information, can be accessed repeatedly at times when the practitioner needs them, and contain information of high learning value (demonstrations, role plays, etc.). The Internet is a powerful tool for disseminating such training.

To address the need for training, two of us (Smith and Saunders) spearheaded the development of **TF-CBT*Web*** (www.musc.edu/tfcbt), a ten-hour web-based, multimedia, distance education course for mental health professionals seeking to learn trauma-focused cognitive-behavioral therapy (TF-CBT; Cohen, Mannarino, and Deblinger, 2006; Deblinger and Heflin, 1996). It was developed for professionals holding a master's degree or above, or graduate students in a mental health discipline such as clinical social work, professional counseling, clinical psychology, psychiatry, marital and family therapy, or psychiatric nursing. It was designed to be used by busy, frontline practitioners who often have little time and few resources for traditional approaches to professional education. The asynchronous, modular, self-study approach of **TF-CBT*Web*** allows practitioners to learn at their own pace when it is convenient for them. They can access the training whenever they have time, and from virtually any computer with Internet access. The modular approach means they can space their learning over time, and return to the course whenever they like.

**TF-CBT*Web*** follows the general organization of the TF-CBT treatment protocol and presents information about each of the components that make up TF-CBT in a modular format. Modules include psychoeducation, stress management (including progressive muscle relaxation, controlled breathing, and thought stopping), affect identification and expression, cognitive coping, creating a trauma narrative, cognitive processing of the trauma narrative, behavior management, and conjoint parent-child sessions. Each module of **TF-CBT*Web*** includes:

- a streaming video introduction to the technique;
- pre- and posttests of knowledge of the treatment component that is the content of the module;
- an overview of the module's learning objectives;
- a description of the techniques of the treatment component and step-by-step instructions for how to implement them, including sample scripts for introducing the techniques to clients;
- multiple streaming video demonstrations of the techniques being used;
- suggested homework assignments or follow-up exercises that can be used with clients;
- cultural considerations that might be relevant in using the technique with diverse client groups;
- discussion of common clinical challenges that often arise in real-life practice; and
- directions for including parents or guardians in the therapeutic activities of the treatment component.

Below we present data regarding the usage of **TF-CBT***Web* by users who registered for the course during its first twelve months of availability (October 1, 2005–September 30, 2006). We present information about the types of learners who registered for and those who completed the course, the typical timing of course completion, and user evaluation data regarding the course format and content. Completion results reflect those who completed the entire course by December 31, 2006. Therefore, learners had a minimum of three months to complete some of the course modules or the full course. It should be noted that some **TF-CBT***Web* learners who registered on or before September 30, 2006, likely completed other modules or the entire course after December 31, 2006. Therefore, all completion statistics may underestimate actual rates of course completion.

Between October 1, 2005, and September 30, 2006, 9,149 learners registered for **TF-CBT***Web*. Of these, 3,558 completed the entire **TF-CBT***Web* course by December 31, 2006, a completion rate of 39 percent. An average of 25.1 new learners registered for **TF-CBT***Web* each day, and each day an average of 9.7 learners completed the course. Over the course of the year, both the daily registration and completion rates increased. Between July 1, 2006, and September 30, for example, 2006 new registrations averaged 32.2 per day and daily completions averaged 14.6.

Of the registered learners, 727 came from sixty different countries outside of the United States. Of the 727, 160 completed the full course by December 31, 2006, a completion rate of 22 percent. Learners from outside the United States were much less likely to complete the entire course than U.S. learners. While many reasons likely account for this difference, an important one is probably language. Though **TF-CBT***Web* contains some material in Spanish, the course is written in English, which may limit its utility in non-English-speaking countries. Because **TF-CBT***Web* was written primarily for American users, the remaining data presented are limited to the U.S. learners.

## U.S. Registrations

A total of 8,422 first-year registered learners resided in the U.S. or were Department of Defense personnel stationed overseas ($n = 22$). Of these U.S. learners, 3,398 (40.3 percent) completed the entire **TF-CBT***Web* course. These learners represented all fifty states and Washington, DC. Most registered U.S. learners (75 percent) held master's degrees in a mental health profession. Social workers were the most prevalent professional group in the learning cohort, representing two out of five learners. Professional counselors were the next most prevalent (28 percent), and psychologists represented about 20 percent of learners. Course completion rates were relatively the same for psychologists, social workers, and counselors, but lower for marriage and family therapists, nurses, and psychiatrists.

## Learner Attrition

Of the 8,422 registered learners from the United States, 2,467 (29.3 percent) did not complete the initial pretest for the first learning module. Of the 4,804 learners who completed the pretest for the second module, 71 percent eventually completed the entire course (before December 31, 2006). Thus registered learners appeared to fall into two distinct groups: those who examined the introductory material and perhaps the first learning module but went no further, and those who entered the course with sufficient motivation to complete it in its entirety. Almost two out of five registrants fell into the "looker" category.

## Completion Statistics

Of the 783 learners who registered in October 2005, 32 percent had completed the course by the end of the first year. Similarly, 555 learners registered in January 2006, and 40 percent had completed it by the end of the year. Generally, monthly completion rates hovered around the 40 percent overall rate with no clear increasing or decreasing trend. Over the full year, those who completed the course took an average of forty-three days to do so and a median of seventeen. However, the standard deviation of the days to completion was very large (SD = 61), indicating that a proportion of learners took quite a long time to complete the course. The longest time to complete was 419 days. However, 10 percent of all course completers did so within one day.

## Learner Knowledge Change

Prior to taking each learning module, learners completed a pretest composed of four questions related to the content of the module. At the end of the module they completed the same four questions as a posttest. Summary scores are the percentage of the four items answered correctly. Results indicated that on average, learners made significant knowledge gains in all ten content modules of **TF-CBT*Web***. It is encouraging that learners in all modules achieved significant knowledge gains, and that there were substantial knowledge gains in about one-half of the modules.

## Learner Satisfaction

After completing the entire course, **TF-CBT*Web*** learners were asked to complete a twenty-item evaluation of the course. Learners were asked to comment on the quality and helpfulness of each module, each module component (e.g., streaming videos, printable scripts, cultural considerations), and the "look and feel" and navigability of the web course. Virtually all learners (over 90 percent) indicated either "agree" or "strongly agree" to every question asking about how helpful various aspects of the course and site were. The large majority of learners agreed that all aspects of the course were helpful. Of course, this result is skewed by the fact that only those completing the course were asked the evaluation questions. Opinions of those who dropped out of the course before completing it obviously may be different from the completers. We are currently fielding evaluation research projects aimed at (a) surveying learners regarding their usage of TF-CBT following completion of the course, and (b) surveying non-completers about their reasons for not continuing with the course.

Overall, we are extremely pleased with both the volume of registrants that have sought training in TF-CBT via **TF-CBT***Web*, the 40 percent completion rate for learners who registered, the increased knowledge about TF-CBT modules evinced by learners, and the overwhelmingly positive evaluation data that has been provided to date by completers. We are currently exploring additional elements to be added to the course in order to increase the depth of information provided. Also, at present **TF-CBT***Web* does not provide any opportunity for consultation or clinical supervision, both of which may be important elements of clinical learning. Innovations in web-based conferencing might make such training elements increasingly feasible on a limited basis, although considerable logistical and ethical issues would clearly need to be addressed prior to initiating them. However, should ongoing evaluation data support the proposition that learners who complete **TF-CBT***Web* demonstrate clinical mastery of TF-CBT similar to or better than (or at least no worse than) those who learn the intervention in more traditional settings (e.g., workshop attendance, learning from a treatment manual), this would have enormous implications for training clinicians who lack knowledge of evidence-based practices, not only for PTSD-related interventions, but for mental health services across a broad spectrum of disorders and conditions.

## CONCLUSION

In sum, numerous characteristics of the trauma, individual, and social context have been identified as potential risk factors for the development of PTSD in child trauma victims. However, individually, these variables account for a relatively small percentage of the variance in subsequent PTSD symptoms, limiting confidence in our ability to identify trauma victims at high likelihood of developing PTSD. Additional research into multifactorial models of risk may inform identification efforts. In contrast, we are currently optimistic about methods of treating PTSD in children who suffer from the disorder. Empirically supported therapies consistently demonstrate treatment gains in victims of a variety of traumatic events. However, this enthusiasm is dampened by findings that many trauma victims with PTSD are not receiving gold-standard treatments. Current translational research examining ways of training and disseminating appropriate treatment procedures are showing promise, including web-based training into cognitive-behavioral techniques for treating child trauma victims.

## REFERENCES

Aaron, J., Zaglul, H., and Emery, R. E. (1999). Posttraumatic stress in children following acute physical injury. *Journal of Pediatric Psychology, 24*, 335–43.

American Psychiatric Association. (2002). *Diagnostic and statistical manual of mental disorders* (fourth ed., text rev.). Washington, DC: American Psychiatric Association.

Boney-McCoy, S., and Finkelhor, D. (1995). Psychosocial sequelae of violent victimization in a national youth sample. *Journal of Consulting and Clinical Psychology, 63*, 726–36.

Breslau, N., Lucia, V. C., and Alvarado, G. F. (2006). Intelligence and other predisposing factors in exposure to trauma and posttraumatic stress disorder. *Archives of General Psychiatry, 63,* 1238–45.

Bryant, R. A. (2003). Early predictors of posttraumatic stress disorder. *Biological Psychiatry, 53*, 789–95.

Chadwick Center for Children and Families. (2004). *Closing the Quality Chasm in Child Abuse Treatment: Identifying and Disseminating Best Practices.* San Diego, CA: Chadwick Center for Children and Families.

Chaffin, M., Wherry, J. N., and Dykman, R. (1997). School age children's coping with sexual abuse: Abuse stresses and symptoms associated with four coping strategies. *Child Abuse and Neglect, 21*, 227–40.

Cohen, J. A., Mannarino, A. P., and Deblinger, E. (2006). *Treating trauma and traumatic grief in children and adolescents.* New York: Guilford Press.

Cohen, J. A., Mannarino, A. P., and Rogal, S. (2001). Treatment practices for childhood posttraumatic stress disorder. *Child Abuse & Neglect, 25*, 123–35.

Cohen, J. A., Perel, J. M., DeBellis, M. D., Friedman, M. J., and Putnam, F. W. (2002). Treating traumatized children: Clinical implications of the psychobiology of posttraumatic stress disorder. *Trauma, Violence, and Abuse, 3*, 91–108.

Crouch, J. L., Smith, D. W., Ezzell, C. E., and Saunders, B. E. (1999). Measuring reactions to sexual trauma among children: Comparing the Children's Impact of

Traumatic Events Scale and the Trauma Symptom Checklist for Children. *Child Maltreatment, 4*, 255–63.

Davidson, P. R., and Parker, K. C. (2001). Eye movement desnsitization and reprocessing (EMDR): A meta-analysis. *Journal of Consulting and Clinical Psychology, 69*, 305–16.

Daviss, W. B., Mooney, D., Racusin, R., Ford, J. D., Fleischer, A., and McHugo, G. J. (2000). Predicting posttraumatic stress after hospitalization for pediatric injury. *Journal of the American Academy of Child and Adolescent Psychiatry, 39*, 576–83.

DeBellis, M. D., Baum, A. S., Birmaher, B., Keshavan, M. S., Eccard, C. H., Boring, A. M., et al. (1999). Developmental traumatology part I: Biological stress symptoms. *Biological Psychiatry, 45*, 1259–70.

Deblinger, E., and Heflin, A. H. (1996). *Treating sexually abused children and their non-offending parents: A cognitive behavioral approach.* Thousand Oaks, CA: Sage Publications.

Delahanty, D. L., Nugent, N. R., Christopher, N. C., and Walsh, M. (2005). Initial urinary epinephrine and cortisol levels predict acute PTSD symptoms in child trauma victims. *Psychoneuroendocrinology, 30*, 121–28.

Ehlers, A., and Clark, D. M. (2000). A cognitive model of posttraumatic stress disorder. *Behavior Research and Therapy, 38*, 319–45.

Ehlers, A., Mayou, R. A., and Bryant, B. (2003). Cognitive predictors of posttraumatic stress disorder in children: Results of a prospective longitudinal study. *Behavior Research and Therapy, 41*, 1–10.

Feeny, N. C., Foa, E. B., Treadwell, K. R. H., and March, J. (2004). Posttraumatic stress disorder in youth: A critical review of the cognitive and behavioral treatment outcome literature. *Professional Psychology: Research and Practice, 35*, 466–76.

Feeny, N. C., and Kahana, S. Y. (2008). PTSD in child and adult populations: A review of the cognitive behavioral treatment outcome literature. In Douglas G. Delahanty (Ed.), *The psychobiology of trauma and resilience across the lifespan.* Lanham, MD: Lexington Books.

Feiring, C., Taska, L., and Chen, K. (2002). Trying to understand why horrible things happen: Attributions, shame, and symptom development following sexual abuse. *Child Maltreatment, 7*, 26–41.

Finkelhor, D., and Hashima, P. (2001). The victimization of children and youth: A comprehensive overview. In S. O. White (Ed.), *Handbook of youth and justice* (49–78). New York: Kluwer/Plenum.

Finkelhor, D., Ormrod, R., Turner, H., and Hamby, S. L. (2005). The victimization of children and youth: A comprehensive national survey. *Child Maltreatment, 10*, 5–25.

Fitzgerald, M. F., Danielson, C. K., Saunders, B. E., Kilpatrick, D. G. (2007). Youth victimization: Implications for prevention, intervention, and public policy. *The Prevention Researcher, 14*, 3–7.

Gerring, J. P., Slomine, B., Vasa, R. A., Grados, M., Chen, A., Rising, W., et al. (2002). Clinical predictors of posttraumatic stress disorder after closed head injury in children. *Journal of the American Academy of Child and Adolescent Psychiatry, 41*, 157–65.

Giaconia, R. M., Reinherz, H. Z., Silverman, A. B., Pakiz, B., Frost, A. K., and Cohen, E. (1995). Traumas and posttraumatic stress disorder in a community population of older adolescents. *Journal of the American Academy of Child and Adolescent Psychiatry, 34*, 1369–80.

Hedtke, K. A., Ruggiero, K. J., Saunders, B. E., Resnick, H. S., and Kilpatrick, D. G. (2007). A longitudinal analysis of the relation between interpersonal violence types and mental health outcomes: Results from the National Women's Study. Manuscript submitted for publication.

Kaplow, J. B., Dodge, K. A., Amaya-Jackson, L., and Saxe, G. N. (2005). Pathways to PTSD, part II: Sexually abused children. *American Journal of Psychiatry, 162*, 1305–10.

Kassam-Adams, N., Garcia-Espana, J. F., Fein, J. A., and Winston, F. K. (2005). Heart rate and posttraumatic stress in injured children. *Archives of General Psychiatry, 62*, 335–40.

Kassam-Adams, N., and Winston, F. K. (2004). Predicting child PTSD: The relationship between acute stress disorder and PTSD in injured children. *Journal of the American Academy of Child and Adolescent Psychiatry, 43*, 403–11.

Kazak, A. E., Barakat, L. P., Meeske, K., Christakis, D., Meadows, A. T., Casey, R., et al. (1997). Posttraumatic stress, family functioning, and social support in survivors of childhood leukemia and their mothers and fathers. *Journal of Consulting and Clinical Psychology, 65*, 120–29.

Keane, T. M., Kaufman, M., and Kimble, M. O. (2001). Peritraumatic dissociative symptoms, acute stress disorder, and the development of posttraumatic stress disorder: Causation, correlation or epiphenomena. In L. Sanchez-Planell and C. Diez-Quevedo (Eds.), *Dissociative states* (21–43). Barcelona, Spain: Springer-Verlag.

Keppel-Benson, J. M., Ollendick, T. H., and Benson, M. J. (2002). Posttraumatic stress in children following motor vehicle accidents. *Journal of Child Psychology and Psychiatry, 43*, 203–12.

Kilpatrick, D. G., Saunders, B. W., and Smith, D. W. (2003). *Child and adolescent victimization in America: Prevalence and implications.* Washington, DC: National Institute of Justice—Research in Brief.

Kliewer W., Lepore, S. J., Oskin D., and Johnson, P. D. (1998). The role of social and cognitive process in children's adjustment to community violence. *Journal of Consulting and Clinical Psychology, 66*, 199–209.

Koenen, K., et al. (2008). Genetic risk factors for PTSD. In Douglas G. Delahanty (Ed.), *The psychobiology of trauma and resilience across the lifespan.* Lanham, MD: Lexington Books.

Labor, N., Wolmer, L., and Cohen, D. J. (2001). Mother's functioning and children's symptoms 5 years after a SCUD missile attack. *American Journal of Psychiatry, 158*, 1020–26.

LaGreca, A. M., Silverman, W. K., Vernberg, E. M., and Prinstein, M. J. (1996). Symptoms of posttraumatic stress disorder in children after Hurricane Andrew: A prospective study. *Journal of Consulting and Clinical Psychology, 64*, 712–23.

Landolt, M. A., Vollrath, M., Timm, K., Gnehm, H. E., and Sennhauser, F. H. (2005). Predicting posttraumatic stress symptoms in children after road traffic accidents. *Journal of the American Academy of Child and Adolescent Psychiatry, 44*, 1276–83.

Lonigan, C. J., Shannon, M. P., Taylor, C. M., Finch, A. J., and Sallee, F. R. (1994). Children exposed to disaster: II. Risk factors for the development of posttraumatic symptomatology. *Journal of the American Academy of Child and Adolescent Psychiatry, 33*, 94–105.

Lynskey, M. T., and Fergusson, D. M. (1997). Factors protecting against the development of adjustment difficulties in young adults exposed to childhood sexual abuse. *Child Abuse and Neglect, 21*, 1177–90.

March, J. S., Amay-Jackson, L., Murray, M. C., and Shulte, A. (1998). Cognitive-behavioral psychotherapy for children and adolescents with post-traumatic stress disorder following a single-incident stressor. *Journal of the American Academy of Child and Adolescent Psychiatry, 37*, 585–93.

McCart, M. R., Smith, D. W., Saunders, B. E., Kilpatrick, D. G., Resnick, H. S., and Ruggiero, K. J. (2007). Do urban adolescents habituate to interpersonal and community violence? Data from a national survey. *American Journal of Orthopsychiatry, 77*, 434–42.

McDermott, B., and Cvitanovich, A. (2000). Posttraumatic stress disorder and emotional problems in children following motor vehicle accidents: An extended case series. *Australian and New Zealand Journal of Psychiatry, 34*, 446–52.

Nugent, N. R., Christopher, N. C., and Delahanty, D. L. (2006). Emergency medical service and in-hospital vital signs as predictors of subsequent PTSD symptom severity in pediatric injury patients. *Journal of Child Psychology and Psychiatry, 47*, 919–26.

Overstreet, S., Dempsey, M., Graham, D., and Moely, B. (1999). Availability of family support as a moderator of exposure to family violence. *Journal of Clinical Child Psychology, 28*, 158–59.

Pelcovitz, D., Libov, B. G., Mandel, F., Kaplan, S., Weinblatt, M., and Septimus, A. (1998). Posttraumatic stress disorder and family functioning in adolescent cancer. *Journal of Traumatic Stress, 11*, 205–21.

Pine, D. S., and Cohen, J. A. (2002). Trauma in children and adolescents: Risk and treatment of psychiatric sequelae. *Biological Psychiatry, 51*, 519–31.

Pynoos, R. S., and Nader, K. (1989). Children's memory and proximity to violence. *Journal of the American Academy of Child and Adolescent Psychiatry, 28*, 236–41.

Resnick, H. S., Kilpatrick, D. G., Dansky, B. S., Saunders, B. E., and Best, C. L. (1993). Prevalence of civilian trauma and PTSD in a representative national sample of women. *Journal of Consulting and Clinical Psychology, 61*, 984–91.

Ruggiero, K. J., Morris, T. L., and Scotti, J. R. (2001). Treatment for children with posttraumatic stress disorder: Current status and future directions. *Clinical Psychology: Science and Practice, 8*, 210–27.

Saigh, P. A. (1986). In vitro flooding in the treatment of a 6-year-old boy's posttraumatic stress disorder. *Behaviour Research and Therapy, 24*, 685–88.

Saunders, B. E. (2003). Understanding children exposed to violence: Toward an integration of overlapping fields. *Journal of Interpersonal Violence, 18*, 356–76.

Saxe, G. N., Stoddard, F., Hall, F., Chawla, N., Lopez, C., Sheridan, R., et al. (2005). Pathways to PTSD, part I: Children with burns. *American Journal of Psychiatry, 162*, 1299–1304.

Scheeringa, M. S., Wright, M. J., Hunt, J. P., and Zeanah, C. H. (2006). Factors affecting the diagnosis and prediction of PTSD symptomatology in children and adolescents. *American Journal of Psychiatry, 163*, 644–51.

Shapiro, F. (2001). *Eye movement desensitization and reprocessing (EMDR): Basic principles, protocols, and procedures* (second ed.). New York: Guilford Press.

Singer, M. I., Anglin, T., Song, L. Y., and Lunghofer, L. (1995). Adolescents' exposure to violence and associated symptoms of psychological trauma. *Journal of the American Medical Association, 273*, 477–82.

Springer, C., and Padgett, D. K. (2000). Gender differences in young adolescents' exposure to violence and rates of PTSD symptomatology. *American Journal of Orthopsychiatry, 70*, 370–79.

Stallard, P., Velleman, R., and Baldwin, S. (1998). Prospective study of posttraumatic stress disorder in children involved in road traffic accidents. *British Medical Journal, 317*, 1619–23.

Stein, B. D., Jaycox, L. H., Kataoka, S. H., Wong, M., Tu, W., Elliott, M. N., et al. (2003). A mental health intervention for school children exposed to violence. *Journal of the American Medical Association, 290*, 603–11.

Stoddard, F. J. (1995). Care of infants, children, and adolescents with burn injuries. In M. Lewis (Ed.), *Child and adolescent psychiatry: A comprehensive textbook* (1016–37). Baltimore: Williams and Wilkins.

Stoddard, F. J., Norman, D. K., Murphy, J. M., and Beardslee, W. R. (1989). Psychiatric outcome of burned children. *Journal of the American Academy of Child and Adolescent Psychiatry, 28*, 589–95.

Stoppelbein, L. A., Greening, L., and Elkin, T. D. (2006). Risk of posttraumatic stress symptoms: A comparison of child survivors of pediatric cancer and parental bereavement. *Journal of Pediatric Psychology, 31*, 367–76.

Vrana, S., and Lauterbach, D. (1994). Prevalence of traumatic events and posttraumatic psychological symptoms in a non-clinical sample of college students. *Journal of Traumatic Stress, 7*, 289–302.

Winston, F. K., Kassam-Adams, N., Garcia-Espana, F., Ittenbach, R., and Cnaan, A. (2003). Screening for risk of persistent posttraumatic stress in injured children and their parents. *Journal of the American Medical Association, 290*, 643–49.

# 5

# Modeling Pathways to Posttraumatic Stress Disorder

*Glenn N. Saxe, Meaghan Geary, Erin Hall, and Julie Kaplow*

## UNDERSTANDING THE COMPLEX
## BIOBEHAVIORAL PROCESSES OF PTSD

The emergence and persistence of PTSD symptomatology is a complex
biobehavioral process influenced by a great many factors relating to the individual within their environment (Pynoos, 1993; Cicchetti and Rogosch, 1994;
Yehuda, 1999). As such, methodologies designed to capture the complex
etiology of PTSD must include approaches that explore how these disparate
variables may "fit together." This chapter describes some of our work over
the last ten years conducting studies to understand the complex etiology of
PTSD and some of the converging findings from these studies. We present
findings from three published studies by our group that used similar methodologies and yielded converging findings in separate cohorts of traumatized
individuals. These three studies describe cohorts of (1) children with burns
(Saxe, Stoddard, Hall, Chawla, Lopez, Sheridan, et al., 2005), (2) parents of
children with burns (Hall, Saxe, Stoddard, Kaplow, Koenen, Chawla, et al.,
2005), and (3) sexually abused children (Kaplow, Dodge, Amaya-Jackson and
Saxe, 2005). The methodologies used by these studies are similar and involve
(1) assessments that occur around the time of the trauma, (2) multimodal assessments, (3) longitudinal research methods, and (4) data analytic procedures
that allow for the modeling of variables. The results of these respective studies point to two discrete pathways to PTSD related to the respective symptom
groupings of acute anxiety and acute dissociation. As we will review, these

Address correspondence to Glenn Saxe, M.D.; Department of Child and Adolescent Psychiatry; Harvard Medical School; 715 Albany St., Dw11; Boston, MA 02118. E-mail: glenn.saxe@bmc.org

two pathways appear to point to separate underlying biobehavioral systems. This chapter is written both to highlight the methodology used to identify these pathways and the meaning of the pathways themselves.

## METHODOLOGICAL ISSUES

A growing number of researchers (e.g., Koss and Figueredo, 2004; Saxe et al., 2005; Shalev, Sahar, Freedman, Peri, Glick, Brandes, et al., 1998) have relied on longitudinal designs in PTSD research, in which the issue of temporal presence and the direction of causality may be better addressed (King, King, McArdle, Saxe, Doron-LaMarca, and Orazem, 2006). For example, a prospective, longitudinal design allows researchers to assess the victim in the acute wake of a trauma, and again at various time intervals, to enhance understanding of how and when certain factors influence the course of symptomatology following a traumatic event (King et al., 2006). As Mezzich and colleagues (1994) explained, prospective, longitudinal strategies are necessary to "allow the possibility of investigating the unfolding of psychopathological processes and testing etiologic hypotheses, pathogenic pathways of interest, prognostic considerations, patient trajectories, and outcomes of illness." Prospective, longitudinal designs allow researchers to assess children acutely following trauma and at various intervals posttrauma, helping us to better understand the sequential "unfolding" of certain pathologic processes throughout the progression of PTSD development.

Using such longitudinal methodologies, variables may be organized according to a time-based classification within the categories of the trauma itself, and pretrauma, peritrauma, and posttraumatic variables. Accordingly, the variables in each of the three studies represented in this chapter are sequentially organized along the temporal sequence of trauma.

## PATHWAYS TO PTSD IN THREE COHORTS

Using the above methodological approach, our research team has explored pathway models in three different cohorts of traumatized individuals. The first study investigated pathways to PTSD in children suffering from burn trauma, the second in parents of burned children, and the third in child victims of sexual abuse. Details on the methodology of each of these respective studies are beyond the scope of this chapter. The reader is referred to the original published research articles for methodological detail (Saxe et al., 2005; Kaplow et al., 2005; Hall et al., 2005).

## Pathway to PTSD Part I: Children with Burns (Saxe et al., 2005)

### Basic Description

The primary objective in this study was to develop a model of risk factors for posttraumatic stress disorder in a cohort of acutely burned children.

### Method

Seventy-two children (ages seven to seventeen) suffering from acute burns were recruited for this study during their inpatient stay. Families completed the Child Posttraumatic Stress Disorder Reaction Index (CPTSD-RI; Frederick, Pynoos, and Nader, 1992), the Multidimensional Anxiety Scale for Children (MASC; March, Parker, Sullivan, Stallings, and Conners, 1997) and other self-report and parent-report measures of psychopathology and environmental stress both during hospitalization for an acute burn and three months following discharge from the hospital.

A series of hierarchically nested multiple regression analyses were used to estimate direct and indirect effects among variables. Accordingly, we chose two primary variables that, together, accounted for 60 percent of the variance of PTSD: acute separation anxiety and acute dissociative symptoms. Once these variables were chosen we began building a model including more "upstream" or antecedent variables that would place acute separation anxiety and acute dissociation in the roles of mediators. We specified a fully saturated model and then removed paths that were not significant.

### Results

Two pathways to PTSD were discerned in children with burns. One pathway was mediated by separation anxiety, the other by acute dissociative symptoms measured within days of the burn. Results identified the following two independent pathways to PTSD in burned children:

(1) from the size of the burn (total burn surface area—TBSA) and child's pain level following burn to the child's level of acute separation anxiety, and then to the child's level of PTSD at three months post-burn, and (2) from the size of the burn (TBSA) to the child's level of acute dissociation following the burn, and then to the child's level of PTSD at three months post-burn. The magnitude of the trauma, measured by the size of the burn, was not related to PTSD directly but exerted its influence indirectly via both pathways. The pathway mediated by separation anxiety was influenced by acute pain, size of burn, and age at acute interview. The pathway mediated by the acute dissociative response was only influenced by the size of the burn. Together,

these pathways accounted for close to 60 percent of the variance in PTSD symptoms, and constituted a pathways model with excellent fit indices.

## Conclusions

These findings supported a model of complex etiology for childhood PTSD in which two independent pathways, acute anxiety and acute dissociation, explained significant variance in PTSD symptoms. Regarding the controversy over whether acute anxiety or dissociation is the more important predictor of PTSD, our data suggested that both anxiety and dissociative symptoms independently contributed to the risk of developing PTSD.

## Pathway to PTSD Part II: Parents of Burned Children (Hall et al., 2005)

### Basic Description

The primary aim of this study was to develop a model of risk factors for PTSD symptoms in parents of children with burns.

### Method

Sixty-two parents (fifty-four mothers, eight fathers) of children who were hospitalized for an acute burn participated in the study. None of the parents were burned in the incident that led to the hospitalization of their children. Parents were interviewed acutely following their child's burn incident (during child's hospitalization) and again three months following the burn incident. Parents were asked to report on their own psychosocial functioning as well as their child's psychosocial functioning following the burn trauma.

A series of hierarchically nested multiple regression analyses were used to estimate direct and indirect effects among variables. Accordingly, we chose three primary variables, all measured three months posttrauma that together accounted for 57 percent of the variance of PTSD, including parents' acute dissociation, children's PTSD symptoms, and increased parent-child conflict. Once again, we began building a model including more "upstream" or antecedent variables that would place parents' dissociation, child's PTSD symptoms, and increased parent-child conflict in the roles of mediators. We specified a fully saturated model and then removed insignificant paths.

### Results

Results identified three independent pathways to PTSD in parents of children with burns: (1) from conflict with extended family and size of burn to acute dissociation and to PTSD symptoms at three months; (2) from acute anxiety to conflict with children after hospital discharge, to PTSD symptoms at three months; and (3) from the size of the burn to the children's acute dissociation to the children's PTSD symptoms and to the parents' PTSD symptoms.

Parents' acute dissociation and children's PTSD symptoms mediated the relationship between total body surface area burned and parents' PTSD symptoms, and children's PTSD symptoms also mediated the relationship between children's dissociation and parents' PTSD symptoms. Moreover, increased conflict between parents and children mediated the relation between parents' acute anxiety and their PTSD symptoms. The relationship between pretrauma conflict with extended family and parents' PTSD symptoms was mediated by parents' dissociation.

## Conclusions

These findings supported a model of complex etiology for PTSD in parents of children with burns in which three independent pathways related to acute anxiety, acute dissociation, and the burned child's acute dissociation and PTSD symptoms independently contribute to the risk of developing PTSD in parents of children with burns.

## Pathway to PTSD Part III: Sexually Abused Children (Kaplow et al., 2005)

### Basic Description

The main goal in this study was to delineate a model of risk factors for posttraumatic stress disorder in a cohort of children following the disclosure of sexual abuse.

### Methods

One hundred fifty-six sexually abused children ages eight to thirteen years. At the time 2 follow-up (seven to thirty-six months following the initial interview), the children were assessed for posttraumatic stress symptoms. Each child was videotaped while undergoing a forensic interview, during which the child was asked to recollect and discuss potentially traumatic memories of the sexual abuse. Avoidant behavior was assessed through the utilization of a behavioral coding technique during videotaped, forensic interviews. Psychopathology was assessed at both interviews using the Trauma Symptoms Checklist for Children (TSCC: Briere, 1996), which assessed specifically for PTSD, dissociation, and anxiety.

A path analysis involving a series of hierarchically nested ordinary least squares multiple regression analyses indicated three direct paths to PTSD symptoms: avoidant coping, anxiety/arousal, and dissociation, all measured during or immediately after disclosure of sexual abuse. Accordingly, we chose three primary variables, all measured three months posttrauma that together accounted for 57 percent of the variance of PTSD, including avoidant coping, anxiety/arousal, and dissociation. Once these three variables were chosen we began building a model including antecedent variables that would place avoidant coping, anxiety/arousal, and dissociation in the roles of mediators. We specified a fully saturated model and then removed paths that were not significant.

*Results*

Path analyses indicated three direct paths to PTSD symptoms: avoidant coping, anxiety/arousal, and dissociation, all measured during or immediately after disclosure of sexual abuse. Additionally, age and gender predicted avoidant coping, while life stress and age at abuse onset predicted symptoms of anxiety/arousal. Taken together, these pathways accounted for 57 percent of the variance in PTSD symptoms. They also show four indirect paths to PTSD symptoms from pretrauma and trauma variables: age, gender, life stress, and age at onset of abuse. More specifically, anxiety/arousal served as a mediator between life stress and PTSD and between age at onset and PTSD. In addition, avoidance served as a mediator between age and PTSD and between gender and PTSD. Dissociation was not only a direct predictor of PTSD but also an indirect predictor of PTSD symptoms by way of anxiety symptoms. Given the high explanatory value of these pathways, the model helps to shed light on the relatively unknown course of PTSD in sexually abused children.

*Conclusions*

Symptoms measured at the time of disclosure constitute direct, independent pathways by which sexually abused children are likely to develop later PTSD symptoms. Specifically, the results indicate that sexually abused children who exhibit symptoms of avoidance, anxiety/arousal, or dissociation either during or immediately following disclosure of abuse are at increased risk of developing PTSD symptoms later on in life.

## DISCUSSION

This chapter is written both to highlight the methodology we use to identify pathways that lead to PTSD in acutely traumatized individuals and the identification and meaning of the pathways themselves. Using a process of categorizing potentially influential variables temporally, and using prospective, longitudinal designs, we were able to identify and replicate specific pathways to PTSD in three cohorts of traumatized individuals. Although there were some differences in variables identified in the three studies, there was important convergence of findings identifying these discrete acute anxiety and acute dissociative pathways.

What does the identification of independent pathways of acute anxiety and acute dissociation mean? Obviously, these are the symptom groupings of the DSM-IV diagnosis of acute stress disorder (ASD) (American Psychological Association, 1994), supporting the validity of this diagnosis; more fundamentally, these two symptom groups may be the phenotypes of distinct biobehavioral systems related to posttraumatic stress disorder, a hypothesis raised before in the literature (Perry, Pollard, Blakley, Baker, and Vigilante, 1995; Perry, 1997; Saxe et al., 2005). These fundamental symptoms may be "built" upon evolutionarily refined adaptations of the human nervous system for the processing of threatening events. A number of writers have drawn connections between the hyperarousal symptoms and the sympathetically mediated fight-or-flight response and between the symptoms of dissociation and the parasympathetically mediated "freeze" or "immobilization" response (Perry, 1999; Perry et al., 1995; Van der Kolk, 1994). For example, Perry has described the hierarchical response to threat in biological theories of children's responses to trauma (Perry, 1999; Perry et al., 1995). He describes the initial fight or flight "hyperarousal response" in children faced with acute threat and a "freeze or surrender" immobilized response when a child is not able to impact the environment and is helpless to respond (Perry et al., 1995). He further states that there are two major neuronal response patterns important for the traumatized child: the hyperarousal continuum and the dissociative continuum. Evidence suggests that hyperarousal symptoms and dissociative symptoms may be subserved by different biological systems, the hyperarousal/anxiety symptoms by the fight-or-flight mediated sympathetic/ HPA axis system and the dissociative symptoms by the freeze/immobilization mediated parasympathetic nervous system.

These ideas fit closely with ideas of the evolution of the autonomic nervous system. In his polyvagal theory, Porges proposes a hierarchical response strategy to environmental challenges based on three elements of the autonomic nervous system, where the most adaptive responses are employed first followed sequentially by less adaptive (phylogenetically older) responses (Porges, 1995; Porges, 1997; Porges, 2001; Porges, Matthew, and Pauls, 1992). This form of dissolution (Jackson, 1958) occurs when the organism's response strategy is sequentially overwhelmed. Thus, the initial response of mammals to environmental threat is via the myelinated vagus. Strong mobilization responses from the sympathetic nervous system are inhibited, and systems related to signaling and social communication are engaged. If this strategy is not effective and threat continues, strong mobilization (fight-or-flight) strategies ensue. This involves withdrawal of vagal inhibition of the heart and mobilization of the norepinephrine and HPA axis to prepare the organism for action. If this strategy is not effective, the organism adapts a metabolically conservative strategy in the face of life threatening challenge, mediated by the unmyelinated vagus. In this "immobilization" strategy, heart rate is decreased, breathing is slowed, locomotor activity stops, and gut motility increases, as the organism is immobile and frozen and anticipates a life threatening challenge (Porges, 2001).

An important element of these ideas is their testability in humans. Heart rate variability (HRV) and respiratory sinus arrhythmia (RSA) are relatively easy to measure and are thought to be indices of an intact polyvagal system (Beauchaine, 2001; Porges, 1991; Porges, 1992; Porges and Byrne, 1992). HRV and RSA have been associated with many parameters of emotional regulation in infants, children, and adults (Porges, 1995; Porges, 1997; Porges, 2001; Porges, 1992; Beauchine, 2001; Porges, 1991; Degangi, Breinbauer, Dousarrd-Roosevelt, Porges, and Greenspan, 2000; Doussard-Roosevelt, McClenny and Porges, 2001; Suess, Porges, and Plude, 1994), and reductions in heart rate variability have been found in studies of individuals with anxiety disorders (McLeod, Hoehn-Saric, Porges, and Zimmerli, 1992).

Our ongoing research is measuring these types of physiologic parameters in order to determine whether such disparate vagal responses may underlie the acute anxiety and acute dissociative responses that appear to explain so much of the variance in PTSD symptoms. Whichever mechanism accounts for the converging findings of independent pathways to PTSD related to acute anxiety and acute dissociative symptoms, the identification of these pathways is critical for hypothesis generation and research to understand the biobehavioral processes that underlie PTSD.

## REFERENCES

American Psychiatric Association. (1994). *Diagnostic and statistical manual of mental disorders: DSM-IV* (fourth ed.). Washington, DC: American Psychiatric Association.

Beauchaine, T. (2001). Vagal tone, development, and Gray's motivational theory: Toward an integrated model of autonomic nervous system functioning in psychopathology. *Development and Psychopathology, 13,* 183–214.

Briere, J. (1996). *Trauma Symptom Checklist for Children (TSCC): Professional Manual.* Odessa, FL: Psychological Assessment Resources, Inc.

Cicchetti, D., and Rogosch, F. A. (1994). The toll of child maltreatment on the developing child: Insights from developmental psychopathology. *Child and Adolescent Psychiatric Clinics of North America, 3,* 759–76.

DeGangi, G. A., Breinbauer, C., Dousarrd-Roosevelt, J., Porges, S., and Greenspan, S. (2000). Prediction of childhood problems at three years in children experiencing disorders of regulation during infancy. *Infant Mental Health Journal, 21*(3), 156–75.

Doussard-Roosevelt, J. A., McClenny, B. D., and Porges, S. W. (2001). Neonatal cardiac vagal tone and school-age developmental outcome in very low birth weight infants. *Psychobiology, 38,* 56–66.

Frederick, C., Pynoos, R. S., and Nader, K. (1992). *Child Post-Traumatic Stress Disorder Reaction Index (CPTSD-RI).* Los Angeles: University of California at Los Angeles Department of Psychiatry.

Hall, E., Saxe, G. N., Stoddard, F., Kaplow, J., Koenen, K., Chawla, N., et al. (2005). Posttraumatic stress symptoms in parents of children with acute burns. *Journal of Pediatric Psychology, 31*(4), 403–12.

Jackson, J. H. (1958). Evolution and dissolution of the nervous system. In J. Taylor (Ed.), *Selected writings of Johan Hughlings Jackson* (45–118). London: Staples Press.

Kaplow, J., Dodge, K. A., Amaya-Jackson, L., and. Saxe, G. N. (2005). Pathways to PTSD, part II: Sexually abused children. *The American Journal of Psychiatry, 162,* 1305–10.

King, L. A., King, D. W., McArdle, J. J., Saxe, G. N., Doron-LaMarca, S., and Orazem, R. J. (2006). Latent difference score approach to longitudinal trauma research. *Journal of Traumatic Stress, 19*(6), 771–85.

Koss, M. P., and Figueredo, A. J. (2004). Change in cognitive mediators of rape's impact on psychosocial health across two years of recovery. *Journal of Consulting and Clinical Psychology, 72,* 34–64.

March, J. S., Parker, J. D., Sullivan, K., Stallings, P., and Conners, C. K. (1997). The Multidimensional Anxiety Scale for Children (MASC): Factor structure, reliability, and validity. *Journal of American Child & Adolescent Psychiatry, 36,* 554–64.

McLeod, D. R., Hoehn-Saric, R., Porges, S. W., and Zimmerli, W. D. (1992). Effects of alprazolam and imipramine on parasympathetic cardiac control on patients with generalized anxiety disorder. *Psychopharmacology, 107,* 535–40.

Mezzich, J. E., Jorge, M. R., and Salloum, I. M. (1994). *Psychiatric epidemiology: Assessment methods.* Baltimore: Johns Hopkins Press.

Perry, B. D. (1997). Incubated in terror: Neurodevelopment factors in the "cycles of violence." In J. Osofsky (Ed.), *Children, youth and violence: The search for solutions* (124–48). New York: Guilford Press.

———. (1999). The memories of states. In J. Goodwin and R. Attias (Eds.), *Splintered reflections: Images of the body in trauma* (9–38). Boulder, CO: Basic Books.

Perry, B. D., Pollard, R. A., Blakley, T. L., Baker, W. L., and Vigilante, D. (1995). Childhood trauma, the neurobiology of adaptation and use-dependent development of the brain: How states become traits. *Infant Mental Health Journal, 16*(4), 271–91.

Porges, S. W. (1991). Vagal tone: An autonomic mediator of affect. In J. Garber and K. Dodge (Eds.), *The development of emotional regulation and dysregulation* (11–27). Cambridge, MA: Cambridge University Press.

———. (1992). Vagal tone: A physiologic marker of stress vulnerability. *Pediatrics, 90*(3), 498–504.

———. (1995). Orienting in a defensive world: Mammalian modification of our evolutionary heritage. A polyvagal theory. *Psychophysiology, 32*, 301–18.

———. (1997). Emotion: An evolutionary by-product of the neural regulation of the autonomic nervous system. *Annals of the New York Academy of Sciences, 807*, 62–77.

———. (2001). The polyvagal theory: phylogenetic substrates of a social nervous system. *International Journal of Psychophysiology, 42*, 123–46.

Porges, S. W., and Byrne, E. A. (1992). Research methods for measurement of heart rate and respiration. *Biological Psychology, 34*, 93–130.

Porges, S. W., Matthew, K. A., and Pauls, D. L. (1992). The biobehavioral interface in behavioral pediatrics. *Pediatrics, 90*(5), 789–97.

Pynoos, R. S. (1993). Traumatic stress and developmental psychopathology in children and adolescents. In J. Oldham et al. (Eds.), *American psychiatric press review of psychiatry* (205–38). Washington, DC: American Psychiatric Press.

Saxe, G. N., Stoddard, E., Hall, N., Chawla, C., Lopez, R., Sheridan, D., et al. (2005). Pathways to PTSD part I: Children with burns. *American Journal of Psychiatry, 161*, 1299–1304.

Shalev, A. Y., Sahar, T., Freedman, S., Peri, T., Glick, N., Brandes, D., et al. (1998). A prospective study of heart rate response following trauma and the subsequent development of posttraumatic stress disorder. *Archives of General Psychiatry, 55*(6), 553–59.

Suess, P., Porges, S. W., and Plude, D. (1994). Cardiac vagal tone and sustained attention in school-age children. *Psychobiology, 31*, 17–22.

Van der Kolk, B. A. (1994). The body keeps the score: Memory and the evolving psychobiology of posttraumatic stress. *Harvard Review of Psychology, 8*(4), 505–25.

Yehuda, R. (1999). *Risk Factors for Posttraumatic Stress Disorder*. Washington, DC: American Psychiatric Publishing, Inc.

# 6

## The Long Reach of Trauma Across the Lifespan: Mechanisms for the Signature of Abuse

*Ana-Maria Vranceanu, Lisa Stines, Jeremiah A. Schumm, Brittain E. Lamoureux, and Stevan E. Hobfoll*

**P**erhaps a combination of the cognitive revolution, increased chemicalization of trauma treatment, and decreased emphasis on psychodynamic approaches has led to a forgetting of childhood and developmental processes in trauma research, in favor of approaches that emphasize the here and now. An appreciation of the lifetime impact of trauma forces us to consider lifelong processes and the long footprint of childhood events, as well as those occurring in adulthood. For childhood trauma survivors, their childhood is not only in their past. The present chapter focuses on the relationship of resource loss and gain with risk and resiliency in the face of various life traumas. We will use conservation of resources (COR) theory (Hobfoll, 1988; 1998; 2002) as a theoretical backdrop to frame an understanding of the impact of trauma on women's lives, with special emphasis on a lifespan developmental perspective.

A great deal of research has supported the application of COR theory in understanding the response of not only individuals, but of families and communities, and their interconnected nature, to traumatic life circumstances (Benight and Harper, 2002; Benight et al., 1999; Burnett et al., 1997; Hobfoll, 2001; Hobfoll, Canetti-Nisim, and Johnson, 2006; Ironson et al., 1997; Sattler, 2006; Sattler et al., 2002; Smith and Freedy, 2000). We have embarked on a particular line of research to examine how childhood trauma might reverberate to impact vulnerability in adulthood, focusing our research on women. Prior to presenting that research, we will delineate the principles of

Address correspondence to Stevan Hobfoll, Ph.D.; Department of Psychology; 378 Kent Hall; Kent State University; Kent, OH 44242. E-mail: shobfoll@kent.edu

COR theory, as has been done elsewhere in greater detail (Hobfoll, 1988, 1989, 1998, 2002).

## COR THEORY: PRINCIPLES AND COROLLARIES

COR theory rests on the basic tenet that individuals strive to obtain, retain, foster, and protect those things they value and that support the individual-nested in families-nested in tribe. These centrally valued entities are termed resources and they include object, condition, personal, and energy resources. *Object* resources include resources that have a physical presence and are either necessary for survival or highly valued within a culture. This includes such objects as shelter, transportation, the means to process food (stove, refrigerator) and to satisfy basic hygiene (washing machine, plumbing). *Condition* resources are valued as they either are important for survival or bring status that is secondarily linked to survival. These include marriage, a supportive social network, job security, and educational status. *Personal* resources are divided into two categories—personal traits and skills. These resources highlighted by COR theory are either linked to survival or resiliency, so not all resources are considered critical. This includes such traits as optimism (Carver, 2000), self-efficacy (Benight and Bandura, 2004) and self-esteem (Rosenberg, 1965) and such skills as those necessary for work (e.g., job skills) and social skillfulness. Finally, *energy* resources are resources that have value in their ability to be used or exchanged for object or condition resources or for their protection and maintenance. These include such resources as knowledge, credit, money, and insurance.

It follows from COR theory that psychological stress will occur in one of three instances:

(1) when individuals' resources are threatened with loss,
(2) when individuals' resources are actually lost, or
(3) where individuals fail to gain sufficient resources following significant resource investment.

COR theory rests on several principles and corollaries that must be delineated to further specify the nature of stressful circumstances. It is important to underscore that although COR theory involves, in part, the element of appraisal, unlike other stress theories (Lazarus and Folkman, 1984), these appraisals are first and foremost conceptualized as a product of shared cultural space, and are not individual, idiographic appraisals. Said another way, what individuals find stressful, what they value, and the behaviors they perform individually, in families, and organizationally are principally determined by their shared culture. Individual, idiographic appraisals are important, but quite secondary to shared ones.

### Principle 1: The primacy of resource loss. Resource loss is disproportionately more salient than resource gain

Resource loss is more potent than resource gain and resource losses accumulate at greater velocity or momentum than resource gains. The greater potency of resource loss over gain has been shown on cognitive (Tversky and Khaneman, 1981), emotional (Cacioppo and Gardner, 1999) and neurological levels (Ito, Larsen, Smith, and Cacioppo, 1998). The extent of this loss sensitivity is extensive and is of increased weight and occurs at greater speed in traumatic circumstances (Hobfoll, 1991). This cross-domain greater saliency of loss over gain suggests that it is biologically based, especially when one considers that it cross cultures. Although evolutionary theory is inferential, it has been argued that the primacy of loss is a product of the evolutionary scarcity of resources and the cost of resource loss for survival. Traumatic circumstances heighten this imbalance and its biological underpinnings are further accelerated. Trauma increases our hardwired response system to its more primitive levels.

Many studies have shown the impact of resource losses on symptoms of posttraumatic stress in both adults and children in the aftermath of traumatic circumstances (Asarnow et al., 1999; Sattler 2006; La Greca, Silverman, Vernberg, and Prinstein, 1996). Resource losses and resource loss spirals were found to be significant predictors of symptoms of acute stress disorder following Hurricane Georges across four cultural locations impacted by the hurricane. (Sattler et al., 2002). Similarly, following the Northridge earthquake, symptoms of posttraumatic stress disorder (PTSD) in children and adults were directly associated with resource losses (Asarnow et al., 1999). Resource loss was similarly vital to victim's psychological well-being following the hurricane-tsunami in 2004, where individuals who displayed the most symptoms of PTSD and depression were more likely to have been displaced from their homes in affected villages and were subject to ongoing threat of destruction (Tang, 2006). Following the terrorist attacks of September 11 (Galea et al., 2002) and in response to the Al Aqsa Intifada in Israel (Hobfoll et al., 2006), resource loss was found to be the principle environmental or personal predictor of PTSD. As we will detail later, for women experiencing childhood abuse and adult rape, resource loss had a central mediating role on outcomes (Schumm, Briggs-Phillips, and Hobfoll, 2006; Schumm, Stines, Hobfoll, and Jackson, 2005; Vranceanu, Hobfoll, and Johnson, 2007; Vranceanu, Hobfoll, and Johnson, under review).

**Principle 2: Resource investment. People must invest resources in order to protect against resource loss, recover from losses, and gain resources**

Corollary 1 of COR theory is that those with greater resources are less vulnerable to resource loss and more capable of orchestrating resource gain. Conversely, those with fewer resources are more vulnerable to resource loss and less capable of resource gain.

Given that traumatic stressful circumstances involve profound resource loss, the means of protection of resources or their reinstatement is critical. This investment of resources can emanate from the self or from resources available to individuals from their environment. Unfortunately, the very circumstances of trauma often act to limit the availability of resources that could potentially be available to offset resource loss, limit its secondary repercussions, and move to stabilize the individual.

**Principle 3: Although resource loss is more potent than resource gain, the salience of gain increases under situations of resource loss**

The paradoxical increase in saliency of resource gain is accentuated during traumatic situations. This follows because under conditions of high loss germane to trauma circumstances, even small gains may have major impact (Hobfoll, Lavin, and Wells, 1999). Hence, resource gains that would under normal circumstances be appraised as trivial may offer a lifeline to survival (e.g., "I am not alone," "They will make me safe") or may be imbued with meaning (e.g., "I am loved," "I have value").

## RESOURCE LOSS AND GAIN SPIRALS

The first two principles of COR theory concerning loss primacy and investment of resources, in turn, lead to two further corollaries pertaining to resource loss and gain spirals (Hobfoll, 1988; 1998). Corollary 2 of COR theory states that those who lack resources are not only more vulnerable to resource loss, but that initial loss begets future loss. Trauma brings a wave of demands that attack a weakened state, leading to further weakening and decreased ability to respond at each iteration of the cycle. COR theory further states that not only are individuals less able to respond as their resources diminish, this process also increases in momentum as trauma entails a wave of losses that attack an already weakened system.

Corollary 3 mirrors corollary 2, stating that those who possess resources are more capable of gain, and that initial resource gain begets further gain. However, because loss is more potent than gain, loss cycles will have a bigger impact than gain cycles. Luckily, gain cycles also occur in spirals. However, because resource gain is less potent and moves more slowly than resource loss, this process is more fragile than loss cycles. Gains tend to require major resources to occur, and they occur slowly. Critically, because people conserve resources for the "worse that might yet come," they often are risk aversive to invest resources to increase gain cycles. Resource loss cycles, being less volitional, take all they can in their wake.

The final corollary (corollary 4) of COR theory posits that those who lack resources are likely to adopt a defensive posture to conserve their resources. The fourth corollary of COR theory is critical, but actually the most understudied. Under circumstances of major resource loss, a new "logic" occurs—the logic of defense. Defensive postures are especially likely when people lack practiced, accepted avenues of response, or where these avenues are blocked. When trauma occurs, the comparative template, whereby known repertoires can be adapted to the new, novel situation, is too far removed to facilitate the adaptive process, or where adaptive coping is tried, it is often blocked (e.g., a controlling parent or spouse). Under such conditions, it is best not to act, to cope by not coping, outwardly at least.

## CHILDHOOD TRAUMA AND LOSS OF THE PROTECTIVE SHIELD

Trauma in childhood challenges both the reality and the perception of what has been called the "protective shield" (Bell, Flay, and Paikoff, 2002; Pynoos, Steinberg, and Wraith, 1995). Children and adolescents' protective shield is largely based on the belief and the physical reality that their parents and the social institutions that they interact with (e.g., schools, the police) will make them safe. For children facing ongoing individual trauma, this belief system may actually never germinate. For other children in war-ravaged areas or where family members perpetrate abuse, the very institutions of safety and protection (e.g., schools, adults, police, government) may be seen as sources of danger and distress.

The protective shield is constituted by the interweaving of resources that the family and culture naturally provide to children in safe circumstances. This shield is a perceived shield, but such perceptions are reality-based. Our personal resiliency resources (hope, self-efficacy, and optimism) emanate from these conditions. It is our thesis that during childhood and adolescence such personal resources are being shaped along with the ability to successfully commerce in social interactions with the basic building blocks of trust, sharing, and caring. Children who experience trauma, we argue, are vulnerable to a long footprint of difficulties both personal and social, which are sapping resiliency resources. This, in turn, increases their likelihood of encountering new traumas, as resources provide a lifetime protective shield. Moreover, when stress occurs they are less able to translate personal and social resources into resilient thought, emotions, and behaviors.

## RESOURCE CARAVANS AND THE CONCEPT OF "GOOD ENOUGH"

The concept of resource caravans is also derived from COR theory and it leads to the concept of "good enough." Social scientists typically study their own pet resources—support, optimism, self-esteem, self-efficacy, or hope. However, like caravans in the desert, resources aggregate and are interconnected across time. Studies suggest that self-esteem, optimism, and self-efficacy are highly correlated (Cozzarelli, 1993) and are impacted in similar ways when an individual encounters trauma (Sumer, Karanci, Berument, and Gunes, 2005). When you have one personal resource you are likely to have others; they travel in packs. Even social support, which is a social resource, is highly related to possessing strong personal resources (Hobfoll, 2002). Having this resource base means that people will use what resources are "good enough," even if they are not perfectly suited. They will use resources in combination and creatively, because resiliency and rebound are expected and this may also help illuminate why "good enough" coping is commonplace (Bonanno, Rennicke, and Dekel, 2005). That is, people will use what resources they can to obtain reasonable outcomes. They do not need ideal resource fit to achieve a good outcome.

This means that trauma will tend to have a generalized negative impact on resources for decades after it occurs. The resource caravan, once assaulted, has difficulty reconstituting itself. If aided by a supportive environment and treatment, recovery is possible. Too often, however, the traumas of childhood are buried or the persons who might provide aid are themselves the perpetrators. Added to this, childhood abuse is often accompanied by neglect, poor family relations, and outright sadism—ground that is poisonous to positive growth and recovery.

## TRACKING THE REACH OF TRAUMA AMONG WOMEN

We embarked upon a series of studies in order to examine the impact of trauma across the lifespan among women. In searching the literature, we found many studies that illustrated that childhood trauma was related to

PTSD, depression, and psychological distress during adulthood. However, we were surprised to find only theory, with little research supporting it, to explain the mechanism by which this occurred. Without understanding the mechanism, both clear models of how trauma translates to impairment and how to treat the active ingredients that generate impairment are difficult. These observations led us to pursue research examining the impact of trauma across the lifespan.

## Study 1

In the first study (Stines, Suniga, Keogh, and Hobfoll, 2005), our goal was a preliminary examination of the signature of abuse hypothesis. The tenets of the signature hypothesis are as follows: (1) childhood abuse leads to resource loss that is likely to be congruent in nature to the abuse experienced (i.e., undermining condition resources of an interpersonal nature and contributing to relationship dysfunction), and (2) this resource loss is cyclical, in that it decreases survivors' abilities to cope with the trauma, thereby leading to an increased vulnerability for further trauma and resource loss. Interpersonal resource loss and current romantic relationship maladjustment were examined as potential mediators using hierarchical multiple regression with PTSD symptom severity as the criterion variable.

Participants were 105 women recruited from two community substance abuse treatment facilities. Women were primarily European American (63.8 percent), thirty-eight years of age with two children on average. 72 percent had a high school education or less, 66 percent had incomes below $15,000 per year, and 77 percent were unemployed. 66 percent of women reported at least one episode of sexual abuse during childhood, and 57 percent experienced physical abuse as children. Dissatisfaction with current romantic relationships was common, with only 36 percent reporting satisfaction with their current relationship. 30 percent of women indicated they had experienced at least some recent threat or loss in the interpersonal domains assessed by the Conservation of Resources—Evaluation scale (COR-E; Hobfoll, Lilly, and Jackson, 1991). Almost half of the women in the sample met criteria for current PTSD (49 percent).

Results from the regression analyses lent support to the signature of abuse hypothesis. Overall, childhood physical abuse was a stronger predictor of PTSD than childhood sexual abuse, though sexual abuse perpetrated by a parent was a strong predictor of PTSD. In this regard, when abuse from all perpetrators was considered, the impact of child physical abuse was the dominant determinant of PTSD levels. However, when we compared the impact of parental sexual abuse and parental physical abuse, removing both types of abuse by other perpetrators, sexual abuse was the more powerful predictor of PTSD symptoms. Interpersonal resource loss, but not relationship adjustment (which was not correlated with child abuse measures), mediated the relationships between childhood abuse and PTSD. This may be due to the different kinds of interpersonal resources measured in the study. Women who have suffered childhood abusive experiences may be able to adjust to a relationship on a short-term level and, in fact, their perception of the relationship may be idealized while it exists. However, the COR-E taps the difficulties these women have in sustaining different kinds of close relationships. This interpersonal loss and persistent difficulty within relationships can impact PTSD among women with histories of childhood abuse, whereas the ephemeral satisfaction within one romantic relationship, which is often short-term, is not related to their childhood abuse or current PTSD.

## Study 2

In a subsequent study we examined how women in a community obstetrics and gynecology clinic were affected by traumatic events in their lives (Vranceanu, Hobfoll· and Johnson, 2007). We focused on women in inner-city ob-gyn clinics because they are quite representative of low-income women in the community. These clinics offer free medical services, and most of their population are physically well and coming for normal care such as birth control, checks on pregnancy, minor sexually transmitted diseases, minor infections, and wellness checkups. We proposed and developed an overarching model that specified how social support and stress could mediate between multiples types of child abuse and maltreatment and depression and PTSD (see figure 6.1). We hypothesized that child abuse and maltreatment deeply marks the victims and thus may decrease their ability to develop, sustain, and benefit from social support and also increase stress during adulthood. This decreased social support and increased stress, in turn, ultimately increases vulnerability to depression and PTSD. Our model was novel and explored comprehensively, within a single model, the role of stress and social support in the development of depression and PTSD in survivors of child abuse and maltreatment.

Participants were one hundred women recruited from a gynecological treatment center for low-income women located in an inner city. Women were mostly European American (48 percent) or African American (47 percent), with a mean age of 28.92 (SD = 10.52). The majority of women were married (52 percent), unemployed (73 percent), and poor, with yearly income of less than $15,000 (67 percent). This inner-city, low-income sample was well-suited for testing our model, given the predicted high rates of childhood

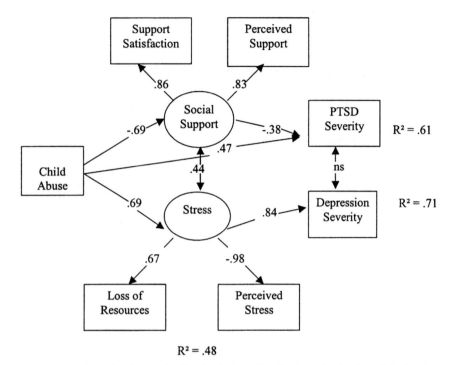

R² = .48

**Figure 6.1.** Completely standardized solutions for the hypothesized model showing the mediating role of stress and social support between child abuse and depression and PTSD severity. All depicted paths are significant at the .01 level. $\chi 2$ (7, N = 100) = 10.45, *p* = .16 AGFI = .90 RMSEA = .05

trauma, and the high risk for inner-city women to experience stressful life events and acute resource losses that occur in the wake of chronically diminished economic conditions (Eckenrode, 1984; Ennis, Hobfoll, and Schroder, 2000; Hobfoll, Johnson, Ennis, and Jackson, 2003).

Using structural equation modeling, we looked at the relationships between variables within a single model, which had an excellent fit. An examination of the path coefficients showed partial support for our hypothesis. Specifically, we found that social support partially mediated the impact of child abuse on PTSD, but not depression. Stress in women's current lives, in turn, was a strong mediator of the impact of child abuse on depression, but did not directly impact PTSD. Child abuse and maltreatment also had significant and direct effects on PTSD, but we did not find that it directly impacted depression. Clearly, child abuse and maltreatment acted to undermine social resources and increase current stress, which in turn, affected women's ongoing psychological distress.

The fact that social support mediated the relationship between child abuse and PTSD highlights the importance of interpersonal resources such as social support in women's adult lives, long after their childhood abuse experience. This is consistent with COR theory which depicts social support as a primary resource necessary for adjustment and survival. It appears that victims of abuse may become unable either to develop or sustain the supportive ties they might need when stress occurs in their lives. This may be related to their developing unhealthy coping mechanisms such as withdrawal or avoidance. Future research should explore the degree to which this influences their perceptions of support, their actual support-seeking behavior, and how others react to them (e.g., if they act overly needy they may repel support).

We found that current stress fully mediated the relationship between childhood maltreatment and adult depression. This suggests that child abuse and maltreatment may increase vulnerability to depression via increased stressful life experiences. In this manner, victims of abuse may become more susceptible to resource loss and may perceive their lives as more stressful. This finding is consistent with previous research on trauma victims and women with histories of child abuse (e.g., King, King, Foy, Keane, and Fairbank, 1999). Finding that child abuse and maltreatment directly predicted social support, but social support did not directly predict depression, suggests that social support may impact depression indirectly. As COR theory suggests, stressful life experience results in a deterioration of resources, which results in loss cycles, further increasing stressful life experience. Hence we found that abused women's vulnerability to stress and loss of resources may be initiated not only directly from the abuse, but also indirectly, via loss cycles as noted in depletion of social resources.

## Study 3

In our next study (Vranceanu, Hobfoll, and Johnson, under review), we thought to expand our prior work by assessing the role of social and personal resources in the development of depression and PTSD in women survivors of child abuse. Consistent with COR theory's prediction that resources travel together in packs, we predicted that child abuse would have a double whammy effect by depleting both social and personal resources, which would, in turn, increase vulnerability to depression and PTSD. Because of the interrelation between social and personal resources, loss associated with one category begets loss in other categories, thus leading to loss cycles, as predicted by COR theory.

We used a sample of 646 women recruited from two clinics serving lower-income, inner-city women. Women were mostly Caucasian (64.5 percent), unemployed (63 percent), with a yearly income of less than $10,000 (54 percent). Only 25.3 percent graduated college or had some college education.

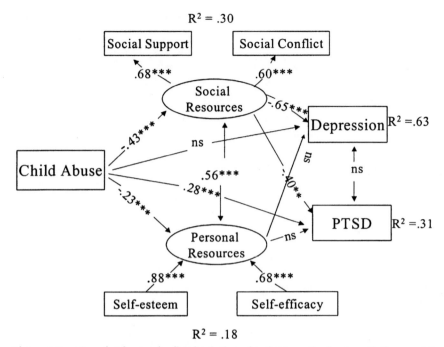

**Figure 6.2.  Completely standardized solutions for the hypothesized mediation model depicting personal and social resources as mediators between child abuse and depression and PTSD; * p < .05 ** p < .01 *** p < .001, 2-tailed tests. $\chi^2$ (17) = 36.71, p = .004, RMSEA = .04 NFI = .99, GFI = .99**

Our model (figure 6.2) fit the data very well. An examination of the path co-efficients showed that social resources partly mediated the association between child abuse and depression and PTSD. Although personal resources did not directly mediate the child abuse—depression and PTSD relationship, they acted as indirect mediators. Specifically, child abuse negatively impacted personal resources, which were significantly interrelated with social resources, and, through social resources, increased vulnerability to depression and PTSD. Consistent with COR theory, our findings show the centrality of social resources in the development of depression and PTSD. This suggests that psychological and social resources interdependently lead to depression and PTSD.

## Study 4

In the next study, we examined the impact of childhood sexual and physical abuse on loss of psychosocial resources and retraumatization through rape in adulthood (Schumm, Hobfoll, and Keogh, 2004). We integrated a mediational model of abuse, revictimization, and PTSD (Nishith, Mechanic, and

110 Ana-Maria Vranceanu et al.

Resick, 2000) along with the social support deterioration model (Kaniasty and Norris, 1995; Norris and Kaniasty, 1996) to improve understanding of PTSD's etiology and maintenance during adulthood. Following COR theory, Kaniasty and Norris have further and in more detail explored how stressful events result in deterioration of interpersonal resources, precisely when people need them for coping. We predicted that child physical and sexual abuse would increase women's likelihood of experiencing adulthood assault. This follows from their lack of resources in the form of poor relationship patterns and more limited relationship opportunities. Further, we hypothesized that women with histories of childhood abuse would also experience deterioration of their interpersonal resources, making them less capable of coping with either childhood events from their past, or the current considerable stressors impinging on their lives. Figure 6.3 depicts our model.

The hypothesized model whereby revictimization and interpersonal resource loss results in PTSD was partially supported. Although adulthood rape was not supported as a full mediator of the impact of childhood abuse on PTSD, our results confirmed an indirect pathway of this proposed causal

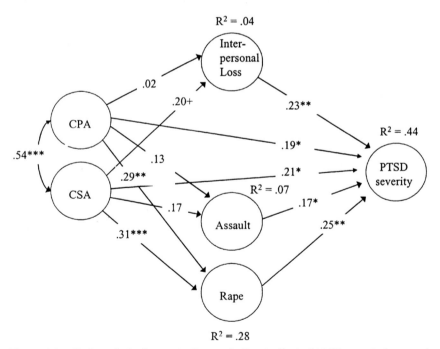

Figure 6.3. Path analysis demonstrating an indirect effect of child sexual abuse and child physical abuse on PTSD via adulthood rape (+$p$ = .08, *$p$ < .05, **$p$ < .01, ***$p$<.001). $\chi^2$ (3, $N$ = 105) = 3.10, *ns*; CFI = 1.00, RMSEA = .02.

relationship. Our findings clearly indicated that CSA and CPA directly impacted PTSD, as many have found. But it is important to note that these early traumatic experiences also were related to a recurrent cycle of violence in the form of rape. In this manner, these childhood and adult traumas further contributed to current PTSD severity. In addition, we found indication of an indirect effect of child sexual abuse on PTSD by its leading to interpersonal resource losses in adulthood. Finally, although partner-produced physical assault was not found as a mediator, these traumatic experiences independently exacerbated PTSD severity.

## Study 5

We further extended this work to a larger sample of inner-city women, again drawn from an ob-gyn clinic in order to draw a more general community sample (Schumm, Stines, Hobfoll, and Jackson, 2005). Based on COR theory, we hypothesized that women who were abused as children would both experience more stress as adults and be more sensitive to these stressors, referring to this as the kindling hypothesis. We examined our model among 176 women, interviewed twice over a period of six months. Outcomes were measured in terms of PTSD and depression using standardized questionnaires administered in an interview format. Figure 6.4 depicts our model.

Participants averaged twenty-two years of age and about 60 percent were African American and 40 percent were European American. All were single or cohabitating with a partner for less than 6 months and unmarried as we viewed this group at high risk for violence and at risk for sexually transmitted disease. Most were unemployed (52 percent) and poor, with 76 percent having family income under $15,000 annually.

We found high rates of childhood abuse and psychological distress. 63 percent of women reported child physical abuse having occurring rarely or more often. 25 percent of women reported child sexual abuse as occurring at least rarely, and 20 percent reported both CPA and CSA as occurring at least rarely. At initial assessment, 61 percent of women scored above the suggested cutoff of 16 for risk of major depression (Radloff, 1977). Similar proportions of women reported at least moderate levels of PTSD severity (25–28 percent), with severe levels being relatively rare (about 6 percent).

Using structural equation modeling (see figure 6.5), we found that women's resource losses over recent months were significantly and strongly predictive of both depressive mood and PTSD severity. These results are especially noteworthy as this relationship occurred after accounting for the effects of initial depressive mood, initial PTSD, and childhood abuse. Consistent with COR theory, the experience of ongoing resource loss was found to be the

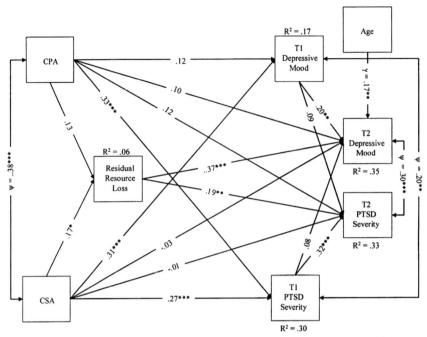

**Figure 6.4.** Completely standardized LISREL path solution for mediation model. To control for its effects, age is entered into the γ matrix of the equation. Except for where indicated, pathways involving age were non-significant. Residual loss to T1 depressive mood ψ = .14, *p* < .05. Residual loss to T1 PTSD ψ = .06, *p* > .30. Unless otherwise denoted, reported values are β matrix pathways. *\*p* < .05. *\*\*p* < .01. *\*\*\*p* < .001. All model variables are observed providing a perfectly fitting model; therefore, fit statistics are not reported.

strongest predictor of later depressive mood and demonstrated twice the predictive effect size of initial depressive mood. This lends credence to the supposition that the process of resource loss is integral to the ongoing process of depression. It is further notable that resource loss was the sole significant predictor of later PTSD severity, after accounting for the significant initial impact of earlier PTSD severity.

Our hypothesis that resource loss would fully mediate the impact of child abuse on later PTSD and depressive mood was not supported, but partial support was found for its basis. Specifically, although child sexual abuse was not significantly associated with later PTSD or depressive mood, it significantly predicted resource loss, which, in turn, predicted later PTSD and depressive mood. This suggests that child sexual abuse acts on PTSD symptoms and depressive mood by affecting a process of ongoing resource loss.

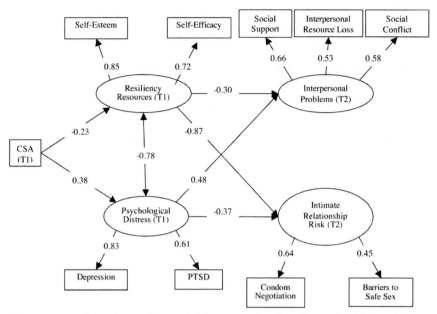

**Figure 6.5.** Structural equation model demonstrating the effects of child sexual abuse on interpersonal problems and intimate relationship risk via resiliency and psychological distress. All paths are significant at $p < 0.05$. $\chi^2$ (29, $N = 485$) = 73.21, $p < .001$; CFI = .96, RMSEA = .06, Standardized RMR = .04.

Our second hypothesis, that child abuse would sensitize women to resource loss was partially supported. Specifically, resource loss demonstrated a high effect size at moderate to high levels of child physical abuse frequency, in contrast to its moderate effect size at low levels of CPA. This indicates that higher levels of resource loss were especially linked to women's psychological distress among those who experienced greater levels of child physical abuse. The high levels of CPA served as experiential kindling that raised women's vulnerability to current losses. We had not expected that child physical abuse, but not child sexual abuse would sensitize women to the negative influence of later resource loss. It is possible that the comparatively higher frequency of child physical abuse and the greater likelihood of chronicity of this kind of abuse might have resulted in stunted psychosocial resource development. These deficiencies might, in turn, carry over into adulthood, leaving women less able to cope with additional losses. In this manner, chronic survivors of physical abuse might be especially damaged due to their already depleted resource caravans.

## TRAUMA, RESILIENCY RESOURCES, AND INTERPERSONAL RISK

We further explored these pathways with an eye to interpersonal risk behavior and sexual risk behavior as outcomes. Often, research has focused on psychological distress as the final outcome, ignoring that the fabric of how people live their lives is also truly important.

### Study 6

We examined the effect of child sexual abuse on both general interpersonal problems and intimate relationship risk (Lamoureux, Jackson, Palmieri, Johnson, and Hobfoll, 2007). We proposed that these effects would be mediated by women's resiliency resources, in terms of their self-esteem and self-efficacy, and psychological distress, in terms of their depressive and PTSD symptomatology. Our model suggested the following predictions in respect to these relationship outcomes (see figure 6.5). We hypothesized that, overall, the experience of child sexual abuse would be related to poorer adulthood relationship outcomes. This effect of child sexual abuse on interpersonal relationships was predicted to be mediated by resiliency resources, such that abuse would lower self-esteem and self-efficacy, but that to the extent women retained these resources they would have better interpersonal outcomes. We further hypothesized that the effect of child sexual abuse on interpersonal relationships would be mediated by psychological distress, such that child sexual abuse would be related to increased depressive and PTSD symptomatology, which would in turn be related to poorer interpersonal relationship outcomes.

A sample of 504 women was recruited from two obstetrics and gynecological clinics serving primarily low-income, inner-city populations. Participants were recruited as part of an ongoing HIV risk reduction project. Women were considered eligible to participate if they were between the ages of sixteen and thirty-nine, not living with a partner for more than six months, and not in the third trimester of pregnancy. They were further required to endorse one or more of the following sexual risk factors: (1) having unprotected sex in the past six months, (2) having sex with more than one person in the past six months, (3) partner possibly having sex with more than one partner in the past six months, (4) self or partner using intravenous drugs, (5) partner in prison during the past five years, or (6) ever having a sexual transmitted disease. We interviewed women on four occasions and the current study focused on their initial interviews and their responses six months later.

Of women participating in the study, 69 percent were African American and 26 percent were European American. The mean age of participants was twenty-one years, ranging from sixteen to thirty-one years of age. 58 percent of women had attained at least high school degree. Approximately half (56 percent) of participants reported an annual household income of less than $10,000. Most women had never been married (90 percent) and over half (52 percent) had at least one child.

We used structural equation modeling to examine our model. In the initial model, we examined both the direct and indirect effects of CSA on interpersonal outcomes. We also controlled for the influence, which was modest, of the different health related interventions. A respecified, indirect effects model was found to have excellent fit as indicated in figure 6.4. Our results suggest that the experience of child sexual abuse undermines women's personal resiliency resources and psychological functioning, which in turn impact women's conduct of adulthood interpersonal relationships and their sexual risk behavior.

Although our hypotheses were largely supported, not all findings were as expected. First, CSA was related to lower levels of resiliency resources and higher levels of distress as expected based on past research. Also as predicted, higher levels of resiliency resources predicted fewer interpersonal problems and less intimate relationship risk. Psychological distress did exhibit the hypothesized negative effect on interpersonal problems, yet was unexpectedly linked to less intimate relationship sexual risk. This finding, however, can be understood better when examining the zero-order relationships, wherein psychological distress is linked to greater sexual risk in relationships. This means that when the independent impact of resiliency resources and interpersonal relationship problems is removed, what is left over is a negative impact of psychological distress on sexual risk behavior. This might suggest that women who have psychological distress, but do not have interpersonal relationships may actually be avoiding relationships altogether. and in this way lowering their sexual risk behavior. Further, as resiliency resources and psychological distress are negatively related, it is likely that resiliency resources are mediating the impact of psychological distress on sexual risk behavior.

Our findings are notable in several respects. First, this is one of the largest prospective studies of the impact of child sexual abuse on a period of high-risk women's lives. The confirmed model strongly supports COR theory. As suggested by the theory, child sexual abuse largely influences interpersonal problems and interpersonal sexual risk through its impact on resiliency resources. Abuse results in a long-term deterioration of resiliency resources that, in turn, result in women's ongoing difficulties in interpersonal functioning. Simultaneously, their psychological distress makes them vulnerable to interpersonal difficulties, which acts to limit both their quality of life and perpetuate their symptomatology. As relationship success is so important throughout the lifespan and especially at this time in women's lives, we get a better glimpse at the fabric of women's lives and the signature of abuse than just focusing on psychopathology would offer.

## IMPLICATIONS FOR INTERVENTION

It is generally beyond the scope of this paper to also discuss intervention in great detail. Nevertheless, a brief discussion of implications for intervention can also serve as a general conclusion of our chapter.

Clearly, we are at an early stage of understanding how childhood trauma reverberates into adulthood. What we have learned is that because childhood trauma undermines women's resources, that this is a primary mechanism for their lifelong difficulty. It disturbs their relationships, perpetuates their psychological distress, increases their sexual risk, and makes them vulnerable to new stressors and revictimization. These findings give particular support for COR theory's principles and corollaries regarding loss cycles. It also, however, points to the more recently added principle of "good enough." That is, women who sustain resources appear to continue to do better, and even in many instances to thrive. This provides an inroad for intervention, as it would appear that intervention should increasingly focus on bolstering and supporting abuse survivors' resiliency resources. This should also include educating them as to how their lack of resources and resource loss may precipitate further highly stressful life circumstances.

This, in turn, places more emphasis on psychoeducation and training. Many resources can be focused on through training. Self-efficacy, for example, can be translated to efficacy skills at targeted life circumstances. By a process of "small wins," women's sense of personal agency will grow. With increased efficacy they may have not only a reduction in symptoms, but may also be more likely to succeed in the challenging circumstances that are a part of life's daily bread. Similarly, social support can be broken down into a series of relationship skills. It is a complicated dance, but one that we have learned much about through the past three decades of research on social support. It includes identifying when and how social support can help, how to ask for help, how to give supporters' feedback, and how to grow more supportive relationships. Treatment seldom takes this "life lessons" approach. After cognitive distortions are corrected and insights are made, there are many skills that these women may need to develop in order to disentangle themselves from further loss cycles.

## ACKNOWLEDGEMENTS

Studies included in this chapter were funded by the NIH/NIMH grant # 5 R01 MH045669-13, "AIDS Prevention Among Inner-city Women: Focus on Conflict." We wish to thank Janice Gaumer for her editing of this manuscript.

## REFERENCES

Asarnow, J., Glynn, S., Pynoos, R. S., Nahum, J., Guthrie, D., Cantwell, D. P., et al. (1999). When the earth stops shaking: Earthquake sequelae among children diagnosed for pre-earthquake psychopathology. *Journal of the American Academy of Child and Adolescent Psychiatry, 38,* 1016–23.

Bell, C. C., Flay, B., and Paikoff, R. (2002). Strategies for health behavior change. In J. C. Chunn (Ed.), *The health behavioral change imperative: Theory, education, and practice in diverse populations* (17–39). New York: Kluwer Academic/Plenum Publishers.

Benight, C. C., and Bandura, A. (2004). Social cognitive theory of posttraumatic recovery: The role of perceived self-efficacy. *Behaviour Research and Therapy, 42,* 1129–48.

Benight, C. C., and Harper, M. L. (2002). Coping self-efficacy perceptions as a mediator between acute stress response and long-term distress following natural disasters. *Journal of Traumatic Stress, 15,* 177–86.

Benight, C. C., Ironson, G., Klebe, K., Carver, C. S., Wynings, C., Burnett, C. S., et al. (1999). Conservation of resources and coping self-efficacy predicting distress following a natural disaster: A causal model analysis where the environment meets the mind. *Anxiety, Stress and Coping, 12,* 107–26.

Bonanno, G. A., Rennicke, C., and Dekel, S. (2005). Self-enhancement among high-exposure survivors of the September 11th terrorist attack: Resilience or social maladjustment? *Journal of Personality and Social Psychology, 88,* 984–98.

Burnett, K., Ironson, G., Benight, C., Wynings, C., Greenwood, D., Carver, C. S., et al. (1997). Measurement of perceived disruption during rebuilding following Hurricane Andrew. *Journal of Traumatic Stress, 10,* 673–81.

Cacioppo, J. T., and Gardner, W. L. (1999). Emotion. *Annual Review of Psychology, 50,* 191–214.

Carver, C. S. (2000). Optimism and pessimism. In A. E. Kazdin (Ed.), *Encyclopedia of psychology* (vol. 6, 1–3). Washington, DC: American Psychological Association.

Cozzarelli, C. (1993). Personality and self-efficacy as predictors of coping with abortion. *Journal of Personality and Social Psychology, 65*(6), 1224–36.

Eckenrode, J. (1984) Impact of chronic and acute stressors on daily reports of mood. *Journal of Personality and Social Psychology, 46,* 907–18.

Ennis, N. E., Hobfoll, S. E., and Schroder, K. E. E. (2000). Money doesn't talk, it swears: How economic stress and resistance resources impact inner-city women's depressive mood. *American Journal of Community Psychology, 28,* 149–73.

Galea, S., Ahern, J., Resnick, H., Kilpatrick, D., Bucuvalas, M., Gold, J., et al. (2002). Psychological sequelae of the September 11 terrorist attacks in New York City. *New England Journal of Medicine, 13*, 982–87.

Hobfoll, S. E. (1988). *The ecology of stress*. New York: Hemisphere.

———. (1989). Conservation of resources: A new attempt at conceptualizing stress. *American Psychologist, 44*, 513–24.

———. (1991). Traumatic stress: A theory based on rapid loss of resources. *Anxiety Research: An International Journal, 4*, 187–97.

———. (1998). *Stress, culture, and community: The psychology and philosophy of stress*. New York: Plenum.

———. (2001). The influence of culture, community, and the nested-self in the stress process: Advancing Conservation of Resources Theory. *Applied Psychology: An International Review, 50*, 337–70.

———. (2002). Alone together: Comparing communal versus individualistic resiliency. In E. Frydenberg (Ed.), *Beyond coping: Meeting goals, visions, and challenges* (63–81). New York: Oxford University Press.

Hobfoll, S. E., Canetti-Nisim, D., and Johnson, R. J. (2006). Exposure to terrorism, stress-related mental health symptoms, and defensive coping among Jews and Arabs in Israel. *Journal of Consulting and Clinical Psychology, 74*, 207–18.

Hobfoll, S. E., Johnson, R. J., Ennis, N., and Jackson, A. P. (2003). Resource loss, resource gain and emotional outcomes among inner city women. *Journal of Personality and Social Psychology, 84*, 632–43.

Hobfoll, S. E., Lavin, J., and Wells, J. D. (1999). When it rains it pours: The greater impact of resource loss compared to gain on psychological distress. *Personality and Social Psychology Bulletin, 25*, 1172–82.

Hobfoll, S. E., Lilly, R. S., and Jackson, A. P. (1991). Conservation of social resources and the self. In H. O. Vans and U. Baumann (Eds.). *The meaning and measurement of social support* (125–41). Washington, DC: Hemisphere.

Ironson, G., Wynings, C., Schneiderman, N., Baum, A., Rodriguez, M., Greenwood, D., et al., (1997). Posttraumatic stress symptoms, intrusive thoughts, loss, and immune function after Hurricane Andrew. *Psychosomatic Medicine, 59*, 128–41.

Ito, T. A., Larsen, J. T., Smith, N. K., and Cacioppo, J. T. (1998). Negative information weighs more heavily on the brain: The negativity bias in evaluative categorizations. *Journal of Personality and Social Psychology, 75*, 887–900.

Kaniasty, K. and Norris, F. H. (1995). In search of altruistic community: Patterns of social support mobilization following hurricane Hugo. *American Journal of Community Psychology, 23*, 447–77.

King, D. W., King, L. A., Foy, D. W., Keane, T. M., and Fairbank, J. A. (1999). Posttraumatic stress disorder in a national sample of female and male Vietnam veterans: Risk factors, war-zone stressors, and resilience-recovery variables. *Journal of Abnormal Psychology, 108*(1), 164–70.

La Greca, A. M., Silverman, W. K., Vernberg, E. M., and Prinstein, M. J. (1996). Symptoms of posttraumatic stress in children after Hurricane Andrew: A prospective study. *Journal of Consulting and Clinical Psychology, 64*(4), 712–23.

Lamoureux, B. E., Jackson, A. P., Palmieri, P. A., Johnson, R. J., and Hobfoll, S. E. (2007). *The impact of child sexual abuse on adult relationships.* Manuscript in preparation, Kent State University, Ohio.

Lazarus, R. S., and Folkman, S. (1984). *Stress, appraisal and coping.* New York: Springer Publishing Company.

Nishith, P., Mechanic, M. B., and Resick, P. A. (2000). Prior interpersonal trauma: The contribution to current PTSD symptoms in female rape victims. *Journal of Abnormal Psychology, 109,* 20–25.

Norris, F. H., and Kaniasty, K. (1996). Received and perceived social support in times of stress: A test of the social support deterioration deterrence model. *Journal of Personality and Social Psychology, 71,* 498–511.

Pynoos, R. S., Steinberg, A. M., and Wraith, R. (1995). A developmental model of childhood traumatic stress. In D. Cicchetti and D. J. Cohen (Eds.), *Developmental psychopathology: Vol. 2. Risk, disorder, and adaptation* (72–95). Oxford: John Wiley & Sons.

Radloff, L. S. (1977). The CES-D scale: A self-report depression scale for research in the general population. *Applied Psychological Measurement, 1,* 385–401.

Rosenberg, M. (1965). *Society and the adolescent self-image.* Princeton, NJ: Princeton University Press.

Sattler, D. N. (2006). Family resources, family strains, and stress following the Northridge earthquake. *Stress, Trauma, and Crisis, 9,* 187–202.

Sattler, D. N., Preston, A. J., Kaiser, C. F., Olivera, V. E., Valdez, J., and Schlueter, S. (2002). Hurricane Georges: A cross-national study examining preparedness, resource loss, and psychological distress in the U.S. Virgin Islands, Puerto Rico, Dominican Republic, and the United States. *Journal of Traumatic Stress, 15,* 339–50.

Schumm, J. A., Briggs-Phillips, M. L., and Hobfoll, S. E. (2006). Abuse and assault of women over the lifespan: The cumulative impact of multiple traumas on PTSD and depression. *Journal of Traumatic Stress, 19,* 825–36.

Schumm, J. A., Hobfoll, S. E., and Keogh, N. J. (2004). Revictimization and interpersonal resource loss predicts PTSD among women in substance-use treatment. *Journal of Traumatic Stress, 17,* 173–81.

Schumm, J. A., Stines, L. R., Hobfoll, S. E., and Jackson, A. P. (2005). The double-barreled burden of child abuse and current stressful circumstances on adult women: The kindling effect of early traumatic experience. *Journal of Traumatic Stress, 18,* 467–76.

Smith, B. W., and Freedy, J. R. (2000). Psychosocial resource loss as a mediator of the effects of flood exposure on psychological distress and physical symptoms. *Journal of Traumatic Stress, 13,* 349–57.

Stines, L. R., Suniga, S. O., Keogh, N. J., and Hobfoll, S. E. (2005). Childhood abuse, interpersonal resource loss, and PTSD in women: An examination of the signature of abuse hypothesis. Unpublished manuscript.

Sumer, N., Karanci, A. N., Berument, S. K., and Gunes, H. (2005). Personal resources, coping self-efficacy, and quake exposure as predictors of psychological

distress following the 1999 earthquake in Turkey. *Journal of Traumatic Stress, 18,*
   331–42.
Tang, C. S. (2006). Positive and negative postdisaster psychological adjustment
   among adult survivors of the Southeast Asian earthquake-tsunami. *Journal of Psychosomatic Research, 61,* 699–705.
Tversky, A., and Kahneman, D. (1981). The framing of decisions and the psychology
   of choice. *Science, 211,* 453–58.
Vranceanu, A. M., Hobfoll S. E., and Johnson, R J. (2007). Child multitype maltreatment and associated depression and PTSD symptoms: The role of social support
   and stress. *Child Abuse & Neglect, 31*(1), 71–84.
———. (under review). Personal and social resources as mediators between child
   abuse and adult depression and PTSD. *Journal of Interpersonal Violence.*

# 7

# Biological Risk and Resilience Factors

*Ann Rasmusson*

## INTRODUCTION

Although much is known concerning psychosocial predictors and correlates of PTSD, research examining biological pathways involved with PTSD is in its relative infancy. The majority of research examining the biology of PTSD has focused on the determination of biological factors that differentiate people with chronic PTSD from similarly traumatized individuals who did not develop the disorder; in other words, the elucidation of biological risk factors. And indeed, research over the past fifteen years has yielded some exciting findings regarding neurobiological systems that appear to influence stress resilience. However, some of these neurobiological systems have been studied only in adults, and should be reconsidered in light of known changes in their function across the lifespan. In addition, there are significant gender differences in the function of these systems that may bear on the risk for negative outcomes in the face of extreme stress. The following chapter will therefore discuss both developmental and gender influences on neurobiological factors implicated in stress resilience and stress vulnerability. Hopefully, understanding the role of these factors in immediate and long-term responses to extreme stress, and understanding the variable role that they may play depending on stage of development and gender, will help us develop new strategies to prevent and treat the negative sequelae of extreme stress, including posttraumatic stress disorder (PTSD).

Address correspondence to Ann Rasmusson, M.D.; Yale University School of Medicine; Department of Psychiatry; 950 Campbell Avenue; West Haven, CT 06516-2770. E-mail: ann.rasmusson@yale.edu

## NEUROBIOLOGICAL FACTORS OF
## RELEVANCE TO STRESS RESILIENCE

### Neuropeptide Y (NPY)

NPY, a 36 amino acid peptide, is among the most abundant peptides in the peripheral and central nervous systems. It is co-localized with norepinephrine in most sympathetic nerve fibers involved in the mammalian fight or flight response, as well as with other neurotransmistters in nonadrenergic systems (Wahlestedt and Reis, 1993). In the brain, NPY is co-localized with norepinephrine in the locus coeruleus, a brain area that mediates arousal. It is stored with a variety of other neurotransmitters in the amygdala, cortex, hippocampus, serotonergic raphe nuclei, and periaqueductal grey—also structures that play important roles in mediating the mammalian stress response (Heilig and Widerlov, 1990).

Extensive basic research has demonstrated that NPY is released when the sympathetic nervous system is intensely activated (Archelos, Xiang, Reinecke, and Lang, 1987; Dahlof, Tarizzo, Lundberg, and Dahlof, 1991; Haass et al., 1991; Lundberg, Rudehill, and Sollevi, 1989; Pernow, 1986; Pernow and Lundberg, 1989; Wahlestedt and Reis, 1993). Indeed, plasma NPY levels have been shown to increase in humans in response to activation of the sympathetic nervous system by intense exercise (Pernow, 1986), electroconvulsive therapy (Hauger et al., personal communication), the alpha$_2$ noradrenergic receptor antagonist, yohimbine (Rasmusson, Southwick, Hauger, and Charney, 1998; Rasmusson et al., 2000), and mock interrogation training exercises conducted during military survival school (Morgan et al., 2000; Morgan, Rasmusson, Wang, Hauger, and Hazlett, 2002). Recent data acquired during maximum load exercise testing (Rasmusson et al., unpublished observations) suggest that release of NPY during sympathetic system activation occurs at the lactate threshold when oxidative metabolism can no longer support energy demands and anaerobic metabolic systems are engaged.

During low, baseline levels of neuronal activity, NPY inhibits the release of neurotransmitters with which it is co-localized. When neuronal firing rates increase to the threshold at which NPY is released, NPY enhances the post-synaptic receptor responses to the neurotransmitters with which it is co-localized (Colmers and Bleakman, 1994). Thus, NPY appears to increase the bio-efficiency of stress responsive neuronal systems by functioning like a high pressure valve: adequate baseline levels reduce baseline system "sputter" while high levels achieved during stress enhance peak system function and power.

It would not be surprising then, that numerous animal and human studies have shown the NPY system to influence behavior under stress as well as to be stress-responsive. The intracerebroventricular (ICV) administration of NPY reduces anxiety-like behaviors via activity at brain $NPY-Y_1$ receptors in the amygdala (Britton et al., 1997; Heilig, Soderpalm, Engel, and Widerlov, 1989; Heilig et al., 1993; Heilig, 1995; Kask, Rago, and Harro, 1996, 1997; Nakajima et al., 1998; Wahlestedt and Reis, 1993). In addition, the ICV administration of NPY blocks increases in anxiety-like behaviors induced by the ICV administration of corticotropin releasing factor (CRF) (Britton et al., 2000), a peptide found at increased levels in the CSF of male combat veterans with PTSD (Baker et al., 1999; Bremner et al., 1997). In response to chronic restraint stress, however, Thorsell et al. (1998) showed that NPY mRNA levels in the amygdala and cortex decrease. Similarly, life-threatening and/or chronic severe stress is associated with reductions in *baseline* plasma NPY levels in male humans and animals (Corder, Castagne, Rivet, Mormede, and Gaillard, 1992; Rasmusson et al., 2000; Morgan, Rasmusson, Winters, Hauger, and Hazlett, 2003). In turn, reductions in *baseline* plasma NPY levels were associated with increased norepinephrine (NE) release during activation of the peripheral sympathetic system (Corder et al., 1992; Rasmusson et al., 2000).

Since the marked mobilization of NE is necessary to support adaptive cardiovascular responses, as well as to promote increases in arousal and defensive vigilance during stress, reductions in baseline plasma NPY levels in response to chronic or severe stress may be considered adaptive. On the other hand, reductions in baseline NPY levels may be most adaptive when less extreme. As seen in figure 7.1, participants in the U.S. military Special Forces Assessment and Selection (SFAS) program ultimately *selected* for Special Forces maintained near-normal baseline plasma NPY levels in response to extremely stressful survival school training procedures, while participants *not selected* showed marked reductions in plasma NPY levels.

Achievement of higher peak NPY responses along with high NE response during extreme stress also appears to be adaptive. Special Forces soldiers, who as a group perform more optimally than general forces soldiers during military survival training, had higher plasma NPY levels than general forces soldiers immediately after extremely stressful mock interrogation exercises (Morgan et al., 2000, 2002; Morgan et al., 2001). Furthermore, higher post-interrogation NPY levels were associated with fewer dissociative symptoms, lower levels of subjective distress, and better military performance during the mock interrogation (Morgan et al., 2000, 2002). In contrast, male combat veterans with chronic posttraumatic stress disorder (PTSD) compared to healthy control subjects had lower baseline plasma NPY levels, increased 3-methyl-4-hydroxyphenolglycol (MHPG) responses (MHPG is the primary metabolite of NE), and markedly blunted NPY release in response to activation of the sympathetic nervous system by the $alpha_2$ antagonist, yohimbine (Rasmusson

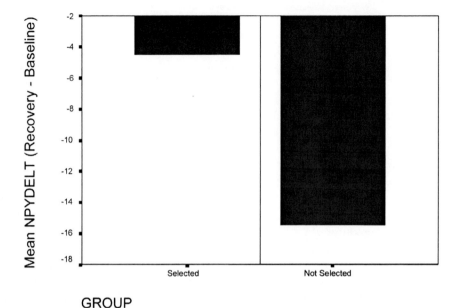

GROUP

Figure 7.1. Change in plasma NPY levels between the pre-stress baseline and completion of military survival school training in Special Forces Assessment and Selection
participants selected (left) and not selected (right) for inclusion in the Special Forces. Of
note, selection status was not known at the time of the NPY measurements. See Morgan
et al., 2000 and 2002 for details regarding survival school training procedures.

et al., 2000). Marked increases in anxiety, as well as flashbacks and panic
attacks, were simultaneously seen in the veterans with PTSD, while healthy
non-combat and combat-exposed veterans without PTSD experienced little if
any anxiety during the yohimbine challenge (Southwick et al., 1993).

We also found several interesting relationships between baseline and
post-yohimbine NPY levels, MHPG levels, and cardiovascular parameters
(Rasmusson et al., 2000). For instance, NPY levels after yohimbine correlated strongly with pulse in the healthy non-traumatized and combat control
groups, but not in the PTSD group. It is well known that the heart rate response to sympathetic nervous system activation reflects a balance between
parasympathetically mediated and sympathetically mediated inputs to the
heart (Korner, 1977). NPY appears to play a role in the mediation of both,
exerting a bradycardic effect in the nucleus tractus solitarius (Shih, Chan, and
Chan, 1992; Ergene, Dunbar, and Barraco, 1993), and inhibiting vagal action
at the heart during sympathetic stimulation (Shine, Potter, Biden, Selbie, and
Herzog, 1994; Ulman, Potter, McCloskey, and Morris, 1997). The lack of a
correlation between yohimbine-induced increases in plasma NPY and maxi-

mum heart rate in the PTSD group may be due to the blunted NPY response in this group.

Plasma NPY levels also correlated positively with systolic blood pressure in the PTSD group, but not in the combat control and non-traumatized groups. Direct effects of NPY at post-synaptic NPY-Y1 receptors that mediate vasoconstriction may explain this (Han et al., 1998). The greater strength of this relationship in the PTSD group is consistent with observations of vasoconstrictor hyperresponsivity to NPY in other hyperadrenergic states such as congestive heart failure (Zukowska-Grojec, 1995).

## *NPY and Genetics*

Given the capacity of NPY to play a consistent role in such a wide variety of neuronal subsystems, it may not be surprising that the structure of NPY is highly conserved across species: structural changes would be expected to have rather wide-ranging consequences. Indeed, NPY deriving from the ray, *Torpedo marmorata*, and from man share 92 percent sequence homology (Larhammer et al., 1993). Consistent with the conservation of NPY peptide structure across species, only a few functional NPY gene polymorphisms have been identified thus far in man. One polymorphism was identified in 14 percent of Finnish and 6 percent of Dutch subjects and was significantly associated with high serum total and LDL cholesterol levels independent of age, sex, obesity, smoking, and medication (Karvovnen et al., 1998).

## *Possible Long-Term Health Risks Associated with Alterations in NPY Responses*

Since the half-life of plasma NPY is much greater than that of norepinephrine (Pernow, 1986), and since systolic blood pressure in PTSD subjects appears to be hyperresponsive to circulating plasma NPY levels, stress-induced increases in plasma NPY may result in more sustained elevations of blood pressure in this group. Under conditions of combat or other prolonged exposure to physical stress, this may be adaptive. However, if persistent over time, stress-induced increases in plasma NPY could result in more persistent ischemic risk to end-organs such as the heart and brain and could account for increased rates of stroke and other circulatory diseases such as peripheral neuropathy observed in persons with histories of trauma (Bao et al., 1997; Brass and Page, 1996; Boscarino, 1997). Our preliminary data from the yohimbine study also raise potential ways in which severe stress-exposed subjects with or without PTSD could be at increased risk for cardiovascular complications over the long haul. Both groups may easily trigger the sympathetic response, but the PTSD group would be expected to do so on a more frequent basis due to the overinterpretation of threat cues. Traumatized subjects without PTSD may not be indiscriminant in activating the sympathetic nervous system, but rapid triggering of high NPY responses to repeated real threats could also result in long-term vascular impact.

## Gender-Effects on NPY Physiology

Research suggests that there may be sexual dimorphism in the NPY response to stress. Testosterone increases both tissue stores of NPY and NPY release and male rats release more NPY in response to cold stress than female rats (Zukowska-Grojec, 1995). These findings are consistent with a study in humans showing increased exercise-induced NPY release in men compared to age-matched ovariectomized women with and without estrogen replacement in whom testosterone levels are significantly reduced (Laughlin, Barrett-Connor, Kritz-Silverstein, and von Muhlen, 2000). Testosterone influences on NPY release also may account for findings by Lewandowski et al. (1998) wherein plasma NPY levels increased significantly during maximum exercise in the immediate pre-ovulatory phase of the menstrual cycle when plasma testosterone levels peak, but not during the luteal phase. In turn, relative decreases in NPY release during the luteal phase of the menstrual cycle may contribute mechanistically to increased NE levels or stress responses observed in women during this phase (Goldstein, Levinson, and Keiser, 1983; Zuspan and Zuspan, 1973). It is therefore possible that sex hormone-based gender differences in NPY physiology could contribute to an increased susceptibility of women to stress-related disorders such as PTSD and depression which have prevalence rates that are two to three times higher in women compared to men (Kessler, Sonnega, Bromet, Hughes, and Neslon, 1995). It is also conceivable that stress experienced during different phases of the menstrual cycle or within different reproductive states could have different effects at a neurobiological level and thereby variably induce negative stress sequelae.

However, it should be noted that, in contrast to findings in men, reductions in baseline plasma NPY levels have not been observed in women with PTSD. Further studies controlling for the chronicity and intensity of stress exposure, as well as menstrual cycle influences, will be necessary to confirm possible gender differences in the adaptation of NPY system physiology to stress. In addition, studies of NPY in children and adolescents should be undertaken; no such studies have been conducted thus far.

## Dehydroepiandrosterone (DHEA)

Increased plasma DHEA and DHEAS (a metabolite of DHEA that forms a storage pool for DHEA) levels have been positively related to vigor and negatively to depression in a variety of populations (Yaffe et al., 1998; Goodyer, Herbert, and Altham, 1998; Cruess et al., 1999; Heinz et al., 1999; Michael, Jenaway, Paykel, and Herbert, 2000; Young, Gallagher, and Porter, 2002). More recent studies suggest that the ratio of DHEA(S) to cortisol may be a more robust indictor of psychological health and resistance to the negative effects of stress (Goodyer et al., 1998; Cruess et al., 1999; Morgan et al., 2004; Rasmusson et al., 2004; Rasmusson, Wu, Paliwal, Anderson, and Krishnan-Sarin, 2006). For example, the salivary DHEA(S) to plasma cortisol ratio was found to be negatively correlated with dissociative symptoms and positively related to military performance in men undergoing stressful mock interrogation exercises during military survival training (Morgan et al., 2004). In premenopausal women, the ratio of plasma DHEA to cortisol after maximum adrenal stimulation by adrenocorticotropic hormone (ACTH) correlated negatively with negative mood (Rasmusson et al., 2004). Similarly, a decrease in the plasma DHEA/cortisol ratio in female smokers was associated with increases in negative mood during a week of biochemically verified smoking abstinence and with abstinence lapse the following week (Rasmusson, Wu, Paliwal, Anderson, and Krishnan-Sarin, 2006).

Interestingly, the study by Rasmusson et al. (2004) showed that adrenal gland activation by ACTH resulted in an upward shift in the ratio of DHEA to cortisol in subjects endorsing previous trauma, but a downward shift in subjects without previous trauma. In addition, greater DHEA responses to ACTH were associated with lower avoidance, hyperarousal, and total PTSD symptoms among subjects with PTSD. Similarly, in a study of refugees from Kosovo, increasing DHEAS levels over time were associated with greater sleep disturbance and the development of PTSD without comorbid depression, while lower DHEAS levels were associated with PTSD comorbid with major depression (Sondergaard, Hansson, and Theorell, 2002), a condition that essentially constitutes more severe PTSD (Breslau, Davis, Peterson, and Schultz, 2000). Increased morning plasma DHEAS levels were also seen in male combat veterans with current or lifetime PTSD compared to those without (Yehuda, Brand, Golier, and Yang, 2006). In the study by Yehuda et al. (2006), higher plasma DHEA levels were predicted by greater retrospectively rated improvements in PTSD symptoms over time.

DHEA administration studies also support a role for DHEA in promoting mental health. At doses of either 50 or 25 mg administered daily over six months, DHEA compared to placebo improved mood and vasomotor instability in early and late menopausal women (Stomati et al., 2000; Genazanni et al., 2003). In a study by Wolkowitz et al. (1999), six weeks of DHEA at 100 mg/day added to previously stable psychotropic medications led to a $30.5 \pm 29.1$ percent decrease in Hamilton Depression (HAM-D) scale scores compared to a $5.3 \pm 20.2$ percent reduction in the placebo group. The large variability in response was reflected in the fact that five of the eleven DHEA-treated subjects were considered treatment responders while none of the placebo-treated subjects were responders. More recently, Schmidt et al. (2005) administered placebo or DHEA at a dose of 90 mg/day for three weeks followed by 450 mg/day for three weeks to middle-aged men and women with dysthymia or mild to moderate major depression. DHEA significantly improved depression symptoms. In the DHEA-treated group, 50 percent of the subjects showed a 50 percent reduction in HAM-D scores while only 28 percent of the placebo-treated subjects showed this level of improvement. Sexual functioning was also improved in the DHEA-treated group. Finally, Strous et al. (2003) found that DHEA at a dose of 100 mg per day reduced negative symptoms in subjects with schizophrenia maintained on stable atypical or typical antipsychotics. DHEA reduced symptoms of affective "blunting," "alogia," and "anhedonia"; it had no effects on "apathy" and "attention." DHEA-treated subjects also showed improvements in depression and anxiety scores. Of note, women were more responsive to the therapeutic effects of DHEA than men.

Thus, there is an emerging literature suggesting that DHEA plays an important role in the mediation of stress resilience and wellness. Further, it appears that achievement of higher DHEA/cortisol levels during adrenal activation by stress may mitigate stress-induced degradation of cognition, mood, and behavioral function.

## Possible Mechanisms by Which DHEA May Confer Stress Resilience

Peripherally derived DHEA is thought to be the only source of brain DHEA and DHEAS in humnas (Compagnone and Mellon, 2000). DHEA released by the adrenal gland crosses the blood brain barrier, after which it is sulfated in the brain, thereby preventing it from crossing back into the periphery. Within the brain, region-specific metabolism of DHEA likely controls the nature of DHEA effects on cognition, mood, and behavior (Rose et al., 1997). For example, 7-hydroxylated DHEA interferes with the nuclear uptake of activated glucocorticoid receptors in hippocampal neurons (Morfin and Starka, 2001), possibly accounting for its neuroprotective and "antiglucocorticoid" effects. Indeed, DHEA protects against excitatory amino acid- and oxidative stress-induced damage, restores cortisol-induced decrements in long-term potentiation, regulates programmed cell death, and promotes neurogenesis in the hippocampus (Kimonides, Khatibi, Svendsen, Sofroniew, and Herbert, 1998; Bastianetto, Ramassamy, Poirier, and Quirion, 1999; Kaminska et al., 2000; Karishma and Herbert, 2002; Zhang et al., 2002). An enhancement of neurogenesis in the hippocampus, in turn, has been associated with resistance to the development of stress-related depressive behaviors in animals (Duman, 2004). DHEA and DHEAS also antagonize gamma-amino-butyric acid $(GABA)_A$ receptors and facilitate N-methyl-D-aspartate (NMDA) receptor function. Thus they may potentiate activation of monoamine systems in response to stress and influence mood, cognition, and behavior in this manner (Heninger, 1997; Aston-Jones, Chen, Zhu, and Oshinsky, 2001; Mattson, Maudsley, and Martin, 2004; Rajkowski, Majczynski, Clayton, and Aston-Jones, 2004; Tobler, Fiorillo, and Schultz, 2005).

DHEA administration studies also suggest that DHEA alters levels of neuroactive steroids that impact mood and behavior. Kroboth et al. (2003) demonstrated decreases in baseline plasma cortisol levels with maintenance of the normal twenty-four-hour diurnal cortisol rhythm in elderly men and women treated with 200 mg of DHEA each morning over two weeks. The cortisol-lowering effect of DHEA was more pronounced in women than in men. Administration of 50 mg of DHEA per day to women in early and late menopause was associated with progressive decreases in cortisol, and with increases in DHEAS, testosterone, estradiol, estrone, progesterone, beta-endorphin and allopregnanolone (Stomati et al., 2000). Allopreganolone has potent anxiolytic, sedative, and anesthetic properties (Rupprecht, 2003) and recent data show that cerebrospinal fluid levels of allopregnanolone and its equipotent stereoisomer pregnanolone (collectively termed "ALLO") are strongly and negatively associated with negative mood and PTSD re-experiencing symptoms in women (Rasmusson, Pinna, Paliwal, Weisman, Gottschalk, Charney, et al., 2006). Finally, administration of 100 mg of DHEA per day to young men for two weeks was associated with an increase in the peak ACTH, cortisol, and arginine vasopressin (AVP) responses to near maximum load exercise stress and a normal return of these hormones to baseline afterward. Of interest, AVP mediates the increase in reactivity of ACTH to novelty in mammals previously exposed to chronic stress (Aguilera, 1994). Thus it appears that DHEA may enhance cortisol reactivity while decreasing baseline cortisol levels. This is consistent with effects of another compound having antiglucocorticoid activity: RU-486 increases the diurnal cortisol peak but decreases the diurnal cortisol nadir (Van Haarst, Oitzl, Workel, and DeKloet, 1996).

*DHEA Across the Lifespan*

Plasma DHEA levels are high at birth then drop and remain low until adrenarche (ages six to eight years). DHEA levels rapidly increase from adrenarche through adolescence and peak in the second to third decade, a time during which sexual activity and the mating agenda, as well as the capacity to endure sleep deprivation, are often at a peak. Thereafter, DHEA levels progressively decline with further aging. Thus, we suggest that blunted DHEA responses to traumatic stress prior to adrenarche or later in life may limit the degree to which the HPA axis can adaptively upregulate. In addition, a lack of neuroprotection by DHEA during periods of life when DHEA levels are low may contribute to more toxic effects of stress on the brain (e.g., in the hippocampus).

## Gender Effects on DHEA(S) Physiology

Plasma DHEA(S) regulation is influenced by gender and may vary with menstrual status. DHEA levels are similar in females and males, but levels of DHEAS are 50–75 percent lower in females (Frye et al., 2000), possibly due to the fact that DHEA sulfation is inhibited by estrogen and facilitated by testosterone (Nestler, 1996). In addition, levels of factors that facilitate DHEA metabolism to inactive substrates are substantially higher in women compared to men (Wang, Napoli, and Strobel, 2000; Lamba et al., 2004). Thus, females may incur greater increases in the rate of DHEA metabolism during stress. This idea is supported by a study showing enhanced induction of DHEA metabolism by oral DHEA administration in women compared to men (Frye et al., 2000). Increased rates of DHEA metabolism also may be induced in women during the luteal phase of the menstrual cycle when progesterone levels exceed those achieved during maximum stress.

Perhaps then, women may be at greater risk for depletion of DHEA(S) in the aftermath of stress, a factor that could contribute to the increased rates of depression and PTSD in women. In turn, this would increase the risk for the development of psychiatric and substance abuse disorders, as well as physical health conditions observed among traumatized persons (reviewed by Gill and Page, 2006).

## Allopregnanolone/Pregnanolone (ALLO)

Two derivatives of progesterone produced by the brain, ovary, and adrenal gland [3-alpha-hydroxy-5-alpha-pregnan-20-one (allopregnanolone) and 3-alpha-hydroxy-5-beta-pregnan-20-one (pregnanolone), collectively termed ALLO] are the most potent and selective positive endogenous modulators of the action of GABA at brain $GABA_A$ receptors (Puia et al., 1990; Puia et al. 2003; Lambert, Belelli, Peden, Vardy, and Peters, 2003). Through this mechanism, ALLO exerts potent anxiolytic, anti-conflict, anticonvulsant, anesthetic, sedative, and neuroprotective effects (Guidotti et al., 2001).

Recently, our work revealed that CSF ALLO levels in premenopausal women with PTSD were <39 percent of CSF ALLO levels in healthy nontraumatized women (Rasmusson, Pinna, Paliwal, Weisman, Gottschalk, Charney, et al., 2006). Further, CSF ALLO levels correlated negatively with PTSD re-experiencing symptoms in the PTSD group and with negative mood symptoms (particularly depression) among all subjects. Interestingly, the ratio of CSF ALLO to DHEA was an even more robust predictor of PTSD and mood symptoms, suggesting that a balance between inhibitory and excitatory tone in the CNS is critical to the maintenance of good psychological function.

Low CSF ALLO levels or a low ratio of ALLO to DHEA, resulting in a relative decrease in CNS inhibitory vs. excitatory tone, could contribute directly to hyperreactivity of the amygdala, as well as increased CRF and monoaminergic responses during trauma exposure or exposure to trauma reminders (reviewed in Rasmusson, Pinna, Paliwal, Weisman, Gottschalk, Charney, et al., 2006). A decrease in extrasynaptic $GABA_A$ receptor mediated tonic inhibition also may facilitate phasic increases in glutamatergic and GABAergic activity that disrupt frontal lobe-mediated inhibition of the amygdala. This may contribute to enhanced fear conditioning and resistance to extinction of fearful conditioned responses and promote the development of PTSD (Southwick, Rasmusson, Barron, and Arnsten, 2005). As allopregnanolone is thought to provide neuroprotection, subjects with a diminished capacity for ALLO release also may be prone to stress-induced structural and functional damage of brain areas such as the hippocampus—as seen in some populations with PTSD (Bonne et al., 2001; De Bellis, Hall, Boring, Frustaci, and Moritz, 2001; Gilbertson et al., 2002; Hull, 2002).

Dysregulation of the HPA axis in PTSD (reviewed in Yehuda, 2002; Rasmusson, Vythilingam, and Morgan, 2003; Young and Breslau, 2004) also may be related to low CNS ALLO levels. Decreased cortisol release during stress could limit adaptive increases in ALLO production during stress (Hou, Lin, and Penning, 1997). On the other hand, ALLO release during stress provides delayed negative feedback control over activation of the HPA axis (Barbaccia, Serra, Purdy, and Biggio, 2001) and reduces expression of the CRF and arginine vasopressin (AVP) genes in the hypothalamus (Patchev, Shoaib, Holsboer, and Almeida, 1994), Thus, low ALLO levels might account for the increases in HPA axis reactivity and increases in twenty-four-hour urinary cortisol output observed in some populations with PTSD, such as premenopausal women with comorbid lifetime or current MDD (Heim et al., 2000; Rasmusson et al., 2001; Lipschtiz et al., 2003; Young and Breslau, 2004).

Interestingly, CSF ALLO levels in the women with PTSD correlated positively with hypervigilance and increased startle, hyperarousal symptoms that cluster together according to recent confirmatory factor analyses of DSM-IV PTSD symptoms (APA, 1994; Simms, Watson, and Doebbeling, 2002). While this correlation is preliminary and did not reach statistical significance when subjected to conservative Bonferroni corrections, it is consistent with the idea that development of hypervigilance and increased startle in the aftermath of intensely threatening experiences is adaptive. Support for this idea comes from recent animal research showing that suppression of fear-potentiated startle by pharmacological manipulations interferes with the extinction of conditioned fear. Thus, we hypothesize that high ALLO levels achieved during or subsequent to severe stress will contribute to natural extinction of conditioned fear and recovery from stressful experiences.

## ALLO Across the Lifespan

Our data (Rasmusson, Pinna, Paliwal, Weisman, Gottschalk, Charney, et al., 2006) and that of Genazzani et al. (1998) demonstrate age-related decreases in plasma or serum levels of ALLO through adulthood. However, while Genazzani et al., (1998) showed ALLO decreases between the ages of nineteen and sixty years in males only, Rasmusson, Pinna, Paliwal, Weisman, Gottschalk, Charney, et al. (2006), showed decreases between the ages of nineteen and forty-five in premenopausal women as well. Therefore, such studies will thus have to be repeated. It is possible that the age-related decline in ALLO levels in the premenopausal women in the study by Rasmusson, Pinna, Paliwal, Weisman, Gottschalk, Charney, et al. (2006) was due to (a) the small sample size, (b) differences in ALLO metabolism between CSF and blood, or (c) methodological differences in assessing ALLO levels.

It also will be important to investigate ALLO physiology in childhood and adolescence. It would not be surprising if ALLO levels increased along with DHEA levels during adrenarche in children (Genazzani et al., 2003) or along with progesterone, estrogen, and testosterone levels during puberty (Mitev et al., 2003). We might also speculate that a pathological limitation in the capacity for ALLO synthesis during these developmental epochs might be associated with increased risk for the development of anxiety or mood disorders, including PTSD.

## Gender Effects on ALLO Physiology

A number of studies have shown that *acute*, physically threatening stress, such as swim stress in rats, increases brain ALLO levels in male as well as female rodents (Purdy, Morrow, Moore, and Paul, 1991; Vallee, Rivera,

Koob, Purdy, and Fitzgerald, 2000). Increases in brain ALLO levels have been attributed to ALLO contributions by the adrenal gland since they do not occur in adrenalectomized animals. However, it is also possible that reduced plasma cortisol levels secondary to adrenalectomy reduces brain expression of 3-alpha-HSD, the enzyme that synthesizes ALLO (Hou et al., 1998). Indeed such work suggests that limitations in cortisol production under stress could increase the risk for PTSD in some populations (e.g. see Delahanty, Raimonde, and Spoonster, 2000; Yehuda et al., 2006) by preventing stress-protective increases in ALLO production.

Animal work, however, suggests that sex-specific mechanisms also should be investigated in regard to stress and ALLO physiology. Mitev et al. (2003) showed that brain 3-alpha-HSD expression is testosterone dependent in male rats, but estrogen responsive in ovariectomized females. Other work has modeled sex-specific effects of *chronic stress* on brain ALLO levels. Dong et al. (2001) found decreased brain ALLO levels in male mice exposed to six weeks of social isolation. Isolation stress-induced reductions in brain ALLO levels did not occur in normal female mice, but were reproduced in testosterone-treated ovariectomized female mice (Pinna, Costa, and Guidotti, 2005).

Other work will be necessary though to characterize sex-specific effects of chronic, *high stimulation* stress (such as repeated footshock or a prolonged series of different stressors) on brain or plasma ALLO levels, as this may have greater relevance to traumatic human experiences such as combat stress, chronic child abuse, or domestic violence. In addition, an examination of stress effects on ALLO physiology across the menstrual cycle in women may be fruitful. We have preliminary data from two healthy subjects showing two- to three-fold increases in CSF progesterone, as well as ALLO, levels during the luteal phase of the menstrual cycle when peripheral progesterone levels are approximately an order of magnitude higher than in the follicular phase. In contrast, the only PTSD subject studied showed a negligible increase in CSF ALLO levels between the follicular and luteal phases despite having a ~six-fold increase in CSF progesterone levels, consistent with a possible block in ALLO synthesis.

## SUMMARY

It can be seen from the preceding discussion that several neurobiological factors may contribute to resilience in the face of traumatic stress exposure. Further, these factors may vary in their relationship to stress outcomes depending on age or stage of development, sex, and reproductive status. In addition, and perhaps most interestingly, these factors interact. While this complexity may contribute to the apparent variability in findings from different studies conducted in different subpopulations or species, it also bodes well for our capacity to intervene when one or another pathway becomes dysregulated in response to severe or chronic stress. In future research then we will be challenged to characterize precise points of dysregulation *within individuals*, so that we can optimally target such therapeutic interventions.

## REFERENCES

Aguilera, G. (1994). Regulation of pituitary ACTH secretion during chronic stress. *Frontiers of Neuroendocrinology, 15*, 321–50.

American Psychiatric Association. (1994). *Diagnostic and Statistical Manual of Mental Disorders* (fourth ed.). Washington, DC: American Psychiatric Association.

Archelos, J., Xiang, J., Reinecke, M., and Lang, R. (1987). Regulation of release and function of neuropeptides in the heart. *Journal of Cardiovascular Pharmacology, 12*, S45–50.

Aston-Jones, G., Chen, S., Zhu, Y., and Oshinsky, M. L. (2001). A neural circuit for circadian regulation of arousal. *Nature Neuroscience, 4*, 732–38.

Baker, D. G., West, S. A., Nicholson, W. E., Ekhator, N. N., Kasckow, J. W., Hill, K. K., et al. (1999). Serial CSF corticotropin-releasing hormone levels and adrenocortical activity in combat veterans with posttraumatic stress disorder. *American Journal of Psychiatry, 156*, 585–88.

Bao, L., Kopp, J., Zhang, X., Xu, S-Q. D., Shang, L-F., Wong, H., et al. (1997). Localization of neuropeptide Y Y1 receptors in cerebral blood vessels. *Processing National Academy Science, 94*, 12661–66.

Barbaccia, M. L., Serra, M., Purdy, R. H., and Biggio, G. (2001). Stress and neuroactive steroids. *International Review of Neurobiology, 46*, 243–72.

Bastianetto, S., Ramassamy, C., Poirier, J., and Quirion, R. (1999). Dehydroepiandrosterone (DHEA) protects hippocampal cells from oxidative stress-induced damage. *Molecular Brain Research, 66*, 35–41.

Bonne, O., Brandes, D., Gilboa, A., Gomori, J. M., Shenton, M. E., Pitman, R. K., et al. (2001). Longitudinal MRI study of hippocampal volume in trauma survivors with PTSD. *American Journal of Psychiatry, 158*, 1248–51.

Boscarino, J. A. (1997). Diseases among men 20 years after exposure to severe stress: Implications for clinical research and medical care. *Psychosomatic Medicine, 59*, 605–14.

Brass, L. M., and Page, W. F. (1996). Stroke in former prisoners of war. *Journal of Stroke Cerebrovascular Disease, 6*, 72–78.

Bremner, J. D., Licinio, J., Darnell, A., Krystal, J. H., Owens, M. J., Southwick, S. M., et al. (1997). Elevated CSF corticotropin-releasing factor concentrations in posttraumatic stress disorder. *American Journal of Psychiatry, 154*, 624–29.

Breslau, N., Davis, G. C., Peterson, E. L., and Schultz, L. R. (2000). A second look at comorbidity in victims of trauma: the posttraumatic stress disorder-major depression connection. *Biological Psychiatry, 48*, 902–9.

Britton, K. T., Akwa, Y., Southerland, S., Koob, G. F. (2000). Neuropeptide Y blocks the anxiogenic-like behavioral action of corticotrophin-releasing factor. *Peptides, 21*, 37–44.

Britton, K. T., Southerland, S., Van Uden, E., Kirby, D., Rivier, J., and Koob, G. (1997). Anxiolytic activity of NPY receptor agonists in the conflict test. *Psychopharmacology, 132*, 6–13.

Colmers, W., and Bleakman, D. (1994). Effects of neuropeptide Y on the electrical properties of neurons. *Trends in Neurosciences, 17*, 373–79.

Compagnone, N. A., and Mellon, S. H. (2000). Neurosteroids: Biosynthesis and function of these novel neuromodulators. *Frontiers of Neuroendocrinology, 21*, 1–56.

Corder, R., Castagne, V., Rivet, J-M., Mormede, P., and Gaillard, R. C. (1992). Central and peripheral effects of repeated stress and high NaCl diet on neuropeptide Y. *Physiology & Behavior, 52*, 205–10.

Cruess, D. G., Antoni, M. H., Kumar, M., Ironson, G., McCabe, P., Fernandez, J. B., et al. (1999). Cognitive-behavioral stress management buffers decreases in dehydroepiandrosterone sulfate (DHEA-S) and increases in the cortisol/DHEA-S ratio and reduces mood disturbance and perceived stress among HIV-seropositive men. *Psychoneuroendocrinology, 24*, 537–49

Dahlof, P., Tarizzo, V., Lundberg, J., and Dahlof, C. (1991). Alpha- and beta-adrenoceptor-mediated effects on nerve stimulation-evoked release of neuropeptide Y (NPY)-like immunoreactivity in the pithed guinea pig. *Journal of Autonomic Nervous System, 35*, 199–210.

De Bellis, M. D., Hall, J., Boring, A. M., Frustaci, K., and Moritz, G. (2001). A pilot longitudinal study of hippocampal volumes in pediatric maltreatment-related posttraumatic stress disorder. *Biological Psychiatry, 50*, 305–9.

Delahanty, D. L., Raimonde, A. J., and Spoonster, E. (2000). Initial Posttraumatic Urinary Cortisol Levels Predict Subsequent PTSD Symptoms in Motor Vehicle Accident Victims. *Biological Psychiatry, 48*, 940–47.

Dong, E., Matsumoto, K., Uzunova, V., Sugaya, I., Takahata, H., Watanabe, H., et al. (2001). Brain 5α-dihydroprogesterone and allopregnanolone synthesis in a mouse model of protracted social isolation. *Proceedings of the National Academy of Sciences of the United States, 98*, 2849–54.

Duman, R. S. (2004). Depression: a case of neuronal life and death? *Biological Psychiatry, 56*, 140–45.

Ergene, E., Dunbar, J. C., and Barraco, R. A. (1993). Visceroendocrine responses elicited by neuropeptide Y in the nucleus tractus solitarius. *Brain Research Bulletin, 32*, 461–65.

Frye, R. F., Kroboth, P. D., Kroboth, F. K., Stone, R. A., Folan, M., Salek, S. F., et al. (2000). Sex differences in the pharmacokinetics of dehydroepiandrosterone (DHEA) after single and multiple dose administration in healthy older adults. *Journal of Clinical Pharmacology, 40*, 596–605.

Genazzani, A. R., Petraglia, F., Bernardi, F., Casarosa, E., Salvestroni, C., Tonetti, A., et al. (1998). Circulating allopregnanolone levels in humans: gender, age, and endocrine influences. *Journal of Clinical Metabology and Endocrinology, 88*, 2099–2103.

Genazzani, A. D., Stomati, M., Bernardi, F., Pieri, M., Rovati, L., and Genazzani, A. R. (2003). Long-term low-dose dehydroepiandrosterone oral supplementation in early and late postmenopausal women modulates endocrine parameters and synthesis of neuroactive steroids. *Fertility and Sterility, 80*, 1495–1501.

Gilbertson, M. W., Shenton, M. E., Ciszewski, A., Kasai, K., Lasko, N. B., Orr, S. P., et al. (2002). Smaller hippocampal volume predicts pathologic vulnerability to psychological trauma. *Nature Neuroscience, 5*, 1242–47.

Gill, J. M., and Page, G. G. (2006). Psychiatric and physical health ramifications of traumatic events in women. *Issues in Mental Health Nursing, 27*, 711–34.

Goldstein, D. S., Levinson, P., and Keiser, H. R. (1983). Plasma and urinary catecholamines during the human ovulatory cycle. *American Journal of Obstetrics and Gynecology, 146*, 824–29.

Goodyer, I. M., Herbert, J., and Altham, P. M. E. (1998). Adrenal steroid secretion and major depression in 8- to 16-year-olds, III. Influence of cortisol/DHEA ratio at presentation on subsequent rates of disappointing life events and persistent major depression. *Psychological Medicine, 28*, 265–73.

Guidotti, A., Dong, E., Matsumoto, K., Pinna, G., Rasmusson, A. M., and Costa, E. (2001). The socially-isolated mouse: a model to study the putative role of allopregnanolone and 5alpha-dihydroprogesterone in psychiatric disorders. *Brain Research Reviews, 37*, 110–15.

Haass, M., Cheng, B., Richardt, G., Lang, R., and Schomig, A. (1991). Characterization and presynaptic modulation of stimulation-evoked exocytotic co-release of noradrenaline and neuropeptide Y in guinea pig heart. *Naunyn-Schmiedeberg's Archives of Pharmacology, 339*, 71–78.

Han, S., Chen, X., Cox, B., Yang, C-L., Wu, Y-M., Naes, L., et al. (1998). Role of neuropeptide Y in cold stress-induced hypertension. *Peptides, 19*, 351–58.

Heilig, M. (1995). Antisense inhibition of neuropeptide Y (NPY)-Y1 receptor expression blocks the anxiolytic-like action of NPY in amygdala and paradoxically increases feeding. *Regulatory Peptides, 59*, 201–5.

Heilig, M., McLeod, S., Brot, M., Heinrichs, S., Menzaghi, F., Koob, G., et al. (1993). Anxiolytic-like action of neuropeptide Y: mediation by Y1 receptors in amygdala, and dissociation from food intake effects. *Neuropsychopharmacology, 8*, 357–63.

Heilig, M., Soderpalm, B., Engel, J., and Widerlov, E. (1989). Centrally administered neuropeptide Y (NPY) produces anxiolytic-like effects in animal anxiety models. *Psychopharmacology, 98*, 524–29.

Heilig, M., and Widerlov, E. (1990). Neuropeptide Y: an overview of central distribution, functional aspects, and possible involvement in neuropsychiatric illnesses. *Acta Psychiatrica Scandinavica, 82*, 95–114.

Heim, C., Newport, D. J., Heit, S., Graham, Y. P., Wilcox, M., Bonsall, R., et al. (2000). Pituitary-adrenal and autonomic responses to stress in women after sexual and physical abuse in childhood. *The Journal of the American Medical Association, 284*, 592–97.

Heinz, A., Weingartner, H., George, D., Hommer, D., Wolkowitz, O. M., and Linnoila, M. (1999). Severity of depression in abstinent alcoholics is associated with monoamine metabolites and dehydroepiandrosterone-sulfate concentrations. *Psychiatry Research, 89*, 97–106.

Heninger, G. R. (1997). Serotonin, sex, and psychiatric illness. *Proceedings of the National Academy of Sciences of the United States of America, 94*, 4823–24.

Hou, Y. T., Lin, H. K., and Penning, T. M. (1998). Dexamethasone regulation of the rat 3-alpha hydroxysteroid/dihydrodiol dihydrogenase (3 alpha-HSD/DD) gene. *Molecular Pharmacology, 53*, 459–66.

Hull, A. M. (2002). Neuroimaging findings in post-traumatic stress disorder. Systematic review. *British Journal of Psychiatry, 181*, 102–10.

Kaminska, M., Harris, J, Gilbers, K., Dubrovsky, B. (2000). Dehydroepiandrosterone sulfate (DHEAS) conteracts decremental effects of corticosterone on dentate gyrus LTP. Implications for depression. *Brain Research Bulletin, 52*, 229–34.

Kaminski, R. M., Livingood, M. R., and Rogawski, M. A. (2004). Allopregnanolone analogs that positively modulate GABA receptors protect against partial seizures induced by 6-Hz electrical stimulation in mice. *Epilepsia, 45*, 864–67.

Karishma, K. K., and Herbert, J. (2002). Dehydroepiandrosterone (DHEA) stimulates neurogenesis in the hippocampus of the rat, promotes survival of newly formed neurons and prevents corticosteroneinduced suppression. *European Journal of Neuroscience, 16*, 445–53.

Karvovnen, M. K., Pesonen, U., Koulu, M., Niskanen, L., Laakso, M., Rissanen, A., et al. (1998). Association of a leucine(7)-to-proline(7) polymorphism in the signal peptide of neuropeptide Y with high serum cholesterol and LDL cholesterol levels. *Nature Medicine, 4*, 1434–37.

Kask, A., Rago, L., and Harro, J. (1996). Anxiogenic-like effect of the neuropeptide Y Y1 receptor antagonist BIBP3226: antagonism with diazepam. *European Journal of Pharmacology, 317*, R3–R4.

———. (1997). Alpha-helical CRF9-41 prevents anxiogenic-like effect of NPY Y1 receptor antagonist BIBP3226 in rats. *NeuroReport, 8*, 3645–47.

Kessler, R. C., Sonnega, A., Bromet, E., Hughes, M., and Nelson, C. B. (1995). Post-traumatic stress disorder in the National Comorbidity Survey. *Archives of General Psychiatry, 52*, 1048–60.

Kimonides, V. G., Khatibi, N. H., Svendsen, C. N., Sofroniew, M. V., and Herbert, J. (1998). Dehydroepiandrosterone (DHEA) and DHEA-sulfate (DHEAS) protect hippocampal neurons against excitatory amino acid-induced neurotoxicity. *Proceedings of the National Academy of Sciences of the United States of America, 95*, 1852–57.

Korner, P. I. (1977). Central nervous control of autonomic cardiovascular function. In *Handbook of physiology* (691–739). Bethesda, MD: American Physiological Society.

Kroboth, P. D., Amico, J. A., Stone, R. A., Folan, M., Frye, R. F., Kroboth, F. J., et al. (2003). Influence of DHEA administration on 24-hour cortisol concentrations. *Journal of Clinical Psychopharmacology, 23*, 96–99.

Lamba, V., Yasuda, K., Lamba, J. K., Assem, M., Davila, J., Strom, S., et al. (2004). PXR (NR1I2) splice variants in human tissues, including brain, and identification of neurosteroids and nicotine as PXR activators. *Toxicology and Applied Pharmacology, 199*, 251–65.

Lambert, J. J., Belelli, D., Peden, D. R., Vardy, A. W., and Peters, J. A. (2003). Neurosteroid modulation of $GABA_A$ receptors. *Progress in Neurobiology, 71*, 67–80.

Larhammar, D., Soderberg, C., Blomvist, A. G. (1993). Evolution of the neuropeptide Y family of peptides. In W. F. Colmers and C. Wahlestedt (Eds.), *The Biology of Neuropeptide Y and Related Peptides*. Totawa, NJ: Humana Press.

Laughlin, G. A., Barrett-Connor, E., Kritz-Silverstein, D., and von Muhlen (2000). Hysterectomy, oophorectomy, and endogenous sex hormone levels in older women: the Rancho Bernardo Study. *Journal of Clinical Endocrinology Metabolism, 85*, 645–51.

Lewandowski, J., Pruszczyk, P., Elaffi, M., Chodakowska, J., Wocial, B., Switalska, H., et al. (1998). Blood pressure, Plasma NPY and catecholamines during physical exercise in relation to menstrual cycle, ovariectomy, and estrogen replacement. *Regulatory Peptides, 75–76*, 239–45.

Lipschitz, D. S., Rasmusson, A. M., Yehuda, R., Wang, S., Anyan, W., Gueoguieva, R., et al. (2003). Salivary cortisol responses to dexamethasone in adolescents with posttraumatic stress disorder. *Journal of American Academy of Child Adolescent Psychiatry, 42*, 1310–17.

Lundberg, J., Rudehill, A., and Sollevi, A. (1989). Pharmacological characterization of neuropeptide Y and noradrenaline mechanisms in sympathetic control of pig spleen. *European Journal of Pharmacology, 163*, 103–13.

Mattson, M. P., Maudsley, S., and Martin, B. (2004). BDNF and 5-HT: a dynamic duo in age-related neuronal plasticity and neurodegenerative disorders. *Trends of Neuroscience, 27*, 589–94.

Michael, A., Jenaway, A., Paykel, E. S., and Herbert, J. (2000). Altered salivary dehydroepiandrosterone levels in major depression in adults. *Biological Psychiatry, 48*, 989–95.

Mitev, Y. A., Darwish, M., Wolf, S. S., Holsboer, F., Almeida, O. F., and Patchev, V. K. (2003). Gender differences in the regulation of 3 alpha-hydroxysteroid dehydrogenase in rat brain and sensitivity to neurosteroid-mediated stress protection. *Neuroscience, 120*, 541–49.

Morfin, R., and Starka, L. (2001). Neurosteroid 7-hydroxylation products in the brain. *International Review of Neurobiology, 46*, 79–95.

Morgan, C. A. III, Hazlett, G. A., Rasmusson, A., Zimolo, Z., Southwick, S. M., and Charney, D. S. (2004). Relationships among plasma dehydroepiandrosterone sulfate and cortisol levels, symptoms of dissociation and objective performance in humans exposed to acute stress. *Archives of General Psychiatry, 61*, 819–25.

Morgan, C. A. III, Rasmusson, A., Wang, S., Hauger, R., and Hazlett, G. (2002). Neuropeptide-Y, cortisol and subjective distress in humans exposed to acute stress: replication and extension of a previous report. *Biological Psychiatry, 52*(2), 136–42.

Morgan, C. A., Rasmusson, A. M., Winters, B., Hauger, R. L., and Hazlett, G. (2003). Trauma exposure rather than PTSD is associated with reduced baseline plasma neuropeptide-Y levels. *Biological Psychiatry, 54*, 1087–91.

Morgan, C. A. III, Wang, S., Hazlett, G., Rasmusson, A., Anderson, G., and Charney, D. S. (2001). Relationships among cortisol, catecholamines, neuropeptide Y and human performance during uncontrollable stress. *Psychosomatic Medicine, 63*, 412–42.

Morgan, C. A. III, Wang, S., Southwick, S. M., Rasmusson, A., Hauger, R., and Charney, D. S. (2000). Plasma neuropeptide-Y in humans exposed to military survival training. *Biological Psychiatry, 47*, 902–9.

Nakajima, M., Inui, A., Asakawa, A., Momose, K., Ueno, N., Teranishi, A., et al. (1998). Neuropeptide Y produces anxiety via Y2-type receptors. *Peptides, 19*, 359–63.

Neslter, J. E. (1996). Advances in understanding the regulation and biologic actions of dehydroepiandrosterone. *Current Opinion in Endocrinology and Diabetes, 3*, 202–11.

Patchev, V. K., Hassan, A. H., Holsboer, D. F., and Almeida, O. F. (1996). The neurosteroid tetrahydroprogesterone attenuates the endocrine response to stress and exerts glucocorticoid-like effects on vasopressin gene transcription in the rat hypothalamus. *Neuropsychopharmacology, 15*, 533–40.

Patchev, V. K., Shoaib, M., Holsboer, F., and Almeida, O. F. (1994). The neurosteroid tetrahydroprogesterone counteracts corticotropin-releasing hormone-induced anxiety and alters the release and gene expression of corticotropin-releasing hormone in the rat hypothalamus. *Neurosciences, 62*, 265–71.

Pernow, J. (1986). Co-release and functional interactions of neuropeptide Y and noradrenaline in peripheral sympathetic vascular control. *Acta Physiologica Scandinavica Supp., 568*, 1–56.

Pernow, J., and Lundberg, J. (1989). Modulation of noradrenaline and neuropeptide Y (NPY) release in the pig kidney in vivo: involvement of alpha 2, NPY and angiotensin II receptors. *Naunyn-Schmiedebergs Archives Pharmacology, 340*, 379–85.

Pinna, G., Costa, E., and Guidotti, A (2005): Changes in brain testosterone and allopregnanolone biosynthesis elicit aggressive behavior. *Proceedings of the National Academy of Sciences of the United States of America, 102*, 2135–40.

Puia, G., Mienville, J-M., Matsumoto, K., Takahata, H., Watanabe, H., Costa, E., et al. (2003). On the putative physiological role of allopregnanolone on $GABA_A$ receptor function. *Neuropharmacology, 44*, 49–55.

Puia, G., Santi, M. R., Vicini, S., Pritchett, D. B., Purdy, R. H., Paul, S. M., et al. (1990). Neurosteroids act on recombinant human $GABA_A$ receptors. *Neuron, 4*, 759–65.

Purdy, R. H., Morrow, A. L., Moore, P. H. Jr., and Paul, S. M. (1991). Stress-induced elevations of gamma-aminobutyric acid type A receptor-active steroids in the rat brain. *Proceedings of the National Academy of Sciences of the United States of America, 88*, 4553–57.

Rajkowski, J., Majczynski, H., Clayton, E., and Aston-Jones, G. (2004). Activation of monkey locus coeruleus neurons varies with difficulty and performance in a target detection task. *Journal of Neurophysiology, 92*, 361–71.

Rasmusson, A. M., Hauger, R. L., Morgan, C.A. III, Bremner, J. D., Charney, D. S., and Southwick, S. M. (2000). Low baseline and yohimbine-stimulated plasma neuropeptide Y (NPY) in combat-related posttraumatic stress disorder. *Biological Psychiatry, 47*, 526–39.

Rasmusson, A. M., Lipschitz, D. S., Wang, S., Hu, S., Vojvoda, D., Bremner, J. D., et al. (2001). Increased pituitary and adrenal reactivity in premenopausal women with PTSD. *Biological Psychiatry, 50*, 965–77.

Rasmusson, A. M., Pinna, G., Paliwal, P., Weisman, D., Gottschalk, C., Charney, D. S., et al. (2006). Decreased cerebrospinal fluid allopregnanolone levels in women with PTSD. *Biological Psychiatry, 60*, 704–713.

Rasmusson, A. M., Southwick, S. M., Hauger, R. L., and Charney, D. S. (1998). Plasma neuropeptide Y (NPY) increases in response to the alpha2 antagonist yohimbine. *Neuropsychopharmacology, 19*, 95–98.

Rasmusson, A. M., Vasek, J., Lipschitz, D., Mustone, M. E., Vojvoda, D., Shi, Q., et al. (2004). An increased capacity for adrenal DHEA release is associated negatively with avoidance symptoms and negative mood in women with PTSD. *Neuropsychopharmacology, 29*, 1546–57.

Rasmusson, A. M., Vythilingam, M., and Morgan, C. A. III. (2003). The neuroendocrinology of PTSD—new directions. Shalev A. (ed), *CNS Spectrums: The International Journal of Neuropsychiatric Medicine, 8*, 651–67.

Rasmusson, A., Wu, R., Paliwal, P., Anderson, G., and Krishnan-Sarin, S. (2006). Smoking abstinence-induced decreases in the ratio of plasma DHEA to cortisol may predict smoking relapse. A preliminary study. *Psychopharmacology, 186*, 473–80.

Rose, K. A., Stapleton, G., Dott, K., Kieny, M. P., Best, R., Schwarz, M., et al. (1997). Cyp7b, a novel brain cytochrome P450, catalyzes the synthesis of neurosteroids 7alpha-hydroxy dehydroepiandrosterone and 7alpha-hydroxy pregnenolone. *Proceedings of the National Academy of Sciences of the United States of America, 94*, 4925–30.

Rupprecht, R. (2003). Neuroactive steroids: Mechanisms of action and neuropsychopharmacological properties. *Psychoneuroendocrinology, 28*, 139–68.

Schmidt, P. J., Daly, R. C., Bloch, M., Smith, M. J., Danaceau, M. A., St. Clair, L. S., et al. (2005). Rubinow, Dehydroepiandrosterone monotherapy in midlife-onset major and minor depression. *Archives of General Psychiatry, 62*, 154–62.

Shih, C-D., Chan, J. Y. H., and Chan, S. H. H. (1992). Tonic suppression of baroreceptor reflex response by endogenous neuropeptide Y at the nucleus tractus solitarius of the rat. *Neuroscience Letters, 148*, 169–72.

Shine, J., Potter, E. K., Biden, T., Selbie, L. A., and Herzog, H. (1994). Neuropeptide Y and regulation of the cardiovascular system. *Journal of Hypertension, 12*(10), S41–45.

Simms, L. J., Watson, D., and Doebbeling, B. N. (2002). Confirmatory factor analyses of posttraumatic stress symptoms in deployed and nondeployed veterans of the Gulf War. *Journal of Abnormal Psychology, 111*, 637–47.

Sondergaard, H. P., Hansson, L-O., and Theorell, T. (2002). Elevated blood levels of dehydroepiandrosterone sulphate vary with symptom load in posttraumatic stress disorder: findings from a longitudinal study of refugees in Sweden. *Psychotherapy and Psychosomatics, 71*, 298–303.

Southwick, S. M., Krystal, J. H., Morgan, C. A., Johnson, D., Nagy, L. M., Nicolauuo, A., et al. (1993). Abnormal noradrenergic function in posttraumatic stress disorder. *Archives of General Psychiatry, 50*, 266–74.

Southwick, S. M., Rasmusson, A. M., Barron, J., and Arnsten, A. (2005). Neurobiological and neurocognitive alterations in PTSD: a focus on norepinephrine, serotonin, and the HPA axis. In J. Vasterling and C. Brewin (Eds), *Neuropsychology of PTSD* (27–58). New York: Guilford Publications.

Stomati, M., Monteleone, P., Casarosa, E., Quirici, B., Puccetti, S., Bernardi, F., et al. (2000). Six-month oral dehydroepiandrosterone supplementation in early and late postmenopause. *Gynecological Endocrinology, 14*, 342–63.

Strous, R., Maayan, R., Lapidus, R., Stryjer, R., Lustig, M., Kotler, M., et al. (2003). Dehydroepiandrosterone augmentation in the management of negative, depressive, and anxiety symptoms in schizophrenia. *Archives of General Psychiatry, 60*, 33–141.

Thorsell, A., Svensson, P., Wiklund, L., Sommer, W., Ekman, R., and Heilig, M. (1998). Suppressed neuropeptide Y (NPY) mRNA in rat amygdala following restraint stress. *Regulatory Peptides, 75–76*, 247–54.

Tobler, P. N., Fiorillo, C. D., and Schultz, W. (2005). Adaptive coding of reward value by dopamine neurons. *Science, 307*, 1642–45.

Ulman, L. G., Potter, I. K., McCloskey, D. I., and Morris, M. J. (1997). Post-exercise depression of baroreflex slowing of the heart in humans. *Clinical Physiology, 17*, 299–309.

Vallee, M., Rivera, J. D., Koob, G. F., Purdy, R. H., and Fitzgerald, R. (2000). Quantification of neurosteroids in rat plasma and brain following swim stress and allopregnanolone administration using negative chemical ionization gas chromatography/mass spectrometry. *Analytical Biochemistry, 287*, 153–66.

Van Haarst, A. D., Oitzl, M. S., Workel, J. O., and DeKloet, E. R. (1996). Chronic brain glucocorticoid receptor blockade enhances the rise in circadian and stress-induced pituitary-adrenal activity. *Endocrinology, 137*, 4935–43.

Wahlestedt, C., and Reis, D. (1993). Neuropeptide Y-related peptides and their receptors—are the receptors potential therapeutic drug targets? *Annual Reviews of Pharmacology and Toxicology, 32*, 309–52.

Wang, H., Napoli, K. L., and Strobel, H. W. (2000). Cytochrome P450 3A9 catalyzes the metabolism of progesterone and other steroid hormones. *Molecular Cellular Biochemistry, 213*, 127–35.

Wolkowitz, O. M., Reus, V. I., Keebler, A., Nelson, N., Friedland, M., Brizendine, L. et al. (1999). Double-blind treatment of major depression with dehydroepiandrosterone. *American Journal of Psychiatry, 156*, 646–49.

Yaffe, K., Ettinger, B., Pressman, A., Seeley, D., Whooley, M., Schaefer, C., et al. (1998). Neuropsychiatric function and dehydroepiandrosterone sulfate in elderly women: A prospective study. *Biological Psychiatry, 43*, 694–700.

Yehuda, R. (2002). Current status of cortisol findings in post-traumatic stress disorder. *Psychiatric Clinics of North America, 25*, 341–68.

———. (2006). Advances in understanding neuroendocrine alterations in PTSD and their therapeutic implications. *Annals of the New York Academy of Sciences, 1071*, 137–66.

Yehuda, R., Brand, S. R., Golier, J. A., and Yang, R. K. (2006). Clinical correlates of DHEA associated with post-traumatic stress disorder. *Acta Psychiatrica Scandinavica, 114*, 187–93.

Young, A. H., Gallagher, P., and Porter, R. J. (2002). Elevation of the cortisol-dehydroepiandrosterone ratio in drug-free depressed patients. *American Journal of Psychiatry, 159,* 1237–39.

Young, E. A., and Breslau, N. (2004). Cortisol and catecholamines in posttraumatic stress disorder: An epidemiologic community study. *Archives of General Psychiatry, 61,* 394–401.

Zhang, L., Li, B., Ma, W., Barker, J. L., Chang, Y. H., and Zhao, W. (2002). Dehydroepiandrosterone (DHEA) and its sulfated derivative (DHEAS) regulate apoptosis during neurogenesis by triggering the Akt signaling pathway in opposing ways. *Brain Research Molecular, 98,* 58–66.

Zukowska-Grojec, Z. (1995). Neuropeptide Y. A novel sympathetic stress hormone and more. *Annals of the New York Academy of Science, 771,* 219–33.

Zuspan, F. P., and Zuspan, K. J. (1973). Ovulatory plasma amine (epinephrine and norepinephrine) surges in the woman. *American Journal of Obstetrics and Gynecology, 117,* 654–61.

# 8

## Age-Related Changes in Neuroendocrine, Cognitive, and Neuroanatomic Aspects of PTSD

*Rachel Yehuda*

### INTRODUCTION

One of the underlying principles of the chapters presented in this volume is that phenomenologic and biologic studies of PTSD generally present a static picture of pathophysiology. However, PTSD symptoms can change over time, raising the possibility that biologic correlates of PTSD can also change with time, and/or in association with aging. Since PTSD may affect age-related psychological or medical conditions, it is necessary to understand its pathophysiology as it continues to develop and change over the lifespan. The question of whether and how biologic markers of PTSD pathophysiology change in relation to age is particularly interesting since at least three important biological domains that have been implicated in PTSD pathophysiology—relating to neuroendocrine, cognitive, and neuroanatomic measures—are also associated with normal aging, but in different ways. Thus, one question that arises concerns how changes associated with normal aging are superimposed on biological parameters associated with PTSD. This question can be best answered by longitudinal studies of aging persons with PTSD, but these are very scarce. Longitudinal biologic studies are even more scant (with the exception of those to be reviewed below). In the absence of such studies, much can be learned by cross-sectional analyses of the relationships among cognitive, endocrine, and neuroanatomic measures in aging trauma survivors with and without PTSD. This chapter will present a review of some of our work in this area. Since we have generally utilized similar protocols to those used in

Address correspondence to Rachel Yehuda, Ph.D. ; Bronx VA OOMH; 130 West Kingsbridge Road; Bronx, NY 10468. E-mail: Rachel.Yehuda@med.va.gov studies of younger persons with PTSD, it is possible to speculate about possible age-related differences in these domains, and generate hypotheses about the nature of longitudinal change in these measures.

## DOES PTSD GET BETTER OR WORSE WITH AGE?

Both longitudinal (Tennant et al., 1997) and cross-sectional (Fontana and Rosenheck, 1994) studies have demonstrated that PTSD symptoms diminish in severity in association with aging. For example, one prospective longitudinal study found a marked diminution in the percent of subjects meeting criteria for PTSD forty and fifty years following exposure compared to earlier time points (Kluznik, Speed, Van Valkenburg, and Magraw, 1986). In our own studies of Holocaust survivors we similarly noticed that older subjects tended to endorse mild to moderate symptom severity on diagnostic assessments rather than symptom severity in the extreme range (Yehuda, Kahana, Binder-Byrnes, et al., 1995; Yehuda, Kahana, Schmeidler, et al., 1995; Yehuda, Schmeidler, et al., 1997). This finding contradicted our experience with treatment-seeking Vietnam combat veterans, who generally reported higher PTSD symptom severity as measured by the same instruments (e.g., the Clinician Administered PTSD Scale [Blake et al., 1995]). In that we had recruited from a non-treatment-seeking community-dwelling sample, we attributed the rather moderate symptom severity in Holocaust survivors with PTSD (4–5 on a scale of 1–8) to cohort differences in treatment seeking. However, as we began to recruit from a treatment-seeking cohort (once we had established a clinic for Holocaust survivors at the Mount Sinai School of Medicine), we were able to confirm that even treatment-seeking Holocaust survivors with PTSD showed relatively lower CAPS scores than what we had noted in younger combat Vietnam veterans (Yehuda, Golier, Halligan, and Harvey, 2004; Golier et al., 2002). Moreover, studies of aging combat veterans—treatment-seeking at the VA—demonstrated CAPS scores in the same range as Holocaust survivors (e.g., Yehuda, Halligan, Grossman, et al., 2002). Putting these findings together, it appeared to us, at least impressionistically, that CAPS scores were lower in older PTSD subjects, consistent with an age-related decline in symptom severity. Yet only a longitudinal study could confirm this impression.

Interestingly, though CAPS scores were in the moderate range, it was clear to us that many older trauma survivors were quite symptomatic on both self-report and interviewer-rated measures of depression and anxiety. Thus, by contrast, PTSD scores seemed to suggest a lower level of severity than that obtained on other more general measures of state depression and anxiety. As we began to analyze this more carefully, we wondered whether some of the relatively reduced PTSD symptom scores were a function of how difficult it was to discern "symptoms" from what had become stable traits. For example, one Korean War veteran seemed extremely perplexed by the question on the CAPS of whether the respondent had experienced less interest in activities he used to enjoy before the trauma. "You mean, like baseball?" he asked. Another Holocaust survivor answered the question about if she felt there was no need to plan for the future (i.e., foreshortened sense of future), by explaining that, at her age, she didn't really make plans knowing that "anything could happen" that might disrupt them. Even intrusive symptoms were harder to measure because survivors indicated they had "gotten used to" such memories, and, in some cases, the constant reminders of the past, and even the distress that such reminders brought, became so routine as to render it difficult to differentiate these experiences from what might have been their functioning prior to trauma exposure.

Indeed, when the decades of life since the trauma well exceed those that preceded the trauma, there are unique challenges in trying to identify a symptom—generally conceptualized as a change from a known baseline—from what has become internalized as fact of the survivor's existence. Furthermore, the extraordinarily positive coping traits that survivors often endorse, and/or the stoicism or acceptance of chronic symptoms as a fact of life, can make it difficult to determine the extent of symptoms and their attendant disability, and might, in some cases, lead to diminished urgency with respect to mental health treatment of these symptoms. It therefore becomes important to examine not only alternate methods of the assessment of PTSD symptomatology in older trauma survivors, but also changes in pathophysiology.

## GAPS IN OUR UNDERSTANDING OF THE LONGITUDINAL COURSE OF SYMPTOM CHANGE

In addition to the difficulty inherent in differentiating "symptoms" from stable traits, there are other challenges in both cross-sectional and longitudinal evaluation of the long-term effects of trauma exposure. One such major challenge is that survivors are often classified based on the presence or absence of PTSD (measured either at a random interval posttrauma, or reflecting a retrospective assessment). Even if symptoms are quantified accurately, this classification can present a false dichotomy. Because the diagnosis of PTSD requires a specified number of symptoms in each of the three core clusters, people who fail to meet diagnostic criteria for PTSD may be very symptomatic within a narrower range of symptoms, while those qualifying based on the required number and constellation of symptoms may express mild severity. The potential overlap in symptom severity based on the PTSD dichotomy can obscure group differences. Accordingly, PTSD severity can be a dimensional, rather than categorical, variable in biological studies. To the extent that biological measures reflect normal stress physiology, correlations with symptom severity would be expected. However, if this alteration reflects a pathophysiological process, its relationship with symptom severity may not be linear across trauma survivors.

In addition to the issue of the overlap in symptoms based on the dichotomous classification of PTSD, evaluating biological alterations in PTSD, whether dimensionally or categorically, can also be challenging in cross-sectional biological studies that do not consider PTSD status in the context of the longitudinal course of a person's illness, since it may be important to differentiate between people who develop and sustain PTSD, who develop but then recover, and who never develop symptoms. In cross-sectional studies, the latter two groups can be similar in current symptom severity, but, since they represent different lifespan trajectories, may show distinct biological profiles when observed longitudinally (Yehuda and Flory, at press). In longitudinal studies there is also the additional trajectory of developing delayed PTSD or redeveloping this condition after a sustained remission. Failing to distinguish between factors that predict stable outcomes and those that reflect capacity to change may constitute a source of biological heterogeneity in trauma exposed subjects with or without PTSD. For example, biological alterations associated with risk for developing PTSD (e.g., smaller hippocampal volume; low IQ) may be present in a non-PTSD group that is comprised of persons that once had, but then recovered from, PTSD, or even persons who have not yet been exposed to trauma. It is important to keep these different lifespan trajectories in mind, even in studies that do not purport to address aging per se so as to differentiate measures that are associated with risk for, or resistance to PTSD, symptom severity, and recovery.

## CONCEPTUAL SUPPORT FOR PREDICTING A SUPERIMPOSITION OF AGING AND PTSD

A prevailing theory of aging explains normal cognitive decline in the elderly as resulting from hippocampal atrophy induced by age-related increases in glucocorticoid release (Sapolsky, 2000; Miller and O'Callaghan, 2005). This theory is supported by reductions in hippocampal size observed in longitudinal studies of normal aging (Lupien et al., 1998; Golomb et al., 1994). Smaller hippocampal volumes have been associated with both cognitive decline (De

Leon et al., 1997; Rusinek et al., 2003) and high levels of cortisol (Lupien et al., 1998; O'Brien, Lloyd, McKeith, Gholkar, and Ferrier, 2004). While PTSD has also been associated with smaller hippocampal volume (Kitayama, Vaccarino, Kutner, Weiss, and Bremner, 2005; Shin et al., 2004) and poor memory performance (Horner and Hamner, 2002; Buckley, Blanchard, and Neill, 2000), these are not generally accompanied by high levels of cortisol. In fact, the causal relationships among neuroendocrine, cognitive, and neuroanatomic alterations in PTSD have been more difficult to establish in cross-sectional studies of PTSD subjects than in studies of aging, but the correlations among these measures are certainly not similar in younger PTSD subjects as they are in normal aged subjects (Neylan et al., 2003; Yehuda, 1999). For this reason, there is much to learn about PTSD pathophysiology by studying aged subjects.

It could be assumed that the same changes in neuroendocrine, cognitive, and neuroanatomic measures observed in normal aging are applicable in persons with PTSD. If so, it would be reasonable to speculate that lower cortisol in PTSD might protect trauma survivors from damaging effects of age-related hippocampal atrophy and memory decline. Alternatively, in PTSD there might be accelerated age-related memory impairments, due to smaller hippocampal volume and/or poor cognitive functioning relatively early in life. These might be exacerbated by increased glucocorticoid receptor sensitivity, even in the absence of high cortisol levels. However, it is not clear that aging subjects with PTSD demonstrate similar relationships among neuroendocrine, cognitive, and neuroanatomic measures as the normal elderly. This is a gap that must be filled by studies of aging trauma survivors. As a first step to such studies, it is useful to delineate differences in PTSD related measures in young vs. older subjects, or at least to generate hypotheses about the specific dimensions in PTSD that are most vulnerable to age-related effects. These are, of course, related to neuroendocrine, cognitive, and neuroanatomic alterations.

## NEUROENDOCRINE (HPA) ALTERATIONS IN PTSD

Our prior work in younger trauma survivors with PTSD suggested that PTSD is associated with increased glucocorticoid responsiveness, even though ambient levels of cortisol are not elevated compared to controls, and are often even lower than in healthy controls (Yehuda, Teicher, Trestman, et al., 1996; Yehuda et al., 1990; Yehuda, 2002). Increased glucocorticoid responsiveness has been demonstrated by *in vivo* (Yehuda, Boisoneau, Lowy, and Giller, 1995; Yehuda et al., 1993) and *in vitro* (Yehuda, Golier, Yang, and Tischler,

2004) studies using DST in PTSD compared to controls. An augmented ACTH response to metyrapone administration in high enough doses to completely suppress cortisol production for several hours was also reported in combat Vietnam veterans compared to controls (Yehuda, Levengood, et al., 1996) consistent with observations of increased corticotropin releasing factor (CRF) release in PTSD (Bremner et al., 1997; Baker et al., 1999; Sautter et al., 2003). One interpretation of these findings is that under ambient conditions, CRF hypersecretion does not culminate in cortisol hypersecretion due to increased cortisol negative feedback inhibition, which could readily be achieved if GR were more responsive to glucocorticoids (Yehuda, 2002). Although a competing explanation for lower cortisol levels in the face of increased CRF levels in PTSD is that of a reduced adrenal activity (Kanter et al., 2001), this possibility has not been supported by the demonstration that the ACTH-to-cortisol ratio does not differ between PTSD and comparison subjects before or after the administration of 0.50 mg DEX. Indeed, if low cortisol levels reflected reduced activity, the administration of DEX might preferentially affect the adrenal and pituitary glands (Yehuda, Golier, Halligan, Meaney, et al., 2004).

It is certainly the case that cortisol levels have not been found to be lower than comparisons in all studies of PTSD, nor even in all studies of combat veterans (Bremner et al., 1997; Bachmann et al., 2005; Pitman and Orr, 1990). Even in studies where lower cortisol levels in PTSD have been reported, the effect sizes have been modest (Boscarino, 1996). This may reflect that cortisol levels are only prominent in subgroups of PTSD, or that cortisol levels vary in relation to type and severity of trauma, age at traumatization, duration of PTSD, current age, or other individual differences, or even PTSD risk factors (e.g., gender, smoking status, medication use, BMI, parental PTSD status, or other relevant family history) (Yehuda, Morris, Labinsky, Zemelman, and Schmeidler, at press; Resnick et al., 1995; Yehuda, Golier, and Kaufman, 2005). However, what has been most interesting about the HPA axis findings in younger combat veterans is that there appears to be a discrepancy between the increased CRF levels in PTSD, reflecting central neuroendocrine overactivity, and ACTH and cortisol levels, which are not comparably increased. Together, these findings suggest that there may be differences in cortisol regulation in PTSD resulting from enhanced glucocorticoid responsiveness, altered cortisol metabolism or signaling, and/or other regulatory influences originating within or outside of the HPA axis.

Since cortisol exerts its effects by binding to, and activating, Type II GRs (de Kloet, Joels, Oitzl, and Sutanto, 1991), our group was initially interested in examining the responsiveness of these receptors as a way of understanding the low and sometimes normal cortisol levels in the face of increased

CRF release. Once receptors are maximally activated, other steps proceed in this cascade. Accordingly, if a decreased number or sensitivity of GR accompanies high circulating cortisol levels, this might protect against some of the potentially damaging effects of cortisol. Conversely, increasing the responsiveness of the system might amplify the deleterious effects of even low levels of cortisol. In theory (e.g., in healthy controls), circulating cortisol levels should be inversely related to GR number and sensitivity, as steroid receptors are partially regulated by circulating hormone concentrations (Zhou and Cidlowski, 2005). In practice, these two measures are not always associated. In Cushing's disorder, GR number does not decrease in relation to cortisol increases, amplifying the effects of hypercortisolism (Huizenga et al., 2000). In major depression (MDD), however, CRF hypersecretion leads to both increased cortisol and reduced number and responsiveness of GR (e.g., as measured by a diminished cortisol suppression to DEX), which is thought to prevent patients from the development of Cushingoid stigmata (Neigh and Nemeroff, 2006; Juruena, Cleare, and Pariante, 2004). Thus, it is critical to evaluate the potential impact of cortisol in the context of understanding glucocorticoid and GR responsiveness.

The effects of cortisol have generally been linked with hippocampal damage and cognitive impairment. Cortisol presumably accomplishes these effects by stimulating events that impair activities of neurons that prevent neuronal degeneration (McEwen and Sapolsky, 1995). For example, high levels of cortisol inhibit glucose transport, depriving brain regions of the energy needed for oxidative damage repair, a process that forestalls cell death (Sapolsky, 1994). High levels of cortisol can also result in metabolic changes that increase the need for protection of hippocampal neurons since, quite independently of its effects on glucose, cortisol levels initiate a cascade of events that result in preventing the removal of glutamate from synapses, which then increases activation of N-methyl-D-aspartate (NMDA) receptors, increases intracellular calcium, and ultimately increases the production of the oxygen radicals that need to be removed with increased energy that is no longer available because of direct effects of cortisol on glucose transport (Landfield and Eldridge, 1994). Of note, blocking NMDA receptors with dilantin reverses hippocampal atrophy and the associated memory impairments (Watanabe et al., 1992). This indicates that there are causes of hippocampal neuronal loss more proximal than high cortisol levels, and possibly even independent of them. Thus, it is at least theoretically possible that the smaller hippocampal volume observed in PTSD (summarized below) reflects altered mechanisms other than high cortisol. Furthermore, with aging, there may be different associations between cortisol levels and parameters reflecting the hippocampus or related structures. The hippocampus is vulnerable to these effects of cortisol because it is an area that is unusually rich in Type II GRs (Juruena et al., 2004; McEwen and Sapolsky, 1995; Sapolsky, 1994; Land-field and Eldridge, 1994). An increased number of GRs in the hippocampus could facilitate all the biological events described above even in the absence of high cortisol. On the other hand, low cortisol levels over the longitudinal course of a person's life might eventually result in neuroprotection with respect to hippocampal damage or other adverse metabolic effects.

## HPA ALTERATIONS IN AGING AND OLDER PERSONS WITH PTSD

Neuroendocrine alterations associated with aging are generally opposite of those reported in PTSD. Aging is associated with decreased circadian rhythm due to increased levels of cortisol at the trough of the diurnal cycle (Van Cauter, Leproult, and Kupfer, 1996; Deuschle et al., 1997; Dori et al., 1994; Dallman et al., 1987). Some studies examining the cortisol response to DEX in the elderly have shown a reduced feedback sensitivity (Zimmerman and Coryell, 1987), but frank hypercortisolism is not commonly associated with age, except in very aged normal individuals (Halbreich et al., 1984). The relatively stable cortisol levels over the normal life span may be due to compensatory changes in the clearance and production of cortisol (Deuschle et al., 1997; Dori et al., 1994; Dallman et al., 1987; Zimmerman and Coryell, 1987; Halbreich et al., 1984). Emerging work does appear to identify a distinct pattern of HPA axis alterations in elderly trauma survivors with PTSD. In particular, we observed that older trauma survivors with PTSD showed a flattening of the circadian rhythm of cortisol, which is similar to what has been described in normal aging but overall levels of cortisol remained lower than normal (Yehuda, Teicher, Golier, and Bierer, in preparation; Yehuda, Golier, and Kaufman, 2005). Other HPA axis alterations, such as the percent suppression of cortisol following DEX administration were still present in older trauma survivors with PTSD, similar to what has been reported in younger survivors (Yehuda et al., 2002). Thus, older subjects with PTSD appear to have neuroendocrine features of both PTSD and aging.

In a recently completed ten-year longitudinal study of cortisol levels in aging Holocaust survivors we demonstrated a strong correlation between cortisol levels at initial assessment and follow-up, and a general decline in cortisol levels in Holocaust survivors who maintained their diagnostic status or developed PTSD (subjects whose diagnostic status changed from meeting to not meeting criteria for PTSD at follow-up showed increased cortisol levels from their baseline assessment). At the ten-year follow-up, there appeared to be less of a gap between cortisol levels in Holocaust survivors with and without PTSD (Yehuda and Flory, at press). These findings are comparable to a cross-sectional study of salivary cortisol over the circadian cycle since that study demonstrated that while Holocaust survivors with PTSD showed significantly lower cortisol levels than non-exposed subjects, cortisol levels in Holocaust survivors with and without PTSD were not significantly different (Yehuda, Golier, and Kaufman, 2005). Interestingly, in the longitudinal study, cortisol levels at the initial assessment were strongly predictive of improvement in clinical status at the follow-up. Thus, cortisol levels in trauma survivors may influence the longitudinal course of PTSD and/or interactions between PTSD and age-related neuroendocrine alterations.

## NEUROCOGNITIVE FINDINGS IN PTSD: ARE THERE AGING EFFECTS?

Most, but not all, investigators have found evidence of significant cognitive deficits in combat PTSD using standard neuropsychological tests, primarily in measures related to verbal learning, attention, and working memory (Vasterling et al., 2002; Sachinvala et al., 2000; Gilbertson et al., 2001; Barrett, Green, Morris, Giles, and Croft, 1996; Golier et al., 1997; Yehuda, Keefe, et al., 1995; Jelinek et al., 2006; Gurvits et al., 1993; Neylan et al., 2004). It is noteworthy that similar to the issues that have been raised by the cortisol findings in PTSD, there are questions regarding whether neuropsychological impairments observed in PTSD are fundamentally related to trauma exposure/PTSD or reflect pretraumatic risk. It has long been known, for example, that (pretrauma) low IQ is a risk factor for PTSD. More recently, an examination of Vietnam veterans and non-exposed co-twins found evidence to support the idea that some cognitive alterations associated with PTSD may have predated trauma exposure, serving as risk factors rather than consequences of trauma (Gilbertson et al., 2006).

Our recent longitudinal data on Holocaust survivors demonstrate that changes in at least some cognitive parameters over time are associated with changes in symptom severity in the direction that symptom improvement is associated with improvement in memory performance over time (Yehuda, Tischler, et al., 2006). These parameters reflect cognitive alterations in attention and long-delay recall that have also been noted in younger trauma survivors with PTSD, and are in contrast to cognitive deficits we have observed that are associated with aging or superimposition of aging and PTSD (Golier et al., 2002; Golier, Yehuda, Lupien, and Harvey, 2003). Furthermore, a recent study of Iraqi war veterans looking at pre- and post-deployment found decrements in cognitive performance related to war zone severity (Vasterling et al., 2006). Since changes in cognitive variables can occur in relation to exposure, symptom severity, and age, it seems that those who have not recovered from PTSD could be differentiated from other veterans on cognitive performance later in life. However, the issues involved in evaluating age effects are complex. Since there are effects of glucocorticoids with age in PTSD (described above), and since cognitive performance is thought to be influenced by glucocorticoids (described below), it is of interest to determine whether subjects with current or lifetime PTSD will show different patterns of cognitive performance in relation to symptom trajectories and/or age than neuroendocrine parameters.

## COGNITIVE AND HIPPOCAMPAL
## MEASURES IN AGING COMBAT VETERANS

We initially examined the memory performance of older combat veterans because results in Holocaust survivors demonstrated a greater range of memory deficits in PTSD than we had previously reported in younger combat veterans, including differences on variables associated with age-related hippocampal volume decline. Similar to Holocaust survivors (Yehuda, Harvey, Buchsbaum, et al., at press), older combat veterans with PTSD showed greater impairments in total learning than comparison subjects that were not accounted for by differences in immediate recall (Yehuda, Golier, Tischler, Stavitsky, and Harvey, 2005). We had previously reported that younger veterans with PTSD showed normal abilities in recall, acquisition of memory, cumulative learning, and active interference from previous learning, all measured by the California Verbal Learning Test (CVLT), but differed from non-exposed controls only in the decrement in retention observed following exposure to an intervening word list (i.e., retroactive interference) (Yehuda, Keefe, et al., 1995). In contrast, older PTSD subjects showed alterations on all of the above-mentioned variables compared to controls, except immediate recall. Thus, the cognitive alterations observed in younger combat veterans did not necessarily reflect PTSD related alterations that were observed in older subjects with PTSD.

More recently, we found that older combat veterans with PTSD also differed on several cognitive measures that are thought to recruit the hippocampus at any age and to be sensitive to the effects of glucocorticoids, compared to veterans without PTSD (Yehuda, Golier, Tischler, et al., 2005). We had also examined these same tests in younger veterans (Grossman et al., 2006), and table 8.1 below demonstrates the comparison between the older and younger sample. Three tests were used: the Wechsler Logical Memory Test

(LMT), the Digit Span Forward Test (DSF), and the Letter Number Sequencing (LNS). The LMT, a test of declarative memory, measures initial and delayed learning of information, as well as retention, reflected by the percent of correctly recalled items at delay compared to those initially recalled. The DSF measures attention, and the LNS measures working memory. Data from the older subjects (mean age, 62.7 ± 8.9; range, fifty-three to eighty-one) are presented in Yehuda, Harvey, Buchsbaum, et al. (at press). The younger subjects (mean age, 35.9 ± 6.7; range twenty-four to fifty-nine) represent a cohort that was studied using the identical protocol on which cognitive measures were recently reported (Grossman et al., 2006). Table 8.1 clearly demonstrates the superimposition of PTSD and aging effects on measures where there were substantial differences between the young and old cohorts and also group differences related to presence or absence of PTSD (i.e., delayed recall, percent savings at delay, and working memory). In contrast, attention was associated with PTSD, but not age. None of these variables were altered by age in the absence of PTSD. There were no interactions between age cohort and PTSD, thus the effects were comparable in their associations with worse cognitive performance. Similar to what had been observed in another younger cohort reported above, there were no group or age effects on immediate recall. These data provide the basis for the assumption that there are specific cognitive impairments associated with PTSD and aging.

## HIPPOCAMPAL ALTERATIONS IN PTSD: ARE THERE ASSOCIATIONS WITH AGE?

Although it is clear that normal aging is associated with hippocampal atrophy, the three studies which have examined older trauma survivors with current or lifetime PTSD have not demonstrated PTSD-related volume deficits in comparison to a non-exposed, similarly aged comparison group. Our group published two studies—one in combat veterans (Yehuda et al., 2007) and one in Holocaust survivors (Golier, Yehuda, DeSanti, et al., 2005). A recent report also failed to find lower hippocampal volume or N-acetylaspartate (NAA) levels in former prisoners of war and concluded that this was evidence of resilience (Freeman et al., 2006). It may be that different biologic alterations associated with trauma exposure have different trajectories. Thus, smaller hippocampal volumes in PTSD may be evident at a time at which healthy subjects are not manifesting atrophy. Furthermore, the alterations associated with atrophy may persist even if discrepancies between groups in hippocampal volume become less prominent over time. This can only be confirmed by performing longitudinal examinations. The idea that a biologic alteration may be

**Table 8.1. Cognitive Measures of Younger and Older Subjects With and Without PTSD. This table presents the mean and standard error for scores on cognitive tests in older and younger subjects with and without PTSD at baseline. The last three columns presents the main effects of age, group, and age x group. There was no interaction of age x group for any of the cognitive measures, however several measures had a main effect of age and group.**

| Measure | PTSD Young n = 15 | Control Young n = 11 | PTSD Older n = 13 | Control Older n = 17 | Main Effect of Cohort | Main Effect of Group | Interaction |
|---|---|---|---|---|---|---|---|
| Imm Recall | 13.8 ± 1.03 | 15.27 ± 1.12 | 12.23 ± 1.07 | 13.18 ± 1.00 | n.s. | n.s. | n.s. |
| Del Recall | 13.27 ± 4.73 | 15.36 ± 2.77 | 9.54 ± 4.65 | 12.12 ± 4.17 | .004 | .046 | n.s. |
| % Saving | 95.43 ± 12.39 | 101.83 ± 11.23 | 75.9 ± 19.76 | 92.63 ± 15.30 | .001 | .007 | n.s. |
| Attention | 10.2 ± 1.86 | 11.5 ± 2.84 | 8.69 ± 3.52 | 10.82 ± 2.3 | n.s. | .019 | n.s. |
| Working | 11.07 ± 1.82 | 12.92 ± 4.03 | 7.69 ± 3.4 | 9.59 ± 2.3 | .022 | .000 | n.s. |

present at an earlier but not a later point in the course of illness, or vice versa, has important implications for understanding risk and pathophysiology of this disorder, and differentiating the effects of trauma from those of PTSD.

## FUNCTIONAL ROLE OF THE HIPPOCAMPUS AND OTHER BRAIN REGIONS IN COGNITION: ARE THERE DIFFERENT ASSOCIATIONS RELATED TO TRAUMA AND/OR PTSD?

Almost all cited studies of hippocampal volume in PTSD have posited associations between hippocampal volumes and cognitive deficits in declarative and working memory (and/or attention), but only rarely have studies actually observed such a correlation between hippocampal volume and memory deficits (Lindauer et al., 2006; McNally and Shin, 1995). In contrast, an association between hippocampal volume decline and cognitive deficits in normal aging has been repeatedly observed in the literature as described above. Thus, it is entirely possible that hippocampal volume and memory-related measures are different in subjects with PTSD compared to those who do not develop this disorder. In this context, it must be mentioned that other brain areas are also important in memory and PTSD. The medial orbitofrontal cortex and anterior cingulate gyrus are regions that inhibit excitatory output of the amygdala in response to fear (which generates emotional memory) (Shin et al., 1997). Thus, decreased activity in these brain regions could have a disinhibiting effect on the amygdala and again result in an increased fear response through inadequate responsive inhibition. These responses, in turn, could affect new learning. The role of the anterior cingulate in failing to disinhibit the amygdala has been confirmed by PET neuroimaging (Shin et al., 1999; Liberzon, Britton, and Phan, 2003). As different brain regions, including the amygdala and anterior cingulate, are identified as important areas in PTSD, it is possible to make a case for an a priori examination of these areas, in tandem with the hippocampus, in searching for brain regions that might be associated with memory-related alterations in PTSD. Moreover, given that different brain areas act to inhibit or facilitate brain centers associated with memory impairment in PTSD, knowledge of the impact of glucocorticoids would be incomplete without information relating to multiple brain regions.

## GLUCOCORTICOIDS AFFECT MEMORY AND THE BRAIN

Studies examining the effects of cortisol on human memory show dose-dependent effects of glucocorticoids on memory though the relationship is not necessarily linear; higher doses can lead either to a greater effect or a different effect than lower doses. For example, in a controlled trial of cortisol (40 and 160 mg/day) in healthy subjects, the higher dose produced reversible decreases in verbal declarative memory without effects on nonverbal memory, sustained, or selective attention as compared with a lower dose and placebo (Newcomer et al., 1999). In another study, early recall was facilitated by all doses used whereas later recall was facilitated by treatment with higher doses and impaired by lower doses (Beckwith et al., 1986).

However, dose differences do not completely account for the discrepancies in the literature regarding the effects of glucocorticoids in humans. Timing of glucocorticoid administration also has an effect. A recent meta-analysis demonstrated that when cortisol was administered before memory retrieval a significant decrease in performance was found, whereas when it was administered before learning such an effect was not observed (Het, Ramlow, and Wolf, 2005). Cortisol effects may also be related to specific memory tasks. Recently, it has been posited that the discrepancies in part relate to the phases of memory tested, that administration of glucocorticoids impairs recall of previously learned information but enhances the formation of new memories (Roozendaal, Hahn, Nathan, de Quervain, and McGaugh, 2004). Thus, there is substantial support for the proposition that glucocorticoids impair or improve memory performance depending on dose, timing, task, and probably also the person to whom glucocorticoids are being administered. Indeed, individual differences, including clinical status, appear to be important factors in predicting the response to glucocorticoids. For example, age may emerge as another important variable influencing response, though few studies have directly investigated the effects of hydrocortisone on cognitive functioning in the healthy elderly. One study of normal elderly subjects showed no significant adverse effects of cortisol on a range of cognitive functions (Porter, Barnett, Iey, McGuckin, and O'Brien, 2002). DEX has been shown to have a beneficial effect on memory performance in depression (Bremner, Vythilingam, Vermetten, Anderson, et al., 2004), a deleterious effect on healthy volunteers, but no effect in PTSD (Bremner, Vythilingam, Vermetten, Afzal, et al., 2004). These findings support the theory that cortisol's effects on memory depend on ambient hormone levels. In elderly subjects with a five-year history of moderate cortisol levels, metyrapone treatment, which acutely *decreases* cortisol, significantly impaired memory performance, while in elderly subjects with a five-year history of high cortisol levels, cortisol administration treatment decreased delayed memory (Lupien et al., 2002). This literature highlights that glucocorticoid effects on memory function in aging depend on ambient HPA axis activity, and also on the ability of the organism to efficiently generate a cortisol response to stress (that serves to mobilize glucose utilization and promote several other functions related to cortisol's facilitation or interference with memory processing).

It is also important to recognize that in addition to having dose and time-related effects, glucocorticoids have different effects in different brain regions (Swanson and Simmons, 1989). For example, glucocorticoids suppress hippocampal glucose metabolism and blood flow in the hippocampus, consistent with the hippocampus as a major organ involved in restraining the HPA axis, but increase activation in other brain areas such as the amygdala, anterior cingulate, and orbitofrontal area (Landgraf, Mitro, and Hess, 1978; Freo et al., 1992). The site-specific effects of glucocorticoid activation have important implications for behavioral and cognitive functions that are mediated by these brain regions. There has been great interest in the idea that extreme stress (via exposure to glucocorticoids) may damage the human brain (i.e., the hippocampus), and this has been supported by animal studies of chronic stress (McEwen, Gould, and Sakai, 1992), and some human studies of PTSD (Starkman et al., 1992). However, it is critical to understand that cortisol's role in the brain is not always toxic or detrimental just because it is released when individuals are under stress. The release of cortisol in response to stress organizes physiological and cognitive responses to stress stimuli and precipitates the regulation of various important neuropeptide systems (e.g., brain CRF, neuropeptide Y, serotonin, norepinephrine, and glutamate) that ultimately help organisms preserve physiological homeostasis (Erickson, Drevets, and Schulkin, 2003). Glucocorticoids also play a role in promoting arousal and attention (Schmidt et al., 1997), which are thought to allow mobilization of cognitive resources and increase survival through enhanced memory for emotionally arousing events. Further, glucocorticoids are involved in anticipation (Schmidt et al., 1999), which promotes focused attention and memory. Thus, it is not without foundation that under some circumstances the administration of glucocorticoids might have beneficial effects.

Cortisol's faciliatory effects on memory at moderate doses have been shown to involve interactions between the basal lateral amygdala, basal ganglia, and hippocampus (Akirav and Richter-Levin, 2002; Roozendaal, 2000). The detrimental effects of cortisol, which have been highlighted by the effects of chronic stress in promoting atrophy of the CA3 region of Ammon's horn in the hippocampus, only occur in response to sustained cortisol increases (Sapolsky, 2000). Furthermore, the mechanisms that might promote neuronal atrophy are different than those involving glucocorticoid effects on memory (Yehuda, 2001). Neural atrophy in the hippocampus appears to be mediated via facilitation of excitatory amino acid-mediated toxicity, whereas glucocorticoids' role in memory appear to depend on glucocorticoid activity in the basolateral amygdala (Spiro, Schnurr, and Aldwin, 1994). What has been more unclear is an understanding of whether effects of glucocorticoids are dependent on the responsiveness of GR, which we believe is enhanced in PTSD. Our studies have been limited to measuring Type II GR activity on human lymphocytes. However, if there were a corresponding change in GR sensitivity in the brain in humans, as has been demonstrated in rats (Lowy, 1989), this could amplify both the positive and negative effects of cortisol even if cortisol levels were not increased (Zhang, Zhou, Li, Ursano, and Li, 2006). For cortisol to exert any of its actions, it must bind to, and activate, Type II GRs. This is the necessary first step in the cascade of events initiated by cortisol (de Kloet et al., 1991). Once receptors are activated, other steps proceed independent of cortisol levels. Generally, information about glucocorticoid responsiveness provides an interpretative context for understanding the relationship between ambient cortisol measures and other neurobiological functions.

## THE CORTISOL CHALLENGE TEST

The above discussion highlights that there are age-related changes in neuroendocrine, cognitive, and neuroanatomic measures, and these may differ according to PTSD status. In some cases the relationship may change with age, whereas in others, with PTSD status. It is possible to examine some of these effects using the cortisol challenge test, which, as we have recently suggested, provides a powerful tool to investigate the relationships among these measures, since cortisol administration affects all three domains (Yehuda, Harvey, Buchsbaum, et al., at press; Yehuda, Yang, et al., 2006).

Below we present some preliminary findings using such a strategy. The details concerning methodology are provided in Yehuda, Harvey, Buchsbaum, et al., at press, and Yehuda, Yang, et al., 2006. Briefly, subjects undergo two test days in which they are administered a bolus of either placebo or 17.5 mg cortisol, in a randomized, double-blind manner. The neuroendocrine, cognitive, and brain metabolic responses on these test days are then examined and compared. Subjects also undergo an evaluation to assess endocrine, cognitive, and brain volume measures at baseline.

Figure 8.1 shows the effect of 17.5 mg cortisol on working memory in our older sample, and specifically compares the subjects for whom baseline values are reported in table 8.1. As described in Yehuda, Harvey, Buchsbaum, et al., at press, the effect of cortisol in this older sample was to improve memory performance. There were significant main effects for immediate and delayed recall on the LMS ($F_{1,28} = 8.9$, $p = .006$), and a trend level effect of cortisol for attention as measured by DSF ($F_{1,27} = 3.07$, $p = .09$). However, the only test showing a group x drug interaction was the LNS test ($F_{1,27}$ = 4.98, p = .034), which occurred in the absence of a main effect of drug ($F_{1,27}$ = .98, n.s.) or Group ($F_{1,27}$ = 1.15, n.s.). This interaction (graphed on the right panel of figure 8.1) demonstrated that although subjects in the PTSD group started out performing more poorly than controls on this relatively difficult task (see also table 8.1 above), cortisol injection significantly improved their performance while having no effect in the controls.

Importantly, the interaction observed in this older cohort represents an effect of glucocorticoids that is opposite to what we previously observed in the younger sample. In the younger sample there was also a significant interaction ($F_{1,25}$ = 6.048, p = .022), but this reflected a decline in performance following cortisol in PTSD and no effect in controls (Grossman et al., 2006). When data from these cohorts were combined, as in table 8.1, to include the effect of cortisol administration, there was a significant group x treatment x cohort interaction ($F_{1,52}$ = 6.38, p = .015). This interaction demonstrated that although performance on the LNS was worse with increasing age for both PTSD and control subjects, cortisol improved performance for older subjects with PTSD, while decreasing performance for young PTSD subjects, but having no effect on young controls (figure 8.1). Thus, the administration

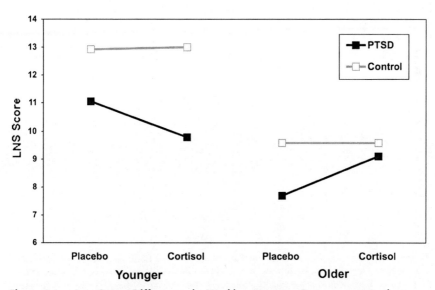

Figure 8.1. **Age Group Differences in Working Memory. Data represents the mean values (corrected for injection order) for number of correct responses on the Letter-Number Sequencing. Data for the PTSD+ and PTSD-groups are depicted in blue and red respectively.**

of cortisol significantly enhanced performance on several hippocampal and glucocorticoid-dependent memory tasks in older PTSD subjects, but had minimal effects in subjects without PTSD. With respect to working memory, cortisol administration actually reversed the poor performance in PTSD observed on the placebo day (Yehuda, Harvey, Buchsbaum, et al., at press). Furthermore, the results in older subjects contrasted with our findings in younger subjects using the identical protocol in which cortisol impaired performance in the PTSD subjects more than controls (Grossman et al., 2006), suggesting that the effects of cortisol in PTSD must be considered in the context of aging.

To confirm that these cohort differences were age-related, we correlated the change in LNS performance with age, and present the results graphically in figure 8.2. The figure shows that the impact of cortisol on performance improves with age for the PTSD group (r = .402, n = 27, p = .038) but not for the control group (r = .227, n = 27, n.s.). These findings are consistent with the possibility that over time, the constellation of neuroendocrine characteristics of PTSD affect cognitive and possibly underlying neuroanatomic alterations. Alternatively, the longitudinal trajectory of changes with age differs for subjects with and without PTSD. Moreover, similar age-related cognitive and neuroanatomic changes may be superimposed on the already existing differences in PTSD, affecting sensitivity to glucocorticoids differ-

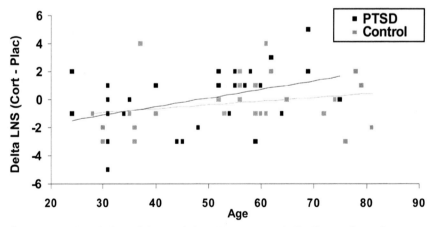

Figure 8.2.   Correlation of Age and Cort Response on LNS. Change in performance on the letter-number sequencing was calculated by taking performance on the cortisol day minus performance on the placebo day. The PTSD + group (n = 18) is represented by dark squares, and the control group (n = 15) by light squares. The dark line shows the trend line for the PTSD + group and the light line shows the trend line for the control group.

ently. Only a longitudinal approach can identify changes within a person over time and see whether these changes differ between groups.

## CONCLUSIONS

Symptoms of PTSD can persist for decades. However, the changes that may occur with age are poorly understood. If there are different biological alterations associated with PTSD in older, compared to younger, trauma survivors, it is critical to establish how biological changes differ in older survivors in order to identify potential neurobiological changes with age and consider their possible treatment implications. The above review highlights critical areas that may be relevant to PTSD in aging trauma survivors as well as the necessity for examining whether the age-related patterns seen in non-trauma-exposed persons are applicable to understanding PTSD as it develops and progresses over time in the elderly. The interface between neuroendocrine, cognitive, and neuroanatomical effects in PTSD and aging are particularly important areas that deserve further inquiry. The above data demonstrate the usefulness of the cortisol challenge test to identify age-related effects of cortisol administration. The pilot data presented here imply that if we mistakenly extrapolate from studies of normal aging that cortisol toxicity results in PTSD-related brain and cognitive deficits, we may miss an opportunity to exploit the potentially beneficial effects of cortisol on cognition and possibly symptom reduction in PTSD.

## ACKNOWLEDGEMENTS

This work was supported by a VA Merit Review Grant and NIMH R01 MH64675-01, and in part by a grant (5 M01 RR00071) for the Mount Sinai General Clinical Research Center from the National Institute of Health.

## REFERENCES

Akirav, I., and Richter-Levin, G. (2002). Mechanisms of amygdala modulation of hippocampal plasticity. *The Journal of Neuroscience: the Official Journal of the Society for Neuroscience, 22*(22), 9912–21.
Bachmann, A. W., Sedgley, T. L., Jackson, R. V., Gibson, J. N., Young, R. M., and Torpy, D. J. (2005). Glucocorticoid receptor polymorphisms and post-traumatic stress disorder. *Psychoneuroendocrinology, 30*(3), 297–306.

Baker, D. G., West, S. A., Nicholson, W. E., Ekhator, N. N., Kasckow, J. W., Hill, K. K., et al. (1999). Serial CSF corticotropin-releasing hormone levels and adrenocortical activity in combat veterans with posttraumatic stress disorder. *The American Journal of Psychiatry, 156*(4), 585–88.

Barrett, D. H., Green, M. L., Morris, R., Giles, W. H., and Croft, J. B. (1996). Cognitive functioning and posttraumatic stress disorder. *The American Journal of Psychiatry, 153*(11), 1492–94.

Beckwith, B. E., Petros, T. V., Scaglione, C., and Nelson, J. (1986). Dose-dependent effects of hydrocortisone on memory in human males. *Physiology & Behavior, 36*(2), 283–86.

Blake, D. D., Weathers, F. W., Nagy, L. M., Kaloupek, D. G., Gusman, F. D., Charney, D. S., et al. (1995). The development of a clinician-administered PTSD scale. *Journal of Traumatic Stress, 8*(1), 75–90.

Boscarino, J. A. (1996). Posttraumatic stress disorder, exposure to combat, and lower plasma cortisol among Vietnam veterans: Findings and clinical implications. *Journal of Consulting and Clinical Psychology, 64*(1), 191–201.

Bremner, J. D., Licinio, J., Darnell, A., Krystal, J. H., Owens, M. J., Southwick, S. M., et al. (1997). Elevated CSF corticotropin-releasing factor concentrations in posttraumatic stress disorder. *The American Journal of Psychiatry, 154*(5), 624–29.

Bremner, J. D., Randall, P., Scott, T. M., Bronen, R. A., Seibyl, J. P., Southwick, S. M., et al. (1995). MRI-based measurement of hippocampal volume in patients with combat-related posttraumatic stress disorder. *The American Journal of Psychiatry, 152*(7), 973–81.

Bremner, J. D., Scott, T. M., Delaney, R. C., Southwick, S. M., Mason, J. W., Johnson, D. R., et al. (1993). Deficits in short-term memory in posttraumatic stress disorder. *The American Journal of Psychiatry, 150*(7), 1015–19.

Bremner, J. D., Vythilingam, M., Vermetten, E., Afzal, N., Nazeer, A., Newcomer, J. W., et al. (2004). Effects of dexamethasone on declarative memory function in posttraumatic stress disorder. *Psychiatry Research, 129*(1), 1–10.

Bremner, J. D., Vythilingam, M., Vermetten, E., Anderson, G., Newcomer, J. W., and Charney, D. S. (2004). Effects of glucocorticoids on declarative memory function in major depression. *Biological Psychiatry, 55*(8), 811–15.

Buckley, T. C., Blanchard, E. B., and Neill W. T. (2000). Information processing and PTSD: A review of the empirical literature. *Clinical Psychology Review, 20*(8), 1041–65.

Dallman, M. F., Akana, S. F., Cascio, C. S., Darlington, D. N., Jacobson, L., and Levin, N. (1987). Regulation of ACTH secretion: Variations on a theme of B. *Recent Progress in Hormone Research, 43*, 113–73.

de Kloet, E. R., Joels, M., Oitzl, M., and Sutanto, W. (1991). Implication of brain corticosteroid receptor diversity for the adaptation syndrome concept. *Methods and Achievements in Experimental Pathology, 14*, 104–32.

De Leon, M. J., George, A. E., Golomb, J., Tarshish, C., Convit, A., Kluger, A., et al. (1997). Frequency of hippocampal formation atrophy in normal aging and Alzheimer's disease. *Neurobiology of Aging, 18*(1), 1–11.

Deuschle, M., Gotthardt, U., Schweiger, U., Weber, B., Korner, A., Schmider, J., et al. (1997). With aging in humans the activity of the hypothalamus-pituitary-adrenal system increases and its diurnal amplitude flattens. *Life Sciences, 61*(22), 2239–46.

Dori, D., Casale, G., Solerte, S. B., Fioravanti, M., Migliorati, G., Cuzzoni, G., et al. (1994). Chrono-neuroendocrinological aspects of physiological aging and senile dementia. *Chronobiologia, 21*(1–2), 121–26.

Erickson, K., Drevets, W., and Schulkin, J. (2003). Glucocorticoid regulation of diverse cognitive functions in normal and pathological emotional states. *Neuroscience and Biobehavioral Reviews, 27*(3), 233–46.

Fontana, A., and Rosenheck, R. (1994). Traumatic war stressors and psychiatric symptoms among World War II, Korean, and Vietnam War veterans. *Psychology and Aging, 9*(1), 27–33.

Freeman, T., Kimbrell, T., Booe, L., Myers, M., Cardwell, D., Lindquist, et al. (2006). Evidence of resilience: Neuroimaging in former prisoners of war. *Psychiatry Research, 146*(1), 59–64.

Freo, U., Holloway, H. W., Kalogeras, K., Rapoport, S. I., and Soncrant, T. T. (1992). Adrenalectomy or metyrapone-pretreatment abolishes cerebral metabolic responses to the serotonin agonist 1-(2,5-dimethoxy-4-iodophenyl)-2-aminopropane (DOI) in the hippocampus. *Brain Research, 586*(2), 256–64.

Gilbertson, M. W., Gurvits, T. V., Lasko, N. B., Orr, S. P., and Pitman, R. K. (2001). Multivariate assessment of explicit memory function in combat veterans with post-traumatic stress disorder. *Journal of Traumatic Stress, 14*(2), 413–32.

Gilbertson, M. W., Paulus, L. A., Williston, S. K., Gurvits, T. V., Lasko, N. B., Pitman, R. K., et al. (2006). Neurocognitive function in monozygotic twins discordant for combat exposure: Relationship to posttraumatic stress disorder. *Journal of Abnormal Psychology, 115*(3), 484–95.

Golier, J., Yehuda, R., Cornblatt, B., Harvey, P., Gerber, D., and Levengood, R. (1997). Sustained attention in combat-related posttraumatic stress disorder. *Integrative Physiological and Behavioral Science: The Official Journal of the Pavlovian Society, 32*(1), 52–61.

Golier, J. A., Yehuda, R., De Santi, S., Segal, S., Dolan, S., and de Leon, M. J. (2005). Absence of hippocampal volume differences in survivors of the Nazi Holocaust with and without posttraumatic stress disorder. *Psychiatry Research, 139*(1), 53–64.

Golier, J. A., Yehuda, R., Lupien, S. J., and Harvey, P. D. (2003). Memory for trauma-related information in Holocaust survivors with PTSD. *Psychiatry Research, 121*(2), 133–43.

Golier, J. A., Yehuda, R., Lupien, S. J., Harvey, P. D., Grossman, R., and Elkin, A. (2002). Memory performance in Holocaust survivors with posttraumatic stress disorder. *The American Journal of Psychiatry, 159*(10), 1682–88.

Golomb, J., Kluger, A., de Leon, M. J., Ferris, S. H., Convit, A., Mittelman, M. S., et al. (1994). Hippocampal formation size in normal human aging: A correlate of delayed secondary memory performance. *Learning and Memory (Cold Spring Harbor, N.Y.), 1*(1), 45–54.

Grossman, R., Yehuda, R., Golier, J., McEwen, B., Harvey, P., and Maria, N. S. (2006). Cognitive effects of intravenous hydrocortisone in subjects with PTSD and healthy control subjects. *Annals of the New York Academy of Sciences, 1071*, 410–21.

Gurvits, T. V., Lasko, N. B., Schachter, S. C., Kuhne, A. A., Orr, S. P., and Pitman, R. K. (1993). Neurological status of Vietnam veterans with chronic posttraumatic stress disorder. *The Journal of Neuropsychiatry and Clinical Neurosciences, 5*(2), 183–88.

Halbreich, U., Asnis, G. M., Zumoff, B., Nathan, R. S., and Shindledecker, R. (1984). Effect of age and sex on cortisol secretion in depressives and normals. *Psychiatry Research, 13*(3), 221–29.

Het, S., Ramlow, G., and Wolf, O. T. (2005). A meta-analytic review of the effects of acute cortisol administration on human memory. *Psychoneuroendocrinology, 30*(8), 771–84.

Horner, M. D., and Hamner, M. B. (2002). Neurocognitive functioning in posttraumatic stress disorder. *Neuropsychology Review, 12*(1), 15–30.

Huizenga, N. A., de Lange, P., Koper, J. W., de Herder, W. W., Abs, R., Kasteren, J. H., et al. (2000). Five patients with biochemical and/or clinical generalized glucocorticoid resistance without alterations in the glucocorticoid receptor gene. *The Journal of Clinical Endocrinology and Metabolism, 85*(5), 2076–81.

Jelinek, L., Jacobsen, D., Kellner, M., Larbig, F., Biesold, K. H., Barre, K., et al. (2006). Verbal and nonverbal memory functioning in posttraumatic stress disorder (PTSD). *Journal of Clinical and Experimental Neuropsychology: Official Journal of the International Neuropsychological Society, 28*(6), 940–48.

Juruena, M. F., Cleare, A. J., and Pariante, C. M. (2004). The hypothalamic pituitary adrenal axis, glucocorticoid receptor function and relevance to depression. *Revista Brasileira de Psiquiatria (Sao Paulo,Brazil: 1999), 26*(3), 189–201.

Kanter, E. D., Wilkinson, C. W., Radant, A. D., Petrie, E. C., Dobie, D. J., McFall, M. E., et al. (2001). Glucocorticoid feedback sensitivity and adrenocortical responsiveness in posttraumatic stress disorder. *Biological Psychiatry, 50*(4), 238–45.

Kitayama, N., Vaccarino, V., Kutner, M., Weiss, P., and Bremner, J. D. (2005). Magnetic resonance imaging (MRI) measurement of hippocampal volume in posttraumatic stress disorder: A meta-analysis. *Journal of Affective Disorders, 88*(1), 79–86.

Kluznik, J. C., Speed, N., Van Valkenburg, C., and Magraw, R. (1986). Forty-year follow-up of United States prisoners of war. *The American Journal of Psychiatry, 143*(11), 1443–46.

Landfield, P. W., and Eldridge, J. C. (1994). The glucocorticoid hypothesis of age-related hippocampal neurodegeneration: Role of dysregulated intraneuronal calcium. *Annals of the New York Academy of Sciences 746*, 308–21; discussion, 321–26.

Landgraf, R., Mitro, A., and Hess, J. (1978). Regional net uptake of 14C-glucose by rat brain under the influence of corticosterone. *Endocrinologia Experimentalis, 12*(2), 119–29.

Liberzon, I., Britton, J. C., and Phan, K. L. (2003). Neural correlates of traumatic recall in posttraumatic stress disorder. *Stress (Amsterdam, Netherlands), 6*(3), 151–56.

Lindauer, R. J., Olff, M., van Meijel, E. P., Carlier, I. V, and Gersons, B. P. (2006). Cortisol, learning, memory, and attention in relation to smaller hippocampal volume in police officers with posttraumatic stress disorder. *Biological Psychiatry, 59*(2), 171–77.

Lowy, M. T. (1989). Quantification of type I and II adrenal steroid receptors in neuronal, lymphoid and pituitary tissues. *Brain Research, 503*(2), 191–97.

Lupien, S. J., de Leon, M., de Santi, S., Convit, A., Tarshish, C., Nair, N. P., et al. (1998). Cortisol levels during human aging predict hippocampal atrophy and memory deficits. *Natural Neuroscience, 1*(1), 69–73.

Lupien, S. J., Wilkinson, C. W., Briere, S., Ng Ying Kin, N. M., Meaney, M. J., et al. (2002). Acute modulation of aged human memory by pharmacological manipulation of glucocorticoids. *The Journal of Clinical Endocrinology and Metabolism, 87*(8), 3798–3807.

McEwen, B. S., Gould, E. A., and Sakai, R. R. (1992). The vulnerability of the hippocampus to protective and destructive effects of glucocorticoids in relation to stress. *The British Journal of Psychiatry Supplement, 15*, 18–23.

McEwen, B. S., and Sapolsky, R. M. (1995). Stress and cognitive function. *Current Opinion in Neurobiology, 5*(2), 205–16.

McNally, R. J., and Shin, L. M. (1995). Association of intelligence with severity of posttraumatic stress disorder symptoms in Vietnam combat veterans. *The American Journal of Psychiatry, 152*(6), 936–38.

Miller, D. B., and O'Callaghan, J. P. (2005). Aging, stress and the hippocampus. *Ageing Research Reviews, 4*(2), 123–40.

Neigh, G. N., and Nemeroff, C. B. (2006). Reduced glucocorticoid receptors: Consequence or cause of depression? *Trends in Endocrinology and Metabolism: TEM, 17*(4), 124–25.

Newcomer, J. W., Selke, G., Melson, A. K., Hershey, T., Craft, S., Richards, K., et al. (1999). Decreased memory performance in healthy humans induced by stress-level cortisol treatment. *Archives of General Psychiatry, 56*(6), 527–33.

Neylan, T. C., Lenoci, M., Rothlind, J., Metzler, T. J., Schuff, N., Du, A. T., et al. (2004). Attention, learning, and memory in posttraumatic stress disorder. *Journal of Traumatic Stress, 17*(1), 41–46.

Neylan, T. C., Schuff, N., Lenoci, M., Yehuda, R., Weiner, M. W., and Marmar, C. R. (2003). Cortisol levels are positively correlated with hippocampal N-acetylaspartate. *Biological Psychiatry, 54*(10), 1118–21.

O'Brien, J. T., Lloyd, A., McKeith, I, Gholkar, A., and Ferrier, N. (2004). A longitudinal study of hippocampal volume, cortisol levels, and cognition in older depressed subjects. *The American Journal of Psychiatry, 161*(11), 2081–90.

Pitman, R. K., and Orr, S. P. (1990). Twenty-four hour urinary cortisol and catecholamine excretion in combat-related posttraumatic stress disorder. *Biological Psychiatry, 27*(2), 245–47.

Porter, R. J., Barnett, N. A., Idey, A., McGuckin, E. A., and O'Brien, J. T. (2002). Effects of hydrocortisone administration on cognitive function in the elderly. *Journal of Psychopharmacology (Oxford, England), 16*(1), 65–71.

Resnick, H. S., Yehuda, R., Pitman, R. K., and Foy, D. W. (1995). Effect of previous trauma on acute plasma cortisol level following rape. *The American Journal of Psychiatry, 152*(11), 1675–77.

Roozendaal, B. (2000). 1999 Curt P. Richter Award. Glucocorticoids and the regulation of memory consolidation. *Psychoneuroendocrinology, 25*(3), 213–38.

Roozendaal, B., Hahn, E. L., Nathan, S. V., de Quervain, D. J., and McGaugh, J. L. (2004). Glucocorticoid effects on memory retrieval require concurrent noradrenergic activity in the hippocampus and basolateral amygdala. *The Journal of Neuroscience: The Official Journal of the Society for Neuroscience, 24*(37), 8161–69.

Rusinek, H., De Santi, S., Frid, D., Tsui, W. H., Tarshish, C. Y., Convit, A., et al. (2003). Regional brain atrophy rate predicts future cognitive decline: 6-year longitudinal MR imaging study of normal aging. *Radiology, 229*(3), 691–96.

Sachinvala, N., von Scotti, H., McGuire, M., Fairbanks, L., Bakst, K., McGuire, et al. (2000). Memory, attention, function, and mood among patients with chronic posttraumatic stress disorder. *The Journal of Nervous and Mental Disease, 188*(12), 818–23.

Sapolsky, R. (1994). Glucocorticoids, stress and exacerbation of excitotoxic neuron death. *Seminars in Neuroscience 6* (1994), 323–31.

———. (2000). Glucocorticoids and Hippocampal Atrophy in Neuropsychiatric Disorders. *Archives of General Psychiatry, 57*(10), 925–35.

Sautter, F. J., Bissette, G., Wiley, J., Manguno-Mire, G., Schoenbachler, B, Myers, L., et al. (2003). Corticotropin-releasing factor in posttraumatic stress disorder (PTSD) with secondary psychotic symptoms, nonpsychotic PTSD, and healthy control subjects. *Biological Psychiatry, 54*(12), 1382–88.

Schmidt, L. A., Fox, N. A., Goldberg, M. C., Smith, C. C., and Schulkin J. (1999). Effects of acute prednisone administration on memory, attention and emotion in healthy human adults. *Psychoneuroendocrinology, 24*(4), 461–83.

Schmidt, L. A., Fox, N. A., Rubin, K. H., Sternberg, E. M., Gold, P. W., Smith, C. C., et al. (1997). Behavioral and neuroendocrine responses in shy children. *Developmental Psychobiology, 30*(2), 127–40.

Shin, L. M., Kosslyn, S. M., McNally, R. J., Alpert, N. M., Thompson, W. L., Rauch, S. L., et al. (1997). Visual imagery and perception in posttraumatic stress disorder. A positron emission tomographic investigation. *Archives of General Psychiatry, 54*(3), 233–41.

Shin, L. M., McNally, R. J., Kosslyn, S. M., Thompson, W. L., Rauch, S. L., Alpert, N. M., et al. (1999). Regional cerebral blood flow during script-driven imagery in childhood sexual abuse-related PTSD: A PET investigation. *The American Journal of Psychiatry, 156*(4), 575–84.

Shin, L. M., Shin, P. S., Heckers, S., Krangel, T. S., Macklin, M. L., Orr, S. P., et al. (2004). Hippocampal function in posttraumatic stress disorder. *Hippocampus, 14*(3), 292–300.

Spiro, A. III, Schnurr, P. P., and Aldwin, C. M. (1994). Combat-related posttraumatic stress disorder symptoms in older men. *Psychology and Aging, 9*(1), 17–26.

Starkman, M. N., Gebarski, S. S., Berent, S., and Schteingart, D. E. (1992). Hippocampal formation volume, memory dysfunction, and cortisol levels in patients with Cushing's Syndrome. *Biological Psychiatry, 32*(9) 756–65.

Swanson, L. W., and Simmons, D. M. (1989). Differential steroid hormone and neural influences on peptide mRNA levels in CRH cells of the paraventricular nucleus: A hybridization histochemical study in the rat. *The Journal of Comparative Neurology, 285*(4), 413–35.

Tennant, C., Fairley, M. J., Dent, O. F., Sulway, M. R., and Broe, G. A. (1997). Declining prevalence of psychiatric disorder in older former prisoners of war. *The Journal of Nervous and Mental Disease, 185*(11), 686–89.

Van Cauter, E., Leproult, R., and Kupfer, D. J. (1996). Effects of gender and age on the levels and circadian rhythmicity of plasma cortisol. *The Journal of Clinical Endocrinology and Metabolism 81*(7), 2468–73.

Vasterling, J. J., Duke, L. M., Brailey, K., Constans, J. I., Allain, A. N. Jr., and Sutker, P. B. (2002). Attention, learning, and memory performances and intellectual resources in Vietnam veterans: PTSD and no disorder comparisons. *Neuropsychology, 16*(1), 5–14.

Vasterling, J. J., Proctor, S. P., Amoroso, S., Kane, R., Heeren, T., and White, R. F. (2006). Neuropsychological outcomes of army personnel following deployment to the Iraq War. *Journal of the American Medical Association, 296*(5), 519–29.

Watanabe, Y., Gould, E., Cameron, H. A., Daniels, D. C., and McEwen, B. S. (1992). Phenytoin prevents stress- and corticosterone-induced atrophy of CA3 pyramidal neurons. *Hippocampus, 2*(4), 431–35.

Yehuda, R. (1999). Linking the neuroendocrinology of post-traumatic stress disorder with recent neuroanatomic findings. *Seminars in Clinical Neuropsychiatry, 4*(4), 256–65.

———. (2001). Are glucocortoids responsible for putative hippocampal damage in PTSD? How and when to decide. *Hippocampus, 11*(2), 85–89; discussion, 82–84.

———. (2002). Post-traumatic stress disorder. *The New England Journal of Medicine, 346*(2), 108–14.

Yehuda, R., Boisoneau, D., Lowy, M. T., and Giller, E. L. Jr. (1995). Dose-response changes in plasma cortisol and lymphocyte glucocorticoid receptors following dexamethasone administration in combat veterans with and without posttraumatic stress disorder. *Archives of General Psychiatry, 52*(7), 583–93.

Yehuda, R., and Flory, J. (at press). Differentiating biological correlates of risk, PTSD, and resilience following trauma exposure. *Journal of Traumatic Stress.*

Yehuda, R., Golier, J. A., Halligan, S. L., and Harvey, P. D. (2004). Learning and memory in Holocaust survivors with posttraumatic stress disorder. *Biological Psychiatry, 55*(3), 291–95.

Yehuda, R., Golier, J. A., Halligan, S. L., Meaney, M., and Bierer, L. M. (2004). The ACTH response to dexamethasone in PTSD. *The American Journal of Psychiatry, 161*(8), 1397–1403.

Yehuda, R., Golier, J. A., Harvey, P. D., Stavitsky, K., Kaufman, S., Grossman, R. A., et al. (2005). Relationship between cortisol and age-related memory impairments in Holocaust survivors with PTSD. *Psychoneuroendocrinology, 30*(7), 678–87.

Yehuda, R., Golier, J. A., and Kaufman, S. (2005). Circadian rhythm of salivary cortisol in Holocaust survivors with and without PTSD. *The American Journal of Psychiatry, 162*(5), 998–1000.

Yehuda, R., Golier, J. A., Tischler, L., Harvey, P. D., Newmark, R., Yang, R. K., et al. (2007). Hippocampal volume in aging combat veterans with and without post-traumatic stress disorder: Relation to risk and resilience factors. *Journal of Psychiatric Research 41*(5), 435–45.

Yehuda, R., Golier, J. A., Tischler, L., Stavitsky, K., and P. D. Harvey. (2005). Learning and memory in aging combat veterans with PTSD. *Journal of Clinical and Experimental Neuropsychology: Official Journal of the International Neuropsychological Society, 27*(4), 504–15.

Yehuda, R., Golier, J. A., Yang, R. K., and Tischler, L. (2004). Enhanced sensitivity to glucocorticoids in peripheral mononuclear leukocytes in posttraumatic stress disorder. *Biological Psychiatry, 55*(11), 1110–16.

Yehuda, R., Halligan, S. L., Grossman, R., Golier, J. A., and Wong, C. (2002). The cortisol and glucocorticoid receptor response to low dose dexamethasone administration in aging combat veterans and Holocaust survivors with and without posttraumatic stress disorder. *Biological Psychiatry, 52*(5), 393–403.

Yehuda, R., Harvey, P. D., Buchsbaum, M., Tischler, L., and Schmeidler, J. (at press). Enhanced effects of cortisol administration on working memory in PTSD. *Neuropsychopharmacology.*

Yehuda, R., Kahana, B., Binder-Brynes, K., Southwick, S. M., Mason, J. W., and Giller, E. L. (1995). Low urinary cortisol excretion in Holocaust survivors with posttraumatic stress disorder. *The American Journal of Psychiatry, 152*(7), 982–86.

Yehuda, R., Kahana, B., Schmeidler, J., Southwick, S. M., Wilson, S., and Giller, E. L. (1995). Impact of cumulative lifetime trauma and recent stress on current posttraumatic stress disorder symptoms in Holocaust survivors. *The American Journal of Psychiatry, 152*(12), 1815–18.

Yehuda, R., Keefe, R. S., Harvey, P. D., Levengood, R. A., Gerber, D. K., Geni, J., et al. (1995). Learning and memory in combat veterans with posttraumatic stress disorder. *American Journal of Psychiatry, 152*(1), 137–39.

Yehuda, R., Levengood, R. A., Schmeidler, J., Wilson, S., Guo, L. S., and Gerber, D. (1996). Increased pituitary activation following metyrapone administration in posttraumatic stress disorder. *Psychoneuroendocrinology, 21*(1), 1–16.

Yehuda, R., Morris, A., Labinksy, E., Zemelman, S., and Schmeidler, J. (at press). Ten year follow-up study of cortisol levels in aging Holocaust survivors with and without PTSD. *Psychoneuroendocrinology.*

Yehuda, R., Schmeidler, J., Siever, L. J., Binder-Brynes, K., and Elkin, A. (1997). Individual differences in posttraumatic stress disorder symptom profiles in Holocaust survivors in concentration camps or in hiding. *Journal of Traumatic Stress, 10*(3), 453–63.

Yehuda, R., Southwick, S. M., Krystal, J. H., Bremner, D., Charney, D. S., and Mason, J. W. (1993). Enhanced suppression of cortisol following dexamethasone administration in posttraumatic stress disorder. *The American Journal of Psychiatry, 150*(1), 83–86.

Yehuda, R., Southwick, S. M., Nussbaum, G., Wahby, V., Giller, E. L. Jr., and Mason, J. W. (1990). Low urinary cortisol excretion in patients with posttraumatic stress disorder. *The Journal of Nervous and Mental Disease, 178*(6), 366–69.

Yehuda, R., Teicher, M. H., Golier, J. A., and Bierer, L. M. (in preparation). Chronobiological analysis of cortisol and ACTH in aging combat veterans. Unpublished Manuscript.

Yehuda, R., Teicher, M. H., Trestman, R. L., Levengood, R. A., and Siever, L. J. (1996). Cortisol regulation in posttraumatic stress disorder and major depression: A chronobiological analysis. *Biological Psychiatry, 40*(2), 79–88.

Yehuda, R., Tischler, L., Golier, J. A., Grossman, R., Brand, S. R., Kaufman, S., et al. (2006). Longitudinal assessment of cognitive performance in Holocaust survivors with and without PTSD. *Biological Psychiatry, 60*(7), 714–21.

Yehuda, R., Yang, R. K., Buchsbaum, M. S., and Golier, J. A. (2006). Alterations in cortisol negative feedback inhibition as examined using the ACTH response to cortisol administration in PTSD. *Psychoneuroendocrinology, 31*(4), 447–51.

Zhang, L., Zhou, R., Li, X., Ursano, R. J., and Li, H. (2006). Stress-induced change of mitochondria membrane potential regulated by genomic and non-genomic GR signaling: A possible mechanism for hippocampus atrophy in PTSD. *Medical Hypotheses, 66*(6), 1205–8.

Zhou, J., and Cidlowski, J. A. (2005). The human glucocorticoid receptor: one gene, multiple proteins and diverse responses. *Steroids, 70*(5–7), 407–17.

Zimmerman, M., and Coryell, W. (1987). The dexamethasone suppression test in healthy controls. *Psychoneuroendocrinology, 12*(4), 245–51.

# 9

# Dissociation Across the Lifespan and Interfaces with Posttraumatic Stress Disorder

*Daphne Simeon and Ashley Braun*

Research examining psychobiological predictors and correlates of PTSD is hindered by the relative absence of trauma victims with "pure" PTSD. That is, a number of mental disorders commonly occur comorbidly with PTSD, potentially clouding relationships between PTSD symptoms and biopsychological variables of interest. Further, research in trauma largely focuses on PTSD, without consideration of additional posttraumatic pathology. Patients with comorbid illness have demonstrated greater distress and dysfunction than patients with PTSD alone (Shalev et al., 1998; Southwick, Yehuda, Giller, and Perry, 1993), underscoring the importance of examining the impact of comorbidities. A recent meta-analysis of pre-, peri-, and posttrauma predictors of PTSD reported that the strongest predictor of PTSD following trauma was the presence of peritraumatic dissociation (weighted $r = .35$: Ozer, Best, Lipsey, and Weiss, 2003). Dissociation, as defined by the DSM-IV (American Psychiatric Association, 1994, 519), refers to "a disruption in the usually integrated functions of consciousness, memory, identity, or perception of the environment." Dissociation has been associated with increased levels of PTSD (Carlson and Rosser-Hogan, 1991), and has been found to mediate the relationship between sexual abuse and psychopathology in children and adolescents (van der Kolk and van der Hart, 1989).

Currently, there is a school of thought that believes that attachment style in infancy may be correlated with dissociation later in life. In order to understand this position, it is helpful to briefly review the Ainsworth Strange

Address correspondence concerning this chapter to Daphne Simeon, M.D.; Mount Sinai School of Medicine Psychiatry, Box 1230; Atran Building, Level E, Rm 26; New York, NY 10029-6574. E-mail: daphne.simeon@mssm.edu

Situation. In this paradigm, an infant is separated from the primary caregiver in the laboratory and presented with toys and a novel individual. The infant's behavior is observed during separation and upon reunion with the caregiver (Ainsworth and Wittig, 1969). The behavior exhibited by the infant in this paradigm results in different attachment styles, one of which is the "insecure-disorganized/disoriented" attachment. This type of attachment is characterized by inconsistent, conflicting, and odd behaviors in the presence of the caregiver. Main and Morgan (1996) describe a number of examples of behaviors that reflect this attachment style. For instance, the infant may at once both reach for the caregiver while also pulling away. Another example of odd behavior exhibited by the infant is a sudden interruption in the child's play with a freezing spell for a number of seconds, followed by a return to playing, as if no break had occurred (Main and Morgan, 1996).

It has been suggested that "insecure-disorganized/disoriented" attachment in infancy may be predictive of dissociative disorders later in life (Liotti, 1992). One explanation is a sort of cycle of events between the parent and child. A parent who has a dissociative experience in the infant's presence may become frightening to the infant (Hesse and Main, 2006). Subsequently, the infant becomes confused or disoriented when the parent, who is usually a source of comfort and support, becomes instead a source of fear. It has been shown that certain types of childhood trauma may lead to dissociation in adulthood (Irwin, 1994). This frightened/frightening behavior may in turn become a source of trauma in the life of the infant that may lead to dissociation later in life (Hesse and Main, 2006).

## DISSOCIATION IN CHILDHOOD AND ADOLESCENCE

The theory that disturbed attachment in early life relates to dissociation in later childhood and adolescence is born out by empirical data. In one longitudinal study, 157 children were followed from infancy to the age of nineteen (Carlson, 1998). The results of this study showed that infants who displayed disorganized attachment styles showed a greater degree of dissociation as older children and adolescents. Likewise, Ogawa et al. (1997) conducted a study entitled the "Minnesota Longitudinal Study" in which 168 high-risk children were studied. They classified certain important developmental periods as follows: Infant (zero to twenty-four months); toddler (thirty to fifty-four months); kindergarten to sixth grade; age 16 to 17.5; and, finally, age nineteen. The authors found certain key findings. First, childhood abuse correlated with dissociation at age nineteen in terms of chronicity, severity, and age of onset. Second, disorganized attachment in infancy (zero to twenty-four months), predicted clinical levels of dissociation (Ogawa et al., 1997).

Similarly, Lyons-Ruth et al. (1993, 1997) conducted the Harvard Longitudinal Study, in which they followed forty-three infants from high-risk families from birth through age nineteen. They too aimed to discover different predictors and developmental pathways leading to dissociation. Certain important variables were targeted, including attachment, childhood maltreatment, trauma history, child IQ, family demographic risk (i.e., single parent, poverty, etc.), as well as the mother's trauma history including sexual and physical abuse, history of psychiatric hospitalization, out-of-home care, and a history of psychiatric diagnoses including Axis I disorders (particularly depression) and dissociation. Of these factors, child maltreatment from birth to age five did not predict dissociation in adolescence. Likewise, adolescent dissociation was not predicted by the mother's psychiatric symptoms assessed through age nine. However, certain positive findings were indicated. Specifically, similarly to Ogawa and colleagues' findings (1997), infant disorganized attachment and maternal disrupted communication during infancy were found to play important roles in later dissociation in adolescence.

Overall, the results of the Harvard Longitudinal Study have shown that the primary caregiver is responsible for the infant's sense of safety and protection. Without such basic needs, the infant is unable to mediate fearful arousal. In an environment where the infant's sense of emotional communications around attachment is repeatedly disturbed, a "hidden trauma" arises in the life of the infant. Data from both animals and humans alike have shown that experiencing such "hidden trauma" in infancy can disrupt proper development of the HPA axis as well as neurotransmitter function. When functioning at such basic levels is interrupted, the consequences are severe as development progresses through childhood and adolescence. Even in the absence of overt maltreatment, dissociative symptomatology arises in the presence of fear-inducing relational events.

Assessing and measuring dissociation in children can be difficult, due to a number of factors. First, the child's inability to accurately verbalize his/her experiences makes it challenging for the clinician to determine whether these experiences are those of dissociation (Hornstein, 1996). Secondly, as a child grows and matures, the child experiences a naturally changing sense of self. The clinician must separate this healthy course of growth from early signs of dissociation (Hornstein, 1996). Furthermore, normative dissociation is higher in younger children, and dissociative symptoms normally decline with age (Ross et al., 1990). Despite the obstacles in obtaining an accurate diagnosis, dissociation in children and adolescents is common, and often underdiagnosed or misdiagnosed. Children with dissociation often present with symptoms such as irritability or depressed mood, suicidal ideation, attentional difficulties, anxiety, temper tantrums, and other inappropriate behavioral conduct, as well as hallucinations (Hornstein and Putnam, 1992). Alternative diagnoses are often made to the neglect of the dissociative component. The Adolescent Dissociative Experiences Scale (A-DES) can measure dissociative experiences in this age group (Armstrong et al., 1997). In addition, the Childhood Dissociation Checklist (CDC) is a widely used measure (Putnam, 1993).

## DISSOCIATION IN ADULTHOOD AND AGING

Studies have shown different types of traumas may impact the presentation of the traumatic disorder in different ways. In general, childhood sexual abuse victims score higher on scales of dissociation than healthy controls (Rodriguez-Srednicki, 2001). However, not all types of abuse exhibit this trend. There is evidence that violence, including physical abuse or witnessing domestic violence, is predictive of PTSD severity (Silva et al., 2000), whereas sexual abuse may lead to more dissociative symptoms than other forms of childhood trauma (Putnam, 1985).

Additionally, having PTSD may be related to dissociative symptoms. One longitudinal study compared three groups: Holocaust survivors with PTSD, Holocaust survivors without PTSD, and a group not exposed to the trauma of the Holocaust (Yehuda et al., 1996). Holocaust survivors with PTSD scored higher on the dissociative experiences questionnaire than either of the other two groups.

Another important factor in determining the course of disease associated with trauma is individual differences. Ross et al. (1990) assessed dissociative symptoms in the general population by giving a random sample of 1,055 adults the dissociative experiences scale (DES) as well as a demographics questionnaire assessing factors such as gender, age, employment status, income, education, religious affiliations, and ethnicity. The results showed that age was the one factor that correlated with DES scores. As age increased, DES scores declined significantly (Ross et al., 1990).

Returning to the data on Holocaust survivors elucidates the importance of individual differences. In the 1996 Yehuda et al. study, in contrast to previous studies showing that the extent of the trauma was related to dissociation, the current study found no such results. The authors posited that this difference could be explained by two important factors: age and culture. As described in the Ross et al. (1990) study, dissociative symptoms have been shown to decrease with age. As Holocaust survivors are older than many other groups of trauma survivors studied in the literature thus far, age may be one plausible explanation for the different results (Yehuda et al., 1996). Another difference stressed by the authors is the unique cultural circumstances surrounding Holocaust survivors. In the Jewish tradition, "Never Forget" is the maxim associated with the Holocaust. Survivors are encouraged to tell their stories of trauma and survival. Therefore, the authors suggest that this too may be an important distinction between Holocaust survivors and other trauma survivors who do not receive such cultural support within their communities (Yehuda et al., 1996).

## DISSOCIATION INTERFACES WITH PTSD

In order to understand the complex interfaces between dissociation and PTSD, it is helpful to first understand four models which have been presented to explain the two disorders and their relationship to one another: a "comorbidity" model, a "shared risk factors" model, a "shared pathogenesis" model, and a "same disorder" model (Simeon, 2007).

### Model 1

The first model, the "comorbidity" model posits that dissociation and PTSD are distinct and separate entities. Both traumatic dissociation and PTSD must be preceded by a "traumatic" event in order to receive a diagnosis that, according to this model, is the common prerequisite that contributes to the high occurrence of comorbidity. Elevations in dissociative symptoms among PTSD samples have been reported in numerous studies (Bremmer et al., 1992; Waller, Putnam, and Carlson, 1996).

Turning to dissociative disorders, their comorbidity with PTSD ranges from almost ubiquitous in Dissociative Identity Disorder (DID) to a very low 4 percent in depersonalization disorder (DPD) (Simeon, Knutelska, Nelson, and Guralnik, 2003). When examined by individual dissociative disorder, the role of trauma can be briefly summarized as follows. In DID several studies clearly document its relationship to childhood interpersonal trauma, in particular extreme and chronic early physical and/or sexual abuse (Braun, 1984; Putnam, 1985; Ross et al., 1990; Spiegel, 1984). In dissociative amnesia, an acute traumatic event is typically identified (Van der Hart and Nijenhuis, 2001). In dissociative fugue, chronic stress is typically described (Coons, 1998). In DPD childhood interpersonal trauma of lesser severity than that encountered in the more severe dissociative disorders, particularly chronic emotional abuse and neglect, have been reported (Simeon, Guralnik, Schmeidler, Sirof, and Knutelska, 2001). In the more culturally bound dissociative disorders, such as ataque and possession/trance states, traumatic stressors are also typically described (Simeon and Hollander, 2000).

Researchers have repeatedly attempted to determine the specific characteristics of trauma that may lead to PTSD vs. dissociative disorder symptoms. Age of abuse onset has been found to be positively correlated with PTSD (r = .19) but negatively with dissociation (r = −.24) (Johnson, Pike, and Chard, 2001). In the same study, degree of trust in the perpetrator did not correlate with PTSD (r = .008) but correlated negatively with dissociation (r = −.19). Early childhood onset and chronicity of trauma have been consistently associated with chronic dissociation (Kirby et al., 1993; Chu and Dill, 1990; Chu, 2000; Ogawa et al., 1997). Younger age at the time of trauma has been significantly related to amnesia and emotional detachment, while older age of trauma onset has been positively correlated with PTSD symptoms (Yehuda et al., 1997).

There seems to be an important distinction when a trauma is perpetrated by someone the victim trusts, although the evidence is inconclusive. According to some, when a trusted individual betrays the victim, dissociative symptoms are more likely to develop than PTSD (Freyd, 1994, 1996). However, others have found that the greater the trust, the less likely dissociative symptoms become (Johnson, Pike, and Chard, 2001).

The extensive comorbidity between PTSD and dissociative disorders especially in the case of more extreme dissociative disorders suggests caution in the complete acceptance of the comorbidity model of PTSD and dissociation.

## Model 2

The "shared risk factors" model says that there are biological, cognitive, and/ or psychological factors that may predispose certain people to develop certain symptoms when confronted by trauma. Studies of identical twins have supported this model (Gilbertson et al., 2002; Gilbertson, 2004). Factors which have been implicated in PTSD symptoms are age, gender, and race in some populations but not others; education, previous trauma, and childhood adversity to a varying extent; and psychiatric history, childhood abuse, and family psychiatric history (Brewin, Andrews, and Valentine, 2000).

Three behavioral genetic studies have examined the heritability of dissociation, and findings are mixed. Results range from no evidence for a genetic component to pathological dissociation (Waller and Ross, 1997) to a 48 percent genetic influence (Jang et al., 1998). Studies suggest that non-pathological dissociation, possibly the precursor to pathological dissocia-tion, has a substantial (greater than 50 percent) heritability (Jang et al., 1998; Becker-Blease et al., 2004).

As with other psychiatric disorders, some propose a stress-diathesis model of dissociation. High hypnotizability, absentmindedness, forgetful-ness, and alexithymia, the inability to identify and describe feelings, are ex-amples of traits that are not pathological themselves, but which may serve as the necessary precursors to pathological dissociation when confronted by substantial stress (Butler et al., 1996; Ray, 1996; Grabe et al., 2000; Irwin and Melbin-Helberg, 1997; Modestin, Lotscher, and Erni, 2002). Findings regarding high hypnotizability, in particular, have been both against this theory (Putnam et al., 1995; Ray, 1996) and in support of it (Frischholz et al., 1992; Bryant, Guthrie, and Moulds, 2001; Sterlini and Bryant, 2002; Waldo and Merritt, 2000).

Yet another powerful unique association is that between backgrounds of emotional neglect and later dissociation (Draijer and Langeland, 1999; Brun-ner et al., 2000). On the contrary, positive parenting may be protective and has negative predictive value (Modestin, Lotscher, and Erni, 2002). As dis-cussed earlier in this chapter, attachment style in infancy may be an important factor in predicting later dissociation (Liotti, 1992; Carlson, 1998; Ogawa et al., 1997). Simeon et al. (2002) reported that cognitive schemata reflective of overconnection and disconnection were associated with depersonalization disorder and depersonalization symptom severity.

Model 2 is only partly supported by empirical data, which indicate both shared but also unique risk factors associated with dissociation and PTSD.

## Model 3

According to the "shared pathogenesis" model, a trauma occurs which then triggers a series of pathogenetic processes, which are different in certain fundamental ways, leading to differential diagnoses, but which share some common features.

Peritraumatic dissociation may be a strong predictor of later PTSD, al-though this is still a matter of debate in recent literature (Marshall, Spitzer, and Liebowitz, 1999; Marshall and Schell, 2002; Gershuny, Cloitre, and Otto, 2003; Ozer et al., 2003). It has been proposed that peritraumatic distress encompasses many different aspects of the traumatic experience, including fears about safety, losing control, helplessness/anger, and guilt/shame (Brunet et al., 2001). However, this theory was not supported in a study of a New York City convenience sample affected by the World Trade Center disaster, which found that peritraumatic "loss of control" and "guilt/shame" feelings were strongly associated with both dissociation and posttraumatic stress at one-year follow-up (Simeon, Greenberg, Nelson, Schmeidler, and Hollander, 2005).

Peritraumatic dissociation may, at times, be a healthy coping mechanism when faced with otherwise inescapable, overwhelming trauma. However, over time, if not taken under control, it can in effect perpetuate the posttraumatic pathology by hindering the emotional and cognitive processing of the original trauma (Foa and Hearst-Ikeda, 1996).

Similarly to peritraumatic distress, cognitive processes such as memory fragmentation, data-driven processing, rumination about the trauma, negative interpretation of intrusions, thought suppression, and angry cognitions, may have an effect on severity of PTSD symptoms (Clohessy and Ehlers, 1999; Halligan et al., 2002, 2003; Mayou et al., 2002; Murray et al., 2002). With regards to dissociation, cognitive aspects such as fear of death and the element of controllability have been implicated as important factors in triggering dissociative reactions (Gershuny and Thayer, 1999; Sterlini and Bryant, 2002).

There are unique cognitive deficits associated with dissociation, and with PTSD. In PTSD, explicit memory has been shown to be generally intact, but the capacity for retention diminishes when tasks involve interference conditions (Yehuda et al., 1995). Siegel (1995) has proposed a resource allocation model to explain these disruptions of explicit memory in PTSD, according to which emotional reactivity resultant from the trauma leads to dividing attentional resources and disturbs focal attention and effortful learning. Interference effects on an emotional Stroop task in response to trauma-related words have been consistently documented in PTSD from various traumatic etiologies (McNally et al., 2000; Cassiday, McNally, and Zeitlin, 1992; Dubner and Motta, 1999; McNally et al., 1990; Foa et al., 1991). These interference effects have not been demonstrated in control groups of trauma survivors without PTSD, suggesting that the abnormality is a feature of the disorder rather than a non-specific sequel to trauma.

Less is known about attentional and memory processes in dissociative disorders. Studies have shown that high dissociators may have deficits in selective attention (Freyd et al., 1998; Simeon, Knutelska, Putnam, and Smith, 2005). However, on a divided attention task, high dissociators showed less interference than low dissociators. In addition, high dissociators did worse than low dissociators in explicitly recalling negative words (DePrince and Freyd, 1999; Simeon, Knutelska, Putnam, and Smith, 2005).

In addition to the actual cognitive processing of the trauma, there are certain endpoint neurobiological and cognitive alterations characteristic of both PTSD and dissociation. The hypothalamic-pituitary-adrenal (HPA) axis, a central system in the body's regulation of stress, has been found to be affected in PTSD in the following ways: altered basal urinary and plasma control (Yehuda et al., 1990, Young and Breslau, 2004), changed cortisol circadian pattern with increased nadir to peak cortisol ratios and decreased cortisol in the evening and night hours (Bremner et al., 2003), elevated corticotrophin releasing factor (CRF) (Bremner et al., 1997), blunted ACTH response to CRF challenge (Smith et al., 1989, Bremner et al., 2003), heightened ACTH response to metyrapone challenge (Yehuda et al., 1996), increased lympho-cyte glucocorticoid receptors (Yehuda et al., 1991), and hypersuppression of cortisol in response to low-dose dexamethasone challenge (Yehuda et al., 1993). These findings are all consistent with a highly sensitized HPA axis in PTSD (Yehuda, 1997), characterized by hypothalamic CRF hypersecretion, downregulated pituitary CRF receptors, enhanced glucocorticoid negative feedback inhibition, and an unresolved question of adrenal insufficiency.

Other biological systems are affected in PTSD as well. Specifically, basal catecholamines, noradrenergic challenges, and receptor binding have gen-erally revealed heightened noradrenergic tone, consistent with the hyper-arousal and intrusive symptomatology characteristic of PTSD (Southwick et al., 1999).

Dissociative disorders may also have a unique set of HPA axis dysregula-tions and biological alterations. Specifically, compared to healthy controls, DPD subjects have shown significantly elevated ambient cortisol, resistance to dexamethasone suppression, and an inverse association between dissocia-tion severity and cortisol reactivity to psychosocial stress (Simeon, Guralnik, Knutelska, Hollander, and Schmeidler, 2001; Simeon, et al., 2007).

Given the "shut-down" amnestic symptomatology typically characteristic of dissociative disorders, one would predict basal autonomic hypoactivity in dissociation. However, limited support for this hypothesis exists in the literature (Griffin, Resick, and Mechnic, 1997; Sierra et al., 2002). Dissocia-tion has been found to be negatively associated with urinary norepinephrine in motor vehicle accident victims (Delahanty et al., 2003), in DPD (Simeon, Guralnik, Knutelska, Yehuda, and Schmeidler, 2003) and in borderline per-sonality disorder (Simeon et al., 2004). Similarly, Morgan et al. (2000) found that acute dissociation severity in response to overwhelming stress was sig-nificantly inversely correlated with plasma neuropeptide Y levels as well.

Neuroimaging studies are also revealing divergent findings between disso-ciative states and classic PTSD. Using fMRI, the dissociative state has been associated with increased activation in the medial prefrontal cortex (BA 9, 10), the inferior frontal gyrus (BA 47), the anterior cingulate (BA 24 and 32), the superior and middle temporal gyri (BA 38), the parietal lobe (BA 7), and the occipital lobe (BA 19) (Lanius et al., 2002). Interestingly, this pattern of activation was distinctly different from that found in a PTSD subgroup, yet

similar to the two published neuroimaging studies in non-PTSD Depersonalization Disorder (Phillips et al., 2001; Simeon et al., 2000).

In summary, there is not much evidence supporting model 3 of a shared
pathogenesis: the experiential, cognitive, and biological processes implicated
in the development of PTSD vs. dissociation are in many ways distinct.


## Model 4

The "same disorder" model differs from the previous models, in that, as its
name implies, it assumes PTSD and dissociation to be essentially the same
disorder, divided merely by our complex and restrictive diagnostic criteria.
While it is true that as it currently stands, the various psychopathologies
which can be traced to a traumatic event are classified relatively arbitrarily
into their respective groups, it seems unlikely that such a large, hetero-
genous group of "traumatic" disorders could be accurately considered as
one and the same.

Bremner (1999) put forth the notion that there may be "two subtypes of
acute trauma response, one primarily dissociative and the other intrusive/
hyperarousal," both representing "unique chronic stress-related psychopathology." In terms of classification, he proposed that either a dissociative
symptom cluster be added to chronic PTSD, or that two separate chronic
posttraumatic disorders be recognized, chronic PTSD (emphasizing intrusion and hyperarousal as currently found in the ICD-10) and chronic dissociative disorder.

Complex PTSD (Herman, 1992; or disorders of extreme stress not otherwise specified—DESNOS; Van der Kolk et al., 1996) is a phenomenological
presentation associated with chronic severe trauma that lies at the interface
of dissociation and PTSD and has not yet been satisfactorily accounted for in
our current classification systems. The four core features of DESNOS include
severe affect and impulse dysregulation, pathological dissociation, somatization including alexithymia, and fundamentally altered beliefs concerning the
self and relationships (Ford, 1999).

The relationship between PTSD and DESNOS has been studied, showing conflicting results. One study led to the conclusion that DESNOS was
more likely to be an associated feature of PTSD than to constitute a separate
diagnosis (Van der Kolk et al., 1996), while in a later study about half the
participants with each diagnosis did not carry the other diagnosis, suggesting that the dissection of PTSD and DESNOS warrants further investigation
(Ford, 1999).

From the standpoint of dissociation, conceptual proposals have also been
put forth which attempt to unify PTSD and traumatic dissociation. A "struc-

tural" dissociation model has been developed, which combines disorders of traumatic descent and frames their phenomenologies in terms of positive and negative symptoms of dissociation (Van der Hart et al., 2004). In this model, there is an "apparently normal part of the personality" (ANP) and an "emotional part of the personality" (EP). As its name implies, the ANP is the aspect of the personality that is dedicated to normal, daily life functioning. The EP is the segregated portion of the personality that is fixated on past trauma and responds to perceived danger.

This model falls short in classifying many of the variants of dissociative disorders, as well as many of the subtypes of PTSD. DID and its milder variants presently classified in the unfortunate DSM-IV-TR category of "dissociative disorders not otherwise specified" are accounted for by this model. However, a variety of "simple" dissociative presentations such as depersonalization disorder, dissociative trance, and dissociative amnesia do not have an appropriate place within this model. The structural dissociation model also claims to encompass all of what is presently known as PTSD, arguing that the two parts of the personality (ANP and EP) are operant even in classic simple PTSD. However, empirical evidence for this kind of structural segregation of the personality in simple PTSD, or for temporal alterations between intrusive and dissociative states in most individuals with simple PTSD, is limited at best.

## CONCLUSION

Dissociation in its normative or non-pathological form (absorption) is ubiquitous and widely distributed in the general population; it is greatest in childhood and diminishes over time into adulthood and possibly old age. Transient, or peritraumatic, dissociation in response to acute severe traumatic stressors is also common, and does not necessarily result in psychopathology. However, vulnerability factors, repeated or overwhelming exposure to trauma, and more lasting acute dissociative responses can result in chronic dissociative symptoms, including dissociative disorders. The evidence presented above most strongly supports the conceptualization of dissociation and PTSD as distinct entities that are often comorbidly associated yet differ in many of their predisposing vulnerabilities, in their pathogenetic mechanisms, and in their neurobiological and cognitive profiles. Many types of trauma can give rise to both PTSD and dissociative symptoms, just as many traumas may give rise to both PTSD and depression. Hardly any trauma characteristics have consistently emerged as unique to either PTSD or dissociation, possibly with the exception of early age, which is more intimately linked to dissociation. Clearly there also exists an area of extensive overlap between the two constructs, variably referred to as PTSD with prominent dissociation, complex PTSD, disorders of extreme stress, dissociative disorder NOS, adult sequalae of serious childhood attachment disorders, or Axis II psychopathology associated with chronic trauma, which need more intensive investigation and accurate classification, since they stretch beyond the limits of our current definitions of both PTSD and dissociation. Future research in PTSD should aim at studying dissociative phenomena in a much more consistent and in-depth fashion, in order to help untangle the often unexplained heterogeneity in PTSD presentations and underlying neurobiological processes, and in order to develop more effective treatment guidelines addressing the dissociative component, when present.

# REFERENCES

Ainsworth, M. D. S., and Wittig, B. A. (1969). Attachment and exploratory behavior of one-year olds in a strange situation. In B. M. Foss (Ed.), *Determinants of infant behavior IV.* London: Methuen.

American Psychiatric Association. (1994). *Diagnostic and statistical manual of mental disorders: DSM-IV* (fourth ed.). Washington, DC: American Psychiatric Association.

Armstrong, J. G., Putnam, F. W., Carlson, E. B., Libero, D. Z., and Smith, S. R. (1997). Development and validation of a measure of adolescent dissociation: The Adolescent Dissociative Experiences Scale. *Journal of Nervous and Mental Disease, 185,* 491–97.

Becker-Blease, K. A., Deater-Deckard, K., Eley, T., Freyd, J. J., Stevenson, J., et al. (2004). A genetic analysis of individual differences in dissociative behaviors in childhood and adolescence. *Journal of Child Psychology Psychiatry, 45,* 522–32.

Braun, B. G. (1984). Towards a theory of multiple personality and dissociative phenomena. *The Psychiatric Clinics of North America, 7,* 171–91.

Bremner, J. (1999). Acute and chronic responses to psychological trauma: Where do we go from here? *American Journal of Psychiatry, 156,* 349–51.

Bremner, J. D., Licinio, J., Darnell, A., Krystal, J. H., Owens, M. J., Southwick, S. M. et al. (1997). Elevated CSF corticotrophin-releasing factor concentrations in post-traumatic stress disorder. *American Journal of Psychiatry, 154,* 624–29.

Bremner, J. D., Southwick, S., Brett, E., Fontana, A., Rosenheck, R., and Charney, D. S. (1992). Dissociation and posttraumatic stress disorder in Vietnam combat veterans. *American Journal of Psychiatry, 149,* 328–32.

Bremner, J. D., Vythilingaam, M., Anderson, G., Vermetten E., McGlashan T., Heninger G., et al. (2003). Assessment of the hypothalamic-pituitary-adrenal axis over a 24-hour diurnal period and in response to neuroendocrine challenges in women with and without childhood sexual abuse and posttraumatic stress disorder. *Biological Psychiatry, 54*, 710–18.

Brewin, C. R., Andrews, B., and Valentine, J. D. (2000). Meta-analysis of risk factors for posttraumatic stress disorder in trauma-exposed adults. *Journal of Consulting and Clinical Psychology, 68*, 748–66.

Brunet, A., Weiss, D. S., Metzler, T. J., Best, S. R., Neylan, T. C., Rogers, C., et al. (2001). The Peritraumatic Distress Inventory: A proposed measure of PTSD criterion A2. *American Journal of Psychiatry, 158*, 1480–85.

Brunner, R., Parzer, P., Schuld, V., and Resch, F. (2000). Dissociative symptomatology and traumatogenic factors in adolescent psychiatric patients. *Journal of Nervous and Mental Disorders, 188*, 71–77.

Bryant, R. A., Guthrie, R. M., and Moulds, M. L. (2001). Hypnotizability in acute stress disorder. *American Journal of Psychiatry, 158*, 600–604.

Butler, L. D., Duran, Ron E. F., Jasiukaitis, P., Koopman, C., and Spiegel, D. (1996). Hypnotizability and traumatic experience: a diathesis-stress model of dissociative symptomatology. *American Journal of Psychiatry, 153*, 42–63.

Carlson, E. A. (1998). A prospective longitudinal study of attachment isorganization/disorientation. *Child Development, 69*, 1107–28.

Carlson, E. B., and Rosser-Hogan, R. (1991). Trauma experiences, posttraumatic stress, dissociation, and depression in Cambodian refugees. *American Journal of Psychiatry, 148*, 1548–51.

Cassiday, K. L., McNally, R. J., and Zeitlin, S. B. (1992). Cognitive processing of trauma cues in rape victims with post-traumatic stress disorder. *Cognitive Therapy and Research, 16*, 282–95.

Chu, J. A. (2000). Psychological defense styles and childhood sexual abuse (letter). *American Journal of Psychiatry, 157*, 170.

Chu, J. A., and Dill, D. L. (1990). Dissociative symptoms in relation to childhood physical and sexual abuse. *American Journal of Psychiatry, 147*, 887–92.

Clohessy, S., and Ehlers, A. (1999). PTSD symptoms, response to intrusive memories, and coping in ambulance service workers. *British Journal of Clinical Psychology, 38*, 251–65.

Coons, P. M. (1998). The dissociative disorders. Rarely considered and underdiagnosed. *Psychiatric Clinics of North America, 21*, 637–48.

Delahanty, D. L., Royer, D. K., Raimonde, A. J., and Spoonster, E. (2003). Peritraumatic dissociation is inversely related to catecholamine levels in initial urine samples of motor vehicle accident victims. *Journal of Traumatic Dissociation, 4*, 65–79.

DePrince, A. P., and Freyd, J. J. (1999). Dissociative tendencies, attention and memory. *Psychological Science, 10*, 449–52.

Draijer, N., and Langeland, W. (1999). Childhood trauma and perceived parental dysfunction in the etiology of dissociative symptoms in psychiatric inpatients. *American Journal of Psychiatry, 156*, 379–85.

Dubner, A. E., and Motta, R. W. (1999). Sexually and physically abused foster care children and posttraumatic stress disorder. *Journal of Consulting and Clinical Psychology, 67*, 367–73.

Foa, E. B., Feske, U., Murdock, T. B., Kozak, M. J., and McCarthy, P. R. (1991). Processing of threat-related information in rape victims. *Journal of Abnormal Psychology, 100,* 156–62.

Foa, E. B., and Hearst-Ikeda, D. (1996). Emotional dissociation in response to trauma: An information-processing approach. In L. K. Michelson and W. J. Ray (Eds.), *Handbook of dissociation: Theoretical, empirical, and clinical perspectives* (207–24). New York: Plenum Press.

Ford, J. D. (1999). Disorders of extreme stress following war-zone military trauma: Associated features of posttraumatic stress disorder or comorbid but distinct syndromes? *Journal of Consulting and Clinical Psychology, 67,* 3–12.

Freyd, J. J. (1994). Betrayal-trauma: Traumatic amnesia as an adaptive response to childhood abuse. *Ethics and Behavioral, 4,* 307–29.

———. (1996). *Betrayal trauma: The logic of forgetting childhood abuse.* Cambridge, MA: Harvard University Press.

Freyd, J. J., Martorello, J., Alvarado, S. R., Hayes, A. E., and Christman, J. C. (1998). Cognitive environments and dissociative tendencies: Performance on the standard Stroop Task for high versus low dissociators. *Applied Cognitive Psychology, 12,* S91–103.

Frischholz, E. J., Lipman, L. S., Braun, B. G., and Sachs, R. G. (1992). Psychopathology, hypnotizability, and dissociation. *American Journal of Psychiatry, 149,* 1521–25.

Gershuny, B. S., Cloitre, M., and Otto, M. W. (2003). Peritraumatic dissociation and PTSD severity: Do event-related fears about death and control mediate their relation? *Behavioral Research Therapy, 41,* 157–66.

Gershuny, B. S., and Thayer, J. F. (1999). Relations among psychological trauma, dissociative phenomena, and trauma-related distress: A review and integration. *Clinical Psychology Review, 19,* 631–57.

Gilbertson, M. (2004). Neurocognitive function in monozygotic twins discordant for PTSD. Presented at the Twentieth Annual Meeting of the International Society for Traumatic Stress Studies (abstract #1720), New Orleans, November 14–18.

Gilbertson, M. W., Shenton, M. E., Ciszewski, A., Kasai, K., Lasko, N. B., Orr, S. P., et al. (2002). Smaller hippocampal volume predicts pathologic vulnerability to psychological trauma. *Nature Neuroscience, 5,* 1242–47.

Grabe, H. J., Rainermann, S., Spitzer, C., Gansicke, M., and Freyberger, H. J. (2000). The relationship between dimensions of alexithymia and dissociation. *Psychotherapy and Psychosomatics, 69,* 128–31.

Griffin, M. G., Resick, P. A., and Mechnic, M. B. (1997). Objective assessment of peritraumatic dissociation: Psychophysiological indicators. *American Journal of Psychiatry, 154,* 1081–88.

Halligan, S. L., Clark, D. M., and Ehlers, A. (2002). Cognitive processing, memory, and the development of PTSD symptoms: Two experimental analogue studies. *Journal of Behavior Therapy and Experimental Psychiatry, 33,* 73–89.

Halligan, S. L., Michael, T., Clark, D. M., and Ehlers, A. (2003). Posttraumatic stress disorder following assault: The role of cognitive processing, trauma memory, and appraisals. *Journal of Consulting and Clinical Psychology, 71,* 419–31.

Herman, J. (1992). Complex PTSD. *Journal of Traumatic Stress, 5*, 377–91.

Hesse, E., and Main, M. (2006). Frightened, threatening, and dissociative parental behavior in low-risk samples: description, discussion, and interpretations. *Developmental Psychopathology, 18*, 309–43.

Hornstein, N. L. (1996). Dissociative disorders in children and adolescents. In L. K. Michelson and W. J. Ray (Eds.), *Handbook of dissociation: Theoretical, empirical, and clinical perspectives.* New York: Plenum.

Hornstein, N. L., and Putnam, F. W. (1992). Clinical phenomenology of child and adolescent dissociative disorders. *Journal of American Academy of Child Adolescent Psychiatry, 31*, 1077–85.

Irwin, H. J. (1994). Proneness to dissociation and traumatic childhood events. *Journal of Nervous and Mental Disease, 4*, 193–99.

Irwin, H. J., and Melbin-Helberg, E. B. (1997). Alexithymia and dissociative tendencies. *Journal of Clinical Psychology, 53*, 159–66.

Jang, K. L., Paris, J., Zweig-Frank, H., and Livesley, W. J. (1998). Twin study of dissociative experience. *Journal of Nervous and Mental Disease, 186*, 345–51.

Johnson, D. M., Pike, J. L., and Chard, K. M. (2001). Factors predicting PTSD, depression, and dissociative severity in female treatment-seeking childhood sexual abuse survivors. *Child Abuse and Neglect, 25*, 179–98.

Kirby, J. S., Chu, J. A., and Dill, D. L. (1993). Correlates of dissociative symptomatology in patients with physical and sexual abuse histories. *Comprehensive Psychiatry, 34*, 258–63.

Lanius, R. A., Williamson, P. C., Boksman, K., Densmore, M., Gupta, M., Neufeld, R. W., et al. (2002). Brain activation during script-driven imagery induced dissociative responses in PTSD: A functional magnetic resonance imaging investigation. *Biological Psychiatry, 52*, 305–11.

Liotti, G. (1992). Disorganized/disoriented attachment in the etiology of the dissociative disorders. *Dissociation, 4*, 196–204.

Lyons-Ruth, K., Alpern, L., and Repacholi, B. (1993). Disorganized infant attachment classification and maternal psychosocial problems as predictors of hostile-aggressive behavior in the preschool classroom. *Child Development, 64*, 572–85.

Lyons-Ruth, K., Easterbrooks, M. A., and Cibelli, C. D. (1997). Infant attachment strategies, infant mental lag, and maternal depressive symptoms: Predictors of internalizing and externalizing problems at age 7. *Developmental Psychology, 33*, 681–92.

Main, M., and Morgan, H. (1996). Disorganization and disorientation in infant strange situation behavior: Phenotypic resemblance to dissociative states. In L. K. Michelson and W. J. Ray (Eds.), *Handbook of dissociation: Theoretical, empirical, and clinical perspectives.* New York: Plenum.

Marshall, G. N., and Schell, T. L. (2002). Reappraising the link between peritraumatic dissociation and PTSD symptom severity: Evidence from a longitudinal study of community violence survivors. *Journal of Abnormal Psychology, 111*, 626–36.

Marshall, R. D., Spitzer, R., and Liebowitz, M. R. (1999). Review and critique of the new DSM-IV diagnosis of acute stress disorder. *American Journal of Psychiatry, 156*, 1677–85.

Mayou, R. A., Ehlers, A., and Bryant, B. (2002). Posttraumatic stress disorder after motor vehicle accidents: 3-year follow-up of a prospective longitudinal study. *Behavioral Research Therapy, 40*, 665–75.

McNally, R. J., Clancy, S. A., Shachter, D. L., and Pitman, R. K. (2000). Cognitive processing of trauma cues in adults reporting repressed, recovered or continuous memories of childhood sexual abuse. *Journal of Abnormal Psychology, 109*, 355–59.

McNally, R. J., Kaspi, S. P., Riemann, B. C., and Zeitlin, S. B. (1990). Selective processing of threat cues in posttraumatic stress disorder. *Journal of Abnormal Psychology, 99*, 398–402.

Modestin, J., Lotscher, K., and Erni, T. (2002). Dissociative experiences and their correlates in young non-patients. *Psychology and Psychotherapy, 75*, 53–64.

Morgan, C. A., Wang, S., Southwick, S. M., Rasmusson, A., Hazlett, G., Hauger, R. L., et al. (2000). Plasma neuropeptide-Y concentrations in humans exposed to military survival training. *Biological Psychiatry, 47*, 902–9.

Murray, J., Ehlers, A., and Mayou, R. A. (2002). Dissociation and post-traumatic stress disorder: Two prospective studies of road traffic accident survivors. *British Journal of Psychiatry, 180*, 363–68.

Ogawa, J. R., Sroufe, L. A., Weinfield, N. S., Carlson, E. A., and Egeland, B. (1997). Development and the fragmented self: Longitudinal study of dissociative symptomatology in a nonclinical sample. *Development and Psychopathology, 9*, 855–79.

Ozer, E. J., Best, S. R., Lipsey, T. L., and Weiss, D. S. (2003). Predictors of posttraumatic stress disorder and symptoms in adults: A meta-analysis. *Psychological Bulletin, 129*, 52–73.

Phillips, M. L., Medford, N., Senior, C., Bullmore, E. T., Suckling, J., Brammer, M. J., et al. (2001). Depersonalization disorder: Thinking without feeling. *Psychiatry Research: Neuroimaging, 108*, 145–60.

Putnam, F. W. (1985). Dissociation as a response to extreme trauma. In R. P. Kluft (Ed.), *The ahildhood antecedents of multiple personality* (65–97). Washington, DC, American Psychiatric Press Inc.

———. (1993). Dissociative disorders in children: Behavioral profiles and problems. *Child Abuse and Neglect, 17*, 39–45.

Putnam, F. W., Helmers, K., Horowitz, L. A., and Trickett, P. K. (1995). Hypnotizability and dissociativity in sexually abused girls. *Child Abuse and Neglect, 19*, 645–55.

Ray, W. J. (1996). Dissociation in normal populations. In L. K. Michelson and W. J. Ray (Eds.), *Handbook of dissociation: Theoretical, empirical, and clinical perspectives* (51–66). New York: Plenum Press.

Rodriguez-Srednicki, O. (2001). Childhood sexual abuse, dissociation, and adult destructive behavior. *Journal of Child Sexual Abuse, 10*, 75–90.

Ross, C. A., Miller, S. D., Reagor, P., Bjornson, L., Fraser, G. A., and Anderson, G. (1990). Structured interview data on 102 cases of multiple personality disorder from four centers. *American Journal of Psychiatry, 147*, 596–601.

Shalev, A.Y., Freedman, S., Peri, T., Brandes, D., Sahar, T., Orr, S. P., and Pitman, R. K. (1998). Prospective study of posttraumatic stress disorder and depression following trauma. *American Journal of Psychiatry, 155*(5), 630–37.

Siegel, D. J. (1995). Memory, trauma and psychotherapy: A cognitive science review. *Journal of Psychotherapy Practice Research, 4*, 93–122.

Sierra, M., Senior, C., Dalton, J., McDonough, M., Bond, A., Phillips, M. L., et al. (2002). Autonomic response in depersonalization disorder. *Archives of General Psychiatry, 59*, 833–38.

Silva, R. R., Alpert, M., Munoz, D. M., Singh, S., Matzner, F., and Dummit, S. (2000). Stress and vulnerability to posttraumatic stress disorder in children and adolescents. *American Journal of Psychiatry, 157*, 1229–35.

Simeon, D. (2007). Relationships between dissociation and posttraumatic stress disorder. In E. Vermetten, M. J. Dorahy, and D. Spiegel (Eds.), *Traumatic dissociation: Neurobiology and treatment* (77–101). Washington, DC: American Psychiatric Press Inc.

Simeon, D., Greenberg, J., Nelson, D., Schmeidler, J., and Hollander, E. (2005). Dissociation and posttraumatic stress 1 year after the World Trade Center disaster: Follow-up of a longitudinal survey. *Journal of Clinical Psychiatry, 66*, 231–37.

Simeon, D., Guralnik, O., Hazlett, E., Spiegel-Cohen, J., Hollander, E., and Buchsbaum, M. S. (2000). Feeling unreal: A PET study of depersonalization disorder. *American Journal of Psychiatry, 157*, 1782–88.

Simeon, D., Guralnik, O., Knutelska, M., Hollander, E., and Schmeidler, J. (2001). Hypothalamic-pituitary-adrenal axis dysregulation in depersonalization disorder. *Neuropsychopharmacology, 25*, 793–95.

Simeon, D., Guralnik, O., Knutelska, M., and Schmeidler, J. (2002). Personality factors associated with dissociation: Temperament, defenses, and cognitive schemata. *American Journal of Psychiatry, 159*, 489–91.

Simeon, D., Guralnik, O., Knutelska, M., Yehuda, R., and Schmeidler, J. (2003). Basal norepinephrine in depersonalization disorder. *Psychiatry Research, 121*, 93–97.

Simeon, D., Guralnik, O., Schmeidler, J., Sirof, B., and Knutelska, M. (2001). The role of childhood interpersonal trauma in depersonalization disorder. *American Journal of Psychiatry, 158*, 1027–33.

Simeon, D., and Hollander, E. (2000). Dissociative disorders not otherwise specified. In B. J. Kaplan and V. A. Sadock (Eds.), *Comprehensive textbook of psychiatry* (seventh ed.) (1570–76). Philadelphia: Lipppincott Williams & Wilkins.

Simeon, D., Knutelska, M., and Hollander, E. (2004). HPA axis function in borderline personality disorder as a function of dissociation. Paper presented at the Twenty-First International Fall Conference of the International Society for the Study of Dissociation, New Orleans, November 18–20.

Simeon, D., Knutelska, M., Nelson, D., and Guralnik, O. (2003). Feeling unreal: A depersonalization disorder update of 117 cases. *Journal of Clinical Psychiatry, 64*, 990–97.

Simeon, D., Knutelska, M., Putnam, F., and Smith, L. M. (2005). Attention and emotional memory processes in individuals with dissociative disorders. Paper presented at the Twenty-Second International Fall Conference of the International Society for the Study of Dissociation, Toronto, Canada, November 6–8.

Simeon, D., Knutelska, M., Yehuda, R., Putnam, F., Schmeidler, J., and Smith, L. M. (2007). Hypothalamic-pituitary-adrenal axis function in dissociative disorders, post-traumatic stress disorder, and healthy volunteers. *Biological Psychiatry, 61*, 966–73.

Smith, M. A., Davidson, J., Ritchie, J. C., Kudler, H., Lipper, S., Chappell, P., et al. (1989). The corticotrophin-releasing hormone test in patients with posttraumatic stress disorder. *Biological Psychiatry, 26*, 349–55.

Southwick, S. M., Bremner, D. J., Rasmusson, A., Morgan, C. A., Arnsten, A., and Charney, D. S. (1999). Role of norepinephrine in the pathophysiology and treatment of posttraumatic stress disorder. *Biological Psychiatry, 46*, 1192–1204.

Southwick, S. M., Yehuda, R., Giller, E. L., and Perry, B. D. (1993). Personality disorders in war veterans with chronic posttraumatic stress disorder. *American Journal of Psychiatry, 150*, 1020–23.

Spiegel, D. (1984). Multiple personality as a posttraumatic stress disorder. *Psychiatric Clinics of North America, 7*, 101–10.

Sterlini, G. L., and Bryant, R. A. (2002). Hyperarousal and dissociation: A study of novice skydivers. *Behavior Research and Therapy, 40*, 431–37.

Van der Hart, O., and Nijenhuis, E. (2001). Generalized dissociative amnesia: Episodic, semantic, and procedural memories lost and found. *Australian and New Zealand Journal of Psychiatry, 35*, 589–600.

Van der Hart, O., Nijenhuis, E., Steele, K., and Brown, D. (2004). Trauma-related dissociation: Conceptual clarity lost and found. *Australian and New Zealand Journal of Psychiatry, 38*, 906–14.

Van der Kolk, B., Pelcovitz, D., Roth, S., Mandel, F. S., McFarlane, A., and Herman, J. L. (1996). Dissociation, somatization, and affect dysregulation: The complexity of adaptation to trauma. *American Journal of Psychiatry, 153*, 83–93.

Van der Kolk, B. A., and van der Hart, O. (1989). Pierre Janet and the breakdown of adaptation in psychological trauma. *American Journal of Psychiatry, 146*, 1530–40.

Waldo, T. G., and Merritt, R. D. (2000). Fantasy proneness, dissociation, and DSM-IV axis II symptomatology. *Journal of Abnormal Psychology, 109*, 555–58.

Waller, N. G., Putnam, F. W., and Carlson, E. B. (1996). Types of dissociation and dissociative types: A taxometric analysis of dissociative experiences. *Psychological Methods, 1*, 300–321.

Waller, N. G., and Ross, C. A. (1997). The prevalence and biometric structure of pathological dissociation in the general population: Taxometric and behavior genetic findings. *Journal of Abnormal Psychology, 106*, 499–510.

Yehuda, R. (1997). Sensitization of the hypothalamic-pituitary-adrenal axis in posttraumatic stress disorder. *Annals of the New York Academy of Sciences, 821*, 57–75.

Yehuda, R., Keefe, R. S. E., Harvey, P. D., Levengood, D. K., Gerber, J., Geni, J., et al. (1995). Learning and memory in combat veterans with PTSD. *American Journal of Psychiatry, 152*, 137–39.

Yehuda, R., Levengood, R. A., Schmeidler, J., Wilson, S., Guo, L. S., and Gerber, D. (1996). Increased pituitary activation following metyrapone administration in post-traumatic stress disorder. *Psychoneuroendocrinology, 21*, 1–16.

Yehuda, R., Lowy, M. T., Southwick, S. M., and Giller, E. L. (1991). Lymphocyte glucocorticoid receptor number in PTSD. *American Journal of Psychiatry, 148,* 499–504.

Yehuda, R., Schmeidler, J., Siever, L. J., Binder-Brynes, K., and Elkin, A. (1997). Individual differences in posttraumatic stress disorder symptom profiles in Holocaust survivors in concentration camps or in hiding. *Journal of Traumatic Stress, 10,* 453–63.

Yehuda, R., Southwick, S. M., Krystal, J. M., Bremner, D., Charney, D. S., and Mason, J. W. (1993). Enhanced suppression of cortisol following dexamethasone administration in combat veterans with posttraumatic stress disorder and major depressive disorder. *American Journal of Psychiatry, 150,* 83–86.

Yehuda, R., Southwick, S. M., Nussbaum, G., Wahby, V., Giller, E. L., and Mason, J. W. (1990). Low urinary cortisol excretion in patients with posttraumatic stress disorder. *Journal of Nervous and Mental Disease, 178,* 366–69.

Young, E. A., and Breslau, N. (2004). Cortisol and catecholamines in posttraumatic stress disorder. *Archives of General Psychiatry, 61,* 394–401.

# 10

## Comorbid PTSD and Major Depression: Does History of Exposure to Interpersonal Violence Contribute to Nonresilience?

*Jesse R. Cougle, Heidi Resnick, and Dean G. Kilpatrick*

As mentioned previously, although PTSD researchers typically focus on predictors and correlates of PTSD alone, presence of comorbid disorders is the rule rather than the exception. The most common diagnoses comorbid with PTSD in MVA victims are affective and anxiety disorders (Koren, Arnon, and Klein, 1999) with rates of comorbid depression and PTSD ranging from 35–50 percent (Breslau, Davis, Peterson, and Schultz, 1997, 2000; Kessler, Sonnega, Bromet, Hughes, and Nelson, 1995). These findings underscore the idea that focusing solely on PTSD as the only posttraumatic outcome may oversimplify the complex array of posttraumatic responses. The present chapter reviews findings concerning the incidence and impact of PTSD and comorbid depression, with a specific focus on the extent to which prior interpersonal trauma may increase risk for developing these comorbid symptoms. Further, unlike much PTSD research, which tends to focus on current mental health status, the present chapter focuses more on resilience in the face of trauma, which takes into account both past and current functioning.

### RESILIENCE AND PTSD

Most people (approximately 40–80 percent; Breslau, Davis, Andreski, and Peterson, 1991; Kessler et al., 1995) will experience at least one traumatic or life-threatening event during their lifetimes, but only a minority will develop emotional problems as a result. The ability to withstand traumatic events free

Address correspondence to Dr. Dean Kilpatrick; Medical University of South Carolina; 67 President St., PO Box 250861; Charleston, SC 29425. E-mail: kilpatdg@musc.edu of emotional sequelae is a concept known as *resilience*, which has been of significant interest to researchers of PTSD. The identification of modifiable variables associated with resilience is particularly important, as it could lead to interventions that would help buffer the effects of trauma exposure. In addition, information on who is likely to be resilient following traumatic exposure could help identify those most in need of prevention services following stressors such as child maltreatment, violent crime, and other traumatic events.

Researchers have generally been more concerned with risk than resilience, and, as a result, have focused more on negative factors that predict PTSD onset instead of those associated with resilience. Meta-analyses of risk factors for PTSD have indicated that psychiatric history (personal and family), prior childhood abuse, trauma severity, and peritraumatic distress and dissociation (Brewin, Andrews, and Valentine, 2000; Ozer, Best, Lipsey, and West, 2003) are all predictors of PTSD onset. There is also much evidence for a "dose effect," such that risk of PTSD is increased with exposure to each additional traumatic event (Ozer et al., 2003). Among the variable (or modifiable) risk factors, low social support and additional life stress following the trauma have been implicated as having the most consistent relationships with PTSD risk.

Positive protective factors that may buffer the impact of trauma have received less attention than risk-related variables. It is true that some negative factors, such as low social support, have an inverse (high social support) related to resilience, but positive variables, such as hardiness (Kobasa, Maddi, and Kahn, 1982), positive emotion, and laughter (Bonanno, Noll, Putnam, O'Neill, and Trickett, 2003) have also been found among resilient individuals. Research on such variables is growing and will likely increase further with the burgeoning movement of positive psychology, which has as its focus some of the positive traits and virtues frequently neglected by researchers (Seligman and Csikszentmihalyi, 2000).

One major limitation of existing research in PTSD involves the conceptual and methodological distinction researchers have often failed to make between resilience and recovery. Bonnano (2004) argued this point forcefully in a recent review. Resilience, properly defined, relates to whether the emotional disorder ever occurs following exposure to a potentially traumatic event (PTE), and recovery involves an occurrence of the disorder posttrauma but then a return to non-clinical status by the time an assessment of current functioning is done. Given this distinction, it is apparent that much of the literature that focuses only on current functioning confounds resilience, recovery, and non-recovery. To neglect "recovered" as a status in its own right neglects the very real suffering many individuals experience following a traumatic event and factors that could lead to recovery among these individuals. Clearly, then, researchers would do well to assess whether disorders ever develop—not whether they are currently present.

## PTSD AND MAJOR DEPRESSIVE DISORDER FOLLOWING TRAUMATIC EVENTS

PTSD and major depressive disorder (MDD) are relatively common psychiatric problems, with lifetime prevalence estimates of 7 percent (Kessler, Berglund, Demler, Jin, and Walters, 2005) and 13 percent (Hasin, Goodwin, Stinson, and Grant, 2005), respectively. Over the past several years, research has accumulated indicating that these disorders often co-occur. For example, Brown and colleagues (2001) assessed lifetime anxiety and mood disorders comorbidity in a community sample of outpatients and found that PTSD was the anxiety disorder most likely to be associated with MDD, with 69 percent of individuals with PTSD also meeting criteria for MDD. High rates of PTSD/MDD comorbidity have also been observed in veteran populations (Kulka et al., 1990; Orsillo et al., 1996), among a sample of female victims of intimate partner violence (Nixon, Resick, and Nishith, 2004), and among U.S. adolescents (Kilpatrick et al., 2003).

A number of explanations have been put forward to account for the high comorbidity between PTSD and MDD. Franklin and Zimmerman (2001) performed an item-analysis of PTSD and MDD symptoms to test whether their co-occurrence could be due to symptom overlap. They found that the rate of "contaminated symptoms" that exist between the two disorders (anhedonia, concentration, and sleep problems) did not differ between individuals with PTSD-only and PTSD/MDD, so they concluded that the high comorbidity rates must have some other explanation.

PTSD/MDD comorbidity may also be explained by the fact that MDD often precedes the occurrence of PTSD and may actually increase the risk of developing PTSD. Research indicates that individuals with MDD are more likely to exhibit PTSD-like symptoms in response to a traumatic event (Breslau et al., 1997; Bromet, Sonnega, and Kessler, 1998). Evidence also suggests that those suffering from MDD are more likely to be exposed to traumatic events (Breslau et al., 1997).

An alternative explanation is that MDD may occur as a consequence of PTSD. Individuals with PTSD often view the world as dangerous (Foa, Ehlers, Clark, Tolin, and Orsillo, 1999) and may isolate themselves in their efforts to maintain a sense of safety. They may avoid different activities that were previously enjoyable because of their associations with the traumatic

event. The absence of positive experiences and social support needed to buffer the impact of different stressors may leave them vulnerable to depression.
Seligman (1972) argued that depression is a consequence of learned helplessness, a type of learning that occurs through the experience of an aversive,
unavoidable event from which there is no escape. The fact that 88 percent of
sexual assault victims described themselves as "feeling helpless" during the
rape (Kilpatrick, Veronen, and Resick, 1982) suggests that such experiences
could lead to depression as a result of this learning.

Further evidence for the hypothesis that PTSD could lead to MDD stems
from Beck's (1976) cognitive theory of depression. This theory proposes that
MDD is a function of a "cognitive triad" consisting of negative views about
the self, the world, and the future. In the case of sexual assault victims, victims are prone to self-blame which may result from internalized myths that
permeate our society; that is, they frequently believe they were in some way
responsible for the assault or did something to deserve it. Victims may be
treated with indifference or hostility by professionals they confided in regarding the rape and could feel much shame and guilt as a result. These negative
self-views, combined with beliefs about the dangerousness of the world and
hopelessness regarding their recovery, may lead many with PTSD to develop
a depressive episode via Beck's triad. Indeed, research has found that beliefs
most strongly related to PTSD involve negative cognitions about the self and
the world, and self-blame (Foa et al., 1999).

The presence of a traumatic stressor is a necessary condition for a diagnosis
of PTSD (APA, 1994), but exposure to traumatic events have also been linked
to MDD. Kilpatrick, Saunders, Veronen, Best, and Von (1987), for example,
noted that lifetime prevalence of depression was approximately 46 percent
in women who experienced one rape and 80 percent in women with multiple
rapes. Duncan, Saunders, Kilpatrick, Hanson, and Resnick (1996) reported a
similar relationship between physical assault and depression. An alternative
account of comorbidity, then, is that the traumatic events that lead to PTSD
may also increase vulnerability to MDD. To test this hypothesis, Breslau and
colleagues (2000) examined rates of MDD without PTSD between people who
were and were not exposed to traumatic events. They found no differences in
MDD between the groups, which suggests that the primary means through
which traumatic events lead to MDD is through a PTSD diagnosis.

One of the most rigorous tests of the temporal relationship between PTSD
and MDD came through a two-year prospective study of Gulf War veterans
(Erickson, Wolfe, King, King, and Sharkansky, 2001). These researchers
found support for a bi-directional model of pathogenesis with MDD symptoms predicting later PTSD and vice versa. However, PTSD symptoms at
time 1 were generally a more reliable predictor of MDD symptoms at time

2 than vice versa. Their analyses also found that symptoms of hyperarousal, in particular, were important predictors of later MDD symptoms. These findings, then, are consistent with retrospective studies indicating that a majority of patients with both diagnoses report that PTSD preceded MDD (Breslau et al., 1997; Kessler et al., 1995).

## PATTERNS OF EXPOSURE TO VIOLENCE AND COMORBIDITY AMONG ADOLESCENTS AND YOUNG ADULTS: AN ANALYSIS OF A NATIONAL PROBABILITY SAMPLE

Research using adult populations has consistently shown an association between exposure to interpersonal violence (IPV) and the development of PTSD. For example, Resnick, Kilpatrick, Dansky, Saunders, and Best (1993) and Kessler et al. (1995) reported that exposure to IPV was a stronger predictor of PTSD than other potentially traumatic events (e.g., accidents, disasters). Exposure to IPV has also been associated with other mental health outcomes, such as MDD (e.g., Kessler, Davis, and Kendler, 1997; Saunders, Kilpatrick, Hanson, Resnick, and Walker, 1999), though evidence for this association is less strong. Recently, Kilpatrick et al. (2003) examined exposure to IPV and certain mental health outcomes (MDD, PTSD, and substance abuse/dependence) in a national probability sample of adolescents. Their findings provided further support for the relationship between IPV and increased risk for MDD and PTSD.

Studies exploring relations between IPV and comorbid mental health outcomes are rare, and patterns of PTSD/MDD comorbidity among adolescents and young adults have received even less attention. Given the absence of research in this area and the limitations of studies examining resilience, we sought to examine patterns of comorbidity among adolescents and young adults using the National Survey of Adolescents (NSA), a national probability sample. Longitudinal data taken from two waves of the NSA are presented that give special attention to the contribution of types of violence suffered by adolescents and young adults and childhood family environment to risk and resilience among those exposed to traumatic events. Because we were interested in examining the role of IPV and comorbid PTSD and MDD in the context of a resilience framework, this dictated two major aspects of the research and data analytical strategy. First, we limited the sample to the NSA participants with exposure to at least one incident of IPV or other PTSD criterion A potentially traumatic event (PTE). This was necessary because it is impossible to determine whether someone is resilient unless they have been exposed to a traumatic event. Second, we focused on patterns of lifetime comorbidity between PTSD and MDD instead of patterns of current comorbidity of the two disorders. As previously noted, current presence or absence of disorders cannot tell us about whether someone is resilient or not, but looking at patterns of lifetime disorders among exposed individuals permits us to look at factors associated with resilience and nonresilience. Based on existing literature, we made the following hypotheses:

1) Most exposed individuals would be resilient;
2) Lifetime PTSD and MDD diagnoses would be highly comorbid;
3) History of adverse family environment (AFE) would be a risk factor for PTSD, MDD only, and PTSD/MDD;
4) History of IPV would be a risk factor for PTSD and PTSD/MDD but not for MDD only;
5) Other life stressors, but not IPV, would be a risk factor for MDD only.

## Methods

Data were examined from 1386 NSA participants who had completed wave 1 at ages twelve to seventeen and wave 2 at ages nineteen to twenty-four and who reported exposure to at least one or more criterion A potentially traumatic events (PTEs). PTEs were coded as IPV or other traumatic stressors (OTS). IPV as defined here included direct exposure to IPV, as well as serious witnessed violence, or being a friend or family member of a homicide victim or a relative killed by a drunk driver. OTS included all non-IPV exposures (e.g., serious accident, disaster, serious injury), and not just those in which the individual reported fear of death or serious injury. The types of stressors were coded more specifically and are described further below, along with prevalence rates. Psychological assessments were also given to identify cases with: (1) lifetime PTSD; (2) lifetime MDD; (3) current PTSD, defined as meeting symptom criteria within the previous six months at the time of the wave 2 assessment; and (4) current MD, defined as meeting criteria within the previous 6 months at the time of the wave 2 assessment. Comorbidity of MDD and PTSD diagnoses was also assessed.

## Results

### Demographic Characteristics

At wave 2, the average age within the *full* sample of 1753 (those who did and did not report the experience of a PTE) was 22.10, SD = 1.74. Women comprised almost half of the sample (49.8 percent). In terms of ethnicity, 160 participants (9.3 percent) said they were of Hispanic origin; 1245 (72.1

percent) reported that they were Caucasian; 220 (12.8 percent) reported being African-American; 3.2 percent said they were Asian; and 2.7 percent reported American Indian or Alaskan Native race/ethnicity.

## Prevalence of Criterion A and Non-Criterion A Stressors across Waves 1 and 2

***Criterion A Stressors.*** Criterion A stressors included interpersonal violence (IPV) exposure and exposure to other traumatic stressors (OTS). IPV was measured by a count of violence types reported at wave 1 that included: (1) molestation; (2) rape; (3) physical assault; and new exposure at wave 2 to (4) rape; (5) physical assault; (6) homicide death of a friend or family member by a drunk driver or by homicide at waves 1 or 2; or (7) witnessing of serious violence incidents including shootings, stabbing, sexual assault, mugging, or attacks with weapons reported at wave 1 or new incidents since wave 1 and reported at wave 2. Scores on this variable ranged from 0 to 8. Based on this classification, 66.7 percent in the full wave 2 sample reported exposure to at least one IPV incident, with an average of 1.39 (SD = 1.41) events. Frequency data indicated that 33.3 percent of the sample reported no IPV, 27.6 percent reported at least one incident, and 39.1 percent reported two or more IPV incidents.

Other traumatic stressors (OTS) were defined as a count of: (1) reported experience of a serious car accident(s); (2) exposure to disaster; (3) other traumatic events that included injury; and (4) other stressful events that included fear of death or injury. Scores on this variable ranged from 0 to 4, and the average number of OTS stressors experienced by the sample was .64 (SD = .81). Frequency data indicated that 943 (53.8 percent) of the sample reported no OTS, 555 (31.6 percent) reported at least one incident, and 255 (14.6 percent) reported two or more types of OTS.

Participants were classified as having exposure to any PTE if they reported being exposed to one or more IPV or OTS incidents. By these criteria, a total of 1386 participants (79.1 percent) in the sample reported at least one PTE.

***Non-Criterion A Stressors.*** Non-criterion A stressors included adverse family environment (AFE) and past year other (non-criterion A) life stressors (OLS). Adverse family environment was defined as reports at either wave 1 or wave 2 of a family member with drug, alcohol, mental health, or legal problems. Scores on this variable ranged from 0 to 4. A total of 592 participants (33.8 percent) from the full sample reported exposure to one or more AFE incidents, and the average score among the sample was .56 (SD = .93). A total of 1161 (66.2 percent) reported no AFE; 336 (19.2 percent) reported one AFE; and 256 (14.6 percent) reported two or more AFE events.

Past year OLS exposure was defined as the count of past year experiences of fourteen events including serious illness of self, close friend, or family member, death of close friend or family member, and major life transitions such as a job loss, with a range of 0 to 14. Participants endorsed an average of 2.49 (SD = 1.93) OLS items. A dichotomous cutoff based on a score of five or more items (reflecting a score of at least one standard deviation above the mean) was used to indicate more vs. less exposure to OLS. A total of 255 (14.6 percent) individuals were classified as positive for OLS exposure based on this cutoff.

### Demographic Characteristics of the Sub-Sample Reporting Exposure to Any PTE (N = 1386)

Characteristics of the sample exposed to any PTE were similar to the full sample. Among this sub-group, average age was 22.15 (SD = 1.76) and 49.1 percent were women. In terms of ethnicity, 141 (10.2 percent) reported that they were Hispanic, 950 (69.7 percent) reported that they were Caucasian, 191 (14.1 percent) reported being African American, 3.1 percent said they were Asian, and 2.9 percent reported American Indian or Alaskan Native race/ethnicity.

### Prevalence of Criterion A and Other Traumatic Stressors and Mental Disorders Among Those with Any PTE Exposure

**Prevalence of Criterion A Events.**    Among this group, 1170 (84.4 percent) reported exposure to one or more IPV events and 810 (58.5 percent) reported exposure to one or more OTS events. A total of 216 participants (15.6 percent) with any PTE reported no IPV; 484 (34.9 percent) reported one IPV, and 686 (49.5 percent) reported two or more IPV events. A total of 576 (42 percent) among those with any PTE exposure reported no OTS, 555 (40 percent) reported one OTS, and 255 (18.4 percent) reported two or more OTS events.

**Prevalence of Non-Criterion A Stressors.**    Among those with a history of any PTE, prevalence of exposure to one or more AFE was 38 percent. More specifically, close to two-thirds reported no AFE exposure, 21 percent reported one exposure; and 17 percent reported exposure to two or more AFE events. Among those with a history of any PTE, prevalence of OLS exposure was 16.8 percent (N = 232).

**Patterns of Exposure to Different Types of Stressors.**    Overlap between IPV, OTS, and AFE indicated that 166 participants (12 percent) reported exposure to OTS only, 374 (27 percent) reported exposure to IPV only, 320 (23.1 percent) reported exposure to both IPV and OTS, 50 (3.6 percent) reported exposure to OTS and AFE, 202 (14.6 percent) reported exposure to both IPV and AFE, and 274 (19.8 percent) reported exposure to IPV, OTS, and AFE. Associations between each of these three types of stressors and the dichotomous OLS cutoff indicated that similar proportions of those with IPV exposure (18.2 percent), OTS exposure (19.5 percent), and AFE (23.6 percent) also had exposure to OLS. The stressor variables were significantly intercorrelated, $p < .01$, with the exception of AFE and OTS, which were not significantly correlated with each other.

## Prevalence of Posttraumatic Stress Disorder (PTSD) and Major Depressive Disorder (MDD) across Waves 1 and 2

Among the subsample reporting any PTE, 302 (21.8 percent) met criteria for lifetime PTSD, while 8.8 percent (N = 122) met for PTSD within the past six months. In addition, the prevalence of a lifetime report of major depressive episode was 39.9 percent (N = 553), while the past six month prevalence of depression was 14.5 percent (N = 200).

Patterns of comorbidity for PTSD and depression were observed. Data indicated that 801 participants (57.8 percent) met neither lifetime diagnosis, 32 participants (2.3 percent) met criteria for PTSD only, 283 participants (20.4 percent) met criteria for MDD without PTSD, and 270 participants (19.5 percent) met criteria for PTSD and MDD. Thus, while lifetime exclusive diagnosis of PTSD rarely occurred, among the 553 participants with lifetime MDD, approximately half (51.2 percent) met criteria for MDD without PTSD while the remainder (48.8 percent) met criteria for both PTSD and MDD.

## Recovery from PTSD and MD

Among 655 participants who had ever met lifetime criteria for either PTSD or MDD, 264 (40.3 percent) met current criteria and 391 (59.7 percent) no longer met criteria for either disorder.

## Associations Between Lifetime PTSD and MD and Exposure to Criterion A and Non-Criterion A Events

Trichotomous variables describing the number of exposures to each stressor as 0, 1, or 2+ were coded for IPV, OTS, and AFE. Multinomial logistic regression analysis was used to examine associations between these variables and the dichotomous OLS variable, and lifetime MD and comorbid PTSD/MDD diagnoses, among the subset of participants exposed to one or more PTEs. This analysis indicated that each lifetime diagnosis was associated with the exposure variables such that the prevalence of diagnosis was higher among those exposed to each type of event. However, the statistical significance of association varied with lifetime diagnosis; AFE (OR = 1.65) and OLS (OR = 1.61) were significant predictors of MD, while AFE (OR = 1.95) and IPV (OR = 2.02) were significant predictors of comorbid PTSD/MDD. OTS was not a significant predictor for either lifetime diagnosis.

When a formal statistical comparison of odds ratios between lifetime diagnoses was performed for each possible variable subset, several of the tests were significant (see table 10.1). That is, the predictors of MDD differed significantly from the predictors of comorbid PTSD/MDD in the multivariate model. It was clear, however, that these results were driven primarily by the strength of the differential effect of IPV; any test that did not include IPV failed to reach significance by a wide margin. This strongly suggests that IPV predicts MD alone differently than it predicts comorbid PTSD/MDD. Examination of table 10.1 hints that the association between IPV and comorbid PTSD/MDD is twice the magnitude of the association with MD alone.

Lifetime prevalence of PTSD/MDD and MDD alone were also examined in terms of IPV experience. Among participants with no IPV exposure, the percentages with no disorder, MDD only, and PTSD/MDD, were 68.1 percent, 19 percent, and 11.6 percent respectively. Among participants reporting one IPV experience, the percentages with no disorder, MDD only, and PTSD/ MDD, were 66.9 percent, 21.3 percent, and 11 percent respectively. Among those reporting more than one IPV experience, the percentages with no dis-

Table 10.1.   Predicting Lifetime "Pure" Depression (MD only, no PTSD) and Comorbid Depression + PTSD by IPV, OTS, AFE, and OLS in a Multivariate Logistic Model

| Depression Only | | | | | | |
|---|---|---|---|---|---|---|
| Step | Variable | Beta | SE | Wald $\chi 2$ | OR | 95% Wald CI |
| 1 | IPV | 0.09 | 0.118 | 0.58 | 1.09 | 0.87 − 1.38 |
| 2 | OTS | 0.03 | 0.109 | 0.08 | 1.03 | 0.83 − 1.28 |
| 3 | AFE | 0.5 | 0.109 | 21.24 | 1.65*** | 1.33 − 2.04 |
| 4 | OLS | 0.48 | 0.22 | 4.8 | 1.61* | 1.05 − 2.47 |
| Comorbid Depression + PTSD | | | | | | |
| 1 | IPV | 0.7 | 0.15 | 23.05 | 2.02* | 1.51 − 2.68 |
| 2 | OTS | 0.19 | 0.11 | 2.77 | 1.21 | 0.97 − 1.51 |
| 3 | AFE | 0.67 | 0.11 | 36.76 | 1.95*** | 1.57 − 2.42 |
| 4 | OLS | 0.13 | 0.23 | 0.32 | 1.14 | 0.73 − 1.77 |

*Note:* IPV: interpersonal violence exposure; OTS: other traumatic stressor exposure; AFE: Adverse family environment exposure; OLS: other lifetime stressor exposure
*$p < .05$, **$p < .01$, ***$p < .001$

order, MDD only, and PTSD/MDD, were 48.2 percent, 20 percent, and 27.9 percent respectively. Thus, MDD only diagnosis did not appear to be affected by frequency of IPV. In contrast, higher rates of PTSD/MDD comorbidity were noted for those with two or more IPV experiences.

## Summary of Findings

The data presented here indicate that exposure to potentially traumatic events (PTE) is particularly common, as 79 percent of the full sample reported such experiences. Among those reporting a history of PTE, 84 percent were exposed to at least one episode of IPV. It was also more common to experience two or more episodes of IPV than just one isolated event. It is noteworthy that these findings were limited to adolescents and young adults; that is, the prevalence of lifetime exposure to PTEs is likely lower among this sample than what would be found among older populations.

The prevalence of PTSD and MDD among this sample is also substantial. Among those exposed to any PTE, 21.8 percent met criteria for PTSD and 39.9 percent met criteria for MDD. Interestingly, among those reporting PTSD, comorbidity appeared to be the rule rather than the exception. That is, participants exposed to PTE were over eight times as likely to have a comorbid PTSD/MDD diagnosis (19.5 percent) as they were to meet criteria for PTSD only (2.3 percent). However, it is also important to note that, as hypothesized, most individuals exposed to PTEs were resilient.

Our analyses also examined the contribution of IPV to PTSD and MDD, when controlling for other traumatic stressors, adverse family environment, and non-criterion A stressors. The pattern of results indicated that IPV did not predict an MDD-only diagnosis, though it was associated with PTSD/MDD comorbidity. These findings are consistent with Breslau and colleagues' (2000) study, which found no relationship between IPV and an MDD-only diagnosis. Our data, thus, add additional support for the hypothesis that the IPV-MDD relationship is mediated by a PTSD diagnosis.

An interesting dose relationship between IPV and mental health outcomes was also noted. No differences in PTSD and MDD diagnoses were observed among participants with no IPV and one IPV event exposure. However, an increase in PTSD/MDD comorbid diagnosis was found among individuals exposed to two or more IPV events. These findings are consistent with previous research showing that prior trauma serves as a risk factor for the development of PTSD following a subsequent traumatic event (Ozer et al., 2003). The fact that cumulative exposure, rather than single exposure, was associated with increased PTSD/MDD diagnoses has important theoretical and clinical implications that will be discussed below.

## IMPLICATIONS

The data presented here have several theoretical and clinical implications. The findings that PTSD/MDD comorbidity was related to episodes of IPV, but MDD only diagnosis was not, suggests that these profiles may be associated with different phenotypes. Twin and adoption studies have implicated moderate degrees of heritability associated with exposure to certain types of traumatic events (Lyons, Goldberg, Eisen, et al., 1993), PTSD (Stein, Jang, Taylor, Vernon, and Lively, 2002; True, Rice, Eisen, et al., 1993) and MDD (Glowinski et al., 2003; Sullivan, Neal, and Kindler, 2000). As discussed in more detail in chapter 2, in terms of specific genes, the serotonin transporter gene (SLC6A4) has been implicated. This gene consists of two common variant alleles (short form: s; long form: l). The short allele appears to convey increased stress response, presumably by a mechanism that leads to increases in amygdala reactivity (Hariri, Goldberg, Mattay, Kolachana, Callicott, Egan, et al., 2003). Human studies have shown an association between the serotonin-transporter-linked polymorphic region and PTSD diagnosis (Lee, Lee, Kang, et al., 2005), and Koenen et al. (2008) reviews research describing the genetic underpinnings of PTSD. Researchers have also found the s allele to be associated with increased risk for several depression-related phenotypes in abused children (Caspi, Sugden, Moffitt, Taylor, Craig, Harrington, et al., 2003; Kaufman, Yang, Douglas-Palumberi, Houshyar, Lipschitz, Krystal, et al., 2004). The fact that this gene has been linked to both PTSD and MDD raises an important question. That is, does this genetic variant represent a common vulnerability to PTSD and MDD, or are researchers linking this gene to MDD simply picking up cases of comorbid PTSD/MDD in their samples? Likewise, many gene x environment interaction studies looking at the serotonin transporter gene and the phenotype of depression may well have an environmental stressor term that is confounded with unmeasured IPV. Further research exploring the relationship between genes such as the serotonin transporter, IPV, and PTSD, MDD, and PTSD/MDD diagnoses is warranted.

The present study's findings also suggest that clinicians and researchers treating MDD would do well to screen for a history of IPV and assess for the presence of PTSD symptoms. Given the unique relationship between IPV and PTSD and the high rates of PTSD/MDD comorbidity, it is possible that many clinicians are treating MDD as such when PTSD may be the more prominent clinical feature. As reviewed earlier, the PTSD/MDD comorbid profile is likely explained by MDD occurring as a consequence of PTSD. The results of a recently published clinical depression trial provide further light on this issue. Researchers found that 33 percent of the depressed sample of women in this study met criteria for comorbid PTSD (Green, Krupnick, Chung, Siddique, Krause, Revicki, et al., 2006). Moreover, these women reported greater anxiety and depression and were more functionally impaired than women without PTSD. Though individuals meeting criteria for PTSD/MDD diagnoses did improve as a result of treatment (cognitive behavior therapy or anti-depressant medication), they remained more impaired than those without comorbid PTSD diagnoses throughout the one-year follow-up period. More work is needed to improve treatment outcomes for these individuals.

It is possible that clients with a comorbid PTSD/MDD profile would benefit from a more specialized treatment than the ones reserved for each specific disorder. There may be certain elements of cognitive-behavior therapy that would lead to decreases in symptoms of both disorders. In particular, behavioral strategies that seek to increase activity levels, opportunities for positive reinforcement, and contact with feared situations (e.g., public settings, crowds) could prove especially beneficial for clients prone to avoidance and social isolation. Some preliminary data provide evidence supporting the use of such strategies. Mulick and Naugle (2004), for example, found eleven weekly sessions of behavioral activation to lead to recovered, non-diagnostic status for an individual military veteran suffering from both disorders. A recent pilot study examining the utility of behavioral activation for the treatment of veterans with PTSD also found it to be effective in reducing PTSD and depressive symptoms (Jakupcak, Roberts, Martell, et al., 2006). Finally, there is some evidence that treating PTSD also results in significant improvement in depression (Resick, Nishith, Weaver, Astin, and Feuer, 2002).

Given that cumulative IPV exposure, rather than single exposure, was associated with increased rates of PTSD/MDD diagnoses, an additional layer of complexity may be implicated in the assessment and diagnosis of PTSD. How should clinicians go about assessing PTSD symptoms associated with multiple traumatic events? Is there such thing as an "aggregate PTSD" with different symptoms associated with different traumatic events? In what way does the impact of these successive traumatic events lead to the onset of PTSD? Additional longitudinal exploration of the impact of different types of IPV incidents, and the manner in which each additional event affects victims would help answer these questions. Given that individuals already exposed to one IPV event may be at risk for comorbid PTSD/MDD should another IPV episode occur, resources should be devoted toward this high risk population to help decrease the risk of subsequent IPV exposure and/or buffer the effects of such exposure.

While previous research has been limited by the confounding of resilience and recovery, our data took into account lifetime diagnoses rather than assessment of current functioning and so was able to accurately determine resilience rates. While exposure to violence was common in this sample, most of those who experienced a PTE did not develop MDD or PTSD, underscoring the importance of additional research identifying factors associated with resilience.

## ACKNOWLEDGEMENTS

The research described in this chapter was supported by NIJ Grant No. 93-IJ-CX-0023 and CDC Grant No. R49-CCR-419810. The preparation of the chapter was also partially supported by NIMH Grant No. MH18869-20.

## REFERENCES

Beck, A. T. (1976). *Cognitive therapy and the emotional disorders*. New York: International Universities Press.

Bonanno, G. A. (2004). Loss, trauma, and human resilience: Have we underestimated the human capacity to thrive after extremely aversive events? *American Psychologist, 59*, 20–28.

Bonanno, G. A., Noll, J. G., Putnam, F. W., O'Neill, M., and Trickett, P. (2003). Predicting the willingness to disclose childhood sexual abuse from measures of repressive coping and dissociative tendencies. *Child Maltreatment, 8*(4), 302–18.

Breslau, N., Davis, G. C., Andreski, P., and Peterson, E. (1991). Traumatic events and posttraumatic stress disorder in an urban population of young adults. *Archives of General Psychiatry, 48*, 216–22.

Breslau, N., Davis, G. C., Peterson, E. L., and Schultz, L. (1997). Psychiatric sequelae of posttraumatic stress disorder in women. *Archives of General Psychiatry, 54*, 81–87.

——. (2000). A second look at comorbidity in victims of trauma: The posttraumatic stress disorder-major depression connection. *Biological Psychiatry, 48*, 902–9.

Brewin, C. R., Andrews, B., and Valentine, J. D. (2000). Meta-analysis of risk factors for posttraumatic stress disorder in trauma-exposed adults. *Journal of Consulting and Clinical Psychology, 68*, 748–66.

Bromet, E., Sonnega, A., and Kessler, R.C. (1998). Risk factors for DSM-III-R posttraumatic stress disorder: Findings from the national comorbidity survey. *American Journal of Epidemiology, 147*, 353–61.

Brown, T. A., Campbell, L. A., Lehman, C. L., Grisham, J. R., and Mancill, R. B. (2001). Current and lifetime comorbidity of the DSM-IV anxiety and mood disorders in a large clinical sample. *Journal of Abnormal Psychology, 110*(4), 585–99.

Caspi, A., Sugden, K., Moffitt, T. E., Taylor, A., Craig, I. W., Harrington, H., et al. (2003). Influence of life stress on depression: Moderation by a polymorphism in the 5-HTT Gene. *Science, 301*, 386–89.

Duncan, R. D., Saunders, B. E., Kilpatrick, D. G., Hanson, R. F., and Resnick, H. S. (1996). Childhood physical assault as a risk factor for PTSD, depression, and substance abuse: Findings from a national survey. *American Journal of Orthopsychiatry, 66*, 437–48.

Erickson, D. J., Wolfe, J., King, D. W., King, L. A., and Sharkansky, E. J. (2001). Posttraumatic stress disorder and depression symptomatology in a sample of Gulf War veterans: A prospective analysis. *Journal of Consulting and Clinical Psychology, 69*, 41–49.

Foa, E. B., Ehlers, A., Clark, D. M., Tolin, D. F., and Orsillo, S. M. (1999). The posttraumatic cognitions inventory (PTCI): Development and validation. *Psychological Assessment, 11*, 303–14.

Franklin, C. L., and Zimmerman, M. (2001). Posttraumatic stress disorder and major depressive disorder: Investigating the role of overlapping symptoms in diagnostic comorbidity. *Journal of Nervous and Mental Disease, 189*, 548–51.

Glowinski, A. L., Madden, P. A. F., Bucholz, K. K., Lynskey, M. T., and Heath, A. C. (2003). Genetic epidemiology of self-reported life-time DSM-IV major depressive disorder in a population based twin sample of female adolescents. *Journal of Child Psychology and Psychiatry, 44*, 988–96.

Green, B. L., Krupnick, J. L., Chung, J., Siddique, J., Krause, E. D., Revicki, D., et al. (2006). Impact of PTSD comorbidity on one-year outcomes in a depression trial. *Journal of Clinical Psychology, 62*, 815–35.

Hariri, A. R., Goldberg, T. E., Mattay, V. S., Kolachana, B. S., Callicott, J. H., Egan, M. F., et al. (2003). Brain-derived neurotrophic factor val66met polymorphism affects human memory-related hippocampal activity and predicts memory performance. *Journal of Neuroscience, 23*, 6690–94.

Hasin, D. S., Goodwin, R. D., Stinson, F. S., and Grant, B. F. (2005). Epidemiology of major depressive disorder: Results from the National Epidemiologic Survey on Alcoholism and Related Conditions. *Archives of General Psychiatry, 62*(10), 1097–1106.

Jakupcak, M., Roberts, L. J., Martell, C., et al. (2006). A pilot study of behavioral activation for veterans with posttraumatic stress disorder. *Journal of Traumatic Stress, 19*(3), 387–91.

Kaufman, J., Yang, B. Z., Douglas-Palumberi, H., Houshyar, S., Lipschitz, D., Krystal, J. H., et al. (2004). Social supports and serotonin transporter gene moderate depression in maltreated children. *Proceedings of the National Academy of Sciences of the United States of America. 101*, 17316–21.

Kessler, R. C., Berglund, P., Demler, O., Jin, R., and Walters, E. E. (2005). Lifetime prevalence and age-onset distributions of DSM-IV disorders in the National Comorbidity Survey Replication. *Archives of General Psychiatry, 62*, 593–602.

Kessler, R. C., Davis, C. G., and Kendler, K. S. (1997). Childhood adversity and adult psychiatric disorder in the US National Comorbidity Survey. *Psychological Medicine, 27*(5), 1101–19.

Kessler, R. C., Sonnega, A., Bromet, E., Hughes, M., and Nelson, C. B. (1995). Posttraumatic stress disorder in the National Comorbidity Survey. *Archives of General Psychiatry, 52*, 1048–60.

Kilpatrick, D. G., Ruggiero, K. J., Acierno, R., Saunders, B. E., Resnick, H. S., and Best, C. L. (2003). Violence and risk of PTSD, major depression, substance abuse/dependence, and comorbidity: Results from the National Survey of Adolescents. *Journal of Consulting and Clinical Psychology, 71*, 692–700.

Kilpatrick, D. G., Saunders, B. E., Veronen, L. J., Best, C. L., and Von, J. M. (1987). Criminal victimization: Lifetime prevalence, reporting to police, and psychological impact. *Crime & Delinquency, 33*, 479–89.

Kilpatrick, D. G., Veronen, L. J., and Resick, P. A. (1982). Psychological sequelae to rape: Assessment and treatment strategies. In D. M. Doleys, R. I. Meredity, and A. R. Ciminero (Eds.), *Behavioral medicine: Assessment and treatment strategies.* New York: Plenum.

Kobasa, S. C., Maddi, S. R., and Kahn, S. (1982). Hardiness and health: A prospective study. *Journal of Personality and Social Psychology, 42*, 168–77.

Koenen, K. C., Fu, Q. C., Ertel, K., Lyons, M. J., Eisen, S. A., True, W. R., Goldberg, J., and Tsuang, M. T. (2008). Common genetic liability to major depression and posttramautic stress disorder in men. *Journal of Affective Disorders, 105*, 109–15.

Koren, D., Arnon, I., and Klein, E. (1999). Acute stress response and posttraumatic stress disorder in traffic accident victims: A one-year prospective, follow-up study. *American Journal of Psychiatry, 156*, 367–73.

Kulka, R., Schlenger, W., Fairbank, J., Hough, R., Jordan, B., Marmar, C., and Weiss, D. (1990). *Trauma and the Vietnam War generation: Report of findings from the National Vietnam Veterans Readjustment Study.* New York: Brunner/Mazel.

Lee, H. J., Lee, M. S., Kang, R. H., et al. (2005). Influence of the serotonin transporter promoter gene polymorphism on susceptibility to posttraumatic stress disorder. *Depression and Anxiety, 21*(3), 135–39.

Lyons, M. J., Goldberg, J., Eisen, S. A., True, W., Tsuang, M. T., Meyer, J. M., et al. (1993). Do genes influence exposure to trauma? A twin study of combat. *American Journal of Medical Genetics, 48*(1), 22–27.

Mulick, P. S., and Naugle, A. E. (2004). Behavioral activation for comorbid PTSD and major depression: A case study. *Cognitive and Behavioral Practice, 11*, 378–87.

Nixon, R. D., Resick, P., and Nishith, P. (2004). An exploration of co-morbid depression among female victims of intimate partner violence with posttraumatic stress disorder. *Journal of Affective Disorders, 82*, 315–20.

Orsillo, S. M., Weathers, F. W., Litz, B. T., Steinberg, H. R., Huska, J. A., and Keane, T. M. (1996). Current and lifetime psychiatric disorders among veterans with war-zone related posttraumatic stress disorder. *Journal of Nervous and Mental Disease, 184*, 307–13.

Ozer, E. J., Best, S. R., Lipsey, T. L., and Weiss, D. S. (2003). Predictors of posttraumatic stress disorder and symptoms in adults: A meta-analysis. *Psychological Bulletin, 129*, 52–73.

Resick, P. A., Nishith, P., Weaver, T. L., Astin, M. C., Feuer, C. A. (2002). A comparison of cognitive-processing therapy with prolonged exposure and a waiting condition for the treatment of chronic posttraumatic stress disorder in female rape victims. *Journal of Consulting and Clinical Psychology, 70*, 867–79.

Resnick, H. S., Kilpatrick, D. G., Dansky, B. S., Saunders, B. E., and Best, C. L. (1993). Prevalence of civilian trauma and posttraumatic stress disorder in a representative national sample of women. *Journal of Consulting and Clinical Psychology, 61*, 984–91.

Saunders, B. E., Kipatrick, D. G., Hanson, R. F., Resnick, H. S., and Walker, M. E. (1999). Prevalence, case characteristics, and long-term psychological correlates of child rape among women: A national survey. *Child Maltreatment, 4*(3), 187–200.

Seligman, M. E. P. (1972). Learned helplessness. *Annual Review of Medicine, 23,* 407–12.

Seligman, M. E. P., and Csiksentmihalyi, M. (2000). Positive psychology: An introduction. *American Psychologist, 55,* 5–14.

Stein, M. B., Jang, K. L., Taylor, S., Vernon, P. A., and Livesley, W. J. (2002). Genetic and environmental influences on trauma exposure and posttraumatic stress disorder symptoms: A twin study. *American Journal of Psychiatry, 159,* 1675–81.

Sullivan, P. F., Neale, M. C., and Kendler, K. S. (2000). Genetic epidemiology of major depression: Review and meta-analysis. *American Journal of Psychiatry, 157,* 1552–62.

True, W. R., Rice, J., Eisen, S. A., Heath, A. C., Goldberg, J., Lyons, M. J., Nowak, J. (1993). A twin study of genetic and environmental contributions to liability for posttraumatic stress symptoms. *Archives of General Psychiatry, 50*(4), 257–64.

# 11

# PTSD in Child and Adult Populations: A Review of the Cognitive Behavioral Treatment Outcome Literature

*Norah C. Feeny and Shoshana Y. Kahana*

As alluded to in prior chapters, a heterogeneous mix of pre-, peri-, and post-traumatic variables have been identified that are associated with increased risk or resilience to posttraumatic stress disorders. Our ability to specifically and sensitively identify those individuals at most risk for developing posttraumatic distress is still quite limited. Thankfully, interventions exist that appear quite effective at reducing chronic PTSD symptoms. The present chapter reviews research into the cognitive behavioral treatment of PTSD highlighting successes and challenges in the clinical treatment of PTSD patients.

In the last ten to fifteen years, there has been an expanding body of research on psychosocial treatments for PTSD in both adult and child populations. Reviews and meta-analyses support the efficacy of psychosocial interventions among adults (Bradley, Greene, Russ, Russ, Dutra, and Westen, 2005; Davidson and Parker, 2001; Keane, Marshall, and Taft, 2006; Van Etten and Taylor, 1998). Much of the research has focused upon cognitive behavioral therapy (CBT), and there now exist multiple randomized controlled trials that have demonstrated both short- and longer-term improvements following CBT in adult populations (e.g., Foa et al., 2005; Resick, Nishith, Weaver, Astin, and Feuer, 2002; Tarrier et al., 1999). In contrast to the substantial body of research on the efficacy of CBT for PTSD in adults, fewer PTSD treatment studies have been conducted with children and adolescents. However, methodologically sound controlled trials (e.g., Deblinger, Mannarino, Cohen, and Steer, 2006; Stein et al., 2003) and recent reviews of the literature (Feeny,

Address correspondence to Dr. Norah Feeny; Division of Child Psychiatry; Case Western Reserve University; University Hospitals of Cleveland; 11100 Euclid Avenue; Cleveland, OH 44216. E-mail: norah.feeny@case.edu

Foa, Treadwell, and March, 2004; Ruggiero, Morris, and Scotti, 2001; for a review specific to child crime victims, see Cohen, Berliner, and Mannarino, 2003) are contributing significantly to our understanding of what treatments work for youth with chronic PTSD.

Because the empirical support for psychosocial treatments of PTSD in adults (Foa and Rothbaum, 1998) and children is strongest for CBT (AACAP, 1998; Cohen, Berliner, and March, 2000), our review will focus on treatment outcome studies evaluating cognitive-behavioral interventions. Among the validated interventions for adults with PTSD are prolonged exposure (PE), stress inoculation training (SIT), cognitive restructuring (CR), cognitive processing therapy (CPT), and eye movement desensitization and reprocessing (EMDR). In the following section, selected outcome studies that evaluate the efficacy of these treatments among adults will be reviewed. After reviewing the treatment outcome data for adults, we will focus on intervention studies for children with PTSD, including cognitive behavioral treatments for sexual abuse survivors, group therapy for various traumas, and EMDR.

We propose that the same mechanisms underlying treatments for PTSD in adults are applicable to children as well. It should be noted that these mechanisms have been more fully elaborated upon in the adult treatment literature (e.g., Ehlers and Clark, 2000; Foa and Kozak, 1986) and limited empirical work has investigated these processes in pediatric populations. Thus, the majority of the proposed treatment mechanisms for PTSD in youth are hypothesized based on what we know about adults. Although elaboration on the specifics of these mechanisms is beyond the scope of this chapter, some of these include: (1) correcting distorted cognitions or schemas about the safety of the world or about self-competence (e.g., Dunmore, Clark, and Ehlers, 1999; Ehlers and Clark, 2000; Tolin and Foa, 1999); (2) organizing and elaborating the trauma narrative more cohesively (Ehlers and Clark, 2000; Foa, Molnar, and Cashman, 1995); and (3) facilitating emotional engagement with, habituation to, and preventing avoidance of traumatic memories, per emotional processing theory (Foa and Kozak, 1986; van Minnen and Hagenaars, 2002).

## ADULT TREATMENT OUTCOME: COGNITIVE BEHAVIORAL TREATMENTS

Most cognitive-behavioral treatments for adults and children with PTSD include some elements of exposure therapy. Such exposure can include imaginally reliving the traumatic event repeatedly and *in vivo* confrontation with avoided trauma-related situations that are not objectively dangerous. Prolonged exposure (PE) consists of a variety of therapeutic components, including psychoeducation, breathing retraining, repeated recounting of the traumatic event (i.e., imaginal exposure [IE]), and encouragement to systematically confront trauma-related reminders (i.e., *in vivo* exposure). SIT teaches various anxiety management and coping tools. Cognitive therapies (cognitive restructuring, cognitive processing therapy) focus on identifying and modifying unhelpful or distorted cognitions thought to maintain PTSD symptoms.

## Assault and Domestic Violence Survivors

Overall, four prospective, large-scale randomized clinical trials (RCT) have evaluated the efficacy of prolonged exposure or a variant of PE, in comparison to other active interventions or waitlists, for sexual and non-sexual assault survivors with chronic PTSD (Foa, Rothbaum, Riggs, and Murdock, 1991; Foa et al., 1999; Foa et al., 2005; Resick et al., 2002). In the first RCT, PE, SIT, supportive counseling (SC), and a waitlist (WL) control were compared with regard to their efficacy in reducing PTSD and associated symptoms (Foa et al., 1991). PE and SIT showed significant pre- to post-treatment reductions on re-experiencing and avoidance symptoms, while SC and waitlist did not. Also, at the end of treatment, 50 percent of patients in SIT and 40 percent of patients in PE no longer met criteria for PTSD; in contrast, only 10 percent of SC patients and none in the waitlist lost their diagnosis. At follow-up, there was a tendency for patients in the PE group to show further improvement in PTSD symptoms whereas patients in SIT and SC did not show such further improvements.

In a second study, the efficacy of PE and SIT were compared to a combination of both treatments (PE/SIT), and a waitlist condition (Foa et al., 1999). All three active treatments were superior to waitlist and resulted in substantial symptom reduction. Following treatment, the majority of those receiving PE (70 percent), SIT (58 percent), and PE/SIT (54 percent) no longer met diagnostic criteria for PTSD diagnosis; in contrast, all participants in the WL condition retained their diagnoses. Interestingly, the percentage of women achieving good end-state functioning (a composite measure of low PTSD, depression, and general anxiety) tended to be higher for PE than for SIT or PE/SIT (52 percent, 42 percent, and 36 percent respectively).

In the third study of assault survivors, Resick et al. (2002) compared the efficacy of cognitive processing therapy (CPT) to PE and a minimal attention control condition among 121 female rape survivors with PTSD. CPT is an intervention utilized with sexual assault survivors that includes cognitive restructuring and written exposure to trauma memories. Results indicated that both treatments were highly effective in reducing PTSD: at post-treatment,

PTSD criteria were met in only 19.5 percent of completers in CPT and 17.5 percent in PE. Among completers, 76 percent of the CPT and 58 percent of the PE clients met criteria for good end state functioning (i.e., low PTSD and depression). Gains were maintained over time as well. At three-month follow-up, 16.2 percent of those who received CPT and 29.7 percent who received PE were PTSD positive. Finally, at nine-month follow-up, 19.2 percent of CPT and 15.4 percent of PE clients were PTSD positive and 64 percent of the CPT and 68 percent of the PE participants experienced improvements meeting criteria for good end-state functioning. In sum, CPT and PE were both quite efficacious on average and had very comparable results (i.e., no statistical differences between them) across most of the relevant outcome domains.

In a fourth large-scale RCT evaluating interventions for assault survivors with PTSD (Foa et al., 2005), PE was compared to a combination treatment including both PE and cognitive restructuring (PE/CR), and to a WL. Results suggested that PE and PE/CR produced improvement on multiple outcome indices: independent evaluator and self-ratings of PTSD severity, depression, general anxiety, and social functioning. Indeed, close to 80 percent of participants (79.8 percent) maintained their gains and displayed stable PTSD symptom scores during follow-up, with a small group of participants (12.4 percent) showing reliable improvement during follow-up. Consistent with the PE/SIT results described above, combining PE with CR did not improve the efficacy or efficiency of PE. Specifically, PE and PE/CR were roughly equivalent in their robustness of various outcomes. Authors have hypothesized that this might result from the fact that all efficacious treatments modify the same dysfunctional cognitions underlying PTSD (Foa, Ehlers, Clark, Tolin, and Orsillo, 1999). Both CR and exposure therapy were designed to modify erroneous interpretations that are thought to maintain symptoms (Beck and Emery, 1985; Foa and Kozak, 1986).

Taken together, these four studies suggest that PE, CPT and SIT are all effective interventions for PTSD resulting from assault. Following these treatments, the majority of participants show symptom improvement and the majority no longer meet criteria for PTSD. Notably, the addition of cognitive therapy to PE does not seem to improve its efficacy.

Finally, in an intervention developed specifically for battered women with PTSD, cognitive trauma therapy for battered women (CTT-BW) has provided initial evidence of efficacy in reducing PTSD symptoms (Kubany et al., 2004). CTT-BW includes trauma history exploration, PTSD education, stress management, exposure to abuse and abuser reminders, self-monitoring of negative self-talk, cognitive therapy for guilt, and modules on self-advocacy, assertiveness, and how to identify perpetrators. One hundred twenty-five ethnically diverse women were randomly assigned to immediate or delayed CTT-BW. At post-treatment, PTSD remitted in 87 percent of women who completed CTT-BW, with large reductions in depression and guilt and substantial increases in self-esteem. Treatment improvements were maintained at three and six-month follow-ups on all relevant outcome measures for women in both conditions, with 81 percent of all participants assessed at six-month follow-up not meeting diagnostic criteria for PTSD. Finally, good end state functioning (defined as the absence of both PTSD and depression within the study) was achieved by 69 percent of participants who completed CTT-BW, and 68 percent and 70 percent of participants at the three and six-month follow-ups.

## Childhood Sexual Assault (CSA) Survivors

In this section, we will discuss three RCTs that have evaluated the efficacy of CBT for adults with PTSD related to childhood sexual assault (CSA; Chard, 2005; Cloitre, Koenen, Cohen, and Han, 2002; McDonagh et al., 2005). Chard (2005) conducted an RCT evaluating CPT for childhood sexual abuse survivors in comparison to a minimal attention waitlist control group. Unlike prior studies of CPT, this study combined both group and individual CBT interventions. Seventy-one patients were assigned to one of the two conditions. Results suggested a significant decrease in PTSD symptoms in the CPT group between pre- and post-treatment. In addition, only 7 percent of those who received CPT met diagnostic criteria for PTSD at post-treatment compared with 74 percent of the control group. This trend continued, with 3 percent meeting criteria at three-month and 6 percent meeting criteria at one-year follow-up. Finally, with respect to good end-state functioning, 79 percent of the CPT participants achieved good end-state functioning compared with 4 percent of the waitlisted control group at the post-treatment assessment. At three-month follow-up, 73 percent of the treatment group met criteria for good end-state functioning, and at one-year follow-up, 75 percent met criteria.

Cloitre, Chase Stovall-McClough, Miranda, and Chemtob (2004) evaluated the outcome of a two-phase treatment for childhood abuse-related PTSD against a waitlist control group. The first phase consisted of skills training in affective and interpersonal regulation (STAIR), which focused on stabilization and preparatory skills building, while the second phase consisted primarily of imaginal exposure to traumatic memories (modified PE). The treatment included sixteen sessions (eight STAIR, eight PE), and was conducted over twelve weeks. The targeted outcomes included affect regulation problems, interpersonal skills deficits, and PTSD symptoms. At post-treatment, differences between the groups on all three domains were in the medium to very large effect range. With respect to good end-state functioning, 46 percent of the participants in the STAIR–modified PE condition achieved good end-state functioning in comparison with only 4 percent of waitlist participants. Treatment gains, particularly in PTSD symptoms, were maintained at three and nine months. The authors report that the most robust predictors of improvements in PTSD symptoms during PE were therapeutic alliance and improvement in negative mood regulation, both of which were developed in the skills-training phase prior to conducting exposure. However, the results do not strongly support the notion that the delivery of STAIR facilitated imaginal exposure. Interestingly, effect sizes for three of the four measures of emotional expression or regulation were as large or larger following imaginal exposure than they were following STAIR. Thus it may be that exposure therapy itself may be an effective intervention for enhancing emotional regulation (for more discussion, see Cahill, Zoellner, Feeny, and Riggs, 2004). A between-group comparison in which exposure therapy alone is compared to skills training prior to exposure is necessary to be able to determine whether such treatment is, in fact, additively helpful (Cahill et al., 2004).

In the third RCT evaluating treatment for CSA survivors with PTSD, McDonagh et al. (2005) compared CBT (including both exposure and cognitive restructuring) with present centered therapy (PCT, a problem-solving therapy) and a waitlist (WL). In the completer analyses, both active treatment groups improved significantly compared with the WL, but did not differ from each other. However, follow-up assessments at three and six months showed significant differences between CBT and PCT in the percentage of participants no longer meeting diagnostic criteria for PTSD at both time points, with the CBT showing superiority (82.4 percent vs. 42.1 percent and 76.5 percent vs. 42.1 percent, respectively).

While many consider CSA survivors with PTSD a particularly complicated clinical population, results from these three studies are encouraging. Across the studies, the majority of those receiving active CBT lost their PTSD diagnosis, and a large minority (Cloitre et al., 2004; 46 percent at post) to a majority (Chard, 2005; 79 percent at post) attained good end-state functioning, a stringent measure of good treatment outcome.

## Mixed Trauma Populations

CBT has also been found to be effective in reducing PTSD resulting from various traumas in men and women (Bryant, Moulds, Guthrie, Dang, and Nixon, 2003; Marks, Lovell, Noshirvani, Livanou, and Thrasher, 1998; Schnurr et al., 2007; Tarrier et al., 1999; Taylor et al., 2003). In a mixed sample of trauma survivors with chronic PTSD, Marks et al. (1998) tested the efficacy of PE, CR, the combination of the two (PE plus CR), and a relaxation control condition (R). Results showed the active treatments (PE, CR, and PE/CR) were all quite effective and superior to the relaxation control. At post-treatment, 53 percent of those who received PE met criteria for good end-state functioning, compared to 32 percent of those who received CR or PE/CR, and 15 percent of those who received relaxation. Similar to the results obtained by Foa and colleagues (2005), both PE and CR were effective, and combining them did not enhance outcome.

In a study of non-sexual assault survivors and motor vehicle accident survivors, Bryant et al. (2003), compared imaginal exposure (IE) alone, IE plus CR, and supportive counseling (SC). Results indicated that IE and IE plus CR were both superior to SC in reducing PTSD and depression at post-treatment and six-month follow-up. Interestingly, in contrast to the Foa et al. 2005 results, at follow-up the combination of IE and cognitive restructuring led to greater reduction in PTSD intensity scores than IE alone. Moreover, intent-to-treat analyses indicated that those who received the combination of IE and CR reported fewer avoidance, depression, and catastrophic cognitions than those receiving supportive counseling. This was not the case for those who received IE alone. It may be that the reason cognitive restructuring was shown to produce added benefit here was that exposure treatment contained only imaginal exposure, rather than both imaginal and *in vivo*. In contrast, other studies reporting no incremental value of adding cognitive restructuring to PE have included the combination of both imaginal and *in vivo* exposure.

Tarrier et al. (1999) compared imaginal exposure to cognitive therapy in a group of patients with PTSD resulting mostly from criminal victimization and automobile accidents. Imaginal exposure and cognitive therapy were equally effective in ameliorating the primary outcome of PTSD symptoms. However, similar to the Bryant et al. (2003) study findings described above, the current study utilized imaginal, but not *in vivo* exposure. Indeed, it may be that the utilization of imaginal exposure alone led to pre-/post-treatment effect sizes (Cohen *d*s in the .8 range) that were considerably more modest than those reported in previous studies (e.g., Foa et al., 1999; Foa et al., 2005).

Another cognitive therapy intervention based on a cognitive conceptualization of PTSD put forth by Ehlers and Clark (2000) was recently evaluated (Ehlers, Clark, Hackmann, McManus, and Fennell, 2005). This cognitive therapy for PTSD specifically highlights the modification of excessively negative appraisals and the correction of autobiographical memory disturbances. Though preliminary, the results are quite good. In both a consecutive case series and RCT, patients treated with cognitive therapy exhibited marked reductions in PTSD, anxiety, and depression symptoms, while the wait list control displayed no improvement. In the intent-to-treat analyses, cognitive therapy yielded quite large effect sizes (ranging from 2.07–2.82) on various outcome measures. Importantly, participants in the cognitive therapy displayed stable symptom improvement, and treatment gains were maintained at the six-month follow-up.

In the most recently published trial, Schnurr et al. (2007) conducted a methodologically rigorous RCT comparing ten sessions of PE to present-centered therapy, a supportive intervention, among 284 women who had served in the military. The type most commonly identified as the worst, or index, event was sexual trauma (n = 194 [68.3 percent]), followed by physical assault (n = 39 [15.8 percent]) and war-zone exposure (n = 16 [5.6 percent]). PTSD symptom severity, comorbid symptoms, functioning, and quality of life were examined as outcomes at post-treatment and three- and six-month follow-ups. Women who received PE experienced greater reduction of PTSD symptoms relative to women who received present-centered therapy. At post-treatment, those who received PE were more likely than those who received present-centered therapy to no longer meet PTSD diagnostic criteria (41.0 percent vs. 27.8 percent) and to achieve total remission (15.2 percent vs. 6.9 percent). The authors indicated that the effects were consistent over time in longitudinal analyses, although in cross-sectional analyses most differences occurred immediately after treatment. However, these results do suggest that PE is a very effective treatment program for reducing PTSD symptoms, particularly in the short-term, among a female military population.

To summarize, both exposure (Bryant et al., 2003; Marks et al., 1998; Schnurr et al., 2007; Tarrier et al., 1999; Taylor et al., 2003) and cognitive therapy programs have been validated for use with PTSD in mixed trauma populations. As reviewed above, three RCTs support the efficacy of cognitive therapy or cognitive restructuring alone in the treatment of PTSD in mixed trauma groups (Ehlers et al., 2005; Marks et al., 1998; Tarrier et al., 1999). In addition, the Resick et al. (2002) and Chard (2005) studies demonstrated that CPT appears to be an efficacious intervention for the short- and long-term treatment of PTSD among assault and CSA survivors.

## ADULT TREATMENT OUTCOME:
## EYE MOVEMENT DESENSITIZATION AND REPROCESSING

One particular type of treatment for PTSD that has received much attention over the past few years is eye movement desensitization and reprocessing (EMDR; Shapiro, 1995). EMDR is a form of exposure accompanied by saccadic eye movements. It has been the focus of considerable controversy due to initial claims regarding remarkable success in only a single session (Shapiro, 1989). Of the studies evaluating the efficacy of EMDR, only some utilized well-controlled designs and thus yielded clearly interpretable results. One well-controlled study evaluated the efficacy of EMDR relative to a waitlist control condition for PTSD in female rape victims (Rothbaum, 1997). Three sessions of EMDR resulted in greater improvement for PTSD symptoms (57 percent reduction in independently evaluated PTSD at post-treatment and 71 percent in self-reported PTSD at follow-up), relative to the waitlist condition (10 percent reduction at post-treatment). A direct comparison between EMDR and a combined treatment of PE plus stress inoculation training (called trauma treatment protocol, TTP) was conducted by Devilly and Spence (1999). Both TTP and EMDR reduced PTSD severity (63 percent and 46 percent, respectively), but TTP clients maintained their gains at follow-up whereas EMDR clients showed higher rates of relapse (symptom reduction at follow-up of 61 percent vs. 12 percent, respectively).

Taylor et al. (2003) compared EMDR to exposure therapy and relaxation training. On average, the three treatments were efficacious in reducing PTSD, and did not differ in attrition rates or rates of symptom worsening. However, exposure tended to yield a higher percentage of participants with clinically significant change and was more effective than EMDR and relaxation in reducing avoidance and re-experiencing symptoms. In addition, exposure therapy tended to yield a greater proportion of participants who no longer had symptoms meeting criteria for PTSD after treatment. EMDR did not differ from the control group (i.e., relaxation) on the clinician-administered measure of PTSD symptoms.

Finally, in the most recently published comparison of EMDR to other treatments, Rothbaum, Astin, and Marsteller (2005) evaluated the relative efficacy of EMDR, PE, and a no-treatment waitlist control in the treatment of PTSD in seventy-four adult female rape victims. Improvement in PTSD, depression, dissociation, and state anxiety as assessed by blind independent assessors was significantly greater in both the PE and EMDR group than the waitlist condition. At post-treatment, 5 percent of PE participants ($n = 1$), 25 percent of EMDR participants ($n = 5$), and 90 percent of the waitlist condition participants ($n = 18$) still met criteria for a diagnosis of PTSD. There were no significant differences between PE vs. EMDR groups at post-treatment in terms of good end-state functioning, but differences were significant between the treatment groups and the control arm. At six-month follow-up, significantly more PE participants (78 percent) met criteria for good end-state functioning than EMDR participants (35.3 percent). The study had few completers for each treatment arm ($n = 20$ completers per group). Results, however, suggested that PE and EMDR did not differ significantly for change from baseline to either post-treatment or six-month follow-up measurement on multiple outcome domains.

Overall then, there is evidence for the efficacy of EMDR. Importantly, however, a meta-analysis found EMDR no more effective than exposure therapy programs (Davidson and Parker, 2001). Moreover, the meta-analysis suggested that the eye movements integral to the treatment are unnecessary (Davidson and Parker, 2001). Indeed, findings from another, more recent meta-analysis (Bradley et al., 2005) did not provide support for any differential efficacy between cognitive behavior treatments and EMDR.

## CHILD TREATMENT OUTCOME: CBT AND CHILD SEXUAL ABUSE

Five studies have directly evaluated PTSD symptoms resulting from sexual abuse. Deblinger and colleagues (Deblinger, McLeer, and Henry, 1990; Deblinger, Lippmann, and Steer, 1996) conducted two studies evaluating the initial efficacy of a CBT treatment protocol for sexually abused children with PTSD and their non-offending parent.

The first evaluation of this treatment included nineteen sexually abused girls, aged three to sixteen years, who met criteria for PTSD based on an interview developed by the investigators (Deblinger et al., 1990). A within-subject design was utilized so that each participant served as her own control via a two- to three-week baseline period. Pre-to-post treatment comparisons revealed significant improvements in the three PTSD clusters of re-experiencing, avoidance, and arousal symptoms.

Some of the prior shortcomings were addressed in a larger RCT conducted by Deblinger, Lippman, and Steer (1996). In this trial, one hundred children between the ages of seven and thirteen (71 percent of whom met PTSD diagnostic criteria) were randomly assigned to one of four conditions: child-only modules, parent-only modules, both child and parent modules, or standard community treatment in which the families were provided with a list of referrals for treatment and were strongly encouraged to seek therapy. Results indicated that children who received treatment (i.e., child-only and child/parent) showed greater decreases in PTSD symptoms than those in the parent-only treatment or standard community treatment conditions. No significant differences were noted between groups however, in terms of remission of PTSD diagnosis: 84 percent of children receiving treatment no longer met diagnostic criteria for PTSD at post-treatment, as compared to 70 percent of children in the parent-only and standard community conditions.

A follow-up study indicated that scores on externalizing behavior problems, depression, and PTSD symptom measures taken at three months, six months, one year, and two years post-treatment were comparable to the posttest scores (Deblinger, Steer, and Lippmann, 1999). Thus, these findings suggest that the pre- to post-treatment improvements held across the two-year follow-up period. However, it is important to note that there was a significant amount of missing data (between 25 percent to 32 percent missing data, depending on measure) in the follow-up period examined in the study.

The largest multi-site RCT for sexually abused youth compared the differential efficacy of trauma-focused CBT (TF-CBT) with child centered therapy (CCT) for treating PTSD and related emotional and behavioral problems (Cohen, Deblinger, Mannarino, and Steer, 2004). Two hundred twenty-nine eight- to fourteen-year-old children and their primary caretakers were randomly assigned to either treatment. Each treatment was provided in twelve weekly individual sessions to parent and child. Treatment sessions lasted ninety minutes, with forty-five minutes for each individual session. In three of the TF-CBT sessions, a joint parent-child session was provided. The TF-CBT components included feeling expression skills, coping skills training, recognizing the relationships between thoughts, feelings, and behaviors, gradual exposure ("trauma narrative"), cognitive processing of the abuse, joint child-parent sessions, psychoeducation, and parent management skills. CCT focused on establishing a trusting therapeutic relationship through which to develop the child and parent's ability to develop positive coping strategies for abuse-related difficulties.

Results suggested that youth in the TF-CBT condition exhibited significant improvement on a host of outcome measures as compared to youth in CCT, including PTSD, depression, behavior problems, shame, and abuse-related attributions. Similarly, parents assigned to TF-CBT showed greater improvement with respect to their own self-reported levels of depression, abuse-specific distress, support of the child, and effective parenting practices. A recently published follow-up study (Deblinger et al., 2006) indicated that children treated with TF-CBT had significantly fewer symptoms of PTSD and described less shame than the children who had been treated with CCT at both six and twelve months after their post-treatment evaluations. The caregivers who had been treated with TF-CBT also continued to report less severe abuse-specific distress during the follow-up period than those who had been treated with CCT.

This study adds to the growing evidence base supporting the efficacy of TF-CBT with children suffering PTSD symptoms as a result of sexual abuse. This study has particularly noteworthy strengths, including its large sample size (drawn from two sites) that includes demographically heterogeneous youth from inner-city, suburban, and rural settings. Thus, the findings are likely generalizeable across symptomatic sexually abused children who present for treatment. Relatedly, the youth involved in the study had high rates of multiple traumas, which is considered representative of sexually abused children seen in community settings. Finally, the authors employed a range of standardized outcome measures (including structured interviews) and a large number of therapists with diverse discipline and theoretical backgrounds were involved. However, one limitation of this study is the lack of a no treatment control group. The authors addressed this issue by citing ethical concerns and previous studies that have demonstrated little to no symptom improvement in sexually abused children during waitlist periods.

A fourth study examining the effects of child and parent treatment for PTSD symptoms following sexual abuse was conducted by Celano, Hazzard, Webb, and McCall (1996). Participants were fifty-six girls ages eight to thirteen, thirty-two of whom completed treatment. Participants were randomly assigned to an eight-week recovering from abuse program (RAP) or eight-week treatment-as-usual (TAU) program. The RAP-structured condition included pictorial exposure to the abuse, modifying self-blame attributions, psychoeducation about sexual maturation and sexual behaviors, and teaching coping self-statements and anxiety management strategies, while TAU was more unstructured and consisted of support, education, and discussion of the child's symptoms, feelings, and thoughts. Following treatment, girls in both groups exhibited similar decreases in PTSD symptoms, beliefs reflecting self-blame and powerlessness, behavior problems, and increases in overall psychosocial functioning. On average PTSD severity was reduced only minimally: 14.6 percent in the RAP condition, and 7.5 percent in the TAU condition. The RAP condition was more effective than TAU in increasing caretaker support of the child and in decreasing caretaker self-blame.

A fifth study (King et al., 2000) evaluated the efficacy of child and caregiver participation in the cognitive-behavioral treatment of sexually abused children with posttraumatic stress symptoms. Thirty-six sexually abused children (aged five to seventeen years) were randomly assigned to a child-alone cognitive-behavioral treatment condition, a family cognitive-behavioral treatment condition, or a waitlist control condition. The child intervention involved twenty fifty-minute individualized sessions and included psycho-education, coping skills, exposure, and personal safety, while parents in the family condition attended an additional twenty sessions, which focused on parent-child communication and behavior management. Compared with controls, both CBT conditions were superior in improving posttraumatic stress disorder symptoms and self-reports of fear and anxiety. Significant improvements also occurred on parent and clinician ratings of global functioning. Maintenance of improvement was evident at a twelve-week follow-up assessment. However, for the most part, there were no significant differences between the CBT conditions with and without parental involvement, causing the authors to conclude that in general, parental involvement did not improve the efficacy of cognitive-behavioral therapy.

## CHILD TREATMENT OUTCOME:
## GROUP CBT FOR VARIOUS TRAUMA POPULATIONS

Five studies have examined the efficacy of group CBT in traumatized youth (Berliner and Saunders, 1996; Chemtob, Nakashima, and Hamada, 2002; Kataoka et al., 2003; March, Amaya-Jackson, Murray, and Schulte, 1998; Stein et al., 2003), all but one of which (Berliner and Saunders, 1996) assessed PTSD symptoms. In four of the studies, CBT consisted of exposure to the trauma narratives and stress inoculation interventions such as psychoeducation, problem solving, relaxation, and cognitive restructuring. In the fifth (Chemto, Nakashima, and Hamada, 2002), no formal exposure was included in treatment. Given that the focus of the current paper is on interventions specifically for PTSD, and not on traumatic grief, the authors are not including several studies (e.g., Brown, Pearlman, and Goodman, 2004; Cohen, Mannarino, and Staron, 2006; Saltzman, Pynoos, Layne, Steinberg, and Aisenberg, 2001) that evaluate the effectiveness of brief trauma/grief-focused psychotherapy.

The first manualized CBT treatment specifically targeting PTSD following single-incident traumas in youth was developed and evaluated by March et al. (1998). The treatment, multimodality trauma treatment (MMTT), included psychoeducation, exposure to trauma narratives, anxiety management training (muscle relaxation, diaphragmatic breathing, training to gauge distress levels), interpersonal problem solving for anger control, development of positive self-talk, and relapse prevention. Treatment consisted of eighteen weekly group sessions conducted in a school setting, with one individual session at week ten. Treatment effects were evaluated via a multiple baseline design. Participants were seventeen children (ten to fifteen years old) diagnosed with PTSD, fourteen of whom completed treatment. Of these, eight (57 percent) no longer met DSM-IV criteria for PTSD immediately after treatment, while twelve (86 percent) of fourteen were free of PTSD at six-month follow-up. In addition, youth exhibited decreases on measures of depression, anxiety, and anger.

In the second study, Chemtob, Nakashima, and Hamada (2002) conducted a community-wide school-based PTSD screening on the island of Kauai two years after hurricane Iniki. Children with the highest levels of trauma-related symptoms were randomized to either individual ($n = 76$) or group treatment ($n = 176$). The manual-guided treatment was four sessions in duration and consisted of the following disaster related modules: safety and helplessness, loss, mobilizing competence and issues of anger, and ending and going forward. In order to address the effects of repeated testing, a sample of forty-two youth with slightly lower PTSD scores was administered a self-report measure of trauma symptoms twice (Kauai Reaction Inventory: KRI), approximately one month apart.

Among treatment completers ($n$ = 214) PTSD scores were reduced substantially following both individual and group intervention, with no difference seen between the two groups in terms of efficacy. At one-year follow-up, both groups evidenced maintenance of gains. Interestingly though, youth were more likely to complete group treatment than individual treatment. Those youth who did not receive any intervention (but completed the KRI twice) did not exhibit any noticeable changes in symptomatology, thus providing support that the interventions themselves were accounting for the reduction in PTSD among those who received treatment. This study represents the first randomized treatment trial conducted among youth with disaster-related PTSD.

In the third study, Kataoka et al. (2003) piloted a school mental health program for 198 third- to eighth-grade Latino students in Los Angeles who had been exposed to either single or multiple incidents of street violence. Youth were randomly assigned to a school-based group CBT or waitlist control condition. The intervention consisted of a manual-based, eight-session, group CBT delivered in Spanish by bilingual, bicultural school social workers. Parents and teachers were eligible to receive psychoeducation and support services. Results suggested a modest reduction in PTSD and depressive symptoms. The study also included a three-month follow-up. Treatment participants had significantly lower depression scores at follow-up as compared to the waitlist control condition. In addition, there was a trend for PTSD symptoms to be more improved among the students in the intervention group in relation to those on the waitlist at three-month follow-up.

In a parallel but more methodologically rigorous study, Stein et al. (2003) evaluated the effectiveness of a collaboratively designed school-based RCT intervention for reducing children's symptoms of PTSD and depression that has resulted from exposure to violence. One hundred twenty-six sixth-grade students at two large middle schools in Los Angeles who reported exposure to violence and exhibited PTSD symptoms in the clinical range were included in the trial. Students were randomly assigned to a ten-session standardized cognitive-behavioral therapy (the cognitive-behavioral intervention for trauma in schools [CBITS]) early intervention group (n = 61) or to a waitlist delayed intervention comparison group (n = 65) conducted by trained school mental health clinicians.

CBITS consists of ten group sessions (six to eight children per group) of approximately an hour in length, conducted once a week in a school setting. In addition to the group sessions, participants receive one to three individual sessions, usually held before the exposure exercises. CBITS also includes two parent education sessions and one teacher education session. CBITS treatment components include psychoeducation about common reactions to trauma, relaxation training, cognitive therapy (including trauma narrative, fear hierarchy, and exposure), and social problem-solving.

At the three-month follow-up, the trauma-focused CBT groups demonstrated significant reductions on PTSD and depression symptoms per self-report measures as well as psychosocial dysfunction as indicated by parent-report. At six months, after both groups had received the intervention, the differences between the two groups were not significantly different for symptoms of PTSD and depression or for ratings of psychosocial functioning. The results of the study are very encouraging and suggest that group interventions delivered within a school context can be effective in reducing PTSD symptoms. Further strengthening confidence in the findings were the strong methodology employed, including the large sample size, a randomized and controlled study design, diverse and psychometrically strong assessments and outcome measures, and the addressing of issues related to treatment fidelity.

Together, these four studies provide good preliminary support for the usefulness of group administered CBT for PTSD. However, they also highlight significant gaps in the treatment outcome literature for youth with PTSD. At this point, additional large scale randomized controlled trials are needed to further evaluate efficacy of group CBT. In addition, it is essential that measures of functioning, not just symptom reduction, be included in such studies.

## CHILD TREATMENT OUTCOME:
## EMDR FOR VARIOUS TRAUMA POPULATIONS

In children with PTSD, one controlled study has examined the efficacy of EMDR (Chemtob, Nakashima, and Carlson, 2002). In this study, thirty-two children exposed to Hurricane Iniki who still met criteria for PTSD one year after participating in an intervention trial (see Chemtob, Nakashima, and Hamada, 2002, described above) received three sessions of EMDR. This study utilized a randomized lagged-groups design, and children were assigned to either immediate or delayed (approximately four weeks later) treatment. Following treatment, reductions in PTSD, anxiety, depression, and visits to the school nurse were seen in both the immediate and delayed treatment groups (Chemtob, Nakashima, and Carlson, 2002). At post-treatment, both groups demonstrated substantial decreases in PTSD symptoms (average range of 42.9 percent–54.9 percent), which were maintained at six-month follow-up (average of 52.3 percent–71.0 percent). Significant pre- to post-treatment differences were also seen in both groups in total anxiety symptoms and these gains were maintained for both groups at follow-up. Six months later, 56.3 percent of the children no longer met criteria for PTSD. Although the study was not designed to establish efficacy, this study provides important initial evidence of the efficacy of EMDR among children with PTSD.

Another study examined the effects of EMDR (one to six sessions) incorporated in a traditional psychodynamic therapeutic approach in the treatment of thirteen traumatized refugee children with PTSD (Oras, De Ezpeleta, and Ahmad, 2004). After treatment, improvement was noted in both PTSD symptoms and overall functioning. However, this pilot study had significant limitations and is thus difficult to interpret. It contained a very small sample size, did not involve a controlled or randomized design, and did not collect any follow-up data. Furthermore, there was considerable variability in the number of sessions allotted to each treatment modality, making it difficult to attribute change to a particular intervention.

## CONCLUSION

The state of the evidence base for treatments for traumatized adult and youth samples with PTSD is varied. For adult populations, several CBT programs have received robust empirical support for their efficacy in decreasing PTSD symptoms, including PE, SIT, CT, CPT, and EMDR (see Bradley et al., 2005, for meta-analysis on the effects of various psychotherapy approaches to treating PTSD in adult samples). Studies have also indicated that the combination of treatments is not superior to single treatments alone in reducing PTSD symptoms (Foa et al., 1999; Foa et al., 2005; Paunovic and Öst, 2001). In a recent review of the treatment outcome studies, Foa, Rothbaum, and Furr (2003), concluded that the addition of cognitive therapy does not improve outcome of exposure treatment that includes both *in vivo* and imaginal exposure. In fact, programs containing too many procedures may even increase dropout rates or reduce efficiency.

Two important issues specific to the treatment of PTSD in adults should continue to be examined in future research. First, pharmacological interventions (e.g., Brady et al., 2000; Davidson, Rothbaum, van der Kolk, Sikes, and Farfel, 2001) have been shown to be helpful for adult populations with chronic PTSD. However, no published randomized trials directly compare any cognitive-behavioral treatment to pharmacotherapy for the treatment of chronic PTSD. Future research comparing these treatments will help us to learn about the treatments' relative efficacy and tolerability. Second, research aimed at understanding patients' preferences for particular interventions as well as the relationship between patient's preferences for and the effectiveness of interventions is also needed. Across a wide variety of disorders and studies, when given a choice, there is a general preference for psychological interventions over pharmacological ones (Barlow, 2004). Two studies have shown similar results for treatment preferences following trauma exposure (Roy-Byrne, Berliner, Russo, Zatzick, and Pitman, 2003; Zoellner, Feeny, Cochran, and Pruitt, 2003) Indeed, the NIMH workshop report on greater public health relevance for psychotherapeutic intervention research (Street, Niederehe, and Lebowitz, 2000) has called for "the study of patient attitudes, knowledge, and beliefs about treatment as they pertain to the decision to enter treatment, subsequent compliance, and satisfaction with care. . . . conducting treatment matching research to target (and provide specific treatments to) patients depending on their particular profile of attitudes and beliefs."

With respect to child populations with PTSD, the research base for efficacious interventions is considerably smaller than for adults. At this time, the strongest evidence base is for cognitive behavioral interventions, as the methodologies of the interventions employing CBT are far more rigorous than those with non-CBT interventions. Larger-scale, randomized trials have supported the efficacy of child and parent CBT programs for PTSD and related symptoms following sexual abuse (e.g., Cohen, Deblinger, Mannarino, and Steer, 2004) as well as group treatment formats in school settings (Stein et al., 2003). Controlled trials also support the efficacy of brief interventions for disaster related PTSD (Chemtob, Nakashima, and Carlson, 2002; Chemtob, Nakashima, and Hamada, 2002). In these studies, CBT decreased PTSD symptoms, along with other outcome measures, relative to control treatments.

There remain a few gaps in the research base for evidence-based child trauma treatment, which have clear and important implications for clinical practice. First, to date, though exposure treatments have been among the most empirically supported treatments for PTSD in adults, there are no RCTs to date that have exclusively focused on the use of exposure treatments in youth. Relatedly, several of the empirically supported treatments for child PTSD (e.g., TF-CBT, CBITS) are multi-component in nature and encompass multiple CBT techniques. In the interest of clinical efficiency and parsimony, future dismantling studies should be conducted in order to identify the "active" ingredients and the particularly effective components in the implemented treatments.

Second, and similar to recommendations for the adult treatment literature, another avenue of research is the study of the efficacy of medication alone and in combination with psychosocial interventions for ameliorating PTSD and related symptoms in youth. Third, it is important that treatment studies conduct long-term follow-ups to explore maintenance of treatment gains and predictors of treatment outcome. The majority of child studies follow their participants for anywhere between zero to twelve months post-treatment; future studies should attempt to track participants for longer periods of time. Fourth, measures of overall global functioning, and not just symptom reduction, should be included to the extent possible in such treatment outcome studies. These types of outcome measures are among the most meaningful to children, families, and clinicians. Finally, to the extent that it is possible, samples of youth with PTSD who have been exposed to different traumas should be compared, rather than merely assuming that treatment strategies would be transferable across trauma types. For example, each trauma type might have associated complex nuances that are important to consider in treatment development. However, it remains an empirical question whether there are shared or common strategies that would be effective across various traumas types and PTSD populations.

Common to both adult and child populations with PTSD is the need for continued dissemination of empirically validated treatments. Far too many individuals with PTSD are left untreated. In a recent special issue, Zoellner, Feeny, and Rothbaum (2006) examined key issues related to dissemination, including conducting translational research (i.e., bridging the gap between basic research and clinical practice toward developing new or improving current treatments), broadening research beyond efficacy to address questions of effectiveness that have broad public health implications, and targeting dissemination methods themselves, specifically through the examination of treatment preferences and the future training of clinicians in the provision of empirically supported interventions. To the extent that clinicians, researchers, and broader systems of clinical care address dissemination efforts, high-quality and empirically supported treatments will become available and accessible to those individuals who may greatly benefit from them.

## REFERENCES

American Academy of Child and Adolescent Psychiatry. (1998). AACAP official action: Practice parameters for the assessment and treatment of children and adolescents with posttraumatic stress disorder. *Journal of the American Academy of Child and Adolescent Psychiatry, 37 (Suppl.),* 4S–26S.

Barlow, D. H. (2004). Psychological treatments. *American Psychologist, 59,* 869–78.

Beck, A. T., and Emery, G. (1985). *Anxiety disorders and phobias: A cognitive perspective.* New York: Basic Books.

Berliner, L., and Saunders, B. E. (1996). Treating fear and anxiety in sexually abused children: Results of a controlled 2-year follow-up study. *Child Maltreatment, 1,* 294–309.

Bradley, R., Greene, J., Russ, E., Dutra, L., and Westen, D. (2005). A multidimensional meta-analysis of psychotherapy for PTSD. *American Journal of Psychiatry, 162,* 214–27.

Brady, K., Pearlstein, T., Asnis, G. M., Baker, D., Rothbaum, B., Sikes, C. R., et al. (2000). Efficacy and safety of Zoloft treatment of posttraumatic stress disorder: A randomized controlled trial. *Journal of the American Medical Association, 283,* 1837–44.

Brown, E. J., Pearlman, M. Y., and Goodman, R. F. (2004). Facing fears and sadness: Cognitive behavioral therapy for childhood traumatic grief. *Harvard Review of Psychiatry, 12,* 187–98.

Bryant, R. A., Moulds, M. L., Guthrie, R. M., Dang, S. T., Nixon, R. D. V. (2003). Imaginal exposure alone and imaginal exposure with cognitive restructuring in the treatment of posttraumatic stress disorder. *Journal of Consulting and Clinical Psychology, 71,* 706–712.

Cahill, S. P., Zoellner, L. A., Feeny, N. C., and Riggs, D. S. (2004). Sequential treatment for child abuse-related posttraumatic stress disorder: Methodological comment on Cloitre, Koenen, Cohen, and Han (2002). *Journal of Consulting and Clinical Psychology, 72,* 543–51.

Celano, M., Hazzard, A., Webb, C., and McCall, C. (1996). Treatment of traumagenic beliefs among sexually abused girls and their mothers: An evaluation study. *Journal of Abnormal Child Psychology, 24,* 1–17.

Chard, K. M. (2005). An evaluation of cognitive processing therapy for the treatment of posttraumatic stress disorder related to childhood sexual abuse. *Journal of Consulting and Clinical Psychology, 73,* 965–71.

Chemtob, C. M., Nakashima, J., and Carlson, J. G. (2002). Brief treatment for elementary school children with disaster-related posttraumatic stress disorder: A field study. *Journal of Clinical Psychology, 58,* 99–112.

Chemtob, C. M., Nakashima, J. P., and Hamada, R. S. (2002). Psychosocial intervention for postdisaster trauma symptoms in elementary school children: A controlled community field study. *Archives of Pediatric and Adolescent Medicine, 156,* 211–16.

Cloitre, M., Chase Stovall-McClough, K., Miranda, R., and Chemtob, C. M. (2004). Therapeutic alliance, negative mood regulation, and treatment outcome in child abuse-related posttraumatic stress disorder. *Journal of Consulting and Clinical Psychology, 72,* 411–16.

Cloitre, M., Koenen, K., Cohen, L. R., and Han, H. (2002). Skills training in affective and interpersonal regulation followed by exposure: A phase-based treatment for PTSD related to childhood abuse. *Journal of Consulting and Clinical Psychology, 70,* 1067–74.

Cohen, J. A., Berliner, L., and Mannarino, A. P. (2003). Psychosocial and pharmacological interventions for child crime victims. *Journal of Traumatic Stress, 16,* 175–86.

Cohen, J. A., Berliner, L., and March, J. S. (2000). Treatment of children and adolescents. In E. B. Foa, T. M., Keane and M. J., Friedman (Eds.), *Effective treatments for PTSD: Practice guidelines from the International Society for Traumatic Stress Studies* (106–38). New York: Guilford Press.

Cohen, J. A., Deblinger, E., Mannarino, A. P., and Steer, R. A. (2004). A multisite, randomized controlled trial for children with sexual abuse-related PTSD symptoms. *Journal of the American Academy of Child and Adolescent Psychiatry, 43*, 393–402.

Cohen, J. A., Mannarino, A. P., and Staron, V. R. (2006). A pilot study of modified cognitive-behavioral therapy for childhood traumatic grief (CBT-CTG). *Journal of American Academy of Child and Adolescent Psychiatry, 45*, 1465–73.

Davidson, J. R. T., Rothbaum, B. O., van der Kolk, B., Sikes, C. R., and Farfel, G. M. (2001). Multicenter, double blind comparison of sertraline and placebo in the treatment of posttraumatic stress disorder. *Archives of General Psychiatry, 58*, 485–75.

Davidson, P. R., and Parker, K. C. H. (2001). Eye movement desensitization and reprocessing (EMDR): A meta-analysis. *Journal of Consulting and Clinical Psychology, 69*, 305–19.

Deblinger, E., Lippman, J., and Steer, R. (1996). Sexually abused children suffering posttraumatic stress symptoms: Initial treatment outcome findings. *Child Maltreatment, 1*, 310–21.

Deblinger, E., Mannarino, A. P., Cohen, J. A., and Steer, R. A. (2006). A follow-up study of a multisite, randomized, controlled trial for children with sexual abuse-related PTSD symptoms. *Journal of the American Academy of Child & Adolescent Psychiatry, 45*, 1474–84.

Deblinger, E., McLeer, S. V., and Henry, D. (1990). Cognitive behavioral treatment for sexually abused children suffering from post-traumatic stress: Preliminary findings. *Journal of the American Academy of Child and Adolescent Psychiatry, 25*, 747–52.

Deblinger, E., Steer, R., and Lippman, J. (1999). Two-year follow-up study of cognitive behavioral therapy for sexually abused children suffering post-traumatic stress symptoms. *Child Abuse and Neglect, 23*, 1371–78.

Devilly, G. J., and Spence, S. H. (1999). The relative efficacy and treatment distress of EMDR and a cognitive-behavior trauma treatment protocol in the amelioration of posttraumatic stress disorder. *Journal of Anxiety Disorders, 13*, 131–57.

Dohrenwend, B. P., Turner, J. B., Turse, N. A., Adams, B. G., Koenen, K. C., and Marshall, R. (2006). The psychological risks of Vietnam for U.S. veterans: A revisit with new data and methods. *Science, 313*, 979–82.

Dunmore, E., Clark, D. M., and Ehlers, A. (1999). Cognitive factors involved in the onset and maintenance of posttraumatic stress disorder (PTSD) after physical or sexual assault. *Behaviour Research and Therapy, 37*, 809–29.

Ehlers, A., and Clark, D. M. (2000). A cognitive model of persistent posttraumatic stress disorder. *Behaviour Research and Therapy, 38*, 319–45.

Ehlers, A., Clark, D. M., Hackmann, A., McManus, F., and Fennell, M. (2005). Cognitive therapy for post-traumatic stress disorder: Development and evaluation. *Behavioral Research and Therapy, 43*, 413–31.

Feeny, N. C., Foa, E., Treadwell, K., and March, J. (2004). Posttraumatic stress disorder in youth: A critical review of the cognitive and behavioral treatment outcome literature. *Professional Psychology: Research and Practice, 35*, 466–76

Foa, E. B., Dancu, C. V., Hembree, E. A., Jaycox, L. H., Meadows, E. A., and Street, G. P. (1999). A comparison of exposure therapy, stress inoculation training, and their combination for reducing posttraumatic stress disorder in female assault victims. *Journal of Consulting and Clinical Psychology, 67*, 194–200.

Foa, E. B., Ehlers, A., Clark, D. M., Tolin, D. F., and Orsillo, S. M. (1999). The posttraumatic cognitions inventory (PTCI): Development and validation. *Psychological Assessment, 11*, 303–14.

Foa, E. B., Hembree, E. A., Cahill, S. P., Rauch, S. A., Riggs, D. S., Feeny, N. C., et al. (2005). Randomized trial of prolonged exposure for posttraumatic stress disorder with and without cognitive restructuring: outcome at academic and community clinics. *Journal of Consulting and Clinical Psychology, 73*, 953–64.

Foa, E. B., and Kozak, M. J. (1986). Emotional processing of fear: Exposure to corrective information. *Psychological Bulletin, 99*, 20–35.

Foa, E., Molnar, C., and Cashman, L. (1995). Change in rape narratives during exposure therapy for posttraumatic stress disorder. *Journal of Traumatic Stress, 8*, 675–90.

Foa, E. B., and Rothbaum, B. O. (1998). *Treating the trauma of rape.* New York: Guilford Press.

Foa, E. B., Rothbaum, B. O., and Furr, J. M. (2003). Augmenting exposure therapy with other CBT procedures. *Psychiatric Annals, 33*, 47–53.

Foa, E. B., Rothbaum, B. O., Riggs, D. S., and Murdock, T. (1991). Treatment of post-traumatic stress disorder in rape victims: A comparison between cognitive-behavioral procedures and counseling. *Journal of Consulting and Clinical Psychology, 59*, 715–23.

Kataoka, S. H., Stein, B. D., Jaycox, L. H., Wong, M., Escudero, P., Tu, W., et al. (2003). A school-based mental health program for traumatized Latino immigrant children. *Journal of the American Academy of Child and Adolescent Psychiatry, 42*, 311–18.

Keane, T. M., Marshall, A. D., and Taft, C. T. (2006). Posttraumatic stress disorder: Etiology, epidemiology, and treatment outcome. *Annual Review of Clinical Psychology, 2*, 161–97.

King, N. J., Tonge, B. J., Mullen, P., Myerson, N., Heyne, D., Rollings, S., et al. (2000). Treating sexually abused children with posttraumatic stress symptoms: A randomized clinical trial. *Journal of the American Academy of Child and Adolescent Psychiatry, 39*, 1347–55.

Kubany, E. S., Hill, E. E., Owens, J. A., Iannce-Spencer, C., McCaig, M. A., and Tremayne, K. J., et al. (2004). Cognitive trauma therapy for battered women with PTSD (CTT-BW). *Journal of Consulting and Clinical Psychology, 72*, 3–18

March, J. S., Amaya-Jackson, L., Murray, M. C., and Schulte, A. (1998). Cognitive-behavioral psychotherapy for children and adolescents with posttraumatic stress disorder after a single-incident stressor. *Journal of the American Academy of Child and Adolescent Psychiatry, 37*, 585–93.

Marks, I., Lovell, K., Noshirvani, H., Livanou, M., and Thrasher, S. (1998). Treatment of posttraumatic stress disorder by exposure and/or cognitive restructuring. *Archives of General Psychiatry, 55*, 317–25.

McDonagh, A., Friedman, M., McHugo, G., Ford, J., Sengupta, A., Mueser, K., et al. (2005). Randomized trial of cognitive-behavioral therapy for chronic posttraumatic stress disorder in adult female survivors of childhood sexual abuse. *Journal of Consulting and Clinical Psychology, 73*, 515–24.

Oras, R., De Ezpeleta, S. C., and Ahmad, A. (2004). Treatment of traumatized refugee children with eye movement desensitization and reprocessing in a psychodynamic context. *Nordic Journal of Psychiatry, 58*, 199–203.

Paunovic, N., and Öst, L.-G. (2001). Cognitive behavioral therapy vs. exposure therapy in treatment of PTSD in refugees. *Behavioral Research and Therapy, 39*, 1183–97.

Resick, P. A., Nishith, P., and Weaver, T., Astin, M. C., and Feuer, C. A. (2002). A comparison of cognitive processing therapy, prolonged exposure, and a waiting condition for the treatment of posttraumatic stress disorder in female rape victims. *Journal of Consulting and Clinical Psychology, 70*, 867–79.

Rothbaum, B. O. (1997). A controlled study of eye movement desensitization and reprocessing in the treatment of posttraumatic stress disordered sexual assault victims. *Bulletin of the Menninger Clinic, 61*, 317–34.

Rothbaum, B. O., Astin, M. C., and Marsteller, F. (2005). Prolonged exposure versus Eye Movement Desensitization and Reprocessing (EMDR) for PTSD rape victims. *Journal of Traumatic Stress, 18*, 607–16.

Roy-Byrne, P., Berliner, L., Russo, J., Zatzick, D., and Pitman, R. (2003). Treatment preferences and determinants in victims of sexual and physical assault. *Journal of Nervous and Mental Disorders, 191*, 161–65.

Ruggiero, K. J., Morris, T. L., and Scotti, J. R. (2001). Treatment for childhood posttraumatic stress disorder: Current status and future directions. *Clinical Psychology: Science and Practice, 8*, 210–27.

Saltzman, W., Pynoos, R., Layne, C., Steinberg, A., and Aisenberg, E. (2001). A developmental approach to trauma/grief focused group psychotherapy for youth exposed to community violence. *Journal of Child and Adolescent Group Therapy, 11*, 43–56.

Schnurr, P. P., Friedman, M. J., Engel, C. C., Foa, E. B., Shea, M. T., Chow, B. K., et al. (2007). Cognitive behavioral therapy for posttraumatic stress disorder in women: A randomized controlled trial. *Journal of the American Medical Association, 297*, 820–30.

Shapiro, F. (1989). Eye movement desensitization: A new treatment for post-traumatic stress disorder. *Journal of Behavior Therapy and Experimental Psychiatry, 20*, 211–17.

Shapiro, F. (1995). *Eye movement desensitization and reprocessing: Basic principles, protocols, and procedures.* New York: Guilford Press.

Stein, B. D., Jaycox, L. H., Kataoka, S. H., Wong, M., Tu, W., Elliott, M. N., and Fink, A. (2003). A mental health intervention for school children exposed to violence. *Journal of the American Medical Association, 290*, 603–11.

Street, L. L., Niederehe, G., and Lebowitz, B. D. (2000). Toward greater public health relevance for psychotherapeutic intervention research: An NIMH workshop report. *Clinical Psychology: Science and Practice, 7*(2), 127–37.

Tarrier, N., Pilgrim, H., Sommerfield, C., Faragher, B., Reynolds, M., Graham, E., et al., (1999). A randomized trial of cognitive therapy and imaginal exposure in the treatment of chronic posttraumatic stress disorder. *Journal of Consulting and Clinical Psychology, 67*, 13–18.

Taylor, S., Thordarson, D. S., Maxfield, L., Fedoroff, I. C., Lovell, K., and Ogrodniczuk, J. (2003). Comparative efficacy, speed, and adverse effects of three PTSD treatments: Exposure therapy, EMDR, and relaxation training. *Journal of Consulting and Clinical Psychology, 71*, 330–38.

Tolin, D. F., and Foa, E. B. (1999). Treatment of a police officer with PTSD using prolonged exposure. *Behavior Therapy, 30*, 527–38.

Van Etten, M. L., and Taylor, S. (1998). Comparative efficacy of treatments for posttraumatic stress disorder: A meta-analysis. *Clinical Psychology & Psychotherapy, 5*, 126–44.

Van Minnen, A., and Hagenaars, M. (2002). Fear activation and habituation patterns as early process predictors of response to prolonged exposure treatment in PTSD. *Journal of Traumatic Stress, 15*, 359–367.

Zoellner, L. A., Feeny, N. C., Cochran, B., and Pruitt, L. (2003). Treatment choice for PTSD. *Behaviour Research and Therapy, 41*, 879–86.

Zoellner, L. A., Feeny, N. C., and Rothbaum, B. O. (2006). Special section: Dissemination: Transforming lives through transforming care. *Journal of Traumatic Stress, 19*, 567–69.

# 12

# Recent Advances in the Pharmacological Treatment/Prevention of PTSD

*Douglas L. Delahanty and Sarah A. Ostrowski*

As we've seen in the previous chapters, PTSD is a complex disorder oftentimes involving comorbid conditions and heterogeneous and protean symptom presentation. Clinical management of PTSD symptoms is also complex, with psychological and pharmacological interventions both demonstrating efficacy. Pharmacotherapy may best be thought of as a component of effective therapy, with choice of medication involving consideration of symptom presentation, response to psychotherapy, comorbid conditions, trauma history, and other patient-related characteristics. A number of medications have been found to be efficacious at reducing the symptoms of chronic PTSD, although few have been tested in randomized controlled trials (RCTs). Existent RCTs have supported the efficacy of selective serotonin reuptake inhibitors (SSRIs), and the FDA has approved sertraline and paroxetine for use in the treatment of PTSD. Similar recommendations have been made for the pharmacological management of PTSD in adults and children, although little research has been conducted on pharmacotherapy for PTSD in children. In this chapter, we will briefly review medications used to reduce/eliminate chronic PTSD symptoms in adult and child trauma victims. We will then focus more on recent advances in early pharmacologic preventive interventions and gaps in the literature involving the secondary prevention of PTSD symptoms.

Address correspondence to Dr. Douglas Delahanty; Department of Psychology; 144 Kent Hall; Kent State University; Kent, OH 44242. E-mail: ddelahan@kent.edu

## PHARMACOLOGIC INTERVENTION FOR CHRONIC PTSD

A number of high quality review articles (Albucher and Liberzon, 2002; Cooper, Carty, and Creamer, 2005; Schoenfeld, Marmar, and Neylan, 2004) and treatment guidelines (Alarcon, Glover, Boyer, and Balon, 2000) have been published to guide practitioners through decision-making steps regarding the appropriate dose and monitoring of pharmacologic regimens in adults with PTSD. Therefore, we will only briefly review findings concerning tertiary pharmacologic interventions for PTSD symptoms. Tertiary interventions are administered to individuals with chronic symptoms in an attempt to reduce or eliminate current symptomatology. In contrast, secondary interventions, which are the focus of the latter half of this chapter, are administered soon after a trauma in an attempt to buffer or prevent the development of PTSD symptoms.

A number of RCT studies (Brady et al., 2000; Davidson et al., 2001; Marshall, Beebe, Oldham, and Zaninelli, 2001; Tucker et al., 2001) have established SSRIs as the first-line treatment of choice for the short-term treatment of PTSD. Large multi-site RCTs have led to the FDA approval of sertraline (Brady et al., 2000; Davidson et al., 2001) and paroxetine (Marshall et al., 2001; Tucker et al., 2001). The majority of studies suggest that SSRIs are equally beneficial with all PTSD symptom clusters, and that their efficacy does not appear to be compromised by comorbid anxiety or depression symptoms. While comorbidities were associated with an approximately one-week increase in mean response time to sertraline, overall efficacy was not affected (Brady and Clary, 2003). However, most studies exclude participants with current substance abuse, limiting the ability to generalize findings to PTSD patients with comorbid substance use.

Although SSRIs are considered the first-line treatment of choice for PTSD, in general, sertraline trials have demonstrated modest effects, with 53–60 percent of sertraline recipients vs. 32–38 percent of placebo recipients responding to the therapy. Further, some evidence suggests that SSRI efficacy may be limited to subgroups of trauma victims (see Schoenfeld et al., 2004). In the initial sertraline trials, women appeared to respond better to sertraline than men; however, subsequent research has not shown a gender difference in efficacy (Marshall et al., 2001). Similarly, whereas SSRIs have consistently been found efficacious in non-combat PTSD, veterans with PTSD did not show a significant benefit to SSRI therapy (Hertzberg, Feldman, Beckham, Kudler, and Davidson, 2000; Zohar et al., 2002; van der Kolk et al., 1994), perhaps due to the more severe levels of PTSD and/or the repetitive nature of combat trauma. Finally, research has raised questions concerning the optimal duration of SSRI treatment for PTSD patients. Pharmacotherapy for PTSD is not typically perceived as curative, as withdrawal of medication often leads to symptom recurrence if concurrent psychotherapy is not provided. The most common medication regimen duration examined is twelve weeks; however, research has suggested that participants treated for longer periods of time exhibit greater and more sustained symptom improvement than those treated for shorter time periods (Davidson, 2000; Rapaport, Endicott, and Clary, 2002). Non-responders to SSRI treatment at twelve weeks may become responders following longer duration therapy (four to six months: Londborg et al., 2001). Due to the somewhat inconsistent pattern of responding to SSRIs across treatment groups (non-combat vs. combat, men vs. women), additional medications continue to be tested as possible treatments for PTSD. Davidson and colleagues (2006) recently examined the efficacy of the serotonin norepinephrine reuptake inhibitor venlafaxine—extended release at decreasing PTSD symptoms in a six-month, double-blind, placebo-controlled trial. Results revealed that venlafaxine was efficacious at reducing symptoms and was well tolerated by participants.

A number of other classes of medications (e.g., non-SSRI anti-depressants, anti-convulsants, anti-psychotics) have also been shown to be efficacious in the short-term treatment of some PTSD symptoms, although this has been found primarily in open label studies with very small samples (see Hageman, Andersen, and Jorgensen, 2001, for a review). Stronger evidence for efficacy comes from double-blind placebo-controlled studies. Medications that have shown treatment effects using this more rigorous testing include monoamine oxidase inhibitors (MAOIs) (Katz et al., 1994; Kosten et al., 1991) and tricyclic antidepressants (Frank, Kosten, Giller, and Dan, 1988), with some suggesting that MAOIs are more effective in treating PTSD than tricyclics (Southwick et al., 1994). Due to side effects and potential toxicity, caution must be employed when administering these older anti-depressants. Additional agents that have shown efficacy at reducing PTSD symptoms in controlled trials include the anti-convulsant lamotrigine (Hertzberg et al., 1999) and anti-psychotic medications used as an adjunct to SSRI therapy (Stein, Kline, and Matloff, 2002). Whereas these medications have shown efficacy at reducing symptoms, they often do not directly target symptoms of PTSD and typically have greater risk of side effects. Therefore, they are best considered as adjunctive therapies useful in targeting comorbid conditions or for use in case of non-response to SSRIs.

In sum, research consistently supports the use of SSRI medications as a first-line treatment for chronic PTSD in adults. Additional medications have been shown to be efficacious, but with greater side effects or limited, open-label support for their use. Symptom presentation and comorbidities should also be taken into account when deciding on a pharmacologic regimen (see Alarcon et al., 2000, for treatment algorithms). Finally, pharmacotherapy should be considered in the context of a comprehensive therapeutic approach combining psychotherapy with medication treatment.

Research examining the pharmacological treatment of childhood PTSD has largely paralleled that conducted in adults, although very few studies have been conducted in children (Cohen, 2001). Moreover, the research that has been conducted on childhood PTSD is often methodologically limited (Cohen, 2001), lacking control groups or randomized treatment assignment (Cohen, Berliner, and Mannarino, 2003). Many clinicians base their treatment practices on findings from the adult literature. A disadvantage in translating the results from adult pharmacological studies into treatment practices for childhood PTSD is that it assumes that the results in adults are applicable to children. It is crucial to take into consideration developmental variations in symptom formation and treatment responsiveness, and physiological differences between children and adults when making decisions concerning the pharmacologic management of PTSD in children (Cohen, 2001). As in adults, appropriate selection of pharmacological treatment for childhood PTSD should be a rational decision based on an adequate understanding of the psychophysiology of PTSD and the particular target symptoms of pharmacological agents, along with an awareness of existing comorbid disorders (Donnelly, Amaya-Jackson, and March, 1999).

In general, there appears to be less variability in medications prescribed to children with PTSD vs. adults with PTSD. Concerns regarding the dangerous side effects of tricyclic anti-depressants and MAOIs have limited their use in children, and a survey of physicians treating children with PTSD revealed that 95 percent of physicians use SSRIs to treat childhood PTSD (Cohen, Mannarino, and Rogal, 2001). Much less frequently, the following were prescribed: alpha- and beta-adrenergic blocking agents (e.g., clonidine, propranolol), tricyclic anti-depressants (e.g., desipramine), anxiolytics (e.g., aloprazolam), anti-convulsants (e.g., carbamazepine), and anti-psychotics (e.g., haloperidol) (Cohen et al., 2001). Although SSRIs are the most commonly prescribed medication for childhood PTSD, treatment decisions appear to be primarily made based on the adult literature as few studies have tested the efficacy of SSRIs in child PTSD. However, Seedat and colleagues have demonstrated the effectiveness of citalopram in treating PTSD in children and adolescents with PTSD (Seedat, Lockhat, Kaminer, Zungu-Dirwayi, and Stein, 2001; Seedat et al., 2002).

Additional medications have been examined in child PTSD and include anti-convulsants and adrenergic agents. Looff and colleagues (1995) found that 300–1200mg/day of carbamazepine decreased PTSD symptoms in twenty-eight children diagnosed with PTSD. However, many of these children suffered from comorbid disorders, such as ADHD, depression, OCD, or polysubstance abuse for which they were receiving other psychotropic medications (eg., Ritalin, clonidine, SSRIs, and/or imipramine). Anti-convulsants may be useful in treating avoidance and hyperarousal symptoms, excessive anger and aggressiveness, and sleep dysregulation in children with PTSD (Donnelly et al., 1999).

As PTSD is characterized by symptoms of hypervigilance and hyperarousal, researchers have hypothesized that adrenergic agonists such as alpha-2 clonidine (Catapres) and guanfacine (Tenex) and the beta antagonist propranolol (Inderal) could reduce sympathetic tone and be effective in reducing PTSD symptoms (Marmar et al., 1993). Harmon and Riggs (1996) conducted an open-trial of the clonidine patch in three- to six-year-old children suffering from PTSD and comorbid disorders such as depression, attentional problems, and reactive attachment disorder. Results suggested that clonidine resulted in improvement in aggression, impulsivity, emotional outbursts, mood lability, hyperarousal, hypervigilance, generalized anxiety, oppositionality, and insomnia (Harmon and Riggs, 1996). A similar open-label trial of clonindine in seventeen abused children with PTSD found that clonidine significantly reduced the children's anxiety, hyperarousal, impulsivity, and depressive symptoms (Perry, 1994). Additionally, a five-week open trial of propranolol found that the medication decreased re-experiencing and hyperarousal symptoms in eight out of eleven children (Famularo, Kinscherff, and Fenton, 1988). However, the symptoms returned once the medication was discontinued.

In sum, limited research in children has revealed that pharmacologic management of PTSD largely parallels that in adults. Additional research is necessary to examine the efficacy of pharmacologic agents in children, as extrapolating from adult treatment studies does not account for the myriad differences in development, symptom presentation, and comorbidities seen in children vs. adults with PTSD.

Although the development of effective tertiary interventions to treat PTSD symptoms has enormous public health relevance, tertiary interventions target patients with chronic PTSD years after traumatic exposure, and after symptoms have taken a toll on academic or work performance, neural and cognitive development, and peer and family relationships. Research into the biology of PTSD and trauma responses has led researchers to hypothesize that pharmacologic interventions administered soon after trauma exposure may be efficacious at reducing/preventing the development of PTSD symptoms.

## SECONDARY PHARMACOLOGICAL INTERVENTIONS TO PREVENT THE DEVELOPMENT OF PTSD SYMPTOMS

Disappointing findings in studies of early psychological interventions have provided additional impetus for the development of early pharmacological interventions to prevent or reduce subsequent PTSD symptoms in trauma victims. Results of methodologically strong RCTs and meta-analyses have found that early psychological debriefing interventions are ineffective at preventing PTSD (Rose, Brewin, Andres, and Kirk, 1999; for reviews, see Litz, Gray, Bryant, and Adler, 2002, as cited in Ruzek and Watson, 2001), and, in some cases, are detrimental (Mayou, Ehlers, and Hobbs, 2000). Delaying interventions to at least two weeks post-trauma has produced more promising results. Foa and colleagues (1995) reported decreased symptoms of PTSD in female assault victims who received four sessions of a cognitive-behavioral intervention. Similarly, cognitive-behavioral interventions have been found to be superior to supportive counseling in preventing PTSD in trauma victims meeting acute stress disorder (ASD) criteria (Bryant, Harvey, Dang, Sackville, and Basten, 1998; Bryant, Sackville, Dang, Moulds, and Guthrie, 1999). However, cognitive-behavioral therapy is relatively time- and labor-intensive. Earlier psychological interventions are not effective at preventing PTSD, creating an initial gap during which no known therapeutic treatment can be administered. Therefore, research has begun to focus on possible pharmacological agents that, if administered in the immediate aftermath of a traumatic event, may reduce or prevent subsequent symptoms of PTSD (Pitman et al., 2002; Schelling et al., 2001; 2004; Vaiva et al., 2003).

Initial examinations of early secondary pharmacologic interventions followed largely from biological theories of the role of stress hormones in memory development. Theories of emotional memory formation stem from the hypothesis that, evolutionarily, our memory storage system provides a means by which more important events (reflected by hormonal consequences) may result in greater strength of memory formation (Charney et al., 1994; Gold, 1984; McGaugh, Liang, Bennett, and Sternberg, 1984; Pitman and Orr, 1995). Animal research has consistently shown that arousal is associated with better retention of stress-related memories (de Wied, 1984; McGaugh, 1985, 1989). Low cortisol levels have been shown to increase the memory-enhancing effects of catecholamines (Bohus, 1984; de Wied, 1984), and high cortisol doses decrease these effects (Borrell, de Kloet, Versteeg, and Bohus, 1983). Human research has demonstrated that blocking β-adrenergic receptors with propranolol abolishes the enhancement of memories of slides presented along with an emotionally arousing narrative but does not impact memory of neutral slides (Cahill, Prins, Weber, and McGaugh, 1994), suggesting that the adrenergic system is integrally involved in facilitating the consolidation of material learned under emotionally arousing conditions.

Pitman (1989) was the first to hypothesize that altered stress hormone levels during traumatic or arousing situations may moderate memory consolidation and subsequent risk for PTSD symptoms. More specifically, he hypothesized that excess adrenergic activity during and immediately after trauma exposure could lead to the development of "overconsolidated" memories, and subsequent symptoms of PTSD (Pitman, 1989; Pitman, Orr, and Shalev, 1993). Yehuda and colleagues expanded this theory by suggesting that, during traumatic stress, exaggerated catecholamine increases without the regulatory influence of accompanying cortisol increases could lead to inappropriate memory formation (either oversalient or fragmented memories) and result in the intrusion symptoms that characterize PTSD (Yehuda and Harvey, 1997; Yehuda, McFarlane, and Shalev, 1998). In other words, lower cortisol levels at the time of the trauma may fail to contain the sympathetic stress response leading to consequent prolonged availability of norepinephrine in the brain (Pacak, Palkovits, Kopin, and Goldstein, 1995), and altered consolidation and retrieval of memory of the traumatic incident (Yehuda, 2002). A number of studies have since tested the extent to which initial physiological responses to trauma are associated with increased risk for the development of subsequent PTSD symptoms.

## ACUTE BIOLOGICAL PREDICTORS OF PTSD IN ADULTS

Research examining whether initial physiological responses to trauma are associated with subsequent PTSD symptoms has typically been conducted in emergency department (ED) settings, as this environment affords the ability to assess physiological responses relatively soon after a traumatic event. A number of studies have taken advantage of readily available medical chart data to examine the extent to which heart rate (HR) levels routinely assessed at varying times following hospital admission were associated with increased risk for subsequent PTSD. Although contradictory findings have been reported in a study of self-selected participants (Blanchard, Hickling, Galovski, and Veazey, 2002) and results may not generalize to seriously injured trauma patients (Buckley et al., 2004), prospective studies of consecutive ED patients have found that patients with higher HRs during their hospital stay are more likely to develop PTSD (Bryant, Harvey, Guthrie, and Moulds, 2000; Shalev et al., 1998; Zatzick et al., 2005).

Few studies have directly tested whether altered cortisol levels soon after trauma increase one's risk for developing PTSD. Resnick and colleagues

(1995) found that rape victims with prior assault or rape histories had lower plasma cortisol levels within fifty-one hours of the rape and were more likely to develop PTSD than women without similar trauma histories. Similarly, motor vehicle accident (MVA) victims who subsequently were diagnosed with PTSD had lower plasma cortisol levels thirty minutes after their accident than victims who subsequently met criteria for major depression (McFarlane, Atchison, and Yehuda, 1997). We have previously found that MVA victims who met acute PTSD diagnostic criteria one month after the accident had significantly lower fifteen-hour urinary cortisol levels in the immediate aftermath of the accident than victims who did not meet diagnostic criteria (Delahanty, Raimonde, and Spoonster, 2000). In addition, initial levels of cortisol were highly negatively correlated with subsequent symptoms of PTSD ($r = -.46, p < .01$). PTSD and non-PTSD patients did not differ in catecholamine levels, although PTSD symptoms were negatively correlated with urinary epinephrine levels. These results supported Yehuda's theory (Yehuda and Harvey, 1997; Yehuda et al., 1998), by suggesting that increased adrenergic activity without the regulatory control of cortisol could lead to subsequent symptoms of PTSD.

### Secondary Pharmacological Interventions for Adult Trauma Victims

Findings of increased risk for PTSD symptoms in trauma victims who display high levels of sympathetic nervous system (SNS) and low levels of hypothalamic pituitary adrenal (HPA) axis activity after trauma have led researchers to hypothesize that altering levels of stress hormones (i.e., blocking sympathetic arousal or boosting circulating cortisol levels) in the immediate aftermath of a traumatic event may lead to a reduction in subsequent symptoms of PTSD. The first studies to examine secondary pharmacological interventions consisted of small studies of patients who received benzodiazepines in the emergency department soon after a traumatic injury. Findings revealed that early benzodiazepine treatment had either little effect on subsequent PTSD severity (Mellman, Bustamante, David, and Fins, 2002) or potentially resulted in adverse effects with regards to subsequent PTSD diagnoses (Gelpin, Bonne, Peri, and Brandes, 1996), suggesting that they should not be considered as potential preventative agents (Cooper et al., 2005).

Currently, the most promising candidate for a secondary intervention that may reduce or prevent PTSD symptoms is the β-blocker propranolol. Propranolol blocks post-synaptic β-adrenergic receptors and reduces sympathetic arousal (Pitman and Delahanty, 2005). Taylor and Cahill (2002) investigated posttraumatic administration of propranolol to prevent re-emergent symptoms of PTSD in a woman with a prior history of PTSD who was experiencing significant PTSD symptoms following an additional trauma. Propranolol administration was initiated forty-eight hours post-trauma following acute reemergence of PTSD symptoms. The woman reported fewer symptoms at two-week, one-month, and nine-month follow-ups, evidencing an 88 percent reduction in symptom severity by nine months post-trauma.

Pitman and colleagues (2002) conducted an initial double-blind placebo-control investigation of propranolol as a secondary intervention for the prevention of PTSD. Participants completed a ten-day (plus taper) medication regimen of propranolol (N = 18) or placebo (N = 23). Although differences between treatment groups were not statistically significant, 30 percent (six out of twenty) of placebo recipients as compared with 10 percent (one out of ten, excluding one outlier) of propranolol recipients met PTSD criteria one month post-trauma. None of the propranolol recipients and eight out of fourteen of the placebo recipients exhibited heightened physiological reactivity to script-driven imagery of their traumatic event, suggesting that early ß-blocker treatment may be especially effective at reducing conditioned fear responses.

A subsequent nonrandomized study also supported the efficacy of early propranolol treatment. Eleven trauma victims who received propranolol for posttraumatic tachycardia were compared to eight victims who refused the medication (Vaiva et al., 2003). Results revealed that rates of diagnostic levels of PTSD and PTSD symptoms were higher in refusers than in participants who received propranolol, suggesting that initial propranolol treatment may buffer against the subsequent development of PTSD.

Whereas propranolol is hypothesized to decrease risk for PTSD by decreasing conditioned fear responses, research examining pharmacologically altering cortisol levels rests on the belief that alterations of cortisol levels may disrupt the retrieval of traumatic memories. Memory formation is a dynamic process, developing over time, and consequently is thought to be susceptible to moderation by internal or external stimuli during consolidation and subsequent retrieval (Lupien and McEwen, 1997). Pitman and colleagues (1993) have suggested that repetitive retrieving, re-experiencing, and restoring of the trauma in the days following a traumatic event may be involved in the pathogenesis of PTSD. Endogenous hypercortisolemia and exogenous glucocorticoid administration have been shown to impair retrieval and declarative memory performance in humans (de Quervain, Roozendaal, Nitsch, McGaugh, and Hock, 2000; Kirschbaum, Wolf, May, Wippich, and Hellhammer, 1996; Mauri et al., 1993; Newcomer, Craft, Hershey, Askins, and Bardgett, 1994; Newcomer et al., 1999; Wolkowitz et al.,

1990; for reviews, see Lupien and McEwen, 1997; Martignoni et al., 1992). This raises the possibility that therapeutic disruption of retrieval mechanisms by exogenous cortisol in the aftermath of a traumatic event might protect against the development of PTSD symptoms.

Support for this hypothesis stems from recent work by Schelling and colleagues indicating that stress doses of cortisol may buffer the development of PTSD in septic-shock patients (Schelling et al., 1999; Schelling et al., 2001). An initial retrospective case-controlled analysis revealed that sepsis patients receiving a 100mg bolus of hydrocortisone (during the sepsis episode) followed by .18mg/kg/hr until shock reversal had a significantly lower incidence of PTSD than patients receiving standard treatment (Schelling et al., 1999). These findings were then replicated in a randomized double-blind study (Schelling et al., 2001). During a sepsis episode, eleven patients were randomly assigned to receive placebo and nine were assigned the above-mentioned dose of hydrocortisone for six days with subsequent tapering. Results revealed that only one of nine from the hydrocortisone group but seven of eleven from the placebo group ($p = .02$) met PTSD criteria assessed thirty-one months after discharge from the intensive care unit (ICU). Although groups did not differ in duration of ICU treatment, there was a trend toward faster shock reversal in the hydrocortisone group. In addition, placebo patients received a higher dose of norepinephrine in the ICU, which could have contributed to higher rates of PTSD in this group. Alternatively, hydrocortisone administration may have interfered with the intensity or emotionality of the traumatic event or disrupted retrieval mechanisms, thus reducing subsequent PTSD. More recently, Schelling and colleagues (2004) have examined the efficacy of peri- and postoperative exogenous hydrocortisone at buffering symptoms of posttraumatic stress in patients following cardiac surgery. Results revealed that patients receiving the hydrocortisone regimen reported significantly fewer PTSD symptoms than comparison patients ($p < .05$).

In sum, both hydrocortisone and propranolol have shown promise as secondary interventions to reduce PTSD symptoms. However, research examining hydrocortisone has been conducted primarily in disease populations. It remains to be seen whether hydrocortisone would exert similar protective effects in injured trauma victims. Hydrocortisone may be more effective at inhibiting early retrieval of traumatic memories and decreasing the intrusive thoughts of PTSD than propranolol. On the other hand, cortisol is not as effective at reducing hyperadrenergic activity, and therefore may not be as effective at decreasing symptoms of hyperarousal. This suggests that, if each of these agents is found to be efficacious in preventing PTSD symptoms in larger-scale examinations, their combination may be even more so.

## ACUTE BIOLOGICAL PREDICTORS OF PTSD IN CHILDREN

As with studies of chronic PTSD, few studies have examined initial biological predictors of PTSD in children. Consistent with the adult literature, elevated HR soon after trauma is associated with increased risk for the development of PTSD in child trauma victims (Kassam-Adams, Garcia-España, Fein, and Winston, 2005; Nugent, Christopher, and Delahanty, 2006). Specifically, HR upon admit to the ED significantly predicted PTSD severity and diagnostic status (odds ratio = 2.5) at follow-up (ranging three- to thirteen-months post-admit) after controlling for age, sex, and injury severity (Kassam-Adams et al., 2005). Similarly, a systematic examination of HR measures across numerous time points soon after trauma injury revealed that HR recorded during emergency medical service (EMS) transport was significantly correlated with subsequent PTSD symptoms at six weeks ($r = .42$ $p < .01$) and at six months posttrauma ($r = .35$, $p < .05$: Nugent et al., 2006). After removing the variance associated with demographic variables and depressive symptoms, both HR during EMS transport and HR averaged over the first twenty minutes following admit continued to predict a significant percentage of the variance in six-week and six-month PTSD symptoms.

These data were collected as part of a study paralleling our adult work, in which we examined initial urinary hormone predictors of PTSD in child trauma victims (Delahanty, Nugent, Christopher, and Walsh, 2005). We collected twelve-hour urine samples initiated upon admission to the trauma unit in eighty-two children (fifty-six boys, twenty-six girls) aged eight to eighteen. Follow-up assessment of PTSD symptoms occurred six-weeks posttrauma. In contrast with the results of our adult study, in children with first-time traumas, *higher* levels of twelve-hour urinary cortisol and epinephrine predicted higher PTSD symptoms six weeks posttrauma. However, these findings seemed to be driven by significant findings in boys (rs = .52 for cortisol, .46 for epinephrine), as the relationships were not significant in girls (rs = .01 for cortisol, −.17 for epinephrine). We have since replicated these findings in a small sample with a more equal gender distribution (thirty-three boys, twenty-eight girls: Ostrowski, Christopher, and Delahanty, 2007). Using identical methods, twelve-hour urinary cortisol was again significantly correlated with PTSD symptoms in boys (r = .52, p < .05) but not girls (r = .27, NS).

In our child studies we typically excluded children with a prior trauma history in order to test the relationship between initial biological responses to trauma and subsequent PTSD in a sample that was not confounded by differing trauma histories. However, due to difficulties inherent in the enforcement of recruitment criteria during emergency triage, we recruited eight children with a prior trauma history (typically abuse or maltreatment) into our initial study (Delahanty et al., 2005). Inspection of the data for these children suggested that children with a prior trauma history tended toward higher PTSD symptom levels and lower urinary cortisol levels (Delahanty, unpublished data). In other words, children with a prior trauma history looked more like our adult trauma victims. We mention this qualifier to our findings to underscore the importance of examining trauma history as a factor in studies examining initial biological predictors of PTSD as well as in early pharmacological interventions.

## Secondary Pharmacological Interventions for Child Trauma Victims

Currently, no published studies have investigated pharmacological secondary interventions for PTSD in children. However, research has suggested that pharmacologic agents administered soon after trauma could impact subsequent PTSD risk in children. For instance, amount of morphine received by child burn victims in hospital has been negatively related to subsequent PTSD symptoms (Saxe et al., 2001). Similarly, we have recently completed a small study examining the efficacy of the ß-blocker propranolol at reducing subsequent PTSD symptoms in child trauma victims. This study was based on our findings of elevated catecholamines and HR in children who subsequently developed more PTSD symptoms as well as on an examination of propranolol as a tertiary treatment for chronic PTSD in children. Famularo, Kinscherff, and Fenton (1988) used an A-B-A design to investigate the effects of propranolol treatment on eleven children with PTSD. The children received four weeks of medication followed by a week of tapering and did not take any other medications throughout the course of the study. Children reported significantly fewer PTSD symptoms while receiving propranolol treatment than either before or after receiving propranolol.

Our study was modeled after Pitman's (2002) initial study in adults. We conducted a randomized, double-blind placebo control design in which twenty-nine children received either ten days of propranolol or placebo (Nugent et al., in preparation). Overall, analyses did not identify significant differences between participants in the placebo vs. the propranolol treatment condition. However, within-gender analyses revealed a different pattern of response to treatment condition, with boys showing fewer symptoms in the propranolol condition relative to the placebo condition and girls showing fewer symptoms in the placebo condition relative to the propranolol condition. Differential responding to propranolol in boys vs. girls was supported by our basic research findings whereby heightened catecholamine levels predicted PTSD symptoms, but only in boys. However, the present findings should be viewed with caution. Our child studies included children ranging in age from eight to eighteen, which includes girls who differ dramatically in hormone levels (due to pubertal status and menstrual phase), coping abilities, and a score of other variables. Additional research is necessary to determine whether any one of these or other variables systematically impacts the efficacy of early pharmacological interventions in traumatized girls.

No research has yet examined the efficacy of hydrocortisone as a secondary intervention in child trauma victims. Given our basic research findings that, especially in boys, children with higher cortisol during the first twelve hours following a traumatic injury are at higher risk for PTSD symptoms (Delahanty et al., 2005), caution should be taken in exogenously increasing child victims' cortisol levels without further understanding of the mechanism through which hydrocortisone may exert protective effects.

In sum, little research has been conducted concerning secondary interventions in child trauma victims. Given that childhood PTSD is associated with significant social impairments (Berman, Kurtines, Silverman, and Serafini, 1996; Stallard, Velleman, and Baldwin, 1998), cognitive deficits (Bremner et al., 1995), poor academic performance (Reinherz, Gianconia, Lefkowitz, Pakiz, and Frost, 1993), and a variety of comorbid behavioral and emotional disorders (Fletcher, 1996) research examining treatments for preventing PTSD before debilitating impairments occur is desperately needed.

## Barriers to Developing Effective Early Interventions

Although the public health relevance of an effective early intervention to prevent PTSD in child and adult trauma victims is obvious, a number of barriers make research in this area difficult. PTSD symptoms appear to be influenced by a complex constellation of environmental and person-specific factors. Prior investigations of predictors of PTSD in children have implicated psychosocial variables such as perceived severity of the stressor, age, gender, ethnicity, and prior trauma experiences as well as myriad event-specific characteristics and initial posttraumatic responses. It is unknown how variability between trauma victims on these dimensions impacts the efficacy of early pharmacologic agents. Perhaps the most important factor to consider when testing a medication as a preventative agent is how to determine who is most likely to benefit from the therapy. Theory and limited empirical data suggest that secondary interventions have the greatest likelihood of success when they can be administered within hours of the traumatic event. This limits the utility of these interventions to trauma groups who can be reached so soon following exposure. Further, the majority of trauma victims recover well without treatment, and alterations of normal stress responses in these individuals can potentially increase risk for the development of posttraumatic symptoms (McCleery and Harvey, 2004). Current screeners for determining at-risk individuals are limited in their sensitivity and specificity, and advances in our ability to identify individuals likely to develop chronic PTSD are necessary to inform early pharmacological trials. An additional barrier to testing novel early interventions concerns the extent to which proposed mechanisms of action are correctly disseminated to the lay public. The popular press, through erroneous depictions of mind-altering mechanisms of medications being tested, has generated negative opinion concerning the "wiping out" of traumatic memories. It is important to underscore that none of the current medications being examined function as amnestic agents. Limited evidence suggests that amnestic agents are potentially harmful (Gelpin et al., 1996). Early propranolol and hydrocortisone treatments do not result in the absence of memory for traumatic events, but rather decrease the saliency of the event and limit the strength of traumatic reminders. This needs to be made clear to potential participants as well as the lay public as a whole.

## SUMMARY OF PHARMACOLOGICAL OPTIONS FOR THE TREATMENT OF PTSD

A rational treatment approach to pharmacological interventions for PTSD should be based on an understanding of the neurobiological underpinnings of PTSD and the drug's mechanism of action (Donnelly et al., 1999). Selection of pharmacological agents should be based, first, on whether the PTSD symptoms are debilitating enough to warrant medication. Second, clinicians must identify comorbid disorders and particular PTSD symptom clusters for treatment and select appropriate interventions that target these particular symptoms. In selecting medications, treating physicians need to identify which symptoms are causing the greatest impairment and balance this with which of the symptoms are most likely to be responsive to medication. SSRIs represent the first-line recommended treatment for chronic PTSD, with adjunctive use of other medications dependent upon comorbid symptoms and treatment response. Prescribing physicians should carefully consider the relative risks and benefits associated with using a particular intervention in relation to other possible treatment approaches (Cohen, 2001). Pharmacotherapy should be considered as one component of effective therapy, with choice of medication involving consideration of symptom presentation, response to psychotherapy, comorbid conditions, trauma history, and other patient-related characteristics.

Additional research is necessary concerning the efficacy of secondary pharmacological interventions, although limited initial findings are suggestive. In particular, beta-blockers have demonstrated limited efficacy at reducing some PTSD symptoms, and early hydrocortisone treatment has been found to decrease rates of PTSD in patients suffering from a variety of physical diseases. Improvements in our ability to identify individuals at high risk for chronic PTSD will aid in the judicious administration of medications informed by continuing research into the neurobiology of PTSD.

## ACKNOWLEDGEMENTS

Preparation of this chapter was supported, in part, by National Institutes of Mental Health grants R34 MH 71201 and R34 73014.

## REFERENCES

Alarcon, R. D., Glover, S., Boyer, W., and Balon, R. (2000). Proposing an algorithm for the pharmacological management of posttraumatic stress disorder. *Annals of Clinical Psychiatry, 12*, 239–46.

Albucher, R. C., and Liberzon, I. (2002). Psychopharmacological treatment in PTSD: A critical review. *Journal of psychiatric research, 36*, 355–67.

Baker, D. G., Diamond, B. I., Gillette, G., Hamner, M., Katzelnick, D., Keller, T. et al. (1995). A double-blind, randomized, placebo-controlled, multi-center study of brofaromine in the treatment of post-traumatic stress disorder. *Psychopharmacology, 122*(4), 386–89.

Berman, S. L., Kurtines, W. M., Silverman, W. K., and Serafini, L. T. (1996). The impact of exposure to crime and violence on urban youth. *American Journal of Orthopsychiatry, 66*(3), 329–36.

Blanchard, E. B., Hickling, E. J., Galovski, T., and Veazey, C. (2002). Emergency room vital signs and PTSD in a treatment seeking sample of motor vehicle accident survivors. *Journal of Traumatic Stress, 15*(3), 199–204.

Bohus, B. (1984). Endocrine influence on disease outcome: Experimental findings and implications. *Journal of Psychosomatic Research, 28*, 429–38.

Borrell, J., de Kloet, E. R., Versteeg, D. H., and Bohus, B. (1983). Inhibitory avoidance deficit following short-term adrenalectomy in the rat: The role of adrenal catecholamines. *Behavioral & Neural Biology, 39*(2), 241–58.

Brady, K. T., and Clary, C. M. (2003). Affective and anxiety comorbidity in posttraumatic stress disorder treatment trials of sertraline. *Comprehensive Psychiatry, 44*, 360–69.

Brady, K., Pearlstein, T., Asnis, G. M., Baker, D., Rothbaum, B., Sikes, C. R., et al. (2000). Efficacy and safety of sertraline treatment of posttraumatic stress disorder:

A randomized controlled trial. *JAMA: Journal of the American Medical Association, 283*(1), 1837–44.

Bremner, J. D., Randall, P., Scott, T. W., Capelli, S., Delaney, R., McCarthy, G., et al. (1995). Deficits in short-term memory in adult survivors of childhood abuse. *Psychiatry Research, 59*(1–2), 97–107.

Bryant, R. A., Harvey, A. G., Dang, S. T., Sackville, T., and Basten, C. (1998). Treatment of acute stress disorder: A comparison of cognitive-behavioral therapy and supportive counseling. *Journal of Consulting and Clinical Psychology, 66*(5), 862–66.

Bryant, R. A., Harvey, A. G., Guthrie, R. M., and Moulds, M. L. (2000). A prospective study of psychophysiological arousal, acute stress disorder, and posttraumatic stress disorder. *Journal of Abnormal Psychology, 109*(2), 341–44.

Bryant, R. A., Sackville, T., Dang, S. T., Moulds, M., and Guthrie, R. (1999). Treating acute stress disorder: An evaluation of cognitive behavior therapy and supporting counseling techniques. *American Journal of Psychiatry, 156*(11), 1780–86.

Buckley, B., Nugent, N., Sledjeski, E., Raimonde, A. J., Spoonster, E., Bogart, L. M., et al. (2004). Evaluation of initial posttrauma cardiovascular levels in association with acute PTSD symptoms following a serious motor vehicle accident. *Journal of Traumatic Stress, 17*(4), 317–24.

Cahill, L., Prins, B., Weber, M., and McGaugh, J. L. (1994). Beta-adrenergic activation and memory for emotional events. *Nature, 371*(6499), 702–4.

Charney, D. S., Southwick, S. M., Krystal, J. H., Deutch, A. Y., Murburg, M. M., and Davis, M. (1994). *Neurobiological Mechanisms of PTSD*. Washington, DC: American Psychiatric Association.

Cohen, J. A. (2001). Pharmacologic treatment of traumatized children. *Trauma, Violence, & Abuse, 2*(2), 155–71.

Cohen, J. A., Berliner, L., and Mannarino, A. P. (2003). Psychosocial and pharmacological interventions for child crime victims. *Journal of Traumatic Stress, 16*(2), 175–86.

Cohen, J. A., Mannarino, A. P., and Rogal, S. (2001). Treatment practices for childhood posttraumatic stress disorder. *Child Abuse & Neglect, 25*, 123–35.

Cooper, J., Carty, J., and Creamer, M. (2005). Pharmacotherapy for posttraumatic stress disorder: Empirical review and clinical recommendations. *Australian and New Zealand Journal of Psychiatry, 39*, 674–82.

Davidson, J. R. T. (2000). Pharmacotherapy of posttraumatic stress disorder: Treatment options, long-term follow-up, and predictors of outcome. *Journal of Clinical Psychiatry, 61*(5), 52–59.

Davidson, J., Baldwin, D., Stien, D. J., Kuper, E., Benattia, I., Ahmed, S., et al. (2006). Treatment of posttraumatic stress disorder with venlafaxine extended release. *Archives of General Psychiatry, 63*(1), 1158–65.

Davidson, J., Pearlstein, T., Londborg, P., Brady, K. T., Rothbaum, B., Bell, J., et al. (2001). Efficacy of sertraline in preventing relapse of posttraumatic stress disorder: Results of a 28-week double-blind, placebo-controlled study. *American Journal of Psychiatry, 158*(1), 1974–81.

Delahanty, D. L., Nugent, N. R., Christopher, N. C., and Walsh, M. (2005). Initial urinary epinephrine and cortisol levels predict acute PTSD symptoms in child trauma victims. *Psychoneuroendocrinology, 30*(2), 121–28.

Delahanty, D. L., Raimonde, A. J., and Spoonster, E. (2000). Initial posttraumatic urinary cortisol levels predict subsequent PTSD symptoms in motor vehicle accident victims. *Biological Psychiatry, 48*(9), 940–47.

de Quervain, D. J., Roozendaal, B., Nitsch, R. M., McGaugh, J. L., and Hock, C. (2000). Acute cortisone administration impairs retrieval of long-term declarative memory in humans. *Nature Neuroscience, 3*(4), 313–14.

de Wied, D. (1984). The importance of vasopressin in memory. *Trends in Neurosciences, 7*(4), 109.

Donnelly, C. L., Amaya-Jackson, L., and March, J. S. (1999). Psychopharmacology of pediatric posttraumatic stress disorder. *Journal of Child and Adolescent Psychopharmacology, 9*, 203–20.

Famularo, R., Kinscherff, R., and Fenton, T. (1988). Propranolol treatment for childhood posttraumatic stress disorder, acute type: A pilot study. *Archives of Pediatrics and Adolescent Medicine, 142*(11), 1244–47.

Fletcher, K. E. (1996). *Childhood posttraumaic stress disorder.* New York: Guilford Press.

Foa, E. B., Hearst-Ikeda, D., and Perry, K. J. (1995). Evaluation of a brief cognitive-behavioral program for the prevention of chronic PTSD in recent assault victims. *Journal of Consulting and Clinical Psychology, 63*(6), 948–55.

Frank, J. B., Kosten, T. R., Giller, E. L., and Dan, E. (1988). A randomized clinical trial of phenelzine and imipramine for posttraumatic stress disorder. *American Journal of Psychiatry, 145*(10), 1289–91.

Gelpin, E., Bonne, O., Peri, T., and Brandes, D. (1996). Treatment of recent trauma survivors with benzodiazepines: A prospective study. *Journal of Clinical Psychiatry, 57*(9), 390–94.

Gold, P. (1984). Memory modulation: Roles of peripheral catecholamines. In R. Squire and N. Butter (Eds.), *Neuropsychology of memory.* New York: Guilford.

Hageman, I., Andersen, H. S., and Jorgensen, M. B. (2001). Post-traumatic stress disorder: A review of psychobiology and pharmacotherapy. *Acta Psychiatrica Scandinavica, 104*, 411–22.

Harmon, R. J., and Riggs, P. D. (1996). Clonidine for posttraumatic stress disorder in preschool children. *Journal of the American Academy of Child & Adolescent Psychiatry, 35*, 1247–49.

Hertzberg, M. A., Butterfield, M. I., Feldman, M. E., Beckham, J. C., Sutherland, S. M., Connor, K. M., and Davidson, J. R. T. (1999). A preliminary study of lamotrigine for the treatment of posttraumatic stress disorder. *Biological Psychiatry, 45*, 1226–29.

Hertzberg, M. A., Feldman, M. E., Beckham, J. C., Kudler, H. S., and Davidson, J. R. T. (2000). Lack of efficacy for fluoxetine in PTSD: A placebo controlled trial in combat veterans. *Annals of Clinical Psychiatry, 12*, 101–5.

Kassam-Adams, N., Garcia-España, J. F., Fein, J. A., and Winston, F. K. (2005). Heart rate and posttraumatic stress in injured children. *Archives of General Psychiatry, 62*(3), 335–40.

Katz, R. J., Lott, M. H., Arbus, P., Crocq, L., Herlobsen, P., et al. (1994). Pharmacotherapy of post-traumatic stress disorder with a novel psychotropic. *Anxiety, 1*, 169–74.

Kirschbaum, C., Wolf, O. T., May, M., Wippich, W., and Hellhammer, D. H. (1996). Stress- and treatment-induced elevations of cortisol levels associated with impaired declarative memory in healthy adults. *Life Sciences, 58*(17), 1475–83.

Kosten, T. R., Frank, J. B., Dan, E., McDougle, C. J., et al. (1991). Pharmacotherapy for posttraumatic stress disorder using phenelzine or imipramine. *Journal of Nervous and Mental Disease, 179*, 366–70.

Litz, B. T., Gray, M. J., Bryant, R. A., and Adler, A. B. (2002). Early intervention for trauma: Current status and future directions. *Clinical Psychology: Science and Practice, 9*(2), 112–34.

Londborg, P. D., Hegel, M. T., Goldstein, S., Goldstein, D., Himmelhoch, J. M., Maddock, R., et al. (2001). Sertraline treatment of posttraumatic stress disorder: Results of 24 weeks of open-label continuation treatment. *Journal of Clinical Psychiatry, 62*, 325–31.

Looff, D., Grimley, P., Kuller, F., Martin, A., and Shonfield, L. (1995). Carbamazepine for PTSD. *Journal of the American Academy of Child and Adolescent Psychiatry, 34*(6), 703.

Lupien, S. J., and McEwen, B. S. (1997). The acute effects of corticosteroids on cognition: Integration of animal and human model studies. *Brain Research. Brain Research Reviews, 24*(1), 1–27.

Marmar, C. R, Foy, D., Kagan, B., et al. (1993). An Integrated Approach for Treating Posttraumatic Stress. In J. M. Oldham, M. B. Riba, and A. Tasman (Eds.), *America Psychiatric Press Review of Psychiatry* (volume 12) (238–72). Washington, DC: American Psychiatric Press.

Marshall, R. D., Beebe, K. L., Oldham, M., and Zaninelli, R. (2001). Efficacy and safety of paroxetine treatment for chronic PTSD: A fixed-dose, placebo-controlled study. *American Journal of Psychiatry, 158*(1), 1982–88.

Martignoni, E., Costa, A., Sinforiani, E., Liuzzi, A., Chiodini, P., Mauri, M., et al. (1992). The brain as a target for adrenocortical steroids: Cognitive implications. *Psychoneuroendocrinology, 17*(4), 343–54.

Mauri, M., Sinforiani, E., Bono, G., Vignati, F., Berselli, M. E., Attanasio, R., et al. (1993). Memory impairment in Cushing's disease. *Acta Neurologica Scandinavica, 87*(1), 52–55.

Mayou, R. A., Ehlers, A., and Hobbs, M. (2000). Psychological debriefing for road traffic accident victims. Three-year follow-up of a randomised controlled trial. *The British Journal of Psychiatry; The Journal of Mental Science, 176*, 589–93.

McCleery, J. M., and Harvey, A. G. (2004). Integration of psychological and biological approaches to trauma memory: Implications for pharmacological prevention of PTSD. *Journal of Traumatic Stress, 17*, 485–96.

McFarlane, A. C., Atchison, M., and Yehuda, R. (1997). The acute stress response following motor vehicle accidents and its relation to PTSD. *Annals of the New York Academy of Sciences, 821,* 437–41.

McGaugh, J. L. (1985). Peripheral and central adrenergic influences on brain systems involved in the modulation of memory storage. *Annals of the New York Academy of Sciences, 444,* 150–61.

———. (1989). Involvement of hormonal and neuromodulatory systems in the regulation of memory storage. *Annual Review of Neuroscience, 12,* 255–87.

McGaugh, J. L., Liang, K. C., Bennett, C., and Sternberg, D. B. (1984). Adrenergic influences on memory storage: Interaction of peripheral and central systems. In G. Lynch, J. L. McGaugh, and N. M. Weinberger (Eds.), *Neurobiology of learning and memory* (313–32). New York: Guilford Press.

Mellman, T. A., Bustamante, V., David, D., and Fins, A. I. (2002). Hypnotic medication in the aftermath of trauma. *Journal of Clinical Psychiatry, 63*(1), 1183–84.

Newcomer, J. W., Craft, S., Hershey, T., Askins, K., and Bardgett, M. E. (1994). Glucocorticoid-induced impairment in declarative memory performance in adult humans. *The Journal of Neuroscience: The Official Journal of the Society for Neuroscience, 14*(4), 2047–53.

Newcomer, J. W., Selke, G., Melson, A. K., Hershey, T., Craft, S., Richards, K., et al. (1999). Decreased memory performance in healthy humans induced by stress-level cortisol treatment. *Archives of General Psychiatry, 56*(6), 527–33.

Nugent, N. R., Christopher, N. C., and Delahanty, D. L. (2006). Emergency medical service and in-hospital vital signs as predictors of subsequent PTSD symptom severity in pediatric injury patients. *Journal of Child Psychology and Psychiatry, 47*(9), 919–26.

Ostrowski, S. A., Christopher, N. C., and Delahanty, D. L. (2007). Brief report: The impact of maternal posttraumatic stress disorder symptoms and child gender on risk for persistent posttraumatic stress disorder symptoms in child trauma victims. *Journal of Pediatric Psychology, 32*(3), 338–42.

Pacak, K., Palkovits, M., Kopin, I. J., and Goldstein, D. S. (1995). Stress-induced norepinephrine release in the hypothalamic paraventricular nucleus and pituitary-adrenocortical and sympathoadrenal activity: In vivo microdialysis studies. *Frontiers in Neuroendocrinology, 16*(2), 89–150.

Perry, B. D. (1994). Neurobiological sequelae of childhood trauma: PTSD in children. In M. M. Murburg (Ed.), *Catecholamine function in posttraumatic stress disorder: Emerging concepts* (223–55). Washington, DC: American Psychiatric Press.

Pitman, R. K. (1989). Post-traumatic stress disorder, hormones, and memory. *Biological Psychiatry, 26*(3), 221–23.

Pitman, R. K., and Delahanty, D. L. (2005). Conceptually driven pharmacologic approaches to acute trauma. *CNS Spectrums, 10,* 99–106.

Pitman, R. K., and Orr, S. P. (1995). *Psychophysiology of emotional and memory networks in posttraumatic stress disorder.* New York: Oxford University Press.

Pitman, R. K., Orr, S. P., and Shalev, A. Y. (1993). Once bitten, twice shy: Beyond the conditioning model of PTSD. *Biological Psychiatry, 33*(3), 145–46.

Pitman, R. K., Sanders, K. M., Zusman, R. M., Healy, A. R., Cheema, F., Lasko, N. B., et al. (2002). Pilot study of secondary prevention of posttraumatic stress disorder with propranolol. *Biological Psychiatry, 51*(2), 189–92.

Rapaport, M. H., Endicott, J., and Clary, C. M. (2002). Posttraumatic stress disorder and quality of life: Results across 64 weeks of sertraline treatment. *Journal of Clinical Psychiatry, 63*, 59–65.

Reinherz, H. Z., Giaconia, R. M., Lefkowitz, E. S., Pakiz, B., and Frost, A. K. (1993). Prevalence of psychiatric disorders in a community population of older adolescents. *Journal of the American Academy of Child & Adolescent Psychiatry, 32*(2), 369–77.

Resnick, H. S., Yehuda, R., Pitman, R. K., and Foy, D. W. (1995). Effect of previous trauma on acute plasma cortisol level following rape. *The American Journal of Psychiatry, 152*(11), 1675–77.

Rose, S., Brewin, C. R., Andrews, B., and Kirk, M. (1999). A randomized controlled trial of individual psychological debriefing for victims of violent crime. *Psychological Medicine, 29*(4), 793–99.

Ruzek, J., and Watson, P. (2001). Early intervention to prevent PTSD and other trauma-related problems. *PTSD Research Quarterly, 12*, 1–3.

Saxe, G., Stoddard, F., Courtney, D., Cunningham, K., Chawla, N., Sheridan, R., et al. (2001). Relationship between acute morphine and the course of PTSD in children with burns. *Journal of the American Academy of Child & Adolescent Psychiatry, 40*(8), 915–21.

Schelling, G., Briegel, J., Roozendaal, B., Stoll, C., Rothenhausler, H., and Kapfhammer, H. (2001). The effect of stress doses of hydrocortisone during septic shock on posttraumatic stress disorder in survivors. *Biological Psychiatry, 50*(1), 978–85.

Schelling, G., Kilger, E., Roozendaal, B., de Quervain, D. J., Briegel, J., Dagge, A., et al. (2004). Stress doses of hydrocortisone, traumatic memories, and symptoms of posttraumatic stress disorder in patients after cardiac surgery: A randomized study. *Biological Psychiatry, 55*(6), 627–33.

Schelling, G., Stoll, C., Kapfhammer, H. P., Rothenhausler, H. B., Krauseneck, T., Durst, K., et al. (1999). The effect of stress doses of hydrocortisone during septic shock on posttraumatic stress disorder and health-related quality of life in survivors. *Critical care medicine, 27*(12), 2678–83.

Schoenfeld, F. B., Marmar, C. R., and Neylan, T. C. (2004). Current concepts in pharmacotherapy for posttraumatic stress disorder. *Psychiatric Services, 55*, 519–31.

Seedat, S., Lockhat, R., Kaminer, D., Zungu-Dirwayi, N., and Stein, D. J. (2001). An open trial of citalopram in adolescents with post-traumatic stress disorder. *International Clinical Psychopharmacology, 16*, 21–25.

Seedat, S., Stein, D. J., Ziervogel, C., Middleton, T., Kaminer, D., Emsley, R. A., et al. (2002). Comparison of response to a selective serotonin reuptake inhibitor in children, adolescents and adults with posttraumatic stress disorder. *Journal of Child and Adolescent Psychopharmacology, 12*, 37–46.

Shalev, A. Y., Freedman, S., Peri, T., Brandes, D., Sahar, T., Orr, S. P., et al. (1998). Prospective study of posttraumatic stress disorder and depression following trauma. *American Journal of Psychiatry, 155*(5), 630–37.

Southwick, S. M., Yehuda, R., Giller, E. L., and Charney, D. S. (1994). Use of tricy-clics and monoamine oxidase inhibitors in the treatment of PTSD: A quantitative review. In M. Michele Murburg (Ed.), *Catecholamine function in posttraumatic stress disorder: Emerging concepts* (293–305). Washington, DC: American Psychiatric Association.

Stallard, P., Velleman, R., and Baldwin, S. (1998). Prospective study of post-traumatic stress disorder in children involved in road traffic accidents. *BMJ: British Medical Journal, 7173*, 1619–23.

Stein, M. B., Kline, N. A., and Matloff, J. L. (2002). Adjunctive olanzapine for SSRI-resistant combat-related PTSD: A double-blind, placebo-controlled study. *American Journal of Psychiatry, 159*(1), 1777–79.

Taylor, F., and Cahill, L. (2002). Propranolol for reemergent posttraumatic stress disorder following an event of retraumatization: A case study. *Journal of Traumatic Stress, 15*, 433–37.

Tucker, P., Zaninelli, R., Yehuda, R., Ruggiero, L., Dillingham, K., and Pitts, C. D. (2001). Paroxetine in the treatment of chronic posttraumatic stress disorder: Results of a placebo-controlled, flexible-dosage trial. *Journal of Clinical Psychiatry, 62*(1), 860–68.

Vaiva, G., Ducrocq, F., Jezequel, K., Averland, B., Lestavel, P., Brunet, A., et al. (2003). Immediate treatment with propranolol decreases posttraumatic stress disorder two months after trauma. *Biological Psychiatry, 54*, 947–49.

van der Kolk, Bessel A., Dreyfuss, D., Michaels, M., Shera, D., et al. (1994). Fluoxetine in posttraumatic stress disorder. *Journal of Clinical Psychiatry, 55*(1), 517–22.

Wolkowitz, O. M., Reus, V. I., Weingartner, H., Thompson, K., Breier, A., Doran, A., et al. (1990). Cognitive effects of corticosteroids. *The American Journal of Psychiatry, 147*(10), 1297–1303.

Yehuda, R. (2002). Post-traumatic stress disorder. *New England Journal of Medicine, 346*(2), 108–14.

Yehuda, R., and Harvey, P. (1997). *Relevance of neuroendocrine alterations in PTSD to memory-related impairments of trauma survivors.* New York: Plenum Press.

Yehuda, R., McFarlane, A. C., and Shalev, A. Y. (1998). Predicting the development of posttraumatic stress disorder from the acute response to a traumatic event. *Biological Psychiatry, 44*(12), 1305–13.

Zatzick, D. F., Russo, J., Pitman, R. K., Rivara, F., Jurkovich, G., and Roy-Byrne, P. (2005). Reevaluating the association between emergency department heart rate and the development of posttraumatic stress disorder: A public health approach. *Biological Psychiatry, 57*(1), 91–95.

Zohar, J., Amital, D., Miodownik, C., Kotler, M., Bleich, A., Lane, R., and Austin, C. (2002). Double blind placebo controlled pilot study of sertraline in military veterans with posttraumatic stress disorder. *Journal of Clinical Psychopharmacology, 22*(2), 190–95.

# 13

## From Childhood to Adult PTSD—
## An Integrative Model

### Douglas L. Delahanty and Leah Irish

The principle focus of this volume was to examine and bridge findings in PTSD research from a developmental standpoint. Up to now, child and adult PTSD researchers have rarely collaborated, and the areas of research were relatively distinct. Our goal was to bring together experts in PTSD across the lifespan in an attempt to increase our understanding of PTSD from a developmental viewpoint. Although there are distinct risk and resilience factors that emerge between child and adult samples, the link between child trauma and adult PTSD is well established. A history of childhood trauma increases one's risk for developing PTSD upon exposure to a subsequent trauma, and research is currently trying to determine why this is. Biological studies focus on genetic predisposition and relatively permanent alterations of stress pathways that could confer increased risk during and after a subsequent trauma. Other studies suggest additional possible mechanisms such as learned deleterious coping techniques, reinforced dissociative responses, and pre-existing risk factors that increase risk at any stage of development. In this final chapter, we attempt to synthesize the prior chapters in order to present a conceptual model of PTSD across the lifespan, highlighting areas in need of future research and possible points for intervention.

Prevalence rates for PTSD appear to differ between adults and children. Children are approximately 1.5 times more likely to develop PTSD in response to a traumatic event than are adults (Fletcher, 1996). Symptom presentation may also differ between adults and children, especially with children

Address correspondence to Douglas L. Delahanty; Department of Psychology; 144 Kent Hall; Kent State University; Kent, OH 44242. Phone: 330-672-2395. Fax: 330-672-3786. E-mail: ddelahan@kent.edu ages six and younger (see chapter 1). Young children suffer from cognitive, emotional, and linguistic limitations that may leave them more vulnerable to posttraumatic distress. Therefore, parents play a key role in assisting their children with processing and recovering from trauma. However, parents are more likely to experience PTSD symptoms after witnessing or being involved in their child's trauma than is the child him/herself, and parental responses can influence the response of the child (Nugent, Ostrowski, Christopher, and Delahanty, 2007). For instance, whereas an adult has some control over avoiding or confronting trauma-reminiscent stimuli, a child's movements and topics of discussion oftentimes depend on the parent's behavior. Although risk factors may impact children and adults differently, certain factors may be influential regardless of developmental stage. One such commonality in risk for PTSD between children and adults may be the influence of genetic factors.

Research investigating genetic predictors of trauma response is still in its early stages. However, findings have provided promising insight into variations in DNA sequence that may help in assessing vulnerability for PTSD (see chapter 2). Twin studies are a valuable tool for parsing out environmental and genetic influences by comparing identical twins, fraternal twins, and siblings. Such research has demonstrated genetic influences on both exposure to trauma (likely due to certain heritable personality traits) and development of PTSD following trauma exposure. Twin studies have also revealed that genetic influences on PTSD may overlap with genetic influences for other psychological disorders. Molecular genetics research has highlighted polymorphisms in serotonergic and dopaminergic systems that are thought to be associated with increased PTSD risk, but additional research is necessary before conclusions can be drawn. In addition, recent research has suggested a possible explanation for the mixed findings concerning the role of genetics in risk for PTSD (see chapter 10). That is, failure to examine gene x environment interactions may have led to equivocal findings as genetic risk can be moderated by other risk and resilience factors.

Whereas genetic predisposition appears to confer some risk for the development of psychopathological symptoms upon exposure to a traumatic event, additional risk factors appear necessary. Numerous psychological and biological factors have been found to increase risk for PTSD and comorbid disorders in a dose-response fashion. That is, presence of more risk factors confers greater risk for the development of PTSD. In general, research examining psychological predictors and correlates of PTSD has been conducted separately from (or at least published separately from) research targeting biological predictors and correlates of PTSD. Therefore, we will present our developmental model from a biological risk viewpoint first, then from a psychological risk viewpoint. Finally, we will incorporate the two viewpoints in an attempt to guide future research toward a more comprehensive examination of risk and resilience factors for PTSD.

## BIOLOGICAL MODELS OF RISK FOR PTSD

The vast majority of research into the biology of PTSD has focused on examining abnormalities of the two primary stress systems: the sympathetic nervous system (SNS) and the hypothalamic-pituitary-adrenal (HPA) axis. Further, the majority of studies have examined adult trauma victims with chronic PTSD. These early studies revealed a number of biological abnormalities in individuals with chronic PTSD in comparison to similarly traumatized individuals who did not develop PTSD. Most consistently observed was exaggerated startle responses, or SNS hyper-reactivity to trauma-reminiscent and non-trauma-reminiscent stimuli (reviewed by Orr, 1994). Further suggestive of a persistent elevation of SNS activity, studies collecting twenty-four-hour urine samples also generally found greater catecholamine levels in adults with chronic PTSD vs. controls (see Southwick, Bremner, Krystal, and Charney, 1994, for a review).

In contrast to the relatively consistent finding of elevated catecholamine excretion in PTSD, studies examining alterations in HPA axis activity have produced more variable findings. Initial studies examining cortisol levels in PTSD produced surprising results. Given that PTSD is a stress disorder, it was hypothesized that patients with PTSD would have very high cortisol levels. However, the first few studies of cortisol levels in PTSD found that victims with PTSD had lower twenty-four-hour urinary cortisol levels than did victims without PTSD and normal controls (see Yehuda, 2002, for a review). However, more recently, contradictory findings have been reported (see Rasmusson, Vythilingam, and Morgan, 2003, for a review). Currently, the literature examining cortisol levels in PTSD is equivocal, with equal numbers of studies finding either PTSD to be associated with high cortisol (Lemieux and Coe, 1995; Pitman and Orr, 1990; Rasmusson and Friedman, 2002), or PTSD to be associated with lower cortisol levels (Yehuda, 2002). Additional research has found no differences in cortisol output between patients with PTSD and controls (Baker et al., 1999; Kosten, Mason, Giller, Ostroff, and Harkness, 1987). Rasmusson and colleagues (2003) have hypothesized a number of possible explanations for these discrepant findings including failure to control for smoking and other pharmacologic agents and possible confounds regarding whether sampling was conducted in a clinical research center or while participants were in their natural environment. Failure to consider the presence of diagnoses comorbid with PTSD may also contribute to the discrepant findings.

Research examining PTSD patients who also met diagnostic criteria for major depressive disorder (MDD) has suggested that each disorder may alter the biological expression of the other (Halbreich et al., 1988; Kudler, Davidson, Meador, Lipper and Ely, 1987; Yehuda, Boisoneau, Mason, and Giller, 1993; Yehuda, Halligan, Golier, Grossman, and Bierer, 2004).

Based largely on findings of biological abnormalities in PTSD, and supported by both animal and human research into arousal and memory, researchers began hypothesizing that the pattern of biological responses found in chronic PTSD, if present soon after trauma, could increase one's risk of developing the disorder. It is important to consider these theories in a historical context, as they were proposed when the majority of studies were reporting higher levels of sympathetic hormones and lower levels of cortisol in PTSD. Pitman was the first to hypothesize that excess sympathetic activity during and soon after exposure to a traumatic event could lead to the development of "overconsolidated" memories, and subsequent symptoms of PTSD (Pitman, 1989; Pitman, Orr, and Shalev, 1993). Yehuda and colleagues extended this theory to suggest that the interplay of SNS and HPA axis hormones might be associated with risk for PTSD. That is, lower cortisol levels at the time of the trauma may fail to contain an exaggerated sympathetic stress response, leading to consequent prolonged availability of norepinephrine (NE) in the brain (Pacak, Palkovits, Kopin, and Goldstein, 1995), and altered consolidation and retrieval of traumatic memories (Yehuda, 2002). This could further lead to inappropriate memory formation and result in the intrusion symptoms that characterize PTSD (Yehuda and Harvey, 1997; Yehuda, McFarlane, and Shalev, 1998)

Research examining acute responses to trauma and subsequent risk for PTSD has largely supported these theories. Generally, prospective studies of hospitalized trauma victims have found an association between higher HR levels measured during a hospital stay and greater risk for PTSD (Bryant, Harvey, Guthrie, and Moulds, 2000; Shalev et al., 1998; Zatzick et al., 2005). However, contradictory findings have been reported (Blanchard, Hickling, Galovski, and Veazey, 2002), and this relationship may not generalize to more seriously injured victims (Buckley et al., 2004).

Studies examining cortisol levels in adults soon after trauma have also been quite consistent, finding that victims with lower cortisol levels in the acute phase of responding to trauma were more likely to develop PTSD symptoms (PTSS: Delahanty, Raimonde, and Spoonster, 2000; McFarlane, Atchison, and Yehuda, 1997; Resnick, Yehuda, Pitman, and Foy, 1995). These findings are in accordance with Yehuda's theory (Yehuda and Harvey, 1997), suggesting that, during and soon after trauma, low levels of cortisol may be insufficient to regulate adrenergic activity, thus leaving individuals more vulnerable to PTSD symptoms.

Despite the progress made in identification of acute and chronic biological correlates of PTSD, it is still unclear why select trauma victims exhibit altered hormonal responses and increased risk for PTSS while others do not. Many researchers have suggested that prior trauma history is an integral part of predicting risk. History of prior traumatic experiences is a consistent predictor of PTSD following a subsequent trauma (Ozer, Best, Lipsey, and Weiss, 2003), and has been shown to alter HPA axis functioning in response to a subsequent stressor in both humans (Heim et al., 2000) and animals (Anisman and Sklar, 1979; Vazquez, 1998). In a study of rape victims, Resnick and colleagues (1995) found that women with a history of interpersonal violence had lower plasma cortisol levels and were more likely to develop PTSS than were women without a history of assault. These findings led Yehuda and colleagues (1998) to hypothesize that exposure to trauma may cause permanent alterations in the primary stress systems, which may reduce their effectiveness in dealing with subsequent traumas. Thus, trauma history, and especially the experience of trauma in childhood, must be taken into account in any model of PTSD risk.

## BIOLOGY OF PTSD IN CHILDREN

Similar to findings in the adult literature, research examining the biopsychology of PTSD in children has produced mixed results. De Bellis, Baum, Birmaher, Keshavan, Eccard, Boring, et al. (1999) compared urinary stress hormone levels in children with chronic PTSD symptoms due to maltreatment with those of children with overanxious disorder (OAD) and those of non-traumatized healthy controls. Children with PTSD had higher levels of cortisol than non-traumatized controls, and cortisol was positively associated with duration of maltreatment and symptom severity. Children with PTSD also had higher levels of epinephrine than children with OAD, and higher norepinephrine and dopamine than both comparison groups. A follow-up study examined neurological deficits in children with PTSD compared to matched controls, and found that cerebral volume was lower in the children with PTSD, suggesting that persistent cortisol elevations may result in neurological vulnerabilities in children with PTSD (DeBellis, Keshavan, Clark, Casey, Giedd, Boring, et al., 1999).

In contrast to DeBellis's findings, some studies of chronic PTSD in children have found lower urinary cortisol levels in children with chronic PTSD (Goenjian et al., 1996; King, Mandansky, King, Fletcher, and Brewer, 2001). However, methodological differences may, at least in part, account for these discrepant findings. Prior studies have differed on a number of variables including recency of the traumatic event, sample age range and gender ratio, and differences in the type and timing of psychological assessments and the manner in which cortisol was collected (saliva vs. urine).

Few studies have examined the extent to which biological variables present soon after trauma are associated with increased risk for PTSD in children. Similar to findings in adults, elevated HR during emergency medical service (EMS) transport and soon after hospital admission is associated with increased risk for PTSS in children (Kassam-Adams, Garcia-España, Fein, and Winston, 2005; Nugent, Christopher, and Delahanty, 2006a). However, studies of acute urinary hormone levels in children have yielded findings opposite from those reported in adult samples. Whereas in adults lower cortisol levels in hospital predicted subsequent PTSS, in children, *higher* cortisol levels were associated with higher PTSS. We have found this in two separate child samples (Delahanty, Nugent, Christopher, and Walsh, 2005; Ostrowski, Christopher, and Delahanty, at press). It is important to note that the children recruited in these studies were victims of a first-time trauma, with no prior trauma history. Further, the urinary hormone effects appear to be driven by a strong relationship in boys; neither study found a significant relationship in girls. One possible explanation for the lack of significant findings in girls involves the failure to consider sex hormone levels and pubertal status as moderators of biological risk factors. Sex hormones interact with and impact the previously discussed biological risk/resilience variables, and it is necessary to incorporate measures of estradiol, testosterone, DHEA, and pubertal status in order to fully understand the impact of trauma during critical developmental stages such as puberty.

Based on findings of biological correlates and predictors of PTSD in adults and children, our proposed model specifically builds upon De Bellis's (2001) developmental traumatology model of PTSD. De Bellis's model was developed in an attempt to account for differing directions of cortisol abnormalities in PTSD initially observed between child and adult samples with chronic PTSD. The model suggested that in some children, initial exposure to trauma might result in HPA axis dysregulation and hypersecretion of cortisol. As cortisol levels increase, they may begin to interfere with normal HPA axis functioning, leading to an enhanced negative feedback loop. Over time, this may result in lower basal cortisol levels, as seen in adult trauma victims. This process likely happens over the course of a few years. Studies examining children within two years of trauma exposure tend to find PTSD symptoms related to higher levels of cortisol (De Bellis, Lefter, Trickett, and Putnam, 1994; De Bellis, Baum, Birmaher, Keshavan, Eccard, Boring, et al., 1999; Delahanty et al., 2005), whereas five years after trauma, lower levels of cortisol have been associated with the development of PTSD symptoms (Goenjian et al., 1996).

Extending De Bellis's model, a biological model of risk across the lifespan would suggest that a subset of child trauma victims who possess genetic predisposition, as well as myriad other possible risk factors, may respond differently to a trauma than victims who are not at risk for PTSD. More specifically, during the hours and days following the traumatic event, these at-risk children may have higher levels of sympathetic arousal and cortisol levels. Additional biological risk resilience factors may also be altered (NPY, DHEA; see chapter 7), although research has yet to examine these factors in children. Further, age, gender, and pubertal status of the child may also impact the risk afforded by biological risk factors.

Over a number of years, continued elevations of catecholamines and cortisol may alter basal HPA axis functioning, eventually leading to a downregulation of the HPA axis and subsequent lower levels of cortisol. Upon exposure to a subsequent trauma in adulthood, adults with a prior trauma history may fail to respond appropriately, exhibiting high levels of sympathetic arousal and lower HPA activity. Whether lower acute phase cortisol levels are causally involved in the development of PTSD in adults or whether they simply serve as a marker of risk afforded by prior traumatic experiences is unknown. However, this model does help to explain the differing direction of relationships between cortisol and PTSD observed between children and adults.

## PSYCHOLOGICAL MODELS OF RISK FOR PTSD

Prior research has identified many risk factors for the development of PTSD in child trauma victims, and many variables that may confound the relationships between initial physiological reactions and persistent child PTSS. PTSS appear to be influenced by a complex constellation of environmental, trauma-specific, and person-specific factors (see chapter 4). Prior investigations of predictors of PTSD in children have implicated variables such as perceived severity of the stressor, age, gender, ethnicity, and prior trauma experiences (see Foy, Madvig, Pynoos, and Camilleri, 1996, for a review). Research in pediatric trauma victims has found that previous traumatic experiences, pre-existing depression and anxiety, and distress during and after the accident are also associated with increased risk for subsequent PTSS (Di Gallo, Barton, and Parry-Jones, 1997; Keppel-Benson, Ollendick, and Benson, 2002; Mirza, Bhadrinath, Goodyer, and Gilmour, 1998; Stallard, Vellerman, and Baldwin, 1998). As mentioned in chapter 4, there have been so many risk factors identified, each accounting for a relatively small percentage of the variance in PTSS, that some researchers doubt whether identifying children who are likely to develop PTSD is possible. However, a number of variables are consistently associated with PTSD risk in children and adults, and a bio-psychological approach to identifying predictors may inform identification efforts. With particular relevance to developmental models, learned negative cognitive or coping strategies could increase risk for the development of PTSD in child trauma victims as well as confer risk for the development of PTSD upon exposure to subsequent trauma. Peritraumatic dissociation is one of the strongest psychological predictors of PTSD in adults (Ozer et al., 2003; see chapter 9), and a child who successfully "avoids" a trauma through dissociation may rely on this response as an adult, increasing the likelihood of developing PTSD. Alternatively, family environment and attachment style may also be correlated with dissociation later in life (see chapter 9).

Parental responses to the trauma may also moderate a child's risk for developing PTSS. As mentioned, parents of children hospitalized with moderate to severe traumatic injuries report high rates of PTSS and other psychosocial consequences. Diagnostic levels of PTSD are found in approximately 15 percent of parents (de Vries et al., 1999; Landolt, Vollrath, Ribi, Gnehm, and Sennhauser, 2003; Winston, Kassam-Adams, Garcia-España, Ittenbach and Cnaan, 2003), while subsyndromal levels of PTSD are more common, with approximately 33 percent of parents meeting at least partial PTSD criteria (Bryant, Mayou, Wiggs, Ehlers, and Stores, 2004; de Vries et al., 1999; Landolt et al., 2003). Higher levels of general distress may result in a parent being less available to their child during the early posttraumatic period (Schwartz, Dohrenwend, and Levav, 1994). However, parental PTSS stemming from the child's trauma has been more strongly related to the development of PTSD in children than general parental distress (Nugent, Christopher, and Delahanty, 2006b; Pelcovitz et al., 1998), suggesting specific risk afforded by parental PTSS. Further, the impact that parental responses have on child recovery most likely differ depending on sex of the parent and child as well as age/developmental stage of the child. Research has found that maternal PTSS exert a more negative impact on girls than boys (Ostrowski, Christopher, and Delahanty, 2007), and that as children go through the pubertal transition, parent-child relationships change (Paikoff and Brooks-Gunn, 1991), which could impact the effect of parental PTSS on child responses to the trauma.

## COMBINATION BIOLOGICAL/PSYCHOLOGICAL MODELS

In effect, a combination model simply combines the prior biological and psychological models, underscoring the importance of examining myriad factors in an attempt to increase understanding of risk and resilience across the lifespan. Figure 13.1 attempts to highlight important biopsychological risk/

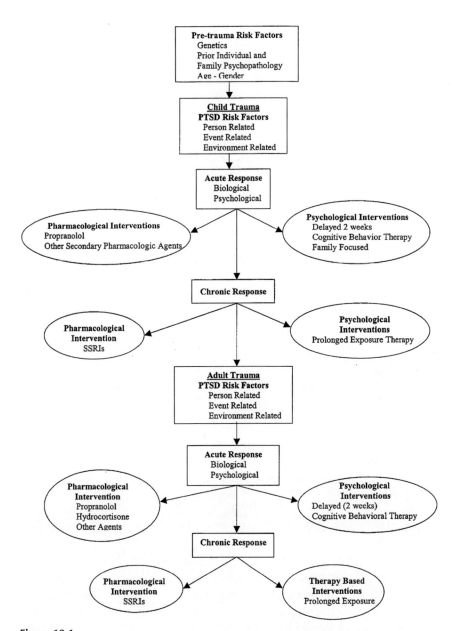

Figure 13.1

resilience factors that have been identified in the prior chapters. In general, this model presumes risk factors of a variety of types including genetic predisposition, person-related factors, event-related factors, and environment-related factors. The model is built on findings of relatively short follow-up and hypothesizes longer-term relationships that have not been tested. That said, it is meant to guide future research that will inform theory, aid in the prediction of individuals at risk for PTSD and comorbid disorders, and contribute to the design of more effective interventions.

The model begins by acknowledging recent research suggesting that there is a likely genetic predisposition to developing PTSD upon exposure to a trauma. Once a trauma occurs during childhood, the experience is filtered through a number of person-, environmental-, and trauma-related risk factors, such as family history of psychopathology, age, gender, perceptions of trauma and/or injury severity, availability of coping resources, and many more. These risk factors will influence the child's acute psychological and physiological responses to the trauma. If the posttraumatic distress is not alleviated by timely interventions and/or is exacerbated by risk factors, chronic symptoms may develop in the most vulnerable children.

Upon exposure to subsequent traumas, initial posttrauma responses are again influenced by a number of risk and resiliency factors, many of which may be impacted by learned or conditioned responses to the prior traumatic event. Without intervention, the acute distress of some adults will manifest itself into chronic PTSD symptoms. Although again, tertiary treatments have demonstrated efficacy, the majority of PTSD patients do not receive adequate treatment. In these cases, PTSD symptoms may persist for decades, severely reducing quality of life. Early research in older adults has suggested that psychobiological and cognitive changes associated with aging may necessitate further examination of appropriate interventions for older individuals (see chapter 8).

## POTENTIAL AREAS FOR FUTURE RESEARCH AND INTERVENTION

Our model highlights a number of areas that are in need of future research as well as illuminating areas at which interventions may be the most successful. With respect to future research, the best test of the proposed developmental model would be a large-scale prospective study following child trauma victims into young adulthood. Such a study would require a large enough sample size to allow for the testing of interactions of risk factors to further inform attempts at early identification of victims at risk for developing PTSD. In addition, such a study should incorporate both biological and psychological risk factors, as the majority of research has just examined one or the other with no attempt to examine how psychological risk/resilience factors could moderate biological risk factors. The necessity of assessing and controlling for sex hormones, pubertal status, maternal and paternal reactions to the trauma, and genetic and environmental influences makes such a study extremely labor intensive. However, it is only through such a design that we can examine the interaction and relative contribution of the various risk/resilience factors in an attempt to design better measures of risk and aid in the design of appropriate, potentially tailored interventions.

With respect to efforts toward intervening to reduce the prevalence and impact of PTSD, in both children and adults, tertiary interventions (interventions designed to reduce symptoms in chronic PTSD patients) demonstrate consistent efficacy. Pharmacological and psychological interventions have been developed that reliably reduce PTSD symptoms in a majority of children and adults with chronic PTSD (see chapters 11 and 12). Although further advances can be made in treating patients with chronic symptoms (i.e., improving relatively high dropout rates and discovering treatments for non-responders), tertiary interventions target patients after symptoms have taken a toll on academic or work performance, neural and cognitive development, and peer and family relationships. More recently, research has attempted to design secondary interventions that can be administered within weeks of a traumatic event to prevent or reduce the subsequent development of PTSS.

Based largely on findings of altered physiological levels soon after trauma in victims who go on to develop PTSD, researchers have examined ways in which they could pharmacologically alter aberrant responses in an attempt to reduce or prevent the development of PTSS. As reviewed in chapter 12, initial evidence suggests that propranolol, a beta blocker that reduces sympathetic arousal, administered within hours following a trauma may have efficacy at reducing some symptoms of PTSD (Pitman et al., 2002). In addition, stemming from findings of lower cortisol levels in trauma victims who go on to develop PTSD as well as basic research on the impact of cortisol on memory, Schelling and colleagues have demonstrated that exogenously elevating cortisol levels may protect against the development of PTSD in a number of disease samples (Schelling et al., 2001; Schelling et al., 2004). Larger scale studies are currently underway examining the extent to which secondary pharmacological interventions are efficacious at reducing or preventing the development of PTSS. Findings of studies examining additional biological risk/resilience factors present in the immediate aftermath of trauma will continue to inform novel secondary pharmacological interventions.

In contrast to findings of initial pharmacological interventions, results of methodologically strong randomized controlled trials and meta-analyses have found that early psychological debriefing interventions are ineffective at preventing PTSD (Rose, Brewin, Andrews, and Kirk, 1999; for reviews, see Litz, Gray, Bryant, and Adler [2002], as cited in Ruzek and Watson, 2001), and, in some cases, are detrimental (Mayou, Ehlers, and Hobbs, 2000). Delaying interventions to at least two weeks posttrauma has produced more promising results. Foa and colleagues (1995) reported decreased symptoms of PTSD in adult female assault victims who received four sessions of a cognitive-behavioral intervention. Similarly, cognitive-behavioral interventions have been found to be superior to supportive counseling in preventing PTSD in adult trauma victims meeting acute stress disorder (ASD) criteria (Bryant, Harvey, Dang, Sackville, and Basten, 1998; Bryant, Sackville, Dang, Moulds, and Guthrie, 1999). Research has yet to examine the efficacy of early psychological interventions at reducing PTSD in at-risk child trauma victims, which is a large limitation. However, although interventions modeled on those found efficacious in adults may also work in child samples, given the impact that parental responses to trauma have on a child's recovery, it is likely that family-focused interventions may be the most efficacious. Much more research is needed in the area of early psychological interventions in children as prior research has suggested differing impact of parental responses on boys vs. girls, suggesting that interventions may have to be tailored depending on a variety of qualities of the child (e.g., gender/developmental stage) and parent (e.g., gender, whether or not parent was a direct victim).

The forum, this book, and the proposed model underscore the limitations inherent in considering snapshot pictures of the impact of trauma on victims. Rather the necessity of taking a developmental approach should now be obvious, as childhood experiences impact the manner in which one responds to traumatic events at later stages of life. In addition, many developmental factors may influence risk afforded by previously documented risk factors, either by increasing or decreasing their saliency. Hopefully, a focus on a lifespan approach to the study of trauma and PTSD will shed light on predictors and consequences of this debilitating disorder.

## ACKNOWLEDGEMENTS

Preparation of this chapter was supported, in part, by National Institutes of Mental Health grants R34 MH 71201 and R34 73014.

## REFERENCES

Anisman, H., and Sklar, L. S. (1979). Catecholamine depletion in mice upon reexposure to stress: Mediation of the escape deficits produced by inescapable shock. *Journal of Comparative and Physiological Psychology, 93*, 610–25.

Baker, D. G., West, S. A., Nicholson, W. E., Ekhator, N. N., Kasckow, J. W., Hill, K. K., et al. (1999). Serial CSF corticotropin-releasing hormone levels and adrenocortical activity in combat veterans with posttraumatic stress disorder. *American Journal of Psychiatry, 156,* 585–88.

Blanchard, E. B., Hickling, E. J., Galovski, T., and Veazey, C. (2002). Emergency room vital signs and PTSD in a treatment seeking sample of motor vehicle accident survivors. *Journal of Traumatic Stress, 15,* 199–204.

Bryant, B., Mayou, R., Wiggs, L., Ehlers, A., and Stores, G. (2004). Psychological consequences of road traffic accidents for children and their mothers. *Psychological Medicine, 34*(2), 335–46.

Bryant, R. A., Harvey, A. G., Dang, S. T., Sackville, T., and Basten, C. (1998). Treatment of acute stress disorder: A comparison of cognitive-behavioral therapy and supportive counseling. *Journal of Consulting and Clinical Psychology, 66,* 862–66.

Bryant, R. A., Harvey, A. G., Guthrie, R. M., and Moulds, M. L. (2000). A prospective study of psychophysiological arousal, acute stress disorder, and posttraumatic stress disorder. *Journal of Abnormal Psychology, 109,* 341–44.

Bryant, R. A., Sackville, T., Dang, S. T., Moulds, M. and Guthrie, R. (1999). Treating acute stress disorder: An evaluation of cognitive behavior therapy and supportive counseling techniques. *American Journal of Psychiatry, 156,* 1780–86.

Buckley, B., Nugent, N. R., Sledjeski, E., Raimonde, A. J., Spoonster, E., and Delahanty, D. L. (2004). Initial cardiovascular predictors are not related to PTSD. *Journal of Traumatic Stress, 17,* 317–24.

De Bellis, M. D. (2001). Developmental traumatology: The psychobiological development of maltreated children and its implications for research, treatment, and policy. *Development and Psychopathology, 13,* 539–64.

De Bellis, M. D., Baum, A. S., Birmaher, B., Keshavan, M. S., Eccard, C. H., Boring, A. M., et al. (1999). Developmental traumatology part I: Biological stress systems. *Biological Psychiatry, 45,* 1259–70.

De Bellis, M. D., Keshavan, M., Clark, D. B., Casey, B. J., Giedd, J., Boring, A. M., et al. (1999). A. E. Bennett Research Award. Developmental traumatology part II: Brain development. *Biological Psychiatry, 45,* 1271–84.

De Bellis, M. D., Lefter, L., Trickett, P. K., and Putnam, F. W. (1994). Urinary catecholamine excretion in sexually abused girls. *Journal of the American Academy of Child and Adolescent Psychiatry, 33,* 320–27.

Delahanty, D. L., Nugent, N. R., Christopher, N. C., and Walsh, M. (2005). Initial urinary epinephrine and cortisol levels predict acute PTSD symptoms in child trauma victims. *Journal of Psychoneuroendocrinology, 30,* 121–28.

Delahanty, D. L., Raimonde, A. J., and Spoonster, E. (2000). Initial posttraumatic urinary cortisol levels predict subsequent PTSD symptoms in motor vehicle accident victims. *Biological Psychiatry, 48,* 940–47.

de Vries, A. P., Kassam-Adams, N., Cnaan, A., Sherman-Slate, E., Gallagher, P. R., and Winston, F. K. (1999). Looking beyond the physical injury: Posttraumatic stress disorder in children and parents after pediatric traffic injury. *Pediatrics, 104*(6), 1293–99.

Di Gallo, A., Barton, J., and Parry-Jones, W. L. (1997). Road traffic accidents: Early psychological consequences in children and adolescents. *British Journal of Psychiatry, 170*(4), 358–62.

Fletcher, K. E. (1996). Childhood posttraumatic stress disorder. In E. J. Marsh and R. Barkley (Eds.), *Child psychopathology* (242–76). New York: Guilford Press.

Foa, E. B., Hearst-Ikeda, D., and Perry, K. J. (1995). Evaluation of a brief cognitive-behavioral program for the prevention of chronic PTSD in recent assault victims. *Journal of Consulting and Clinical Psychology, 63*, 948–55.

Foy, D. W., Madvig, B. T., Pynoos, R. S., and Camilleri, A. J. (1996). Etiologic factors in the development of posttraumatic stress disorder in children and adolescents. *Journal of School Psychology, 34*(2), 133–45.

Goenjian, A. K., Yehuda, R., Pynoos, R. S., Steinberg, A. M., Tashjian, M., Yang, R. K., et al. (1996). Basal cortisol, dexamethasone suppression suppression of cortisol, and MHPG in adolescents after the 1988 earthquake in Armenia. *American Journal of Psychiatry, 153*, 929–34.

Halbreich, U., Olympia, J., Glogowski, J., Carson, S., Axelrod, S., and Yeh, C. M. (1988). The importance of past psychological trauma pathophysiological process as determinants of current biologic abnormalities. *Archives of General Psychiatry, 45*(3), 293–94.

Heim, C., Newport, D. J., Heit, S., Graham, Y. P., Wilcox, M., Bonsall, R., et al. (2000). Pituitary-adrenal and autonomic responses to stress in women after sexual and physical abuse in childhood. *Journal of the American Medical Association, 284*, 592–97.

Kassam-Adams, N. K., Garcia-España, J. P., Fein, J. A., and Winston, F. K. (2005). Heart rate and posttruaumatic stress in injured children. *Archives of General Psychiatry, 62*, 335–40.

Keppel-Benson, J. M., Ollendick, T. H., and Benson, M. J. (2002). Posttraumatic stress in children following motor vehicle accidents. *Journal of Child Psychology and Psychiatry, 43*, 203–12.

King, J. A., Mandansky, D., King, S., Fletcher, K. E., and Brewer, J. (2001). Early sexual abuse and low cortisol. *Psychiatry Clinical Neuroscience, 55*, 71–74.

Kosten, T. R., Mason, J. W., Giller, E. L., Ostroff, R. B., and Harkness, L. (1987). Sustained urinary norepinephrine and epinephrine elevation in post-traumatic stress disorder. *Psychoneuroendocrinology, 12*, 13–20.

Kudler, H., Davidson, J., Meador, K., Lipper, S., and Ely, T. (1987). The DST and posttraumatic stress disorder. *American Journal of Psychiatry, 144*(8), 1068–71.

Landolt, M. A., Vollrath, V., Ribi, K., Gnehm, H. E., and Sennhauser, F. H. (2003). Incidence and associations of parental and child posttraumatic stress symptoms in pediatric patients. *Journal of Child Psychology and Psychiatry, 44*(8), 1199–1207.

Lemieux, A. M., and Coe, C. L. (1995). Abuse related posttraumatic stress disorder: Evidence for chronic neuroendocrine activation in women. *Psychosomatic Medicine, 57*, 105–15.

Litz, B. T., Gray, M. J., Bryant, R. A., and Adler, A. B. (2002). Early intervention for trauma: Current status and future directions. *Clinical Psychology: Science and Practice, 9*(2), 112–34.

Mayou, R. A., Ehlers, A., and Hobbs, M. (2000). Psychological debriefing for road traffic accident victims: Three-year follow-up of a randomised controlled trial. *British Journal of Psychiatry, 176*, 589–93.

McFarlane, A. C., Atchison, M., and Yehuda, R. (1997). The acute stress response following motor vehicle accidents and its relation to PTSD. *Annals of the NY Academy of Science, 821*, 437–41.

Mirza, K. A. H., Bhadrinath, B. R., Goodyer, I. M., and Gilmour, C. (1998). Posttraumatic stress disorder in children and adolescents following road traffic accidents. *British Journal of Psychiatry, 172*, 443–47.

Nugent, N. R., Christopher, N. C., and Delahanty, D. L. (2006a). Emergency medical service and in-hospital vital signs as predictors of subsequent PTSD symptom severity in pediatric injury patients. *Journal of Child Psychology and Psychiatry, 47*(9), 919–26.

———. (2006b). Initial physiological responses and perceived hyperarousal predicts subsequent emotional numbing in child trauma victims. *Journal of Traumatic Stress, 19*(3), 349–59.

Nugent, N. R., Ostrowski, S. A., Christopher, N. C., and Delahanty, D. L. (2007). Parental symptoms of PTSD as a moderator of child's acute biological response and subsequent symptoms of PTSD in pediatric trauma patients. *Journal of Pediatric Psychology, 32*(3), 309–18.

Orr, S. P. (1994). An overview of psychophysiological studies of PTSD. *PTSD Research Quarterly, 5*(1), 1–7.

Ostrowski, S. A., Christopher, N. C., and Delahanty, D. L. (2007). Brief report: The impact of maternal posttraumatic stress disorder symptoms and child gender on risk for persistent posttraumatic stress disorder symptoms in child trauma victims. *Journal of Pediatric Psychology, 32*(3), 338–42.

———. (at press). Acute child and mother psychophysiological responses and subsequent PTSD symptoms following a child's traumatic event. *Journal of Traumatic Stress.*

Ozer, E. J., Best, S. R., Lipsey, T. L., and Weiss, D. S. (2003). Predictors of posttraumatic stress disorder and symptoms in adults: A metal-analysis. *Psychological Bulletin, 129*, 52–73.

Pacak, K., Palkovits, M., Kopin, I. J., and Goldstein, D. S. (1995). Stress-induced norepinephrine release in the hypothalamic paraventricular nucleus and pituitary-adrenocortical and symptathoadrenal activity: In vivo microdialysis studies. *Front Neuroendocrinology, 16*, 89–150.

Paikoff, R. L., and Brooks-Gunn, J. (1991). Do parent-child relationships change during puberty? *Psychological Bulletin, 110*(1), 47–66.

Pelcovitz, D., Libov, B. G., Mandel, F., Kaplan, S., Weinblatt, M., and Septimus, A. (1998). Posttraumatic stress disorder and family functioning in adolescent cancer. *Journal of Traumatic Stress, 11*, 205–21.

Pitman, R. K. (1989). Editorial: Post-traumatic stress disorder, hormones, and memory. *Biological Psychiatry, 26*, 221–23.

Pitman, R. K., and Orr, S. P. (1990). Twenty-four hour urinary cortisol and catecholamine excretion in combat-related post-traumatic stress disorder. *Biological Psychiatry, 27*, 245–47.

Pitman, R. K., Orr, S. P., and Shalev, A. Y. (1993). Once bitten, twice shy: Beyond the conditioning model of PTSD. *Biological Psychiatry, 33*, 145–46.

Pitman, R. K., Sanders, K. M., Zusman, R. M., Healy, A. R., Cheema, F., Lasko, N. B., et al. (2002). Pilot study of secondary prevention of posttraumatic stress disorder with propanolol. *Biological Psychiatry, 51*, 189–92.

Rasmusson, A. M., and Friedman, M. J. (2002). *Gender issues in the neurobiology of PTSD.* New York: Guilford Press.

Rasmusson, A. M., Vythilingam, M., and Morgan, C. A. (2003). The neuroendocrinology of posttraumatic stress disorder: New directions. *CNS Spectrum, 8*, 651–56, 665–67.

Resnick, H. S., Yehuda, R., Pitman, R. K., and Foy, D. W. (1995). Effect of previous trauma on acute plasma cortisol level following rape. *American Journal of Psychiatry, 152*, 1675–77.

Rose, S., Brewin, C. R., Andrews, B., and Kirk, M. (1999). A randomized controlled trial of individual psychological debriefing for victims of violent crime. *Psychological Medicine, 29*, 793–99.

Ruzek, J., and Watson, P. (2001). Early intervention to prevent PTSD and other trauma-related problems. *PTSD Research Quarterly, 12*, 1–7.

Schelling, G., Briegel, J., Roozendaal, B., Stoll, C., Rothenhausler, H., and Kapfhammer, H. (2001). The effect of stress doses of hysrocortisone during septic shock on posttraumatic stress disorder in survivors. *Biological Psychiatry, 50*, 978–85.

Schelling, G., Kilger, E., Roozendaal, B., de Quervain, D., Briegel, J., Dagge, A., et al. (2004). Stress doses of hydrocortisone, traumatic memories, and symptoms of posttraumatic stress disorder in patient after cardiac surgery: A randomized study. *Biological Psychiatry, 55*, 627–33.

Schwartz, S., Dohrenwend, B. P., and Levav, I. (1994). Nongenetic familial transmission of psychiatric disorders? Evidence from children of Holocaust survivors. *Journal of Health and Social Behavior, 35*, 385–402.

Shalev, A, Y., Sahar, T., Freedman, S., Peri, T., Glick, N., Brandes, D., et al. (1998). A prospective study of heart rate response following trauma and the subsequent development of posttraumatic stress disorder. *Archives of General Psychiatry, 55*, 553–59.

Southwick, S. M., Bremner, D., Krystal, J. H. and Charney, D. S. (1994). Psychobiologic research in posttraumatic stress disorder. *Psychiatric Clinics of North America, 17*(2), 251–64.

Stallard, P., Velleman, R., and Baldwin, S. (1998). Prospective study of posttraumatic stress disorder in children involved in road traffic accidents. *British Medical Journal, 317*, 1619–23.

Vazquez, D. M. (1998). Stress and the developing limbic-hypothalamic-pituitary-adrenal axis. *Psychoneuroendocrinology, 23*(7), 663–700.

Winston, F. K., Kassam-Adams, N., Garcia-España, F., Ittenbach, R., and Cnaan, A. (2003). Screening for risk of persistent posttraumatic stress in injured children and their parents. *Journal of the American Medical Association, 290*(5), 643–49.

Yehuda, R. (2002). Post-traumatic stress disorder. *New England Journal of Medicine, 346*, 108–14.

Yehuda, R., Boisoneau, D., Mason, J. W., and Giller, E. L. (1993). Glucocorticoid receptor number and cortisol excretion in mood, anxiety and psychotic disorders. *Biological Psychiatry, 34*, 18–25.

Yehuda, R., Halligan, S. L., Golier, J. A., Grossman, R., and Bierer, L. M. (2004). Effects of trauma exposure on the cortisol response to dexamethasone administration in PTSD and major depressive disorder. *Psychoneuroendocrinology, 29*, 389–404.

Yehuda, R., and Harvey, P. (1997). Relevance of neuroendocrine alterations in PTSD to memory-related impairments of trauma survivors. In D. J. Read and S. D. Lindsay (Eds.), *Recollections of trauma* (221–52). New York: Plenum Press.

Yehuda, R., McFarlane, A. C., and Shalev, A. Y. (1998). Predicting the development of posttraumatic stress disorder from the acute response to a traumatic event. *Biological Psychiatry, 44*, 1305–13.

Zatzick, D. F., Russo, J., Pitman, R. K., Rivara, F., Jurkovich, G., and Roy-Byrne, P. (2005). Reevaluating the association between emergency department heart rate and the development of posttraumatic stress disorder: A public health approach. *Biological Psychiatry, 57*, 91–95.

# Index

abuse hypothesis, signature of, 105
acute stress disorder, 75, 95, 238
adolescents, 69–70, 193; depression
    among, 199, *200*, 200–201;
    dissociation in, 172–73, 174;
    posttraumatic stress disorder
    comorbidity in, 199, *200*, 200–201;
    posttraumatic stress disorder criteria
    and, 5; traumatic events experience
    of, 69–72, 197–99, 201
adrenarche, 129, 130, 132
adrenergic blocking agents, 236, 237,
    238, 240–41, 244
adulthood: older, traumatic stressors in,
    12–13; posttraumatic stress disorder
    in, 11–14, 48, 144–45; prevalence of
    PTSD in, 11, 48
aging, 146–47, 150; posttraumatic stress
    disorder with, 143, 144–45, 147,
    150–51, 152–53, *154*, *160*, 160–61
alcohol. *See* psychoactive substance
    dependence
alexithymia, 55–56
allopregnanolone/pregnanolone
    (ALLO), 129, 130, 132–33;
    dehydroepiandrosterone with,
    131; gender and, 133; HPA axis

interaction with, 131; re-experiencing
    symptoms and, 129, 131
amnestic agents, 246
anti-convulsants, 235, 236–37
ASD, 75, 95, 238
attachment style in infancy, 171–73
avoidance symptoms, 2, 56–57, 60–61,
    62, 74, 217; in children, 3, 7–8, 94,
    218

benzodiazepines, 240

carbamazepine, 236–37
catecholamines, 51, 238, 239, 240, 244,
    257
childhood posttraumatic stress disorder,
    5; acute burns in, 91–93, 244; age
    and, 72–73, 94; cognitive abilities
    and, 8–9; developmental stages and,
    7–9, 38, 236, 260; parental roles and,
    9–10, 92–93, 256, 262; predictors of,
    243–44; prevalence of, 1, 3, 5–6, 70–
    71, 255; symptoms in, 2–3, *4*, 7–9,
    92–94, 259; treatments for, 77–78,
    218–24, 225–26, 236–37 (*see also*
    cognitive-behavioral interventions)
chronic disorders, 30, 32, 37–38, 144–45

273

# List of Contributors

Ananda B. Amstadter, M.S., Medical University of South Carolina, Auburn University.

Ashley Braun, B.S., Department of Psychiatry, Mount Sinai School of Medicine.

Jesse R. Cougle, M.Sc., National Crime Victims Research and Treatment Center, Medical University of South Carolina.

Douglas L. Delahanty, Ph.D., Department of Psychology, Kent State University.

Norah C. Feeny, Ph.D., Division of Child Psychiatry, Case Western Reserve University.

Meaghan Geary, M.S., Children's Hospital Boston, Harvard Medical School.

Erin Hall, Ph.D., Children's Hospital Boston, Harvard Medical School.

Stevan E. Hobfoll, Ph.D., Department of Psychology, Kent State University.

Leah Irish, M.A., Department of Psychology, Kent State University.

Shoshana Y. Kahana, Ph.D., Division of Child Psychiatry, Case Western Reserve University.

Julie Kaplow, Ph.D., Children's Hospital Boston, Harvard Medical School.

Dean G. Kilpatrick, Ph.D., National Crime Victims Research and Treatment Center, Medical University of South Carolina.

Karestan C. Koenen, Ph.D., Harvard School of Public Health, Boston University School of Medicine.

Brittain E. Lamoureux, M.A., Department of Psychology, Kent State University.

Michael R. McCart, Ph.D., National Crime Victims Research and Treatment Center, Department of Psychiatry and Behavioral Sciences, Medical University of South Carolina.

Nicole R. Nugent, Ph.D., Postdoctoral Fellow, Brown Medical School.

Sarah A. Ostrowski, M.A., Department of Psychology, Kent State University.

Nnamdi Pole, Ph.D., Department of Psychology, University of Michigan.

Ann Rasmusson, Ph.D., Department of Psychiatry, Yale University School of Medicine.

Heidi Resnick, Ph.D., National Crime Victims Research and Treatment Center, Medical University of South Carolina.

Benjamin E. Saunders, Ph.D., Family and Child Clinic, National Crime Victims Research and Treatment Center, Medical University of South Carolina.

Genelle K. Sawyer, Ph.D, National Crime Victims Research and Treatment Center, Department of Psychiatry and Behavioral Sciences, Medical University of South Carolina.

Glenn N. Saxe, M.D., Department of Child and Adolescent Psychiatry, Harvard Medical School.

Jeremiah A. Schumm, Ph.D., Harvard Medical School.

Daphne Simeon, M.D., Department of Psychiatry, Mount Sinai School of Medicine.

Daniel W. Smith, Ph.D., Department of Psychiatry and Behavioral Sciences, Medical University of South Carolina.

Lisa Stines, Ph.D., Department of Psychology, Case Western Reserve University.

Ana-Maria Vranceanu, Ph.D., Harvard Medical School, Massachusetts General Hospital.

Rachel Yehuda, Ph.D., Mount Sinai School of Medicine.

Breinigsville, PA USA
06 November 2010
248797BV00002B/3/P